CHANGING THE NEWS

This book examines the difficulties in changing the news processes in response to the struggles of the journalism industry. The editors have put together this volume in an effort to demonstrate why prescriptions to date haven't worked, and to explain how constraints and pressures have fashioned the field's responses to challenges in an uncertain, changing environment. If journalism is to adjust and thrive, the following questions need answers:

* Why do journalists and news organizations respond to uncertainties in the ways they do?
* What forces and structures constrain these responses?
* What social and cultural contexts should we take into account when we judge whether or not journalism successfully responds and adapts?

The book tackles these questions from varying perspectives and levels of analysis, through chapters by scholars of news sociology and media management. Scholars discuss the nature of uncertainties, the tendencies of journalism in the face of these uncertainties, and factors that pressure these tendencies. They address brief case-study reports of specific news industry efforts to change, looking into the consequences of these innovations, as well as reasons they were initiated in the first place. Chapters and case studies come mainly from experiences in American journalism, but most of the problems they explore face news systems across the industrial world.

Wilson Lowrey is an Associate Professor in the College of Communication and Information Sciences at The University of Alabama. Lowrey's research focuses on the sociology of news work, and has been published in a number of journals, including *Journalism & Mass Communication Quarterly*, *Political Communication*, *Journalism*, *Journalism Studies*, and *Journal of Media Economics*.

Peter J. Gade is a Gaylord Family Professor and Journalism Area Head in the Gaylord College of Journalism and Mass Communication at the University of Oklahoma. He is a co-author of *Twilight of Press Freedom: The Rise of People's Journalism* (2001). He is a former newspaper reporter and mid-level manager and has worked as an organizational consultant for newspapers, including the *St. Louis Post-Dispatch*.

Communication Series

Jennings Bryant/Dolf Zillmann, General Editors

CHANGING THE NEWS

The Forces Shaping Journalism
in Uncertain Times

Edited by Wilson Lowrey
and Peter J. Gade

Routledge
Taylor & Francis Group

NEW YORK AND LONDON

Published 2011
by Routledge
270 Madison Ave, New York, NY 10016

Simultaneously published in the UK
by Routledge
2 Park Square, Milton Park, Abingdon, Oxon OX14 4RN

Routledge is an imprint of the Taylor & Francis Group, an informa business

© 2011 Routledge, Taylor and Francis

The right of Wilson Lowrey and Peter J. Gade to be identified as editors of this work has been asserted by them in accordance with sections 77 and 78 of the Copyright, Designs and Patents Act 1988.

Library of Congress Cataloging in Publication Data
A catalog record has been requested for this book

ISBN 13: 978-0-415-87157-0 (hbk)
ISBN 13: 978-0-415-87158-7 (pbk)
ISBN 13: 978-0-203-86857-7 (ebk)

Typeset in Bembo and Stone Sans ITC Pro by Prepress Projects Ltd, Perth, UK

Printed and bound in the United States of America on acid-free paper by Walsworth Publishing Company, Marceline, MO.

SUSTAINABLE FORESTRY INITIATIVE

Certified Sourcing

www.sfiprogram.org

The SFI label applies to the text stock.

CONTENTS

FOREWORD

Certainty and Uncertainty of Change in Journalism

The changing news environment has been clearly evident for the past two decades, forcing news organizations to reconsider and reorganize existing activities and to add new products and functions. It has been a tumultuous time during which organizations have added Internet, social media, and mobile media activities to their portfolios, created flatter and more flexible organizational structures, and laid off workers who previously played important roles in the enterprises.

The changes transpired because news organizations could not sustain the established structures and work flows that were based on nineteenth- and twentieth-century technologies and perspectives on how to organize enterprises. The enterprises have responded to large-scale technical and economic changes that have altered the way information flows in society, as well as to changes in demographics, lifestyles, and media use patterns. These have changed financial support for and demand for traditional news and news delivery methods (Becker & Schönbach, 1999; Currah, 2009; Mindich, 2005; Picard, 2004).

The changes are part of a broader, profound transformation from an industrial to a post-industrial society, which is affecting all aspects of social life (Bergqvist, 1993; Castells, 2000; Clark & Rempel, 1998; Esping-Andersen, 2009; Putnam, 2000; Schlesinger, 1991). This alteration of society and markets is forcing resistant news organizations to change and placing great pressures on traditional journalism values, norms, and practices. Changing the organizational structures and processes in news organizations has proven difficult, but changing the practices and conceptualization of news is proving even harder.

Yet it is a hugely important transformation that must take place if the practice of journalism is to remain relevant in the twenty-first century.

Pressures to change journalistic values, norms, and practices are being produced by the social transformation and by emerging external players with different values and norms, which are challenging the existence and practice of journalism. These are forcing reconsideration of how news is gathered, the sources of news, whom news is intended for, and the uses made of news. At a broader level news organizations are being forced to rethink the nature of community and commonality of experience, where and how leadership and influence are exercised in society, and what it means to be a journalist.

The changes are producing immense discomfort in the news industry because it must confront the fact that the expansive and profitable news organizations of the second half of the twentieth century are no longer sustainable, and recognize the looming uncertainty and risk for news firms and journalists. A number of books have revealed the distress over the changes and their effects on news organizations and journalism (Anderson, 2004; Downie & Kaiser, 2002; Fenton, 2005; Jones, 2009), and some have attempted to deal with how journalism and news organizations must change (Meyer, 2004; Picard, 2010; Pickard, Stearns, & Aaron, 2009; Reilly Center for Media and Public Affairs, 2008).

This book tackles those issues and others with a breadth and depth not previously seen. It combines insights from sociological, organization behavior, management, philosophical, and journalism perspectives to holistically address the issues confronting news enterprises. The book attempts to reduce the uncertainty and risk by clarifying how the changes are affecting society and its values, altering the locations and exercise of power in society, creating new characteristics and roles for audiences, transforming organizations and institutions, reconfiguring information flow, and reshaping journalistic culture and practice. Its chapters provide essential insight for thoughtful consideration of the scale and scope of changes and how journalists and news organizations need to rethink their current positions and act for the future.

Every sailor knows the apprehension of entering uncharted waters because of the potential dangers there. Journalists and news organizations are now leaving the security of the well-mapped navigation lanes of the past century and they must employ all available knowledge and tools and exercise great vigilance while plotting and steering a cautious course toward the unknown world ahead. It will be a perilous passage, with vision obscured by the fog of uncertainty and the disquieting awareness of the certainty of risk. The authors of this book attempt to dissipate the uncertainty by providing understanding of the waters being entered, by providing principles and practices that can be employed to guide enterprises and journalists on their passage.

Like explorers of old, journalists and news organization managers are not sure where they are going, how long the journey will take, or what they will find on arrival. The explorers and their crews made their voyages voluntarily, with vision, hopes, and expectations that gave them the courage and stamina to face the uncertainty ahead. News organizations and journalists have been unwillingly pressed into making their voyage and, unless they develop a positive attitude, embrace the need for the voyage, and concentrate on the potential benefits of the exploration of new methods and practices, they will have a horrific passage, become increasingly pessimistic, frustrated and disgruntled, and increase the risks of self-destruction and ruin.

The future need not produce such a poor outcome. Information and journalism have been vital because they engender community, help the public understand the world about them, facilitate social engagement and interaction, and promote debate and other functions important to democratic processes. In the contemporary world, however, new institutions are emerging to serve some of those functions and journalists and news organizations must focus on functions not served by other institutions and discover and pursue new ones that will keep them relevant and garner the attention and respect of the public in the future.

It is certain there will be more change in the future that will require more agility and willingness to change on the part of news organizations and journalists. Understanding the nature and direction of current changes will help all of us deal with the uncertainty the future poses. This book helps prepare us for the journey.

Robert G. Picard
Reuters Institute for the Study of Journalism
University of Oxford

References

Anderson, B. M. (2004). *News flash: Journalism, infotainment and the bottom line business of broadcast news*. San Francisco: Jossey-Bass.

Becker, L., & Schönbach, K. (1999). *Audience response to media diversification*. Mahwah, NJ: Lawrence Erlbaum.

Bergqvist, W. (1993). *The postmodern organization: Mastering the art of irreversible change*. San Francisco: Jossey-Bass.

Castells, M. (2000). *The rise of networked society* (2nd ed.). Oxford, UK: Blackwell.

Clark, T. N., & Rempel, M. (1998). *Citizen politics in post-industrial society*. Boulder, CO: Westview Press.

Currah, A. (2009). *What's happening to our news: An investigation into the likely impact of the digital revolution on the economics of news publishing in the UK*. Oxford, UK: University of Oxford, Reuters Institute for the Study of Journalism.

Downie, L., Jr., & Kaiser, R. G. (2002). *The news about the news: American journalism in peril*. New York: Alfred A. Knopf.

Esping-Andersen, G. (2009). *Changing classes: Stratification and mobility in post-industrial societies*. London: Sage.

Fenton, T. (2005). *Bad news: The decline of reporting, the business of news, and the danger to us all*. New York: Regan Books.

Jones, A. S. (2009). *Losing the news: The future of news that feeds democracy*. Oxford, UK: Oxford University Press.

Meyer, P. (2004). *The vanishing newspaper: Saving journalism in the information age*. Columbia, MO: University of Missouri Press.

Mindich, D. T. Z. (2005). *Tuned out: Why Americans under 40 don't follow the news*. New York: Oxford University Press.

Picard, R. G. (2004). Environmental and market changes driving strategic planning in media firms. In R. G. Picard (Ed.), *Strategic responses to media market changes* (pp. 1–17). Jönköping, Sweden: Jönköping International Business School.

Picard, R. G. (2010). *Value creation and the future of news organizations: Why and how journalism must change to remain relevant in the 21st century*. Lisbon, Portugal: Media XXI.

Pickard, V., Stearns, J., & Aaron, C. (2009). *Saving the news: Toward a national journalism strategy*. Washington, DC: Free Press.

Putnam, R. (2000). *Bowling alone: The collapse and revival of American community*. New York: Simon & Schuster.

Reilly Center for Media and Public Affairs. (2008). *The Breaux Symposium: New models for news*. Baton Rouge: Louisiana State University Press.

Schlesinger, A. M. (1991). *The disuniting of America: Reflections on a multicultural society*. New York: W. W. Norton.

PREFACE

A number of recent books detail the challenges facing journalism, suggesting ways forward. This book does this as well. However, it does so only after exploring the thicket within which journalists decide and act, overgrown as it is with complexities and uncertainties. Uncertainties can obstruct and disorient journalists and news managers, but uncertainties may also provoke new thinking about changing the news. This tangled environment, and the constraints and motivations it induces, must be better understood before we can see journalism's way forward.

The concept of uncertainty is central to this text. Under some conditions, uncertainties can bewilder and stagnate. Under other conditions, uncertainties can spur a search for understanding, expand the thinkable, and prompt innovation. Our contributors explore the nature of uncertainty as a concept, as well as the antecedents and consequences of particular uncertainties facing journalists. They pursue this understanding across multiple levels of analysis, and from wide-ranging perspectives, including media management and economics, media sociology, and journalism philosophy. Analyses and explanations lie at various levels of analysis, consistent with hierarchical theories of message production and macro-social theories of organizations.

The book also wrestles with the duality of agency and structure as it relates to the work of journalism. The book blends discussions of individual strategic thinking at the heart of media management literature, with the constraining structures found in media sociology and media economics, and with the shifting philosophical and ideological frameworks that frame journalism.

A few points about the book's approach: First, chapters are generally situated within a U.S. context, consistent with the scholarly focus of most of the contributors. However, chapter discussions apply beyond the United States, as many of the complexities and changes described are found throughout the industrial world. Second, authors in this book generally write from an industry vantage point. They also use terms such as "journalist" and "audience" in the legacy sense, while recognizing the debate over the terms. We feel that there is still a generally shared understanding about the meaning of these constructs, which remain socially relevant and alive. (Otherwise we couldn't say things like "audiences cease to act like audiences" and expect others to understand what we mean.) Of course this shared understanding is fraying and fading. The boundaries around these terms are increasingly contested and negotiated, as their social and cultural contexts shift—a fascinating phenomenon. However, rather than have this phenomenon reshape the terms we use, we place these shifting, contested boundaries in an analytical frame, focusing on the uncertainty and jurisdictional disputes that accompany them.

The book is organized into three sections, with Part I serving as an introduction. The first chapter lays out the conceptual premise: Journalism is in an uncertain time, the forces shaping this uncertainty are inter-related and complex, and journalism's interdependency with other social institutions adds to the difficulty of responding to its environment. We discuss these influences on journalism through the dominant paradigms used in research on the news-making process. From sociological approaches, external complexities at macro levels shape and constrain the responses from journalists and managers; from organizational studies and media management approaches, uncertainty is perceived as more manageable and individual efforts to overcome it are more relevant. Issues of power, influence, and control thread through these approaches.

Chapter 2 grounds this conceptual framework in the real and fast-changing world of journalism, dissecting in a fine-grained way the complex forces reshaping journalism, and how these forces foster an uncertain environment and influence journalism practices, routines and values. We explore perceived problems of journalistic culture, such as public inaccessibility, change-resistant processes, and the conflicts that grow from dual missions (democratic and economic).

Parts II and III make up the main body of the book, comprising chapters written by leading journalism and mass communication scholars. We asked authors to explore complexities facing journalism on differing levels of analysis, and to provide theoretically grounded discussions of the uncertainties these cause, likely responses to uncertainties, and factors shaping these responses. Some chapters offer original empirical research. Others are thought essays.

Chapters in Part II, Ideology, Culture, and Institutions, are situated within macro-level contexts. Authors explore ideological, cultural, and institutional environments that shape journalists' uncertainty and responses to it. Journalists tend to respond and adapt to environmental change at these macro levels, as environments become naturalized, institutionalized, and difficult to change.

In Chapter 3, John Merrill grounds his discussion in the dynamic, complex principles of democracy, a form of governance that seeks balance between chaos and order. Merrill says journalists must respond to this turbulence by exercising their professional responsibility to inform citizens—it is not enough to merely amplify the people's voices. In Chapter 4, Peter J. Gade extends this discussion of ideological volatility by probing the implications of postmodernism. He explores journalism's normative and organizational responses to a culture of uncertainty, where truths are multiple, and egalitarian, pluralistic networks are replacing traditional sources of authority. In Chapter 5, George Sylvie applies this notion of pluralistic truth to the complex nature of journalistic diversity, noting the close relationship between diversity and uncertainty. He questions the wisdom of reducing uncertainty and thereby closing off valuable new perspectives.

In Chapter 6, Maggie Rivas-Rodriguez challenges the narrow certainties with which journalists often approach notions of social diversity. She encourages journalists to embrace a complex, nuanced view of American citizenship and identity, and she explores obstacles to such a shift. In Chapter 7, Doug Hindman also points to the value of complexity in journalism, examining a disturbing tendency by journalists to ignore the meaningful nuance and intricacy of local issues in favor of the oversimplified liberal–conservative rhetoric of national political institutions. In Chapter 8, Wilson Lowrey also explores journalism's institutional-level relationships, particularly the challenges that decentralized network structures pose to an uncertain society in need of sensemaking, and in need of a journalistic system that has public legitimacy.

Part III, Markets, Organizations, and Profession, focuses on organizational and individual levels, and includes chapters about changing markets, organizational and technological transformation, and changes related to professionalism and education. Contributors in this section explore levels at which journalists and news managers have some degree of control—in relationships with markets, in the structures and processes of news organizations, and in their daily professional lives. However, this control is elusive, and uncertainty emerges here as well.

In Chapter 9, Steve Lacy and Ardyth Sohn discuss the uncertainty and risk stemming from conflicting dual markets for audiences and advertisers, as well as complex media ownership arrangements. Uncertainty and confusion have led to strategic blunders, and the authors encourage journalists and management to reconnect with the needs and patterns of audiences and their communities, to aid prediction and planning. In Chapter 10, John Dimmick, Angela Powers, and co-authors also encourage managers to adjust media offerings to fit changing audience patterns, focusing especially on changing niches for audience gratifications. They offer a case study of one newsroom's efforts to adapt to changing niches. In Chapter 11, Ann Hollifield wrestles with the uncertainties that changing, complex markets and technologies present to the organization of news work, at both the corporate level and the level of the individual news organization. She notes disturbing as well as hopeful implications for journalism's democratic mission.

Jane Singer focuses in Chapter 12 on changing technologies, particularly on their impact on journalists' control over their work. She says that, although the practices of journalism must change and adapt, core journalism values must persist in a democratic society that needs accurate representations and sense-making. In Chapter 13, Randal Beam and Lindsey Meeks highlight journalists' diminished professional autonomy and increased workload in the face of economic and technological uncertainties. They propose a number of ways that journalists can respond, from the careful monitoring of audiences to an emphasis on the economic value of public interest reporting. In Chapter 14, Lee Becker and Tudor Vlad also discuss journalism's diminishing professional jurisdiction, which they refer to as a weakened "market shelter." They emphasize implications for journalism education, noting movements in media work toward knowledge specialization and entrepreneurialism, both of which show promise for strengthening the shelter.

In the final chapter, we connect the dots of the book's main ideas. We comb through contributors' chapters for thematic patterns that shed light on the complexity in journalism's environment, on the resulting uncertainties, and on the conflicting responses to uncertainty. We close by suggesting a way forward that requires deeper connectedness between journalists and their complex environment, some acceptance of uncertainty, and commitment to core values and principles such as clarity and accuracy.

At the end of each chapter, authors pose thought questions and comments meant to stimulate thoughtful and meaningful exchanges among scholars, students, and journalists. Although the case examples in the book are time-bound, the central concepts and conceptual frameworks are timeless, and adaptable to future contexts.

Finally, most books are shared efforts, and this is certainly true for *Changing the News*. First, we would like to acknowledge our contributors, whose intellectual diversity and scholarly expertise greatly strengthen the book, adding considerable scope and depth. We would also like to acknowledge the help of our colleagues, and our past research assistants (and present peers), including Elina Erzikova, John Latta, Jenn Mackay, and Chang Wan Woo. They provided valuable research assistance and feedback. Finally, we acknowledge the vitality and optimism of our students, who continue to be drawn to journalism despite the uncertainty. They represent the hopeful agency within the structures of the profession.

PART I
INTRODUCTION

1

COMPLEXITY, UNCERTAINTY, AND JOURNALISTIC CHANGE

Wilson Lowrey, University of Alabama, and Peter J. Gade, University of Oklahoma

The litany of journalism's recent troubles—fragmenting audiences, plummeting revenue, the challenges of digital media, declining credibility—has taken on a steady, unnerving cadence to which journalism's decision-makers are expected to march. But in which direction? Owners and managers are not at all certain.

What is certain are the troubles and their complexity. A variety of forces—technological, social, political, and economic—are pushing journalists in many directions, and some of these directions seem dubious or clash with their professional consciences. This is a global phenomenon, and it is certainly evident in the United States, the main regional focus of this book. Uncertainty obscures journalists' future as they try to see a way forward and respond.

Consider some of the complexities. The Internet supports a virtual library of information and a news-on-demand marketplace, fundamentally changing relationships between news media and audiences. In a marketplace teeming with content providers, audiences have short patience for a news media that fall short of expectations. Though mainstream media still strongly shape the news agenda (Picard, 2009), audiences expect media to provide space for their voices in the public sphere, and audiences create their own space through social media. Young people in particular are turning their backs on traditional news media (Adee, 2008; Mindich, 2008). Telling is the story of the young focus group members who declined to subscribe to *The Washington Post* for free because they did not want old papers piling up (Penenberg, 2004).

The Internet is a powerful democratic tool, but it blurs distinctions between trained journalists and all others who seek an audience or simply want to blow off steam. Journalists, educators, and the citizenry in general are questioning if anything clearly distinguishes professional journalists from everybody else.

In some corners, the notion of a diverse and egalitarian media offers reason for optimism (e.g., Gillmor, 2004). Elsewhere are calls for journalism to professionalize, through stricter education standards, accreditation, or certification, so we can tell who the "real journalists" are (Merrill, 2006; Meyer, 2004).

News audiences are becoming fragmented, partisan, and specialized (Dimmick, 2003; Project for Excellence in Journalism, 2010; Tewksbury, 2005), and successful business models have been stubbornly slow to emerge. Communities are less geographically defined, but they are more like-minded and niche. Media firms aim their portfolios of products at audience fragments, hoping to regain the market reach and leverage of the days before digital (Picard, 2005). However, online audiences expect their content for free, and increases in online ad revenue have not offset advertising losses in traditional media (Sass, 2008). News media firms have responded with cost controls and corporate restructuring, but these have led to fewer resources and to evident holes in enterprise and watchdog coverage (Project for Excellence in Journalism, 2009). Just one example of many: A recent survey found no journalists covering such federal bodies as Veterans Affairs or the Nuclear Regulatory Commission full-time, and only four devoted to covering the U.S. Internal Revenue Service (Graves, 2008).

Within this fluid, complex environment, journalists are changing how they work. Across the field, work is becoming more individualized and "contingent," with more and more journalists practicing their craft outside of organizational walls (Deuze, 2009). Within organizations, journalistic routines have been derailed by the need for continual online updating, and by the increased coordination and the new expertise and flexibility of skills required to produce multiple story versions for multiple products aimed at multiple audiences. Big multimedia projects take substantial coordination time—"three or four months" in the case of a recent award-winning package on gambling in the *Las Vegas Sun* (Curley, 2010).

Journalists are networked with one another, the audience, and technology (Beckett, 2008; Deuze, 2009), but this tight web constrains the time needed to gather information, check facts, and interact with sources. Facing economic uncertainty, news managers spend less time with news, and more time with marketing strategy (Farhi, 2010; Gade, 2008). Many lament that public service and the democratic mission are being lost, symptoms of a deprofessionalizing field (Beam, 1996, 2006).

This brief sampling of the forces contributing to journalism's uncertainty does not cover it all, but it begins to illustrate the shifting landscape, the interrelatedness and complexity of the forces and environments, and the challenges the occupation faces in trying to make sense of them. Journalists, like anyone else, make sense of their surroundings through the shared beliefs, practices, and values that constitute their culture, and through the ongoing negotiation of these. So we see journalism's culture change as journalists grope toward a new common understanding in a time of upheaval. Uncertainty, bearing risk as well as opportunity, defines this era of transformation in journalism. No wonder there are no easy solutions.

Uncertainty

A number of recent texts have outlined these difficulties and advocated change (Beckett, 2008; Kovach & Rosenstiel, 2007; McLellan & Porter, 2007; Meyer, 2004). This book also discusses specific challenges facing journalism, broadly suggesting a way forward in the final chapter. However, the book takes a unique path by focusing on the complications, pressures, and uncertainties journalists face in changing the news. In addition to pointing toward possible remedies for journalism's ailments, we examine the factors that complicate these remedies. If journalism is to adjust and thrive, we need to know the answers to a number of questions: What is the conceptual nature of uncertainty, and what are its origins? How do journalists and news managers respond to uncertainties, if at all, and why? What complicating forces, structures, and ideas constrain these responses?

Through a variety of change initiatives over the past 20 years, news managers have tried to reshape newsrooms and newsroom practice so as to gain some predictability in the face of uncertain environments. Efforts are well meaning, and some are well considered. However, many appear frantic and fleeting, and mimicry is epidemic. An example is the convergence bandwagon in the first decade of this century, when hundreds of newsrooms teamed print and broadcast journalists with little direction about how these long-time competitors should learn to collaborate, other than telling them to "get converged" (Silcock & Keith, 2006; Singer, 2004). Convergence extended the newsroom team structure, introduced in the 1990s to encourage staff collaboration and to flatten hierarchies. Today, in newsrooms increasingly focused on multimedia journalism, these structures are becoming the norm, but their effectiveness is suspect (Gade, 2004, 2008). And despite encouraging various forms of citizen-derived content, management's commitment to civic, public, and citizen journalism in newsrooms has rarely led to more than an occasional, isolated project (Massey & Haas, 2002; Nichols, Friedland, Rojas, Cho, & Shah, 2006). A number of high-profile "hyperlocal" citizen journalism efforts by legacy news media have floundered (Adams, 2008; Potts, 2007), and a recent report suggests the path to sustainability for new community news sites is rocky (Schaffer, 2010).

Reasons for these responses and results are complex. We assume that factors on a variety of levels shape decisions about change in times of uncertainty—factors such as shared understandings about news by the news outlet's community; interdependencies with other institutions; ownership demands and shifting markets and competition; continuously changing technologies, news organization structures, and resources; journalists' professional and organizational socialization; and available expertise in the labor market.

This multi-level view of influences on news falls within the normal science of news-making research (Dimmick & Coit, 1982; Hirsch, 1977; McQuail, 2010; Schudson, 2002; Shoemaker & Vos, 2009). Models vary, but generally scholars depict media personnel's decisions as framed by culture and ideology, shaped by larger political and social institutions, constrained by news organization needs, and influenced to a lesser degree by journalists' own characteristics. The various levels of influence are also evident in sociological studies portraying media organizations as porous "open systems" that are creatures of their environments (Peterson & Anand, 2004; Tichenor, Donohue, & Olien, 1980; Turow, 1997).

As suggested in these multi-level perspectives, decision-making by media personnel involves both agency and structure. Agency refers to actions and interactions at the individual human level—arguably, this side of the duality is growing in importance as work arrangements become more flexible (Deuze, 2009). Certainly, the rise of the individual personality (e.g., Arianna Huffington) seems to have the tail wagging the dog, as news structures form around engaging, entrepreneurial agents who are able to gain centrality in the network.

Structure refers to social forces and institutions shaping choices for action on macro levels (Collins, 1981; Mayes, 2005). Some media scholars have called for us to consider new ways to link agency and structure, though they know this is a tough task (Benson & Neveu, 2005; Dimmick & Coit, 1982; Whitney, 1982). And sociologists have increasingly viewed agency and structure as shaping one another. Individuals' cognitive limitations, coupled with the complications of everyday life, make the structure of routines and rules necessary (Collins, 1981), and these structures in turn organize and bind human action (e.g., Bourdieu, 1993; Giddens, 1976, 1984).

The Conceptual Nature of Uncertainty

That we live in a world of uncertainty is not news to journalists. Traditionally, journalism has emoted impermanence, surprise, even adventure and danger—like "trying to tell time by watching the second hand of a clock," said the writer Ben Hecht (Galewitz, 2001, p. 24). Yet according to the classic research on news production, the uncertainty that results from a complex, dynamic world has led journalists and their organizations toward safe routinization—toward categories, typifications, and conventions in their daily work practices, making production and relationships with other organizations stable and predictable (e.g., Epstein, 1973; Ryfe, 2006; Shoemaker, Eichholz, Kim, & Wrigley, 2001; Shoemaker & Reese, 1996; Tuchman, 1978).

Can routinization still characterize news production during times of high uncertainty? What happens to comfortable, familiar work processes when markets wobble, when technologies change and employment patterns become unstable, when distinctions between journalists and audiences blur, and cultural and social contexts shift? The rest of this chapter addresses these questions by exploring the concept of environmental uncertainty across various conceptual frameworks. The chapter maps out the tendencies with which journalists and their organizations respond to uncertainty, and the pressures, constraints, motivations, and knowledge capabilities that constrain and enable these responses. The way journalists think about uncertainty also has an impact on their responses to uncertainty. It influences which wider pressures and motivations come into play.

"Environmental uncertainty" is a potent concept in both sociological and economic research. The concept has been looked at in a number of ways, with most agreeing that uncertainty is not a friend; rather, it is to be avoided, contained, or reduced (Donaldson, 2001; McQuail, 2010; Perrow, 1986; Pfeffer & Salancik, 2003; Turow, 1982, 1997). Uncertainty is sometimes thought of as an extreme condition, in which so little is known about the way things may come out that it is simply not possible to assess risks or figure probabilities (Knight, 1921; Wilson, 2007). "Future states of the world cannot be anticipated and accurately predicted" (Pfeffer & Salancik, 2003, p. 67) because the list of possible choices hasn't been determined (Wilson, 2007). This definition reflects "fundamental" or "strong" uncertainty. When uncertainty is fundamental, relevant information about a complex environment and the odds of possible outcomes can't be known. In fact, actions today influence the environment tomorrow, making the decision environment even murkier (Dequech, 2001, 2004). Technological innovation is one major source of fundamental uncertainty. It is "arguably the best example of non-predetermined, structural change... in the economic sphere" (Dequech, 2004, p. 373) (though the degree to which technology is determined or determining is a topic of much debate [Jones & Orlikowski, 2007]). For sure, digital technology and the democratizing, fragmenting impacts associated with it continue to shake the ground on which news managers make decisions.

Alternatively, uncertainty may be thought of as somewhat conquerable. Here the assumption is that it is possible, though difficult, to assign probability to complex events. This has been called "ambiguity" and "process uncertainty" (Dequech, 2001, 2004), and, because situations are measurable, the concept of risk applies (e.g., Knight, 1921). Others refer to this as merely a less intense type of uncertainty (e.g., Wilson, 2007), one that reflects a gap between the complexity of a knowable situation and a person's ability to grasp this complexity—an ability that is challenged because of a lack of information and partial competence. Within this view, people have meaningful agency. If they can't eliminate uncertainty, they can at least reduce it by gaining knowledge. They can then improve their ability to predict and envision consequences.

Herbert Simon's (1976) "bounded rationality" fits with this view. For Simon, people making decisions in organizations are limited in their ability to think logically through the odds in a complex environment. He said people are more likely to adopt rules of thumb in their decision-making than they are to assess costs and benefits in a thorough way. Decision-makers do take on rational-choice searches for solutions, but these efforts are limited, often resulting in "satisficing"—settling for an OK outcome rather than on an optimal one. In the same vein, psychologists Kahneman and Tversky (1979) observed decision-makers taking mental short cuts, settling on readily available information, and on tried and true practices. As mentioned, news managers and staff often adopt tried and true routines and conventions to deal with uncertainty (Becker, Lowrey, Claussen, & Anderson, 2000; Shoemaker et al., 2001; Tuchman, 1978; Whitney & Becker, 1982). This has been found in online news work as well. To wit, Domingo (2008) found in a study of Spanish newspapers that the routine of immediacy framed decision-making during uncertainty: For example, during a breaking murder story, journalists fell into a cycle of online news filtering and story updating rather than pursuing news actively.

The idea of bounded rationality is also found in Williamson's (e.g., 1983) work on economic transactions. According to this view, the knowledge and information accessible to principal decision-makers differ, as do their motivations and aspirations. Decision-makers do not share an equal, objective base of knowledge, and this leads to unequal knowledge about transactions (Nooteboom, 2000). In uncertain times, individuals and companies negotiate contracts with limited rationality, evidence, and forethought, leaving the door open to opportunism. And so third parties are needed to establish conventions that all involved in the negotiation can follow. This reduces uncertainty, limits opportunism, and helps stabilize markets. This logic suggests merging or acquiring suppliers, buyers, or competitors may reduce uncertainty because it allows firms to monitor other firms on which they depend (Barney & Hesterly, 2001; Perrow, 1986; Williamson, 1983), and to draw on their competencies (Hardy, Phillips, & Lawrence, 2003). Newspaper–TV partnerships have followed this logic: Local competitors collaborate in using emerging online and multimedia technologies, in the hopes this will lessen uncertainty about markets and competition.

These perspectives all assume human shortcomings can lead to problems in handling uncertainty, but that people can overcome shortcomings. However, these perspectives have been criticized for ignoring the way institutional forms of all sorts—other organizations, technologies, and routines—frame and constrain the ways people in organizations attend to, select, organize, and interpret information (e.g., Dequech, 2004; Perrow, 1986). Institutional influences at different levels work in the background, the argument goes, rendering the premises for news work naturalized, unquestioned. A good example is the way the traditional two-party political system in the United States has reinforced journalists' conception of objectivity—as a two-sided balance. This media portrayal then reinforces the system.

Uncertainty and the Nature of Journalism's Environment

Entering the second decade of the twenty-first century, journalists' comfortably obscure surroundings have become highly complex and dynamic, but also uncomfortably transparent. The world is intruding in the form of increasingly active audiences and new audience-centered newsroom tasks, and this world is hard to understand. Society is becoming increasingly postmodern, with collapsing boundaries and multiple, fleeting sources of truth. These changes in the "world out there" are imposing. But are they powerfully determining, or merely troubles to be analyzed and worked through? It depends on how one thinks of journalism's social, cultural, political, and economic environments, and how powerfully constraining the environment is for decision-makers.

Much of the literature examining the impact of uncertainty on news decision-making can be traced to two traditions: media sociology and media management and economics. The sociological literature has focused on broad forces that constrain or channel decision-making, emphasizing culture, and social and organizational structures, and the ways journalists typify and routinize so they can accomplish work in uncertain times. Production routines reduce uncertainty for news organizations even as they may serve powerful forces beyond.

According to traditional media sociology research, decision-making by journalists and their news organizations is subject to the patterns, needs, and dependencies of other powerful organizations and institutions in the news organization's social world. These views are reflected in British media traditions that highlight the influence of resources from political and economic institutions (e.g., Curran, 1996; McQuail, 2010), as well as theoretical approaches such as media dependency theory (Merskin, 1999), the community power structure framework (Hindman, Littlefield, Preston, & Neumann, 1999; Tichenor et al., 1980), and institutional approaches portraying news as an arm of political and economic institutions (e.g., Cook, 2005; Ryfe, 2006).

Intricately interconnected and complicated environments make it tough to calculate odds or control outcomes because decisions hinge on decisions made by others (Dequech, 2004). And the impact of uncertainty in the environment increases as the interdependence and interactivity with an organization's environment increases (Pfeffer & Salancik, 2003). We can see this at the level of the reporter, when a story becomes more complex because it demands esoteric, expert knowledge or because the official agencies involved grow in number and complexity—or even because the reporter's own work structure becomes unstable. And we see this at the managerial level, when a news company's change efforts become entangled in consequences to local commercial or governmental institutions. In such situations, decision-makers may try to find shelter in the tried and true (Lindblom, 1959), in easily available models of what others are doing (Boczkowski, 2010; Lowrey, 2005; Ryan & Peterson, 1982), or by conventionally adopting someone else's guidelines (Perrow, 1986; Williamson, 1983). Routines and conventions can in turn become substitutes for a hard-to-understand world.

In contrast, management literature on decision-making acknowledges pressures and constraints of the social world but most strongly emphasizes agency, or individuals' motivations and actions. The workings of the "world out there" are seen as ambiguous, but not impossible to know, and so news managers and staff try to act on their immediate surroundings in an informed and rational way (Picard, 2004; Sylvie & Witherspoon, 2002). This literature tends to be more prescriptive, less fatalistic, looking for best practices. Media organization managers and owners assess costs and benefits of both action and inaction, and they take calculable risks. However, they avoid diving headlong into the darkness. It is possible to control uncertainty, either by changing the way work tasks are structured, or by monitoring sources of uncertainty beyond the organization, such as competitors, consumers, and suppliers (e.g., Lacy & Martin, 2004; Meyer, 2004; Picard, 2004). Also, it is possible for organizations and individuals to learn and innovate, by engaging fully with diverse networks, and gaining and creating new knowledge (Hardy, Phillips, & Lawrence, 2003; Williamson, 1983).

Change in a Knowable World

How is journalism, as an organizational or occupational enterprise, likely to respond to an intruding, complex world? If environments are seen as intrusive and changing but knowable, then individuals may learn about their situations and gain some control. Prescriptive approaches from research on organizational management, such as structural contingency theory and organizational learning and development, apply here. According to contingency theory, managers assess the environment and then shuffle personnel and tasks accordingly, to help steady the flow of incoming resources so managers can predict and plan. Theoretically, mechanized, predictable organizational processes work best in stable, predictable times. Fluid, less bureaucratic processes work better in dynamic times (Donaldson, 2001). Similar notions have fueled news managers' efforts to flatten newsroom hierarchies into work teams, and to encourage the rank and file to share ideas across networks that transcend organizational boundaries, encouraging innovation (Gade, 2004; Hansen, Neuzil, & Ward, 1998; Williams, 2007).

According to scholarship on organizational learning, intrusive environmental change leads organizations to abandon routines and conventions and to question assumptions, and rethink relationships with the relevant environment (audiences, advertisers, suppliers, news sources, etc.). Managers restructure organizations to help them learn and innovate, by flattening internal hierarchies and creating collaborative work teams (Donaldson, 2001; Kanter, 1983; Weick & Westley, 2001). However, these opportunities are fleeting, and they confuse. Their organizations may too easily fall back into well-worn routines: "On the actual day of battle, naked truths may be picked up for the asking; by the following morning they have already begun to get into their uniforms" (Cohen and Gooch, 1991, p. 44).

Learning and change may take place at the level of the occupation as well (Abbott, 1988; Dooley, 1999). Professions and occupations (or a "semi-profession" in the case of journalism) may find their "jurisdiction" over an area of work threatened by changing technologies, by occupational rivals, or by shifting social conditions. In such cases, professions may wither. However, they may also re-evaluate assumptions on which they base the logic of their decision-making. They may redefine the nature of the problems they claim to solve. In the face of citizen sites and blogs, for example, journalists have tried to reposition their work goals away from mere dissemination, which anyone can now do, and toward news gathering and truth seeking, competencies that are higher-hanging fruit and require resources, legitimacy, and esoteric knowledge. The key, then, is for a profession and its professionals to have a flexible, abstract knowledge base and to use it to redefine practices and purposes. Professions with weak knowledge bases, too strongly tied to transitory technologies or common competencies, will be less successful at rethinking what they're doing. Also, as will be discussed in Chapter 2, the degree to which the organizations that house professionals are structured to allow autonomy, collaboration, and learning can shape a profession's ability to exercise its professional knowledge and reposition itself.

Although "learning" is often portrayed as an inclusive, shared act, it may also be thought of as a tool for gaining control, and, in fact, staff concern over management's motives and a lack of staff input have contributed to failed change efforts in newsrooms (e.g., Daniels & Hollifield, 2002; Hansen et al., 1998). Recall that transaction cost economics predicts firms will buy or merge with other firms in order to monitor them, using knowledge gained to reduce uncertainty (Perrow, 1986; Williamson, 1983). In addition, the "precariousness" inherent in new flexible work arrangements, theoretically conducive to organizational learning, can shift control from workers to management (Deuze, 2009).

These approaches suggest that managers will seek research about audience preferences and will encourage rigorous interaction with audiences to learn more about their preferences and needs, and they will structure their

organizations less hierarchically in order to take advantage of this new information. In fact, news organizations are becoming more integrated on several
levels. Joint ventures across organizations, such as convergence partnerships
between TV stations and newspapers, grow competencies, product base, and
audience reach. Restructuring within organizations removes the walls between
business and journalism, creating interdepartmental teams that mesh marketing research with development of the news product and its content (Gade &
Raviola, 2009). And it's the rare news manager who does not routinely monitor the use patterns of online readers and share these results in news meetings
(Brill, 2001; Lowrey, 2009).

Change in a Complex World

Rational-choice models such as transaction cost economics and organizational
learning tend to assume that managers will seek beneficial change for the
organization during uncertain times, that the environment is not so complex
that it can't be monitored and assessed, and that structure and processes may
be changed based on these assessments.

In contrast, much of the sociological literature on news production portrays
individual managers as having limited autonomy. Decisions reflect the news
organization's dependence on broad cultural, social, political, and economic
structures. These narrowly constrain the range of decisions, and outcomes
tend to reflect the status quo, or serve the powerful, according to critical
approaches. The "world out there" for managers and staffers is thought to
be impossibly complex. So routines, conventions, and easily available models
channel decisions and behavior, becoming taken-for-granted common sense
and a substitute for an unknowable world.

This channeling of decisions and behavior may blind news managers to
new possibilities. Industry analysts have scratched their heads over news
managers' hesitance to change direction when the conventional path seems
to be heading off a cliff. Not surprisingly, the terms "routine" and "convention" are often used pejoratively. However, the consequences of conventions
and routines are not straightforward—they have actually proved helpful in a
number of ways. At the staff level, journalists typify events so they can choose
what's news from an impossibly complex world (Shoemaker et al., 2001;
Tuchman, 1978). As Giddens (1976) says that the conventions of language
enable speech, so may we say that the agreed-upon conventions of journalism
can enable journalistic agency. Audiences and communities also need conventions, as there must be a stable, shared understanding about journalism's
forms and practices so they can "get" the meaning journalists intend (Altheide
& Snow, 1979; Schudson, 2003). So we see that routines and familiar conventions can add clarity to the communication of media messages in a confusing
world; unfortunately they have also tended to constrain the social meaning of

these messages, constrain journalistic practices, and blind news organizations to the need for change.

Production routines and conventions have allowed journalists and their organizations to keep external uncertainty at bay, for better or worse. In the modern era, newsrooms have been at least partly buffered from the complexities of audience likes and dislikes, and from fluctuations in ad revenue. Most journalists don't regularly meet with their "client-audience." So they have created conventional images of audiences and community rather than seek their own systematic evidence, or follow marketing research (Ettema & Whitney, 1994; Lowrey, 2009; McQuail, 2010).

This has upset those who, more recently, crave a responsive and nimble journalism in the face of change; management efforts to "blow up" newsrooms have targeted these very categories, conventions, and routines. However, we should also consider that when news organizations base decisions on audience marketing research, it may erode the value of journalistic professional knowledge, and undercut a publication's long-earned credibility and brand (e.g., Meyer, 2004; Sterling, 2008). Change is often necessary, and it may very well be that the traditional brand needs eroding, but the consequences of radical change should be fully appreciated. Organizations that throw over core values and practices can increase the chance of failure. Older organizations fail less frequently than younger organizations because they have developed valuable external ties, stable competencies, and social and professional legitimacy (Baum, 2001). Attempts to change core practices can rob an "organization's history of its survival value, . . . lowering its performance reliability and accountability back to that of a new organization" (Baum, 2001, p. 100).

Similarly, institutional theorists say that organizations buffer their core activities and processes from the ups and downs of their surroundings so that they can maintain legitimacy and smooth working relations with the wider institutional environment. For example, news organizations' resource commitment to new practices such as convergence and hyperlocal efforts may amount to little more than window dressing (Adams, 2008; Lowrey, 2005; Potts, 2007), and, although this tentativeness may get in the way of large-scale core change, the appearance of progressiveness and innovation can help an organization hold on to legitimacy.

Uncertainty, Power, and Control

We touch on one last aspect of the relationship between uncertainty and decision-making—the issue of control and power over decision-making. If we allow for the possibility of real agency in response to changes and complexities facing the news outlet, then we need to consider that relationships of power and control may be altered, shaping patterns of decision-making within the organization.

Through more predictable times, news organizations gained authority, legitimacy, and stability through strong ties with other powerful institutions. These ties allowed a fairly continuous, predictable source of "raw material"—notably, information and ad revenue—thereby limiting uncertainty and enabling planning. News organization routines have tended to reflect the political and economic status quo, and have tended to serve the information needs of other institutions and organizations (Ryfe, 2006; Shoemaker & Vos, 2009; Singer, 2005; Tuchman, 1978). At the same time, journalism has staked out an area of autonomy for itself. Other institutions have had to work with and through journalistic processes, and recognize and account for journalism's professional norms, in trying to get their messages to the public. Journalism and other institutions have been co-dependent. Shared routines and conventions have made work manageable for the news organization and for dependent institutions, and have also helped establish a shared understanding between news media and their audiences and communities.

However, turbulent times rock the stability of these relationships. Digital, interactive technology allows not only everyday citizens, but also powerful commercial and governmental institutions, easy ways to produce and disseminate messages directly to audiences. So, although diminished journalistic control may allow diverse and marginalized voices to be heard more directly, it has also opened up wider avenues for direct messages from the powerful.

Instability in the environment also affects power dynamics within news organizations. When individuals or subunits within an organization are able to keep resource flow stable and reduce uncertainty for the organization, they gain power within the organization (Pfeffer & Salancik, 2003). So, instead of rigid, bureaucratic rules, policies, and routines giving way to flat, egalitarian, and innovative processes—as predicted by organizational learning approaches—they may instead give way to a capricious, direct form of control by those able to bring order. In such situations, individuals use their organizations as tools for their own purposes: "The resources and the goals of an organization are up for grabs, and people grab for them continually" (Perrow, 1986, pp. 12–13).

Although the concepts of bureaucratic control and rules have become associated popularly with rigidity and with the stifling of innovation, formal rules can actually allow creativity and autonomy within the rules' boundaries. So, as with the consequences of routines, the consequences of rules are not straightforward. Knowledge of boundaries, offered by rules, can free individuals for confident movement within them (Ettema, 1982; Perrow, 1986)—again, Giddens' (1976) observations on the enabling quality of the structure of language are relevant. Collaborative work teams in newsrooms, which are supposed to loosen traditional structure, flatten authority, and encourage creativity, may actually lead to more capricious control. This is because well-known routines and rules are dismissed, causing confusion and frustration over unclear roles and tasks, a phenomenon that has been referred to as the "tyranny of structurelessness" (Freeman, 1972–1973). Staffers must step cautiously to avoid managerial preferences, which still exist but now are obscured; staffers become unnerved, controlled by hidden landmines rather than visible fences (Gade, 2004; Hansen et al., 1998). In addition, the widening of skills that come from fluid, collaborative work arrangements can serve management's need for adaptiveness (though also offering opportunities for workers) (Deuze, 2009).

Power grabs within organizations also point to the possibility of internal conflict over decision-making (Pfeffer & Salancik, 2003). Different subgroups within organizations—for example, reporters and visual journalists—may ascribe to differing norms and practices. Conflict deriving from differentiation of power within organizations may lead to a negotiated and less than optimal outcome. Conversely, normative conflict may set the stage for innovation and constructive change (Lowrey, 2002; Trice, 1993).

Change and Stasis

In dealing with turbulence and uncertainty, the industry and profession must find the right mix of change and stasis, of agency and structure. They must find ways to alter the norms and practices that have constituted journalism culture while also holding on to fundamental, hard-won competencies and connections that enable journalistic agency (Sterling, 2008). News organizations depend on both the fuel of economic capital and the legitimacy that comes from "cultural capital"—reputation, credibility, and professional knowledge (Benson & Neveu, 2005).

Sociology of professions literature suggests professions with a strong base of "abstract knowledge" are better able to secure both cultural/social legitimacy and economic standing because they can successfully define their audiences and markets, as well as the types of problems the profession can address. Such professions can successfully claim control over areas of work in times of change (Abbott, 1988; Dooley, 1999). The degree to which the organization is structured to allow professionals the autonomous use of their knowledge base is an important factor as well, particularly for "semi-professions" such as journalism that are mostly housed within organizations. Insufficient abstract knowledge can lead to abandoning jurisdiction over critical, core areas of work, opening these areas up to competition from other professional/occupational groups.

Within this view, journalism's lurch toward increased entertainment and opinion content—a response to perceived market demands, diminished resources for reporting, and intense online interactivity—could leave the work of gathering public information vulnerable to encroachment by PR professionals, politicians, or bloggers. However, journalism has had previous success in altering its culture and in repositioning itself as a profession. When challenged by an advancing public relations field in the early twentieth century, U.S. journalism successfully altered its goals by embracing the practices of objectivity, balance, and news analysis (Schudson, 1978).

There are real pitfalls in both changing and staying put. Likewise, there are benefits to scrutinizing and responding to environments on the one hand, and to maintaining core competencies on the other. Viewing uncertainty as less than absolute, and the environment as potentially knowable, opens the door to agency by news managers and staffers, and to the possibility of beneficial change. Yet entanglements with larger institutions, rigid organizational structures, tussles over power within the organization, and decision-makers' limited rationality will continue to challenge efforts to make beneficial changes and to deal effectively with uncertainty. The gap between the decision-maker's knowledge and a complex, dynamic, hard-to-predict environment will likely persist. A key may be to develop the knowledge necessary to make wise decisions—to recognize when changes should be core or peripheral, or when cultural capital trumps economic capital, to understand better how to structure organizations for change. Journalists have been able to adjust their culture and exercise "abstract knowledge" to save their profession before. It should be possible again.

Thought Questions: Contemplating Change

In this chapter, we discuss the complexities surrounding journalism, and the resulting uncertainties. We consider assumptions of the dominant theoretical frameworks in the news-making literature, and what these suggest about complexities and uncertainties and their impact on journalistic change. Uncertainty is accompanied by risk, and there are strong forces and convincing rationales that work against change and innovation, even when the need to change seems clear. With these thoughts in mind, we offer these questions for further discussion:

1. Do you think news organizations and journalists can successfully respond to the complexities and uncertainties they face? Why or why not? Are there certain aspects of journalism that must not be changed, or is a complete overhaul needed?
2. How much agency and autonomy do journalists and managers have as they try to bring about change within wider structural constraints?
3. As control over news information ebbs away from professional journalists, everyday citizens have more input into news—but so do powerful commercial and governmental entities. Is this a problem for society? If not, why not? If so, what can be done?

References

Abbott, A. (1988). *The system of professions*. Chicago: University of Chicago Press.

Adams, R. (2008, June 4). Big daily's 'hyperlocal' flop: Loudounextra.com fails to give lift to Washington Post. *The Washington Post*, p. B1.

Adee, B. (2008). Digging into social media to build a newspaper audience. *Nieman Reports, 62*(4), 52–54.

Altheide, D. L., & Snow, R. P. (1979). *Media logic*. Beverly Hills, CA: Sage.

Barney, J. B., & Hesterly, W. (2001). Organizational economics: Understanding the relationship between organizations and economic analysis. In S. Clegg, C. Hardy, & W. R. Nord (Eds.), *Handbook of organization studies* (pp. 115–147). London: Sage.

Baum, J. A. C. (2001). Organizational ecology. In S. Clegg, C. Hardy, & W. R. Nord (Eds.), *Handbook of organization studies* (pp. 77–114). London: Sage.

Beam, R. (1996). How perceived environmental uncertainty influences marketing orientation of U.S. daily newspapers. *Journalism & Mass Communication Quarterly, 73*, 285–303.

Beam, R. (2006). Organizational goals and priorities and the job satisfaction of U.S. journalists. *Journalism & Mass Communication Quarterly, 83*, 169–185.

Becker, L. B., Lowrey, W., Claussen, D. S., & Anderson, W. A. (2000). Why does the beat go on? An examination of the role of beat structure in the newsroom. *Newspaper Research Journal, 21*(4), 2–16.

Beckett, C. (2008). *Supermedia: Saving journalism so it can save the world*. Hoboken, NJ: Wiley-Blackwell.

Benson, R., & Neveu, E. (2005). Introduction: Field theory as a work in progress. In R. Benson & E. Neveu (Eds.), *Bourdieu and the journalistic field* (pp. 1–25). Cambridge, UK: Polity Press.

Boczkowski, P. J. (2010). *News at work: Imitation in an age of information abundance*. Chicago: University of Chicago Press.

Bourdieu, P. (1993). *The field of cultural production*. New York: Columbia University Press.

Brill, A. M. (2001). Online journalists embrace new marketing function. *Newspaper Research Journal, 22*(2), 28–41.

Cohen, E. A., & Gooch, J. (1991). *Military misfortunes: The anatomy of failure in war*. New York: Anchor Books.

Collins, R. (1981). Microfoundations of macrosociology. *American Journal of Sociology, 86*, 984–1014.

Cook, T. E. (2005). *Governing with the news: The news media as a political institution*. Chicago: University of Chicago Press.

Curley, R. (2010, July 27). Bottoming out: A look back at our multimedia journalism package on gambling addiction. Rob Curley: Internet punk. Retrieved November 25, 2010, from http://robcurley.com/2010/07/27/bottoming-out-sun-multimedia-journalism/

Curran, J. (1996). Mass media and democracy revisited. In J. Curran, & M. Gurevitch (Eds.), *Mass media and society* (pp. 81–119). London: Arnold.

Daniels, G. L., & Hollifield, C. A. (2002). Time of turmoil: Short- and long-term effects of organizational change on newsroom employees. *Journalism & Mass Communication Quarterly, 79*, 661–680.

Dequech, D. (2001). Bounded rationality, institutions, and uncertainty. *Journal of Economic Issues, 35*, 911–930.

Dequech, D. (2004). Uncertainty: Individuals, institutions and technology. *Cambridge Journal of Economics, 28*, 365–378.

Deuze, M. (2009). Technology and the individual journalist: Agency beyond imitation and change. In B. Zelizer (Ed.), *The changing faces of journalism: Tabloidization, technology and truthiness* (pp. 82–97). London: Routledge.

Dimmick, J. (2003). *Media competition and coexistence: The theory of the niche*. Mahwah, NJ: Lawrence Erlbaum.

Dimmick, J., & Coit, P. (1982). Levels of analysis in mass media decision making. *Communication Research, 9*, 3–32.

Domingo, D. (2008). Online journalism models in four Catalan newsrooms. In C. Paterson, & D. Domingo (Eds.), *Making online news: The ethnography of new media production*. New York: Peter Lang.

Donaldson, L. (2001). The normal science of structural contingency theory. In S. R. Clegg, C. Hardy, & W. Nord (Eds.), *The handbook of organization studies* (pp. 57–76). London: Sage.

Dooley, P. L. (1999). Journalistic occupational development and discourses of power. In D. Demers, & K. Viswanath (Eds.), *Mass media, social control and social change* (pp. 333–358). Ames: Iowa State University Press.

Epstein, E. J. (1973). *News from nowhere: Television and the news*. New York: Random House.

Ettema, J. S. (1982). The organizational context of creativity: A case study from public television. In J. S. Ettema, & D. C. Whitney (Eds.), *Individuals in mass media organizations: Creativity and constraint* (pp. 91–106). Beverly Hills, CA: Sage.

Ettema, J. S., & Whitney, D. C. (1994). The money arrow: An introduction to audiencemaking. In J. S. Ettema, & D. C. Whitney (Eds.), *Audiencemaking: How the media create the audience* (pp. 1–18). Thousand Oaks, CA: Sage.

Farhi, P. (2010, Fall). Traffic problems. *American Journalism Review, 32*, 46–51.

Freeman, J. (1972–1973). The tyranny of structurelessness. *Berkeley Journal of Sociology, 17*, 151–165.

Gade, P. (2004). Newspapers and organizational development: Management and journalist perceptions of newsroom cultural change. *Journalism and Communication Monographs, 6*, 3–55.

Gade, P. (2008). Journalism guardians in a time of great change: Newspaper editors' perceived influence in integrated news organizations. *Journalism & Mass Communication Quarterly, 85*, 371–392.

Gade, P., & Raviola, E. (2009). Integration of news and the news of integration: A structural perspective on news media changes. *Journal of Media Business Studies, 6*(1), 87–111.

Galewitz, H. (Ed.). (2001). *Jewish wit and wisdom*. Mineola, NY: Dover Publications.

Giddens, A. (1976). *New rules of sociological method*. London: Hutchinson.

Giddens, A. (1984). *The constitution of society*. Berkeley: University of California Press.

Gillmor, D. (2004). *We the media: Grassroots journalism by the people, for the people*. Sebastopol, CA: O'Reilly.

Graves, F. (2008, Spring). Watchdog reporting: Exploring its myth. *Nieman Reports*. Retrieved November 25, 2010, from http://www.nieman.harvard.edu/reportsitem. aspx?id=100065

Hansen, K. A., Neuzil, M., & Ward, J. (1998). Newsroom topic teams: Journalists' assessment of effects on news routines and newspaper quality. *Journalism & Mass Communication Quarterly, 75*, 803–821.

Hardy, C., Phillips, N., & Lawrence, T. B. (2003). Resources, knowledge and influence: The organizational effects of interorganizational collaboration. *Journal of Management Studies, 40*, 321–347.

Hindman, D. B., Littlefield, R., Preston, A., & Neumann, D. (1999). Structural pluralism, ethnic pluralism, and community newspapers. *Journalism & Mass Communication Quarterly, 76*, 250–263.

Hirsch, P. M. (1977). Occupational, organizational and institutional models in mass media research: Toward an integrated framework. In P. M. Hirsch, P. V. Miller, & F. G. Kline (Eds.), *Strategies for communication research* (pp. 13–42). Beverly Hills, CA: Sage.

Jones, M., & Orlikowski, W. J. (2007). Information technology and the dynamics of organizational change. In R. Mansell, C. Avgerou, D. Quah, & R. Silverstone (Eds.), *Information and communication technologies* (pp. 293–313). Oxford: Oxford University Press.

Kahneman, D., & Tversky, A. (1979). Prospect theory: An analysis of decision under risk. *Econometrica, 47*, 263–291.

Kanter, R. M. (1983). *The change masters: Innovation for productivity in the American corporation.* New York: Simon and Schuster.

Knight, F. H. (1921). *Risk, uncertainty and profit.* Boston: Houghton Mifflin.

Kovach, B., & Rosenstiel, T. (2007). *The elements of journalism: What newspeople should know and the public should expect.* New York: Three Rivers Press.

Lacy, S., & Martin, H. (2004). Competition, circulation and advertising. *Newspaper Research Journal, 25*(1), 18–39.

Lindblom, C. E. (1959). The science of muddling through. *Public Administration Review, 19*, 79–88.

Lowrey, W. (2002). Word people vs. picture people: Normative differences and strategies for control over work among newsroom subgroups. *Mass Communication and Society, 5*, 411–432.

Lowrey, W. (2005). Commitment to newspaper–TV partnering: A test of the impact of institutional isomorphism. *Journalism & Mass Communication Quarterly, 82*, 495–514.

Lowrey, W. (2009). Institutional roadblocks: Assessing journalism's response to changing audiences. In Z. Papacharissi (Ed.), *Journalism and citizenship: New agendas* (pp. 44–67). New York: Routledge.

Massey, B. L., & Haas, T. (2002). Does making journalism more public make a difference? A critical review of evaluative research on public journalism. *Journalism & Mass Communication Quarterly, 79*, 559–586.

Mayes, P. (2005). Linking micro and macro social structure through genre analysis. *Research on Language and Social Interaction, 38*, 331–370.

McLellan, M., & Porter, T. (2007). *News, improved: How America's newsrooms are learning to change.* Washington, DC: CQ Press.

McQuail, D. (2010). *McQuail's mass communication theory* (5th ed.). London: Sage.

Merrill, J. C. (2006). *Media, mission and morality.* Spokane, WA: Marquette Books.

Merskin, D. (1999). Media dependency theory: Origins and direction. In D. Demers, & K. Viswanath (Eds.), *Mass media: Social control and social change* (pp. 77–98). Ames: Iowa State University Press.

Meyer, P. (2004). *The vanishing newspaper*. Columbia, MO: University of Missouri Press.

Mindich, D. T. Z. (2008). Journalism and citizenship: making the connections right. *Nieman Reports, 62*(4), 23–25.

Nichols, S. L., Friedland, L. A., Rojas, H., Cho, J., & Shah, D. V. (2006). Examining the effects of public journalism on civil society from 1994–2002: Organizational factors, story frames and citizen engagement. *Journalism & Mass Communication Quarterly, 83*, 77–100.

Nooteboom, B. (2000). *Learning and innovation in organizations and economics*. New York: Oxford University Press.

Penenberg, A. L. (2004, November 11). Newspapers should really worry. *Wired*. Retrieved August 9, 2010, from http://www.wired.com/culture/lifestyle/news/2004/11/65813

Perrow, C. (1986). *Complex organizations: A critical essay*. New York: McGraw-Hill.

Peterson, R. A., & Anand, N. (2004). The production of culture perspective. *Annual Review of Sociology, 30*, 311–334.

Pfeffer, J., & Salancik, G. R. (2003). *The external control of organizations: A resource dependence perspective*. Stanford, CA: Stanford University Press.

Picard, R. G. (2004). Commercialism and newspaper quality. *Newspaper Research Journal, 25*(1), 54–67.

Picard, R. G. (2005). The nature of media product portfolios. In R. G. Picard (Ed.), *Media product portfolios* (pp. 1–22). Mahwah, NJ: Lawrence J. Erlbaum.

Picard, R. G. (2009). Changing structures and organization of newsrooms. *Journal of Media Business Studies, 6*, 1–7.

Potts, M. (2007, July 15). Backfence: Lessons learned. Recovering Journalist. Retrieved November, 23, 2010, from http://tinyurl.com/25u6on

Project for Excellence in Journalism. (2009). *2008 trends. The state of the news media 2009*. Retrieved November 23, 2010, from http://www.stateofthenewsmedia.org/2009/narrative_yearinthenews_intro.php?media=2&cat=0

Project for Excellence in Journalism. (2010). *Overview. The state of the news media 2010*. Retrieved November 25, 2010, from http://www.stateofthemedia.org/2010/overview_intro.php

Ryan, J., & Peterson, R. A. (1982). The product image: The fate of creativity in country music songwriting. In J. S. Ettema & D. C. Whitney (Eds.), *Individuals in mass media organizations: Creativity and constraint* (pp. 11–32). Beverly Hills, CA: Sage.

Ryfe, D. M. (2006). New Institutionalism and the news. *Political Communication, 23*, 135–144.

Sass, E. (2008, March 31). Bad to worse, to worst: Newspaper revenues down 7.9% in 2007, as online growth slows. MediaPost Publications. Retrieved November 23, 2010, from http://tinyurl.com/289bfj3

Schaffer, J. (2010). New voices: What works. Retrieved November 23, 2010, from http://www.kcnn.org/nv_whatworks/pdf/

Schudson, M. (1978). *Discovering the news*. New York: Basic Books.

Schudson, M. (2002). The news media as political institutions. *Annual Review of Political Science, 5*, 249–269.

Schudson, M. (2003). *The sociology of the news*. New York: W. W. Norton.

Shoemaker, P. J., Eichholz, M., Kim, E., & Wrigley, B. (2001). Individual and routine forces in gatekeeping. *Journalism & Mass Communication Quarterly, 78*, 233–246.

Shoemaker, P., & Reese, S. (1996). *Mediating the message: Theories of influence on mass media content*. White Plains, NY: Longman.

Shoemaker, P. J., & Vos, T. P. (2009). *Gatekeeping theory*. New York: Routledge.

Silcock, B. W., & Keith, S. (2006). Translating the Tower of Babel? *Journalism Studies*, 7, 610–627.

Simon, H. (1976). *Administrative behavior* (3rd ed.). New York: Free Press.

Singer, J. B. (2004). Strange bedfellows? The diffusion of convergence in four news organizations. *Journalism Studies*, 5, 3–18.

Singer, J. B. (2005). The political j-blogger: "Normalizing" a new media form to fit old norms and practices. *Journalism*, 6, 173–198.

Sterling, J. (2008). A plan for a U.S. newspaper industry counterattack against disruptive innovators. *Strategy & Leadership*, 36, 20–26.

Sylvie, G., & Witherspoon, P. D. (2002). *Time, change and the American newspaper*. Mahwah, NJ: Lawrence Erlbaum.

Tewksbury, D. (2005). The seeds of audience fragmentation: Specialization in the use of online news sites. *Journal of Broadcasting & Electronic Media*, 49, 332–348.

Tichenor, P. J., Donohue, G. A., & Olien, C. N. (1980). *Community conflict & the press*. Beverly Hills, CA: Sage.

Trice, H. M. (1993). *Occupational subcultures in the workplace*. Ithaca, NY: ILR Press.

Tuchman, G. (1978). *Making the news: A study in the construction of reality*. New York: Free Press.

Turow, J. (1982). Unconventional programs on television: An organizational perspective. In J. S. Ettema & D. C. Whitney (Eds.), *Individuals in mass media organizations: Creativity and constraint* (pp. 107–129). London: Sage.

Turow, J. (1997). *Media systems in society: Understanding industries, strategies and power*. White Plains, NY: Longman.

Weick, K. E., & Westley, F. (2001). Organizational learning: Affirming an oxymoron. In S. R. Clegg, C. Hardy, & W. Nord (Eds.), *The handbook of organization studies* (pp. 440–458). London: Sage.

Whitney, D. C. (1982). Mass communicator studies: Similarity, difference and level of analysis. In J. S. Ettema & D. C. Whitney (Eds.), *Individuals in mass media organizations: Creativity and constraint* (pp. 241–254). Beverly Hills, CA: Sage.

Whitney, D. C., & Becker, L. B. (1982). Keeping the gates for gatekeepers: The effects of wire news. *Journalism Quarterly*, 59, 60–65.

Williams, V. (2007). All eyes forward: How to help your newsroom get where it wants to go faster. American Press Institute. Retrieved November 23, 2010, from http://www.knightfoundation.org/dotAsset/355991.pdf

Williamson, O. (1983). Organizational innovation: The transaction-costs approach. In J. Ronen (Ed.), *Entrepreneurship* (pp. 101–134). Lexington, MA: Heath.

Wilson, M. C. (2007). Uncertainty and probability in institutional economics. *Journal of Economic Issues*, 41, 1087–1097.

2

RESHAPING THE JOURNALISTIC CULTURE

Peter J. Gade, University of Oklahoma, and Wilson Lowrey, University of Alabama

Until recently, news was a product created by professional journalists employed by media companies. Creating news required expensive technology (e.g., a printing press or production studio) and a means of distribution that was not available to the public. News judgments were generally determined by the norms and values of journalism. The public was seldom an active participant. The mass media model that endured throughout the twentieth century positioned journalism as an influential institution. News media reported to citizens the events and actions of other powerful institutions (e.g., government, business), linking these institutions to journalism and journalism to the public. The democratic rationale for journalism is derived from these dissemination, agenda setting, and watchdog functions, and individual journalists have long found that their social and political influence emerges from exclusive access to the powerful and elite (Schudson, 2002; Weaver, Beam, Brownlee, Voakes, & Wilhoit, 2007). This mass media model largely assumed a one-way flow of information from media to audience.

How quickly that model has eroded. Digital media, and their increasingly numerous applications, empower the public in ways that were unforeseen less than a decade ago. Anyone with access to a computer and rudimentary technical expertise can create their own media products—including *news and commentary*—and distribute them to an audience that transcends geographic boundaries. Public officials use online media to communicate directly with their constituents, no longer reliant on news media, and citizens can interact online with elected officials, the journalists who write about them, and one another. This empowerment has affected the media landscape in ways that Pulitzer Prize-winning journalist Thomas Friedman (2007) says are "fundamentally reshaping the flow of creativity, innovation, political mobilization, and information gathering and dissemination" (p. 95). The flow of information is no longer top down (from media and traditional sources of authority to the public) or one way, but side-to-side (from people to people) through mediated social networks, and bubbling up from any level of the social, political, or economic strata.

These technological and social developments have also challenged news media's economic prominence in the information marketplace, adding further complexity to journalism's fast-changing environment, and increasing uncertainty in the minds of journalists. Many basic questions are apparent. How does journalism maintain its influence in this new media landscape? How can news organizations best employ new technologies? Is journalism a skill set that belongs only to journalists? How and to what extent should journalists work with the public? How do journalists help their employers—who are losing audiences and advertising revenue—adapt in this quickly changing environment? What can journalists do to maintain their professionalism as their control over the journalism process is eroding?

In the first chapter we approached the concepts of uncertainty and complexity in a broad, abstract way, mapping possible responses to uncertainty, as suggested by sociological and managerial approaches. In this chapter, we take a fine-grained look at the complex environment that is driving uncertainty for journalism, and we examine specific, possible responses. We discuss particular ways the journalistic environment is being reshaped by macro forces—technological, social, economic—which themselves are undergoing profound changes. Technological innovation is changing the public's media use and expectations of journalism. An abundance of media outlets has altered the market for news, rendering mass media economic models obsolete. We explore how, in the face of such changes, the culture of journalism and the professional values and practices that have traditionally defined it are being challenged and are evolving.

Digital Technology: The Great Equalizer

There is ample evidence to suggest that most uncertainties facing journalism stem from technological innovations that have changed the relationship between legacy media and the public. The Internet gives the public a virtual library of information from a diversity of sources at their fingertips, providing many options for news that no longer have to include legacy media. More important, perhaps, is that the public is no longer confined to being consumers of news—they can do journalism work, creating their own news and commentary. Citizen-based journalism has blurred the distinctions between journalists and audiences, creating "pro-sumers" (Kovach & Rosenstiel, 2007) or "produsers" (Bruns, 2008), interactive citizens who both produce and consume news and information content.

A corollary to increased control by the audience is the redistribution of power away from established journalism outlets and corporations (Friedman, 2007; Schudson, 2009). This shift has sent seismic tremors through news media firms, as they seek to retain their audiences and advertisers. News media have suffered from diminishing levels of public trust for several decades (Project for Excellence in Journalism, 2009), and this credibility crisis is a significant hurdle when so many other sources of information are available. To maintain their community influence, news media have to provide a quality of content that has value to their audiences (Picard, 2009b). However, this task appears difficult as media companies have cut news budgets in response to shrinking audiences and a loss of advertisers (Meyer, 2004, 2008). News media's diminished investment in journalism reinforces public perceptions that legacy media are more interested in profit than public service.

The shifting locus of control toward the audience has had an impact on the public's expectations of journalism. The democratization of media means people are free to pursue news that fits with their values, predispositions, and biases. News consumption transforms from a desire to be informed to a means of reaffirming what we think we already know. The large, mass audience that shared media experiences as a component of the social and political fabric of society has largely vanished, except in rare and extreme cases (e.g., 9/11), replaced by fragmented, niche audiences whose members fit the profile of their like-minded communities (Dimmick, 2003; Hamilton, 2004). Partisan media have re-emerged in the United States. The notion that media should be neutral so they don't offend potential audiences often no longer applies. The existing political culture suggests that partisan-based content is not only viable but also may be an essential element of media business strategy (Hallin, 2009). Citizen-powered media contribute to partisan splintering of content and to selective cognition among the audience (Bowden, 2009; Friedman, 2007).

Two other developments merit discussion: the ways that news is accessed and distributed online, and the idea that online content should be free. Mobile media allow people to access news in close to real time, wherever they are, at all times of day, in formats that facilitate sharing information with others. The networked nature of online journalism is changing how the audience finds news and how the news media distribute it. Legacy news media have found that the majority of their online traffic comes from search engines and links from other websites and blogs (Adee, 2008; Learmonth & Ives, 2009). An online editor at the *Chicago Tribune* offers a good example, writing that harnessing the power of viral journalism and social media has become increasingly important. A story about a small city in Texas posted on the *Tribune's* website drew 16,000 hits the day it was published and quickly the number of hits fell off; however, two weeks later the number began to rise and three weeks after initial publication the story had 126,000 hits in one day. The reason: the story had been linked in 300 blogs and became popular on Digg.com, where visitors post news stories and then vote to rank them. It appears online audiences are networked hunters and gatherers, searching for news the interests them, visiting sites that aggregate news, and sharing it with others.

The public's changing consumption habits have forced news media to reconsider their distribution methods. They must make it easier for audiences to upload and share online information while distributing content in as many platforms, products, and social networks as possible (Vukanovic, 2009). By making these changes, news media are acknowledging the difficulty of getting people to start their news consumption on their websites.

The idea that content on the Internet should be free can be traced to communities of software writers in the 1990s who formed open-source sites where anyone could contribute as long as they made their updates and changes available to the public for free under the same license as the original code (Friedman, 2007). As the Internet grew in reach and scope, legacy news media—eager to get online but unsure of the future of online journalism—followed the free content model, hoping it would bring audiences and eventually advertisers. Today, the most technologically savvy media consumers—young people—have grown up expecting online media to be free (Carroll, 2004). Although some analysts believe the online audience will pay for news if it has added value (Lacy, 2009), the legacy news media have hesitated, apparently with good reason, to create pay walls for online content. A 2009 study found that 82 percent of online news consumers said they would find their news elsewhere if their favorite sites began to charge them for news (Project for Excellence in Journalism, 2010).

Citizen-Based Media

For several hundred dollars, anyone can buy a laptop with broadband, audio and visual media (e.g., a cell phone, video recorder, iPod) and become a multimedia publisher. These reduced barriers open the public sphere to a nearly infinite number of voices. In theory, this creates a broader Enlightenment-style "marketplace of ideas" that is largely free and unregulated. Digital media provide a basis for a potent grassroots journalism, created by the people, for the people, in a way that directly connects the public to their elected officials and powerful institutions (Gillmor, 2004). These media also provide a space for those voices that have been shunned by a commercial media focused on audiences attractive to advertisers (Hamilton, 2004). The extent of this shift cannot be underestimated, as the public no longer has to rely on (or wait for) legacy media to cover issues or provide platforms for discussion, debate, or dissent. The power of citizen media has even drawn praise from *The New York Times*, which reported that "a new kind of Web-based news operation has arisen in several cities, forcing the (local) papers to follow the stories they uncover . . . putting local politicians and businesses on the hot seat" (Perez-Pena, 2008, p. A18).

Journalists see the potential and value of citizens as collaborators in the news process, but they also see the drawbacks and have been quick to point out the differences between what journalists and citizens do in the name of journalism. The positives are apparent. Citizens widen the field of journalistic vision; they can interact with journalists about stories, pass on news tips, and actually report and create their own news. News coverage tends to move in new directions. An international study of journalists who maintain blogs found that fewer story ideas came from editors; journalists used their blogs to put out calls for additional information and sources; and they relied less on official sources in their reporting. The journalists also said that audience interaction helps them better understand their stories (Bradshaw, 2008). Journalists have become avid consumers of social and citizen-based media (Emmett, 2009; Messner & Watson DiStacio, 2008; Phillips, Singer, Vlad, & Becker, 2009). A 2009 study found that 89 percent of journalists used blogs for story research, more than two-thirds used social networking sites (e.g., LinkedIn, Facebook), and slightly more than half used Twitter (Cision, 2009).

On the other hand, journalists recognize that citizen media have become potent competitors with no obligation to standards of journalistic ethics and professionalism (Jones, 2009; Kovach & Rosenstiel, 2007). These reports can divert audiences away from legacy news and information outlets, but more alarmingly they can misinform and confuse. The opportunity exists to circulate rumors and untruths, some of which are motivated by private interests and narrow agendas. Also, many citizens aren't interested in or capable of doing the work of journalists—interviewing, vetting, and verifying public information so it may be processed in a coherent way. Rather, they want to express their personal ideas, and publish and share them with others (Howe, 2008).

Crowdsourcing has become a popular corrective mechanism in the digital, networked, mediated world. Giving the public a chance to correct, edit, and comment on content provides a form of peer review and transparency that strengthens the credibility of information by opening it to broader tests of verification. No doubt errors of fact and falsehoods are published, but subjecting content posted on the Web to public revision "uploads" the power of communities, decentralizes institutional media power and may provide "a better guarantee that the *complete* truth is out there . . . somewhere . . . in pieces" (Friedman, 2007, p. 47).

The growth of citizen-based journalism, combined with a broader integration of news and entertainment content in all media, makes it difficult to define what exactly is journalism and who is (and isn't) a journalist. Schudson and Tifft (2005) write that "news" has become "so conflated with opinion and other cultural commodities that a one-size-fits-all definition no longer applies"; truth and fact are "entirely up for grabs," leaving the notion of who is a journalist "entirely fluid," especially among the young (p. 40). They conclude: "Fewer Americans appeared to value the media's role as surrogates for the public or its function as a filter through which inaccuracy, imbalance and unfairness are sifted out" (p. 42). In a postmodern sense, society appears to have abandoned the idea that truth—as a manifestation of reality that can be observed and defined—is what the news media provide or even strive to provide, making legacy media's embrace of objectivity a suspect and unappreciated value (Merrill, 2006). These social trends contribute to the rise of citizen media that claim to practice journalism, while in a broader sense they explain to some degree the public's dissatisfaction with legacy media.

These tensions noted, the idea that truth will emerge in the marketplace of ideas has its roots in Enlightenment liberalism, the philosophical basis for freedom of speech and the First Amendment (Siebert, Peterson, & Schramm, 1956). Historically, the press found a significant part of its rationale in subjecting those in government and power to tests of truth. In this way, the news media serve as "a stand-in for the public" to ensure the rules that allow a democracy to operate (Schudson, 1995, p. 217). However, the public no longer has to rely solely on legacy media to be stand-ins for them; citizens have greater access to this power themselves (Gillmor, 2004). King (2008), a journalist in the United Kingdom, writes: "To my mind, this revolution can be seen as the next phase of the Enlightenment, which puts publishing and communication in the hands of the many, instead of the few who have traditionally controlled the media" (p. 12).

The New Economics of News

For decades, media firms enjoyed relative stability and market power, attracting significant audiences based on local, regional, and national economic conditions. Media generally, and news media specifically, have been profitable industries, operating in dual markets—selling their content to audiences, and these audiences to advertisers. However, in the era of digital media, the news media's market leverage and economies of scale, and the organizational and journalistic routines that produced efficient production and distribution, have been shattered or fundamentally redefined.

Legacy media have been losing audience share for decades, but the past few years have made clear that superficial efforts to change, while most methods of operation remain largely unaffected, are not enough to sustain them (Picard, 2009a). Daily newspaper circulation in the United States continues a downward trend, dropping in 2009 to about 43 million, with overall circulation down about 20 percent in the first decade of the twenty-first century (Newspaper Association of America, 2009; Project for Excellence in Journalism, 2010). The network television news audience is shrinking even faster, with the three networks (ABC, CBS, NBC) reporting 22.3 million viewers in 2009 for the evening newscast, down from about 32 million in 2000 and 52 million in 1980 (Project for Excellence in Journalism, 2006, 2009,

2010). After a wave of mergers and acquisitions in the 1990s and 2000s, some prominent and respected news firms found themselves burdened with debt; stock prices for public companies tumbled, and well-known firms faced bankruptcy (Morton, 2009). Overall, the newspaper and television news industries remain profitable, although neither medium anticipates a return to the level of profits (around 20 percent for newspaper, higher for broadcast) that were common until about 2005 (Morton, 2009); both industries face declines in advertising as their audiences shrink and they face stronger competition. Newspapers executives have realized that online advertising, once considered the hope for replacing run-of-the-paper ads, is unlikely to reach a level that supports their news gathering (Project for Excellence in Journalism, 2010). Newspapers remain highly reliant on advertising printed in the paper; these ads create more than 90 percent of newspaper advertising revenue (Sass, 2008). Web portals, such as Yahoo, MSN/Microsoft, AOL, and Google News, are among the most visited sites for news (Pew Research Center, 2009). Local legacy media have ad sharing and placement agreements with most of these portals (Helft, 2008; Klaassen, 2008), but the amount of this revenue is small compared with run-of-the-paper ads. Mobile technology is developing and news media are trying to establish a presence in the absence of clear strategies or established business models (Sharma & Wildman, 2009).

However, amid the preponderance of economic uncertainty, opportunities exist. Technological innovation also creates opportunities for developing new products and entering new markets (Chan-Olmsted, 2006). News media are diversifying their portfolio of products to create additional revenue streams (Picard, 2005). To act quickly and reduce risks, media companies are entering strategic alliances with other firms that have complementary resources (Chan-Olmsted, 2006). In this way, firms become more *competitive* by becoming more *collaborative* (Gade & Raviola, 2009), a form of "coopetition" that can increase value by brand extension and reduce costs and risks (Brandenburger & Nalebuff, 1996). Convergence partnerships in the first part of this decade and more recently content sharing and ad placement agreements are examples of strategic alliances (Dailey, Demo, & Spillman, 2005; Perez-Pena, 2009).

Strategically, media firms seek to reconstitute their market share by developing new products that attract audiences who might not have interest in their legacy news products. These new products are more specialized to serve well-defined target audiences and market niches (Dimmick, 2003). A good example is *The Cincinnati Enquirer*, a Gannett-owned newspaper, which boasted 270 niche products in 2007, including websites for moms, local Little League, and specific neighborhoods (Howe, 2007).

As news shifts online, costs associated with non-editorial production (e.g., paper, ink, printing presses, broadcast studios, and production staff) are significantly reduced, as are distribution costs (Hamilton, 2004). For newspapers, production and distribution account for 40–50 percent of total costs, whereas editorial labor (including management) is about 15 percent (Picard, 2004). Production and distribution costs are fixed costs of doing business (some vary, e.g., paper, ink), although the trend has been for these costs to increase over time. What remains uncertain is when (or if) revenue generated by online media will be greater than the savings in production and distribution costs that media would make by ceasing to publish. Until that point is reached or on the horizon, news media (especially newspapers) are unlikely to cease publishing their legacy products, as the production and distribution cost savings by not publishing are less than the losses in advertising and circulation revenue.

The challenge for journalists and news media generally is to make their products attract attention in a crowded digital marketplace. News has become an abundant commodity, easily aggregated (often by non-journalists), and sent to or shared with online audiences for free, diluting the value of news (Hamilton, 2004; Kovach & Rosenstiel, 2007; Picard, 2009b). Legacy news media have lost considerable control over their content, as Web portals and aggregators publish stories created by legacy media, often without compensation to the content creators (Picard, 2009a). One study identified online news as an inferior public good, a product much like fast food. Widely available, its consumption is based on convenience, but as the consumer's income increases the demand for online news decreases (Chyi & Yang, 2009). The abundance and availability of news discourages news media from investing additional time and resources in information gathering. They gain little or no revenue for doing so. Instead, it is simpler and easier to pass on readily available information.

Journalists' value has long come from their ability to determine the significance of events, sort through enormous amounts of information, access sources, and construct stories. These skills are no longer a unique knowledge base, as citizen journalists can now potentially do the same things, often for no pay, and they do not need the support of a news organization to publish. This casts doubt on the value of journalists simply embracing techniques afforded by technology—for example, crowdsourcing, social networking, blogging, and collaborating with audiences to create news content—because these techniques have become so commonplace they do not add marketplace value (Picard, 2009b). Businesses facing commoditization need to find ways to differentiate themselves, which begins with identifying core competencies that add value to their products. For media companies, the focus shifts to those things that cannot be digitized, including product quality, customer relations, and transparency (Friedman, 2007).

All this makes it clear that technological change has broken the business models of established journalism. News executives continue to look for ways to "monetize" their products, and editors openly wonder how they can support existing news and information gathering. News organizations are being restructured and downsized, while they experiment and learn through trial and error (Lacy, 2009; Picard, 2009a; Project for Excellence in Journalism, 2009; Ricchiardi, 2009; Vukanovic, 2009). Emerging business models usually include some combination of these elements:

- *Hyper-local.* News media organizations can find value in being the primary and best source of news and information about their communities, which do not draw the attention of national and regional media. This focus could also attract more local advertising.
- *Collaboration.* Former news competitors work together to expand their resources for information gathering, share content, and offer their audiences more comprehensive coverage.
- *Diversification.* Media firms create broader portfolios of products, and develop multiple forms of content creation and distribution. They are repackaging, repurposing, and bundling information and content, distributing it in cross-media platforms that reach different audiences through different media at different times and places.
- *Specialization.* Media organizations seek to add value by specializing in coverage areas that interest and serve the niches in their markets. High-quality, specialized coverage could also be sold to other news outlets.
- *Mobile media production and distribution.* Mobile media deliver information in convenient, timely, and interactive ways that fit audience wants and needs and extend usage to outside of home and work.
- *Hybrid models.* These include a variety of revenue sources (public donations, corporate sponsors, advertisers) to support their efforts. Many are non-profit, supported by grants or philanthropy.

Professionalism, Environmental Uncertainty, and Journalism Work

Professionalism is an organizing principle of occupational cohorts. The professional's work is based in a theoretical body of knowledge, shared values and norms, and common purpose. Some professions are strictly defined, utilizing *a priori* criteria as a basis for determining standards and membership (e.g., law and medicine), whereas others reject formal definitions and consider the traits, attributes, and functions of the cohort and how they are manifest in the occupational group (Becker & Carper, 1956). U.S. journalism fits with the latter. As mentioned in Chapter 1, it is most accurately described as a "semi-profession," because criteria for entry and professional standards are ambiguous and not legally mandated (Beam, 1993), and connection with a professional knowledge base is tenuous (Abbott, 1988).

Professionalism is a form of occupational control, and the strategies pursued to maintain this control in the face of complexities and uncertainties are a recurring theme throughout this book. The authority and autonomy of a profession is supported by an abstract knowledge base, needed to define and regulate the values, substance, goals, and performance of their work (Abbott, 1988; Van Maanen & Barley, 1984). The professional values that define journalism in the United States and most Western nations are, in a philosophical sense, based in Enlightenment ideas of human rationality, free expression, the relationship between government and citizens, and the relative importance of freedom and social responsibility (Merrill, 1989; Siebert et al., 1956). Journalism professional values include a commitment to truth, public service, objectivity, independence, and fairness (Kovach & Rosenstiel, 2007), and journalists identify their social functions as disseminators, interpreters, watchdogs, and populist mobilizers (Weaver et al., 2007). Journalists are socialized into the profession through education, training, professional organizations, and observing established newsroom practices (Beam, 1990, 1993; Breed, 1955; Gans, 1979; Shoemaker & Reese, 1996; Tuchman, 1978). Russo (1998) found that journalists' professional identification "served as a source of collective inspiration, energy and strength" (p. 101).

Media companies, however, have a "duality" of purpose (as journalistic and commercial enterprises) that can lead to internal tensions between professional and organizational orientations, and shifting levels of influence within news organizations (Achtenhagen & Raviola, 2007; Gade, 2008). These tensions tend to become more acute as environmental complexity and uncertainty increase, resulting in a variety of responses. Beam (1996, 2001) found that high levels of perceived uncertainty prompted newspaper organizations to become more market oriented, which then lowered perceived uncertainty. However, he found no relationship between greater market orientation and increased circulation. This gap is consistent with findings by Lowrey (2005, 2006) that news managers who perceived high levels of environmental uncertainty were likely to resort to familiar routines and easily available models, be risk-averse, and "muddle through." He concluded that environmental uncertainty constrains decision-making, resulting in a level of organizational isomorphism, or mimicry.

News organizations have responded to economic uncertainty by finding ways to cut costs. The number of newspaper and network broadcast journalists shrank by roughly 25 percent in the first decade of the twenty-first century (Project for Excellence in Journalism, 2009). News bureaus were closed in the United States and overseas. Half the states no longer have a newspaper covering the U.S. Congress; the number of journalists covering state legislatures dropped 32 percent since 2003 (Dorroh, 2009). The amount of news covered has decreased, and a loss of veteran journalists has robbed news outlets of their most experienced reporters, contributing to significant drains of organizational knowledge, investigative expertise, and journalistic enterprise (Phillips et al., 2009).

Amid shrinking staffs and fewer resources, journalists find their jobs expanding and their routines vastly altered. Although expectations vary among news organizations, journalists are producing additional content, learning multimedia skills, creating content for multiple platforms, updating continuously for the Web, and interacting more with the audience (Raviola & Hartmann, 2009; Singer, 2004; Witschage & Nygren, 2009). The extent to which journalists need to master multimedia skills remains unclear. Some media organizations—generally larger ones—have taken the approach that multimedia content can best be produced by teams. Team members have basic cross-platform skills (e.g., writing) but are not expected to have the technical expertise to produce content across all platforms (Buttry, 2008). Smaller organizations, with fewer resources, have a need for more versatile employees.

Multimedia's impact on journalism routines is also apparent in the newsroom premium on timeliness. Updating online stories creates continuous deadlines. This pressure means less time for the traditional journalism activities of information gathering, research, and verification. Studies of both U.S. and European journalists have found that expanded job responsibilities and increased emphasis on timeliness fuel journalists' concerns that they are time squeezed in ways that diminish the quality of their work (Phillips et al., 2009; Witschage & Nygren, 2009). A study of Spanish journalists found that those who were expected to master and execute all multimedia skills felt they were under acute pressure (Aviles & Carvajal, 2008), while U.S. journalists say creating cross-platform media products is more time-consuming than their editors realize (Singer, 2004).

The combination of fewer journalism resources and emerging interactive media has news organizations embracing user-generated content and crowd-sourcing as ways to create information and draw audiences. As discussed earlier, these practices place journalists closer to the public and expand the journalistic network; however, user-generated content requires verification, fact-checking, and monitoring for legal issues, activities that can be time-consuming and costly. These tasks generally fall on journalists responsible for producing their own stories, expanding their jobs even further (Phillips et al., 2009). Even advocates of user-generated content do not see it as a replacement for traditional journalism (Howe, 2008). However, integrating the public into journalism does require a realignment of resources and work. News organizations are developing parameters for user-generated content, exercising some traditional gatekeeping roles and closing some processes from citizen involvement (Domingo et al., 2008; Hermida & Thurman, 2008).

The confluence of macro-level forces—social, technical, and economic—discussed thus far has created a "perfect storm" that some scholars assert threatens journalism's status as a profession (Witschage & Nygren, 2009). Journalists are losing a sense of control and autonomy in their work. They have broader jobs, never-ending deadlines, greater marketing orientation, and they collaborate with everyone (with other media, the public, business interests in the news organization, and among divisions within the newsroom).

Journalism now is more focused on technology and associated skills, shifting the emphasis of journalism work from creative inputs (news gathering, creative enterprise, verification, writing, editing, and design) to outputs of content in multiple platforms and products. Waves of downsizings and layoffs have seen many experienced and talented journalists leave journalism. And there is a growing sense that news managers, most of whom have worked their way up the journalism ranks, lack professional training in business and management to lead people and manage complex organizational issues and challenges (McLellan & Porter, 2007; Sylvie & Gade, 2009).

The forces of change are also constraining journalistic responses. Amid these waves of uncertainty many journalists, newsroom managers, and some scholars are calling for a return to professionalism (Kovach & Rosenstiel, 2007; Merrill, 2006; Meyer, 2004; Witschage & Nygren, 2009). As discussed in Chapter 1, professionalism potentially provides an abstract knowledge base that can help members adapt to times of upheaval. Also, journalists see their professional values as anchors that provide stability, distinguish them from others in the public sphere, and give them a sense of purpose in today's shifting seas.

The Culture of Journalism: Shifting Structure and Agency

The values, norms, and professional expectations that make up the culture of journalism are being challenged in arguably unprecedented ways. Journalists are responding by seeking opportunities amid powerful constraints. Journalists understand they must change, and news organizations are undergoing profound change. What remains unclear is the level of change that will be pursued, how changes will impact journalism over the long term, and to what extent the values and norms of professional journalism will endure.

The forces changing journalism are also structures that have empowered it, and can continue to empower it. As a social and political institution, journalism has developed its voice and influence independent of government, a position granted it by government (e.g., the First Amendment). A reciprocal relationship exists: Journalism portrays the acts of government to the people, while public officials recognize press reports' influence and constrain government acts, often simply by the threat of public exposure or bad press (Glasser, 2009; Kaplan, 2006). The government and journalism both achieve a large part of their legitimacy as social institutions—their cultural capital—by their inter-relatedness (Benson, 2006). This symbiosis remains much alive, as the blogosphere, citizen media, and corporate online portals are highly reliant on content produced by traditional news media organizations (Picard, 2009a).

Historically, journalism has found opportunity and evolved (or improved) by adopting innovative technologies and practices—photography, radio, and television are examples. Digital media create new ways to present information, tell stories, and interact with audiences. Technological innovation is disruptive, but can also be a source of creativity and renewal (Day & Shoemaker, 2000; Galbraith, 1994; Schumpeter, 1949, 1950). Although technology has challenged economic models that have served mass media for nearly a century, it is media's embrace of technology and innovation that fueled the growth of global media conglomerates, and provided media firms the substantial economic influence and resources they now find threatened. Initially slow to respond to changing economic conditions, media firms are restructuring, building new competencies, creating new products, and reaching out to new audiences, though the pace of such changes varies across the industry.

These opportunities provide some explanation for the directions journalism has taken and will continue to explore. However, the disruptions associated with these macro forces have also imposed powerful constraints on journalism. As we have discussed in this chapter, technological innovation has reduced journalism's control over the flow of public information and news creation, empowered the public to participate in journalism, had an impact on journalistic norms and routines, created a need for new journalistic skills and competencies, and imploded news media economic models in ways that have resulted in significant reductions in the number of journalists and resources for journalism. How journalism responds to these constraints and embraces opportunities will determine the course of the profession. Much is yet to be worked out.

Journalism is taking steps to adapt at both organizational and professional levels. At the organizational level, change is proceeding largely by trial and error, by processes that economists and organizational scholars first proposed when U.S. manufacturing was threatened by globalization more than a quarter-century ago (Bergquist, 1993; Drucker, 1995; Grant, 1996; Kanter, 1983; Senge, 1990). These processes include restructuring to facilitate innovation, recognizing journalism as a form of knowledge work, redefining jobs and responsibilities, and adding additional competencies and skills bases. All of these initiatives challenge the established culture of journalism, making change a target of skepticism and at times resistance (Gade, 2004; Gade & Perry, 2003; Lowrey, 2006; Phillips et al., 2009; Silcock & Keith, 2006; Singer, 2004; Sylvie & Moon, 2007; Sylvie & Witherspoon, 2002; Witschage & Nygren, 2009).

Scholars generally agree that for innovation to occur there must be a conversation among organizational entities with specialized knowledge. In news media organizations, this knowledge resides among journalists, whose core product is information (journalists are *knowledge manufacturers*); however, specialized knowledge also resides within business/marketing and information technology departments (Raviola & Hartmann, 2009). Organizations leverage their collective knowledge and capacity for innovation by creating structural mechanisms for the exchange of ideas from their diverse sources of expertise. Accordingly, they restructure to facilitate exchanges by professionals across organizational boundaries—a process of *organizational integration* (Grant, 1996; Huber, 2004; Kanter, 1983; Nooteboom, 2000). Successful innovation requires coordination across boundaries (structure), but it also requires a loosening of structural and hierarchical controls to nurture problem-solving at the professional level, by individual experts (agency).

In news media organizations, this integration has spurred the transition to team-based work at several levels: news, business/marketing, and information technology personnel working together to develop products and strategies (interdepartmental teams), and newsroom teams to create specialized content for multiple media platforms and products (multimedia journalism). Beyond intra-organizational teams, news media are teaming with former competitors to develop new competencies and products (e.g., convergence), and they are opening their organizations to the public by encouraging greater access, interactivity, and user-generated content. News production appears increasingly embedded within a network arrangement in which knowledge exists at the "interstices" between entities rather than within entities, and developing the ability to take advantage of such an arrangement is increasingly important for organizational survival (Hardy, Phillips, & Lawrence, 2003; Powell, Koput, & Smith-Doerr, 1996), and for survival of those professions that have largely relied on organizational resources (Abbott, 1988).

The exchange of ideas that integration and team-based work create pose problems for the culture of journalism because they create the basis for shifting levels of organizational influence and introduce new values and practices that may not fit with existing standards of journalism professionalism. The professional culture of journalism (a stabilizing force rooted in journalists' specialized knowledge, authority, and control over the values and practices that support their work) is confronted by agents outside journalism with different areas of specialized expertise. In integrated news organizations, journalism is only one among several areas of specialized knowledge vying for influence (Beam, 1996; Gade, 2004, 2008; Harris, 2004; Stepp, 2000).

Beyond this, restructuring to integrate flattens organizational hierarchies in ways that are intended to let innovation "bubble up," assuming that the expertise of knowledge workers resides at all levels of the organization (Drucker, 1995; Grant, 1996; Kanter, 1983). However, in news organizations, the restructuring, mandates for changes in practices and values, and opening news organizations to outside entities (the public, former competing media) have generally been top-down, authoritative mandates (Project for Excellence in Journalism, 2008; Singer, 2004; Sylvie & Moon, 2007). In other words, restructuring initiatives that should nurture innovation within news organizations are trumped by firm-level mandates that journalists have no choice but to accept. Instead of innovative ideas bubbling up, change initiatives are pushed down. Journalists have not responded positively to teamwork, saying they do not sense empowerment, increased professional autonomy, or enhanced journalism (Gade, 2004, 2008; Neuzil, Hansen, & Ward, 1999). Reductions in the journalism workforce and resources further diminish resources for journalists' agency.

As the focus of news organizations shifts from input to output, new journalistic routines amount to a de-skilling of journalism work (Picard, 2009b). Journalists spend more time in the newsroom and less time out of the office interacting with sources, observing, investigating. News becomes more planned and collaborative (Deuze, 2008). Witschage and Nygren (2009) note that an administrative news culture—one in which journalists find themselves spending more time sitting at their desks recycling and repurposing their stories, wire material, and press releases—is replacing an investigative news culture. They call this phenomenon "churnalism" (p. 38), and note a paradoxical development: although digital technology provides greater opportunity for creativity in storytelling, the expectations for content output and never-ending deadlines mean that personal creativity associated with the professional skills of researching, interviewing, writing, and storytelling is constrained. This has a homogenizing impact on news content, contributing to the commodification of news.

Cultural change is enacted by altering tangible parts of everyday life—practices, policies, and routines. These elements are the basis of daily experience, and changing them eventually changes the way people think and act (Schneider, Brief, & Guzzo, 1996). In news media organizations, this process is well under way. The relative stability of news media industries in the second half of the twentieth century permitted the culture of journalism to solidify, nurturing a professional ideology that became a powerful influence over journalists and somewhat resistant to outside influences. The macro forces changing the journalistic environment and the integration of news media organizations have diluted the power of this professional ideology and opened it to change. Deuze (2008) notes that the tears on the surface of this culture are becoming apparent and the system is increasingly porous. These tears suggest an opportunity for renewal, as changes in the workforce bring more journalists trained in multimedia and socialized into collaborative newsroom cultures, which over time will redefine journalism culture. Journalists are challenged to find ways to assert their specialized and abstract knowledge, their core values and evolving professionalism, to enhance the value of journalism products in a very competitive information marketplace. Doing so creates new opportunities for enhanced journalistic agency.

Thought Questions: Contemplating Change

As change occurs at macro levels it creates uncertainties in the journalism environment, prompting news organizations and journalists to rethink their missions and reorganize their work. Journalism's position as a distinct and influential institution has been challenged by technological innovations that have networked society, democratized news, and rendered mass media business models obsolete. The culture of professional journalism is challenged as journalists respond to their changing environment and seek ways to maintain control over journalism values and practices.

1. What does it mean to say that a "perfect storm" of social, technical, and economic forces is changing journalism's environment? How does this storm add to the complexity of understanding the uncertainties that journalism faces?
2. How have journalism's responses to a complex, changing environment reduced uncertainties or created others? Identify specific ways that journalism might respond differently.
3. How much control does journalism have over its values and practices? How can journalism assert its claims of professionalism? What are the social, political, and economic benefits and pitfalls of doing so?

References

Abbott, A. (1988). *The system of professions*. Chicago: University of Chicago Press.

Achtenhagen, L., & Raviola, E. (2007). Organizing internal tension: Duality management of media companies. In L. Achtenhagen (Ed.), *Organizing media: Mastering the challenges of organizational change* (pp. 127–146). JIBS Research Reports 1. Jonkoping, Sweden: Jonkoping International Business School.

Adee, B. (2008). Digging into social media to build a newspaper audience. *Nieman Reports, 62*(4), 52–54.

Aviles, J. A. G., & Carvajal, M. (2008). Integrated and cross-media newsroom convergence. *Convergence, 14*, 221–239.

Beam, R. (1990). Journalism professionalism as an organizational-level concept. *Journalism Monographs, 121*, 1–43.

Beam, R. (1993). The impact of group ownership variables on organizational professionalism at daily newspapers. *Journalism & Mass Communication Quarterly, 70*, 907–918.

Beam, R. (1996). How perceived environmental uncertainty influences marketing orientation of U.S. daily newspapers. *Journalism & Mass Communication Quarterly, 73*, 285–303.

Beam, R. (2001). Does it pay to be a market-oriented daily newspaper? *Journalism & Mass Communication Quarterly, 78*, 466–483.

Becker, H., & Carper, J. (1956). The elements of identification with an occupation. *American Sociological Review, 21*, 341–347.

Benson, R. (2006). News media as a "journalistic field": What Bourdieu adds to New Institutionalism, and vice versa. *Political Communication, 23*, 187–202.

Bergquist, W. (1993). *The postmodern organization: Mastering the art of irreversible change*. San Francisco: Jossey-Bass.

Bowden, M. (2009, October). The story behind the story. *The Atlantic*, 164–169.

Bradshaw, P. (2008). When journalists blog: How it changes what they do. *Nieman Reports, 62*(4), 50–52.

Brandenburger, A., & Nalebuff, B. (1996). *Co-opetition*. New York: Doubleday.

Breed, W. (1955, May). Social control in the newsroom: A functional analysis. *Social Forces*, 326–335.

Bruns, A. (2008). The active audience: Transforming journalism from gatekeeping to gatewatching. In C. Paterson & D. Domingo (Eds.), *Making online news: The ethnography of new media production* (pp. 171–184). New York: Peter Lang.

Buttry, S. (2008, January). *Multimedia storytelling and collaboration*. American Press Institute. Guidelines distributed at seminar for *The Oklahoman*/NewsOK.com, Oklahoma City, OK.

Carroll, J. (2004, November/December). Be unafraid. Be very unafraid. *The American Editor*, 4–8.

Chan-Olmsted, S. (2006). *Competitive strategy for media firms: Strategic and brand management in changing media markets*. Mahwah, NJ: Lawrence Erlbaum.

Chyi, H. I., & Yang, M. J. (2009). Is online news an inferior good? *Journalism & Mass Communication Quarterly, 86*, 594–612.

Cision. (2009). *2009 Social media & online usage study*. Retrieved March 23, 2010, from http://us.cision.com/journalist_survey_2009/GW-Cision_Media_Report.pdf

Dailey, L., Demo, L., & Spillman, M. (2005). Most TV/newspaper partnerships at cross promotion stage. *Newspaper Research Journal, 26*(4), 36–49.

Day, G. S., & Shoemaker, P. (2000). *Wharton on managing emerging technologies*. New York: Wiley.

Deuze, M. (2008). Understanding journalism as newswork: How it changes, and how it remains the same. *Westminster Papers of Communication & Culture, 5*(2), 1–23.

Dimmick, J. (2003). *Media competition and coexistence: The theory of the niche*. Mahwah, NJ: Lawrence Erlbaum.

Domingo, D., Quandt, T., Heinonen, A., Paulussen, S., Singer, J. B., & Vujnovic, M. (2008). Participatory journalism practices in the media and beyond: An international study of initiatives in online newspapers. *Journalism Practice, 2*, 326–342.

Dorroh, J. (2009, April/May). Statehouse exodus. *American Journalism Review*. Retrieved May 23, 2009, from http://www.ajr.org/Article.asp?id=4721

Drucker, P. (1995). *Managing in a time of great change*. New York: Truman Talley Books/ Dutton.

Emmett, A. (2009, December/January). Networking news. *American Journalism Review*. Retrieved May 30, 2009, from http://www.ajr.org/Article.asp?id=4646

Friedman, T. (2007). *The world is flat: A brief history of the 21st century*. New York: Picador.

Gade, P. (2004). Newspapers and organizational development: Management and journalist perceptions of newsroom cultural change. *Journalism & Communication Monographs, 6*, 5–55.

Gade, P. (2008). Journalism guardians in a time of great change: News editors' perceived influence in integrated news organizations. *Journalism & Mass Communication Quarterly, 85*, 371–392.

Gade, P., and Perry, E. (2003). Changing the newsroom culture: A four-year case study of organizational development at the *St. Louis Post-Dispatch*. *Journalism & Mass Communication Quarterly, 80*, 327–347.

Gade, P., & Raviola, E. (2009). Integration of news and the news of integration: A structural perspective on news media changes. *Journal of Media Business Studies, 6*, 87–111.

Galbraith, J. R. (1994). *Competing with flexible lateral organizations*. Boston, MA: Addison-Wesley.

Gans, H. (1979). *Deciding what's news*. New York: Random House.

Gillmor, D. (2004). *We the media: Grassroots journalism by the people, for the people*. Sebastopol, CA: O'Reilly.

Glasser, T. (2009). Journalism and the second-person effect. *Journalism, 10*, 326–328.

Grant, R. (1996). Prospering in dynamically-competitive environments: Organizational capability as knowledge integration. *Organization Science, 7*, 375–387.

Hallin, D. (2009). Not the end of journalism history. *Journalism, 10*, 332–334.

Hamilton, J. (2004). *All the news that's fit to sell: How the market transforms information in news*. Princeton, NJ: Princeton University Press.

Hardy, C., Phillips, N., & Lawrence, T. B. (2003). Resources, knowledge and influence: The organizational effects of interorganizational collaboration. *Journal of Management Studies, 40*, 321–47.

Harris, J. (2004, April). What business are we in? *The American Editor*, 5–8.

Helft, M. (2008, April 7). Yahoo reveals some details of its new ad sales system. *The New York Times*, p. C6.

Hermida, A., & Thurman, N. (2008). A clash of cultures: The integration of user-generated content with professional journalistic frameworks at British newspaper websites. *Journalism Practice, 2*, 343–356.

Howe, J. (2007, August 15). To save themselves, U.S. newspapers put readers to work. *Wired*. Retrieved May 29, 2009, from http://wired.com/techbiz/media/magazine/15–08/ff_gannett?currentPage=all

Howe, J. (2008). The wisdom of the crowd resides in how the crowd is used. *Nieman Reports, 62*(4), 47–50.

Huber, G. (2004). *The necessary nature of future firms: Attributes of survivors in a changing world*. Thousand Oaks, CA: Sage Publications.

Jones, A. (2009). *Losing the news: The future of the news that feeds democracy*. Oxford, UK: Oxford University Press.

Kanter, R. M. (1983). *The change masters: Innovation for productivity in the American corporation*. New York: Simon & Schuster.

Kaplan, R. (2006). The news about new institutionalism: Journalism's ethic of objectivity and its political origins. *Political Communication, 23*, 173–185.

King, K. (2008). Journalism as conversation. *Nieman Reports, 62*(4), 11–13.

Klaassen, A. (2008, April 7). Yahoo's new ad platform lets newspapers sell its inventory. *Advertising Age*, 4.

Kovach, B., & Rosenstiel, T. (2007). *The elements of journalism: What news people should know and the public should expect*. New York: Three Rivers Press.

Lacy, S. (2009). The future of local journalism. Retrieved May 22, 2009, from http://aejmc.org/topics/2009/05/the-future-of-local-journalism/

Learmonth, M., & Ives, N. (2009, March 30). Aggregation forces journalistic evolution: News outlets must accept that consumers want more content faster – and don't care who creates it. *Advertising Age*, 13–14.

Lowrey, W. (2005). Commitment to newspaper–TV partnering: A test of the impact of institutional isomorphism. *Journalism & Mass Communication Quarterly, 82*, 495–514.

Lowrey, W. (2006). Cognitive shortcuts, the constraints of commitment, and managers' attitudes about newspaper–TV partnerships. *Journal of Media Economics, 19*, 241–258.

McLellan, M., & Porter, T. (2007). *News improved: How America's newsrooms are learning to change*. Washington, DC: CQ Press.

Merrill, J. C. (1989). *The dialectic in journalism*. Baton Rouge: Louisiana State University Press.

Merrill, J. C. (2006). *Media, mission and morality*. Spokane, WA: Marquette Books.

Messner, M., & Watson DiStacio, M. (2008). The source cycle: How traditional media and weblogs use each other as sources. *Journalism Studies, 9*, 447–463.

Meyer, P. (2004). *The vanishing newspaper: Saving journalism in the information age*. Columbia: University of Missouri Press.

Meyer, P. (2008, October/November). The elite newspaper of the future. *American Journalism Review*. Retrieved May 30, 2009, from http://www.ajr.org/Article.asp?id=4605

Morton, J. (2009, December/January). It could be worse. *American Journalism Review*. Retrieved May 30, 2009, from http://www.ajr.org/Article.asp?id=4660

Neuzil, M., Hansen, K., & Ward, J. (1999). Twin cities journalists' assessment of topic teams. *Newspaper Research Journal, 20*(1), 2–16.

Newspaper Association of America. (2009). Total paid circulation: Trends and numbers. Retrieved May 29, 2009, from http://www.naa.org/TrendsandNumbers/Total-Paid-circulation.aspx

Nooteboom, B. (2000). *Learning and innovation in organizations and economies*. New York: Oxford University Press.

Perez-Pena, R. (2008, November 19). Websites that dig for news rise as community watchdogs. *The New York Times*, pp. A1, A18.

Perez-Pena, R. (2009, February 19). Five big papers to share articles and photos. *The New York Times*, p. B7.

Pew Research Center. (2009). *Key news audiences now blend online and traditional sources*. Retrieved March 23, 2010, from http://people-press.org/report/444/news

Phillips, A., Singer, J., Vlad, T., & Becker, L. (2009). Implications of technological change for journalists' tasks and skills. *Journal of Media Business Studies, 6*, 61–85.

Picard, R. G. (2004). The economics of the daily newspaper industry. In A. Alexander, J. Owens, R. Carveth, C. A. Hollifield, & A. Greco (Eds.), *Media economics* (pp. 109–126). Mahwah, NJ: Erlbaum.

Picard, R. G. (2005). The nature of media product portfolios. In Picard, R. G. (Ed.), *Media product portfolios* (pp. 1–22). Mahwah, NJ: Erlbaum.

Picard, R. G. (2009a). Changing structures and organization of newsrooms. *Journal of Media Business Studies, 6*, 1–5.

Picard, R. G. (2009b). Why journalists deserve low pay. *Christian Science Monitor*. Retrieved May 21, 2009, from http://www.csmonitor.com/2009/0519/p09s02-coop.html

Powell, W., Koput, K., & Smith-Doerr, L. (1996). Interorganizational collaboration and the locus of innovation: Networks of learning in biotechnology. *Administrative Science Quarterly, 42*, 116–145.

Project for Excellence in Journalism. (2006). *Network TV audience trends*. Retrieved May 27, 2009, from http://www.journalism.org/node/1197

Project for Excellence in Journalism. (2008). *State of the news media 2008: Journalist survey*. Retrieved April 21, 2008, from http://www.stateofthenewsmedia.org/2008/journalist_survey_commentary.php?ca t=1&media=3

Project for Excellence in Journalism. (2009). *State of the news media 2009: Major trends*. Retrieved May 18, 2009, from http://www.stateofthenewsmedia.org/2009/narrative_overview_majortrends.php? media=1&cat=1

Project for Excellence in Journalism. (2010). *State of the news media 2010: Overview*. Retrieved March 15, 2010, from http://www.stateofthemedia.org/2010/overview_intro.php

Raviola, E., & Hartmann, B. (2009). Business perspectives on work in news organizations. *Journal of Media Business Studies, 6*, 7–36.

Ricchiardi, S. (2009, February/March). Share and share alike. *American Journalism Review*. Retrieved May 30, 2009, from http://www.ajr.org/Article.asp?id=4685

Rosen, J. (2006, June 26). The people formerly known as the audience. PressThink (Web log comment). Retrieved June 23, 2007, from http://journalism.nyu.edu/pubzone/weblogs/pressthink/2006/06/27/ppl_frmr.html

Russo, T. (1998, August). Organizational and professional identification: A case of newspaper journalists. *Management Communication Quarterly, 12*, 72–111.

Sass, E. (2008, March 31). Bad to worse, to worst: Newspaper revenues down 7.9% in 2007, as online growth slows. MediaPost Publications. Retrieved April 1, 2008, from http://publications.mediapost.com

Schneider, B., Brief, A., & Guzzo, R. (1996, Spring). Creating a climate and culture for sustainable organizational change. *Organizational Dynamics*, 7–19.

Schudson, M. (1995). *The power of news*. Cambridge, MA: Harvard University Press.

Schudson, M. (2002). The news media as political institutions. *Annual Review of Political Science, 5*, 249–269.

Schudson, M. (2009). Ten years backwards and forwards. *Journalism, 10*(3), 368–370.

Schudson, M., & Tifft, S. (2005). American journalism in historical perspective. In G. Overholser & K. Hall Jamieson (Eds.), *The press* (pp. 17–47). New York: Oxford University Press.

Schumpeter, J. (1949). *The theory of economic development*. Cambridge, MA: Harvard University Press.

Schumpeter, J. (1950). *Capitalism, socialism, and democracy*. New York: Harper.

Senge, P. (1990). *The fifth discipline: The art and practice of the learning organization*. New York: Doubleday/Currency.

Sharma, R., & Wildman, S. (2009). The economics of delivering digital content over mobile networks. *Journal of Media Business, 6*, 1–24.

Shoemaker, P., & Reese, S. (1996). *Mediating the message: Theories of influence on media content* (2nd ed.). New York: Longman.

Siebert, F., Peterson, W., & Schramm, W. (1956). *Four theories of the press*. Urbana: University of Illinois Press.

Silcock, B. W., & Keith, S. (2006). Translating the tower of Babel? Issues of definition, language and culture in converged newsrooms. *Journalism Studies, 7*(4), 610–627.

Singer, J. B. (2004). Strange bedfellows? The diffusion of convergence in four news organizations. *Journalism Studies, 5*, 3–18.

Stepp, C. S. (2000, July/August). Reader friendly. *American Journalism Review*, 22–43.

Sylvie, G., & Gade, P. (2009). Changes in news work: Implications for newsroom managers. *Journal of Media Business Studies, 6*, 113–148.

Sylvie, G., & Moon, S. J. (2007). Framing change: Who's in charge in the newsroom. In Achtenhagen, L. (Ed.), *Organizing media: Mastering the challenges of organizational change* (pp. 147–162). JIBS Research Reports 1. Jonkoping, Sweden: Jonkoping International Business School.

Sylvie, G., & Witherspoon, P. (2002). *Time, change and the American newspaper*. Mahwah, NJ: Erlbaum.

Tuchman, G. (1978). *Making news: A study in the construction of reality*. New York: Free Press.

Van Maanen, J., & Barley, S. (1984). Occupational communities: Culture and control in organizations. In B. Staw & L. L. Cummings (Eds.), *Research in organizational behavior* (pp. 287–365). Greenwich, CT: Jai Press.

Vukanovic, Z. (2009). Global paradigm shift: Strategic management of new and digital media in new and digital economics. *International Journal of Media Management, 11*, 81–90.

Weaver, D., Beam, R., Brownlee, B., Voakes, P., & Wilhoit, G. C. (2007). *The American journalist in the 21st century*. Mahwah, NJ: Erlbaum.

Witschage, T., & Nygren, G. (2009). Journalistic work: A profession under pressure? *Journal of Media Business Studies, 6*, 37–59.

PART II

IDEOLOGY, CULTURE, AND INSTITUTIONS

3

JOURNALISM AND DEMOCRACY

John C. Merrill, University of Missouri

The postmodern world, with its open and democratic overtones, is at hand. Promises of progress, equality, and new directions flood upon us. How we select and send news is changing. How news is defined promises to change our perception of the world. A certain populist order is seen coming to save increasingly chaotic societies. But where do we find populist wisdom, credibility, and authority? Here and there perhaps in certain universities and religious groups. But seldom where it needs to be: among national political leaders, in giant, multi-national corporations, and in public discourse.

Sociologist Robert Nisbet (2000) has written that our forefathers believed that modern democracy could avoid the kind of erosion and decay endemic in all kinds of states. At this point we are not so sure. We are hard pressed to say that the public media of communication provide credible information and wise counsel. In fact, the more we study the media, the more we realize that they (with a few exceptions) provide little more than entertainment and a surfeit of advertising.

In spite of occasional enlightened and helpful news and comment, our media system is little more than an "opiate" for the public, to appropriate a Marxian reference to religion (actually so termed by John Dewey in the introduction to Corliss Lamont's *The Illusion of Immortality* [Lamont, 1990, p. xiii]). In this view the media provide a narcotic that turns their audiences away from serious affairs and ideas and takes their attention away from serious democratic participation.

Our so-called newspapers give us only snippets of news—the rest being advertising, entertainment, opinion, commentary, features, and sports. TV and radio have even less news content. Helping to establish social order, national progress, and more democracy is not a media priority.

A strong feeling, however, still is found among journalists and ex-journalists that the press is a servant of democracy. Alex Jones (2009), long-time journalist whose book *Losing the News* has garnered considerable attention, writes:

> A successful news media [sic] that does its job for all the nation's citizens is the engine for the news that nourishes democracy. To demand that the news organizations perform this service is a part of American democracy as much as are the principles of tolerance and pursuit of happiness. If the iron core [news] should gradually melt away, Americans will have surrendered part of their birthright. (p. 222)

Normative Values: Freedom and Responsibility

One can question Jones' view whether the news media have been the nation's engine for democracy. However, more clear is that the media's democratic functions—to the extent they exist—are pressured and changing. Impulses both new (e.g., postmodern and technical) and old (e.g., populist and authoritarian) create considerable uncertainty about the media's normative roles, leaving journalism unsure of its moral compass, and casting considerable confusion on the value—and democratic meaning—of a free press.

In many Western societies—mainly those emanating from the eighteenth-century European Enlightenment and nineteenth-century romanticism—a free and independent press was believed important, even essential, to proper journalism, even though it posed serious problems for citizen involvement in journalism. During most of the twentieth century emphasis was given (at least in the West) to *press* freedom, thereby keeping the door open for an emphasis on media power. Developed Western countries of Europe and North America have tried to spread this libertarian gospel of *press* freedom, often with missionary zeal, to the rest of the world. The rationale for press freedom is to make the press independent—or *free from* government control. This independence has been viewed as essential because a democracy requires informed citizens, and citizens rely on news media for much of their information about government. Freedom leads to the truth, truth is essential for credibility, and credibility is essential for faith in government and wise populist decision-making.

However, freedom is a vague concept. Is it meant as freedom for the journalist or for the press? Freedom for the journalist can do great harm: It can destroy reputations, it can unfairly stereotype persons and groups, it can endanger national security, it can fuel public anxiety, and it can encourage extreme and irrational social conduct. Of course, it can also permit the journalist to refrain from participation in any of the above. Also, we know that freedom does not, in many cases, lead to truth. Journalistic freedom provides much room for falsification; in fact, it can legitimize distortions, exaggerations, superficialities, and falsehood. One must remember that control and discipline are also journalistic values, and a free press is not the same as a good press.

In the United States such reminders are worrisome. The shortcomings of a free press conjure up fears of a meddling government getting control of the press system and imposing a monolithic order. For freedom-loving journalists and many publishers, these fears came to life after World War II with the Hutchins Commission report (Commission on Freedom of the Press, 1947). The report, *A Free and Responsible Press*, outlined the licentiousness and elitist practices of the press, declaring that its failures to clarify the goals of society and accurately portray various segments of society could result in government sanctions on freedom. The report demanded that press freedom be tempered with the idea of *responsibility*. This emphasis transitioned the press's freedom to the people's freedom (Merrill, 1974). Democracy assumed a mantle of social control. It became common to hear that the press was simply untrustworthy to bring about responsible journalism. Capitalistic media freedom was increasingly suspect, and *vox populi* assumed a more important position—at least in intellectual rhetoric.

Innumerable writers have also exhaustively proclaimed the importance of social responsibility. In fact, since the days of the Hutchins Commission social responsibility has become a dominant concern for the press. The press must be free *and* responsible. This is a tall order; in fact, it is really an impossible dream. If the press is "free" it is free to be "irresponsible." If it is "responsible," then it is so in terms of some referee or controller. Therefore, it appears that a "free *and* responsible" press can never truly exist. A little freedom, yes; and a little responsibility, yes. But one or the other has got to give. Journalists know this, but continue their misguided dream that they can have a press both free and responsible. The recent concern with media ethics (self-control) may well make the media more responsible in some ways for some people—but even here we have the problem of a pluralism of ethical theories and the subjectivity involved in trying to define "responsibility."

What journalists seem to prize is a pluralistic disorder—a kind of situational ethics—that signifies a truly free press. What about the people? What do they want? The people are diverse and they seem to *want everything*. The truth when they can get it, yes, but also plenty of gossip, sensation, and mythology. And, of course, they are getting increasing doses of it via the Internet. There is little doubt but that the Internet will expand informational triviality and superficiality—and also decrease media credibility—while providing an increase of kernels of truth hidden somewhere in its vast pluralism.

The Internet and associated forces for the democratization of public information undoubtedly change the news (semantically and quantitatively). However, the question remains: Will this "people-determined" news be any more socially helpful than the news determined by the capitalistic media managers of the past? It is true that media-determined news has not been, and has never been, a democratic enterprise with its elitist, institutionalized concept of what the public should be exposed to. And now a more pluralistic, democratic public information system threatens this journalistic monopoly. News has been what the *journalists* say it is. New democratic news will be the cacophonous determinations of the people. It will therefore be more diverse and opinionated.

The Elusive Democracy

Today we may ask: Where are the media messages that suggest how we can *expand democracy* in public life generally or in interpersonal communication? The media themselves, in their own operation, do not point the way. Not only the journalistic staff but the audiences of the media are basically voiceless. The former have no real say in ongoing policy and the vast majority of the latter are silent recipients of the information given them by news determiners. The audiences, at least some few of them, try to get their ideas to the media. However, the media, with recent exceptions, largely ignore public questions about editorial policy. As two journalism educators wrote (Glasser & Ettema, 2008), an occasional writer will complain about the form or content of the news, "but journalists seldom dignify it with a response . . . A handful of news-rooms employ an ombudsman or readers' representative, but their columns, if they write one at all, rarely question journalism's traditions and assumptions" (p. 13).

Glasser and Ettema pull no punches in faulting journalism for its lack of respect for public criticism. They score a deft body punch with these words:

> Journalists' resistance to criticism, particularly criticism intended to solicit a response from them, vivifies a professional ethos that discounts the value of debating to and with the public about what goes on in and around the newsroom. Perhaps more so in the United States than anywhere else, the prevailing view of independent journalism represents the triumph of autonomy over accountability, and this in turn fuels a curious ethic of defiance. (pp. 13–14)

Public Discourse: Where Is It?

Why is all this important? Because even in a capitalistic society, there is a rather deep-rooted belief, resting on democratic ideals, that the citizens should be closely involved in public issues and governance. Theoretically, government power should shrink while citizen power expands. However, as Bertrand de Jouvenel (1993) has documented, democracies have done a poor job in limiting the powers of government. One problem with a discussion of democracy is that various cultures (often without using that people-connected term) have their own self-serving plan for their social involvement. Juergen Habermas, perhaps contemporary Germany's most prominent philosopher, through his interest in public discourse has tried to "bring together various strains of democratic theory to show that there is no predetermined, natural path of development for democratic societies" (as cited in Allen, 2002, p. 100).

In the United States and most Western countries, the main path is investing the people with means of participating in public policy. The public media are often seen as necessary to such involvement—both through their public pronouncements and their symbiotic relationship with the audiences. If we as citizens are to rule wisely, we must have reliable and thorough news. That is the theory. So democracy in the news process is increasingly under pressure to improve. At least one would think so. Sad to say, however, the vast majority of citizens appear to care little about injecting their opinions and ideas into media decision-making. And the nagging question persists: Would such communication from the public (if it did come forth) enhance the validity and credibility of the information available?

In U.S. press theory a main mission of the information media is to facilitate democracy and to expand it. Not everybody, of course, accepts this mission. Some see the media's mission as no more than supplying non-directive information (and that includes advertising). Then there are, at one extreme, the nihilists who say there is *no* mission or public responsibility—the media are simply moneymaking businesses for the owners. In a recent book (Merrill, 2006) I wrote about the nihilist position:

> To speculate about it [public mission] is meaningless . . . Journalism is an assortment of activities going off in all directions and accomplishing a number of things, some socially important and some not. There is no purpose to journalism, or to anything else really . . . for the world and life itself is basically meaningless. Get out the paper but don't expect it to accomplish anything of significance. Forget this talk about mission. (pp. 82–83)

Again, that's the nihilist position, not mine.

Then at the other extreme are the journalists (and audience members) who pay lip service to democracy (they may even vote), but have no real interest in participatory journalism and accept the elitist perspective of "let the experts take care of it." Very seldom do these persons apply Habermas' (1989) "ideal speech situation"—attempting a consensus—to a dialogue between journalism and citizen.

Journalism does seem to have developed in a philosophical vacuum, built largely on a foundation of relativism and subjectivism. Democratizing society may be a main purpose of some media systems, but certainly it is not for many others. A kind of relative pragmatism is to be found among various journalism systems of the world. John Dewey and Niccolo Machiavelli, championing the "what works is good" philosophy, inject a sense of realism into journalism theory and highlight the non-universality of media mission (Merrill, 1994). One great problem with democracy involves the problem of how to find leaders with standards. Harvard professor Irving Babbitt (1924) in his seminal book *Democracy and Leadership* pointed out the danger of unchecked majoritarianism. In 1997 sociologist Edward Shils forcefully echoed Babbitt's concern with public rationality and stressed the need for civility in a free society that is well ordered and democratic (Shils, 1997).

Unfortunately rationality and civility are often ignored in a discussion of democracy. Majoritarianism is what is emphasized, and of course that can result in systems (governments or media) that are mired in moral decay. In the nineteenth century James Fitzjames Stephen (1993), famous critic of Mill's (1986 [1861]) *On Liberty*, proposed that only the constraints of morality, coupled with law, make for a viable society; unlimited liberty and material equality will lead to tyranny. Liberty, he believed, is not as important as morality, and must be accompanied by tradition and custom, and a strong sense of ethics, if a society is to be viable. Hallowell (2007) supports this moral emphasis for the orderly functioning of a democracy. Democracy, he believes, is dependent on citizens being moral, spiritual, and rational actors.

The Importance of Debate

But let us assume here that we want a journalism based on citizen involvement. Essential to a democratically oriented system is the "debate" concept that media can extend to the public. However, it seems increasingly that like-minded individuals and public segments talk to one another and castigate those in opposing camps. And the media are complicit in this. Bowman (2008) writes that we should recognize this media weakness "and begin to re-assert the need for real debate in the place of that which now goes under that name but whose routine accusations of bad faith, corruption, or mental illness are really the death of rational discourse" (pp. 6–7).

Participation in a democratic system is a matter of both habit and conscious reflection. It appears that most of us accept some of the tenets of democracy habitually and unreflectively. Editors and news directors, for example, accept certain benefits of democracy but are hesitant to apply them to their staffs or to their audiences. Democracy it seems, like morality, comes in two forms (Hegel's *sittlichkeit* and *moralitaet),* the first a kind of almost unconscious immersion in at least shallow democratic waters, and the second a deeper, more reflective dive into serious communal depths where egalitarianism merges with self-interest and mass ignorance is overcome by public enlightenment.

Meilaender (2008), commenting on this Hegelian binary emphasis, gives the following challenge to teachers, but it is appropriate for media executives as well:

We should sharpen the intellect the best we can; we should pursue truth . . . we should transmit knowledge and the skills required to gain and extend that knowledge—but we should not try to produce or control what must be contingent and felicitous. (p. 36)

Meilaender is writing in a Catholic journal and his words, especially those after the dash in the above quotation, may not find approval by secular writers and journalists. However, the pursuit of truth, and the transmission of knowledge and skills—for the extension of knowledge—would seem a beneficial journalistic formula. Surely the truth about democracy, its strengths and weaknesses, is needed by the citizenry, and the media should have this as a prime objective.

Public Leadership Problematic

Democracy is a good-sounding word, but the average citizen (and the media) appears to have opted out of it. Some scholars (e.g., Lindbom, 1996) think democracy is a myth. Others, like sociologist Michael Sandel (1996), see our democracy in serious danger of disappearing. Lazar (1996), an even more troubled writer, believes democracy in America is not working: "Problems are mushrooming, conflicts are multiplying, and society seems increasingly out of control" (p. 1). He even believes that the United States cannot "survive much longer with a government that is inefficient and none too democratic by design" (p. 5). Another critic, Ryn, a political science professor, writes: "The problems of Western society are sufficiently severe to raise doubts about democracy's ability to survive" (as cited in Lindbom, 1996, p. 2). Excessive rhetoric? Maybe not. It does appear that citizens are accustomed to being virtually ignored by the media and national leaders, with only the smallest fraction of the population getting representation in the news. Zakaria (2003) contends that a tiny group—perhaps a million—runs most of the American institutions and has "enormous power" (p. 235) compared with that of the average citizens. The media establishment is certainly a part of this tiny group.

Is Democracy a Myth?

Two conflicting concepts of Western democracy are *liberty* and *equality*. And the media seem incapable of recognizing this as they alternately manifest an interest in each. At one moment the media try to put everyone on the same level—sports figures, government officials, truck drivers, scientists, rock stars—editorially endowing them with *equality*. At the same time the media routinely ignore and even disdain certain classes, professions, trades, religions, and races, thus recognizing the obvious inequality among people.

Democracy, in many ways, is nothing but a myth. Horizontal leadership and control, along with people's freedom and equality, are not only contradictory concepts but also invitations to either nihilism or social conformity. As the Swedish philosopher Tage Lindbom (1996) has put it:

> If the democratic myth were only a proclamation of liberty, the whole democratic construction, the whole edifice, would be thrown out of balance and anarchy would result . . . But at the same time, equality is a menace for liberty; it can become a means of oppression in the hands of a central authority. When liberty and equality meet, therefore, conflict is unavoidable. (pp. 80–81)

Journalists have long looked at themselves as somewhat special people, not exactly equal even among themselves. And they perceive that equality (even of opportunity) is impossible and unrealistic in a free society. So they resign themselves to a familiar and shallow democracy defined primarily by the availability of a ballot box. In the face of criticism, however, the idea of "people involvement" has prompted the media in recent years to attempt to bring the citizens into their operations. And the Internet has made this involvement available to most everyone, as most media invite user comments, feedback, and interaction.

Still, however, the media establishment—a small minority—determines what the public receives (outside self-centered blogging) in the way of news and opinion. This is not good, contend two noted media critics (Davidson & Rees-Mogg, 1998), who believe that "the normal information channels cannot be depended on to provide accurate and timely understanding" of the news (p. 337). There are plenty of facts available, but "no broad view" or meaning to what is going on.

The Lure of Platonic Order

Voices are heard in opposition to the postmodern call for more communication democratization. They call for more order, especially in the face of uncertainty—for example, the war on terror, the great recession, the cacophony of voices on the Internet—for more authority in elite hands. For many whose contention is represented by a *Newsweek* writer (Zakaria, 2003), social order is not seen coming from pluralizing power bases; in fact, there "can be too much democracy" (p. 26). The British philosopher Isaiah Berlin (2002) has cogently pointed out the danger to freedom and democracy posed by the lure of such thinkers as Plato, Hegel, Fichte, Rousseau, and Hobbes, exemplars of this non-democratic tradition. As I have discussed in *Call to Order: Plato's Legacy of Social Control* (Merrill, 2009), the magnetic attraction of social stability, strong leadership, and hierarchical authoritarianism has always been powerful. The people are simply not knowledgeable enough or don't desire to have a great impact on editorial or national policies. Besides, how would "the people" in their busy personal lives manage to become public enlightenment servants in any democratically meaningful way? However, in spite of obstacles, citizen-involved communication is in its ascendancy. The state, say the Hegelians and other authoritarians, is in a sense "the people." This is adamantly contradicted by freedom-lovers (e.g., Meyer, 1996; Fukuyama, 1992), the latter saying that the idea that the state is the people is nothing but "a lie" (p. 11).

Postmodern technology—especially cyberspace communication—is encouraging this democratic proclivity by empowering vast numbers of formerly silent citizens to get their voices heard. Social media, e-mail, and other computer-generated technologies have given birth to untold numbers of "citizen journalists." The traditional media are in trouble and limping along, and ordinary citizens, with their new technological potency, are posing a democratically significant challenge to the old information paradigm. If this is true, the new cyberworld of information will certainly be more democratic.

What does this portend for the concept of "news"? It obviously will revolutionize it, and the optimists believe it will change its meaning from items of deviance, negativity, and oddity to a wider scope of local, positive, and citizen-related interests. For serious citizens that is the hope. At least it will take the monopoly out of the hands of a small journalistic elite and engage a much larger public opinion as to what is newsworthy. This is definitely a more hopeful trend in the democratization of news. However, of course, there is no assurance that news determinants will change much if put in the hands of the people, who may very well be generally satisfied with the status quo. At least there is little evidence that they are greatly troubled by what Bowman (2008) has called "media madness."

From Superficiality to Decay?

The media themselves, although conscious of their general superficiality and popular content (Lazar, 1996), are reluctant to upgrade their content. By 2010 the mainline media were aware of their serious problems, and they were cutting staff and groping for ideas to keep them alive. Lombard (2009), a newspaper editor from West Palm Beach, Florida, gave his version of the problem:

> The recent presidential race is telling evidence of the press' problems—the 90 percent negative coverage of Sarah Palin; the adoring puffery for Barack Obama; the constant crying about recession starting two long years before the year it might arrive. (p. 47)

Lombard refers to the news media as being on the "cutting edge" of negativity and moral decay. "We are taught to write that way," he says, "from J-school to boardroom [and] this is hurting the nightly TV news too, and network news, much of it focused on grossly negative news and light feel-good features"

(p. 47). Two media scholars, John Nichols and Robert McChesney (Nichols & McChesney, 2009), long-time critics of capitalistic media, have added their voices to the anti-media critical bombardment. Here are some of their strong expressions:

> Communities across America are suffering through a crisis that could leave a dramatically diminished version of democracy in its wake . . . Journalism is collapsing, and with it comes the most serious threat in our lifetimes to self-government and the rule of law as it has been understood here in the United States . . . newspapers, as we have known them, are disintegrating and are possibly on the verge of extinction . . . the quality of journalism in the United States is dreadful . . . [the media] trade in trivia and reduce everything to spin, even matters of life and death. (pp. 11–16)

These sentiments show a definite antagonism to free-market journalism. However, there is considerable truth in them, and it is interesting that at the same time the public has lost faith in government for its lack of transparency and morality. The authors, although not opposed to commercial ownership, see a great need for municipal ownership, staff ownership, and independent non-profit ownership. They propose greater government involvement, saying that in the next media system "the government should be prepared to rewrite rules and regulations and to use its largesse to aid a variety of sound initiatives" (p. 20).

Entertainment, Democracy, and Profit

Many critics have noted that the media's emphasis on entertainment is harmful to public enlightenment and democracy. At a 2008 ethics summit former vice-president Al Gore in his keynote speech on "democracy" made this point (as cited in Cooper, Christians, & Babbili, 2008):

> The mingling of entertainment values with journalism [is an element] prominent in the American ecosystem that also serves as one of those pressures that can tilt the odds that an outcome in any given set of choices made by journalists will go in a way that ethicists might look back on years from now and say that wasn't the right choice. (p. 173)

The preceding "Faulknerian" sentence, in getting to the point, is much milder than many such criticisms of the media's emphasis on entertainment.

Critical remarks such as those above increasingly pour in on the media. But, for the most part, they fall on deaf ears. News directors know they are in trouble, but ignore the call for more sophisticated and objective coverage and hope to solve their problems through better technology. Spurred on by the profit motive, they want to catch as many fish as possible in their nets. Therefore, with few exceptions, they continue to lower their standards to the attitudinal and political illiterates in society and give slight attention to the socially and morally concerned minority. The government, of course, is basically satisfied with this, for it keeps the public from looking too closely at its operations.

One could contend that this media superficiality is a sign of "democracy" injected into journalism—giving more people what they want. However, the masses don't know what they "really" want, because such a narrow range of options has been given them. This ("give 'em what they want so we can make the most money") kind of democracy does not make the grade. More active participatory democracy is increasingly called for. And news media are opening their websites to citizen voices, encouraging comments and letting citizens create some content. This is commendable, at least in liberal circles, in that it transcends media profit and envisions a wiser, more equitable society. But news media are finding that relatively few citizens participate and too many comments are rude or vulgar (Howe, 2008; Perez-Pena, 2010).

Weakening the Journalistic Core

Communitarianism, the populist and groupist genre related to communication (Christians, Ferre, & Fackler, 1993), would largely replace *press* freedom with a new *community*-oriented freedom. Social responsibility would push press freedom to one side. Of course, the hope is that the "people" will have higher tastes and rationality than the traditional media controllers have had. Editorial self-determination of the press as guaranteed in the First Amendment would recede, to be supplanted by some problematic community-directed media system. Alternatively, it could be that *citizens* would be defined as "the press," further obfuscating the Bill of Rights.

Societies, while talking much of the individual, gravitate toward groups, toward communities, and away from the individual. Listen to Michael Novak, an American Catholic intellectual (as cited in Peikoff, 1982), talking about the tendency to collectivize:

> There is not now, there never was, there never will be, a solitary autonomous self, apart from society. The human being is in a social network, necessarily dependent and psychologically interrelated, a social organism, a political animal. The self is not an "I" but a "we." (p. 288)

But we know that, in spite of such communitarian sentiments, *any* media system must be ultimately hierarchical, with the power not with an amorphous "people" but with a leader, a group of stockholders, or some other powerful elite. Many idealist journalists and academicians today are saying that the acceptance of increasingly populist ideology and anti-market economics will force the media world to open up and grant increasing message control to the public, thereby expanding democracy. This people-involved (everybody a journalist) idea is troublesome—especially for media people who see it as a danger to an institutionalized, self-directed press.

Without a doubt this new populist press concept is more democratic, but the question is whether or not it would work in a nation dotted with discrete institutions with their own authority. What is interesting is that the idea of "citizen journalists" comes at the same time that the idea of professionalizing journalism is gaining momentum. A profession implies institutional self-regulation: If professional doctors direct medical care, why wouldn't professional journalists direct journalism? Traditionally the people have submitted to ostensible experts—the professionals. But as they have done so, what about their freedom? Freedom of the general run of people to perform specialized professional duties is problematic (even irrational) in a complex society.

Two Worlds: Democracy and Authority

It appears that we are caught between two worlds: the democratic or people-dominated world and the authority-dominated world. Actually a "people-dominated" world is purely theoretical, and not realistic. A people-dominated press system would likely be pure chaos, resulting only in the leadership shifting from media managers to everybody—or nobody. It is true that government officials can substitute for independent editors and publishers, but they are still authorities directing and controlling the media.

What is rather obvious is that the American media are drifting in the direction of populism, even socialism. A main rationale for this is that the capitalist media, the laissez-faire, competitive media, are too concerned with profit-making and too little with ethics and public welfare. Implicit in this argument, of course, is that government, the people, or some other controlling agent will be more competent and ethical than editors and news directors. We have no empirical evidence that this would be so, but the lure of "democracy" provides us with a hope that there is a better way.

The profit-making impulse of the capitalist publisher does, unfortunately, often eclipse ethical motivations, but *any* control system will likely sacrifice ethics to pragmatic or political ends. If we are heading toward another type of authoritarian media world, under the name of democracy, the would-be controllers will be aided by a belief that the media will be more efficiently run, more moral, and more public service oriented. Apologists for such a controlled and efficiently run world maintain that stability and community cooperation are more important than individual freedom. As I expressed it at the 2009 International Communication Association convention in Chicago, the communitarian mantra might be worded like this: *Discipline preserves society; freedom destroys it*. Oversimplification, yes, as I heard loudly from my audience, but there is some truth in it.

Now . . . let me make myself clear. I am a freedom lover, but I am also aware that freedom can be dangerous and socially harmful as well as beneficial. When I wrote *The Imperative of Freedom* (Merrill 1974), I perhaps gave too much emphasis to freedom and not enough to responsibility. I tried to remedy this some 15 years later in *The Dialectic in Journalism* (Merrill 1989). Freedom does not mean, in spite of the Founding Fathers' optimism, that freedom of the press necessarily enhances ethical action. Freedom always needs control, and it is safe to say that *every* media system is, to some degree, authoritarian *and* unethical. It just depends where the authority lies and to what extent it is ethical.

Press Freedom, Ethics, and Democracy

Freedom (as essential for democracy) is being lost in subtle ways, not only in countries such as Cuba, Zimbabwe, and Venezuela, but also in the United States. Beyond such blatant cases of government authoritarianism by such leaders as Castro and Mugabe, there are other signs of freedom's loss in advanced capitalist countries of the Western world. A political press theory (Siebert, Peterson, & Schramm, 1963) reflecting "progressive" thinking in the West was the popular "four theories" concept that added "social responsibility" to the authoritarian, Marxist, and libertarian concepts. Although this model has been criticized widely for Western bias throughout the ensuing years, it is still around and very influential. It added fuel to the growing criticism of press freedom and opened the door to a spasm of "democratic" media revisions in the United States—such as press councils, ombudspersons, and critical reviews. The postmodern age had arrived.

Somewhere along the line the concepts of "democracy" and "people's press" have been intermingled and tied to press freedom, perhaps even trumping it. Assumption A: If the press is free, the people are free and have significant representation in the press. Assumption B: "The people" are better journalists and more responsible than the professionals. But nowhere is there evidence for these assumptions. Without the order provided by a media institutional leadership, there is reason to believe that society would dissolve. Social decay was predicted early by Plato and popularized in the last century by writers on cybernetics (e.g. Wiener, 1967) who call for more social discipline to halt the encroachments of democratic chaotic tendencies.

Social Entropy and Platonic Decay

Wiener talked about the process of "entropy" (the tendency of a system to lose information and energy and to run down). And he, like Plato and the pre-Socratic philosopher Heraclitus, who saw all things in motion and tending to run down, talked about slowing this process by creating "islands of decreasing entropy." Authoritarians such as Hegel, Hobbes, and de Maistre endorsed such ideas, believing the people need strong leadership, discipline, and a sense of social cohesion.

To counter the development of such extreme decadent and entropic tendencies, efforts have been under way to develop in the United States a more responsive press system. Mounting criticism provided ample reason to be concerned. As far back as the 1960s, American writers (e.g., Rourke, 1961) were intimating that this country was becoming a "contemporary dictatorship," largely because of the emphasis the government puts on "arousing and maintaining public support." Rourke admitted the media are much better in Western democracies than elsewhere, but says that even here the "influence of government upon the process of opinion formation is very great" (p. 17). Also he laments the growth of secretive government as threatening "the vitality of democracy itself" (p. 18). About this same time, a number of countries were beginning to stress codes of press ethics, ombudspersons, press councils, and media criticism. A journalistic "conscience" seemed to be developing—at least in speeches, conferences, classrooms, and journalism literature.

However, authoritarianism was still alive and well through the final decades of the twentieth century and continues in the present century. Censorship, press harassment, political correctness, press laws, court action, government secrecy, and the whole gamut of controlling mechanisms are still firmly entrenched.

The spirit of Plato's rigid concept of social control (Merrill, 2009)—stalled for centuries by Enlightenment thinkers such as Milton, Mill, Constant, Voltaire, and Kierkegaard—is far from dead in the twenty-first century. The basic appeal of Plato's orderly city-state type of government—described in *The Republic*—has been historically potent. Such a system, for Plato, was highly structured, appropriately censored, wisely led, with each class knowing its place and individual freedom largely sacrificed (as cited in Popper, 1966, pp. 85–90). Most modern institutions (such as the mass media) have retained many of Plato's ideas but wrapped them in democratic rhetoric.

This Platonic demeanor is seductive, with a beguiling quality, a disciplined and organized thinking. In many countries even journalists, usually among a society's individualistic "intellectuals," feel comfortable having someone make editorial decisions for them. In a sense they are beyond democracy and have a longing for power. They (like their governments) see "the people" as having a psychological desire to "escape from freedom" (see Fromm, 1965), thus relieving themselves of the trauma of choice and personal responsibility. Organization (not individualism) still has a hold on societies. "Organization," according to Roderick Seidenberg (1950) in his catalytic *Post-historic Man*, "demands further organization." And the "pressure of this demand will have far-reaching and profoundly significant consequences: In time it will necessarily transform society from an organic into an organizational entity" (p. 107).

Seidenberg continues that the individual, "narrowed by the organized patterns of collectivized society, no longer sustains a sense of inward autonomy: as the wells of inward values are drained, the nuclear sense of the person as the source of free choice and of values must likewise vanish" (p. 112). These individual values are increasingly shifted to the outstretched hands of paternalistic governments.

Socialism at the Gates

It may well be that, as the Hutchins Commission warned in 1947, government may have to step in to correct the media's sins. Again, such a warning comes from Nichols and McChesney (2009), who see the first order of government intervention as the assurance "that no state or region would be without quality local, state, national or international journalism" (p. 19). Maybe so, but it would be nice to think that government might concentrate on its own quality, which is as low or lower than that of the press. However, recent signs point to more external control of the media (e.g., Congress considering in 2009 exempting newspapers from taxes *if they will not take political positions*).

Not a bright prospect for the libertarian. But media managers and journalists fuel the call for external control when they show little interest in expanding democracy—either in the society generally or in their own institutions. Media leaders are often Machiavellians, pursuing their ends by using whatever means will work (see Christians & Merrill, 2009). They are realists, materialists, and individual-pragmatists. They hold on to their power and decision-making activities and fail to provide information that can increase their audience's impact on government and other social institutions. This, of course, is not always bad for the society—especially if their ends overlap with society's ends. Also it must be said that the people—the audiences—give no evidence that they are desirous of more control of the media. The people are seemingly too busy with their own affairs to be concerned about running any social institution such as the press—or even their schools.

Despite the potentialities of traditional autocratic thinking, democratization of the media output is increasing. Largely this is the result of technological developments that make it much easier for the average citizen to be heard. This is a hopeful—although uncertain and problematic—sign. It may well be that we will see a basically "people's press" as democracy increases—and it may mean that the mainline media will either disappear or morph into more stagnant forms that will provide a drabness and dullness, lulling the populace into an ever more passive sleep.

Mass unconcern and alienation can have little value for sustainable society. So the alternative—a democratic public communication system—is seen as an obvious and immediate need. Platonists among us may challenge this view, but their hierarchical and vertical pattern of leadership in the media has led to public lethargy and alienation (Bowman 2008; Lindbom, 1996). Perhaps it is time to establish a new pattern of media direction and responsibility.

During the next decade or so this should be a priority: policing, taming, directing, and influencing the media, making them more ethical or responsible to democratic principles. A Socrates may have to be sacrificed here and there, but we can become true believers in an actively engaged, wise democracy that will reject politicized populist authoritarianism in any of its attractive forms. If we do not want to do this, or find that we cannot do it, then we can continue to stumble along in our plutocratic and elitist society, watching our world crumble around us as we are fed narcotizing crumbs from arrogant media managers.

Thought Questions: Contemplating Change

1. If journalism is a "profession," as it is generally considered, how can it be further democratized without losing its professional identity? If active public participation in media decision-making leads to indecision and chaos (or even danger), what should be done?
2. In a more democratic media system, would the general public determine what is published? What other entities might determine what is published? How could a more "democratic" press system work to provide assurance that information is credible?
3. Is the traditional capitalistic "laissez-faire" press system all right in its theoretical foundation, only needing a better educated and more ethical human dimension? Why should a communication medium (e.g. a newspaper) be any different in structure, purpose, and operation from any other commercial business (e.g., a hardware store)? Why would some say that the very concept of democracy is incompatible with credible, quality journalism?

References

Allen, D. (2002). Juergen Habermas and democratic principles. In C. Christians & S. Bracci (Eds.), *Moral engagement in public life* (pp. 97–122). New York: Peter Lang.

Babbitt, I. (1924). *Democracy and leadership*. Indianapolis, IN: Freedom Fund.

Berlin, I. (2002). *Freedom and its betrayal*. New York: Henry Holt.

Bowman, J. (2008). *Media madness: The corruption of our political culture*. New York: Encounter Books.

Christians, C., Ferre, J. P., & Fackler, P. M. (1993). *Good news*. New York: Oxford University Press.

Christians, C., & Merrill, J. C. (Eds.). (2009). *Communication ethics*. Columbia: University of Missouri Press.

Commission on Freedom of the Press. (1947). *A free and responsible press*. Chicago: University of Chicago Press.

Cooper, T. W., Christians, C., & Babbili, A. (2008). *An ethics trajectory*. Urbana, IL: Institute for Communications Research.

Davidson, J. D., & Rees-Mogg, W. (1998). *The sovereign individual*. New York: Simon & Schuster.

Fromm, E. (1965). *Escape from freedom*. New York: Avon Books.

Fukuyama, F. (1992). *The end of history and the last man*. New York: Avon Books.

Glasser, T., & Ettema, J. (2008, December 31). A philosophy of accountability for journalism. *Media Ethics*, 13–14.

Habermas, J. (1989). *The structural transformation of the public sphere*. Cambridge: Massachusetts Institute of Technology Press.

Hallowell, J. H. (2007). *The moral foundation of democracy*. Indianapolis, IN: Freedom Fund.

Howe, J. (2008). The wisdom of the crowd resides in how the crowd is used. *Nieman Reports, 62*(4), 47–50.

Jones, A. (2009). *Losing the news*. Oxford: Oxford University Press.

Jouvenel, B. de. (1993). *On power*. Indianapolis, IN: Freedom Fund.

Lamont, C. (1990). *The illusion of immortality*. New York: Continuum.

Lazar, D. (1996). *The frozen republic: How the constitution is paralyzing democracy*. New York: Harcourt Brace.

Lindbom, T. (1996). *The myth of democracy*. Grand Rapids, MI: William B. Eerdmans.

Lombard, D. (2009, January). Moral decay [Letter to the editor]. *American Journalism Review*, 47.

Meilaender, G. (2008, November). Education & soulcraft. *First Things*, 36.

Merrill, J. C. (1974). *The imperative of freedom: A philosophy of journalistic autonomy*. New York: Hastings House.

Merrill, J. C. (1989). *The dialectic in journalism*. Baton Rouge: Louisiana State University Press.

Merrill, J. C. (1994). *Legacy of wisdom: Great thinkers and journalism*. Ames: Iowa State University Press.

Merrill, J. C. (2006). *Media, mission and morality*. Spokane, WA: Marquette Books.

Merrill, J. C. (2009). *Call to order: Plato's legacy of social control*. Spokane, WA: Marquette Books.

Meyer, F. S. (1996). *In defense of freedom and related essays*. Indianapolis, IN: Liberty Fund.

Mill, J. S. (1986 [1861]). *On liberty*. New York: Macmillan.

Nichols, J., & McChesney, R. W. (2009, April 6). The death and life of great American newspapers. *The Nation*, 11–20.

Nisbet, R. (2000). *Twilight of authority*. Indianapolis, IN: Freedom Fund.

Peikoff, L. (1982). *The ominous parallels*. New York: New American Library.

Perez-Pena, R. (2010, April 12). Unmasking the commenters: In a rude realm, news sites rethink anonymity. *The New York Times*, p. B1.

Popper, K. R. (1966). *The open society and its enemies*. Princeton, NJ: Princeton University Press.

Rourke, F. E. (1961, May 13). How much should the government tell? *Saturday Review*, 17–19, 21.

Sandel, M. (1996). *Democracy's discontent*. Cambridge, MA: Harvard University Press.

Seidenberg, R. (1950). *Post-historic man: An inquiry*. Chapel Hill: University of North Carolina Press.

Shils, E. (1997). *The virtue of civility*. Indianapolis, IN: Freedom Fund.

Siebert, F., Peterson, T., & Schramm, W. (1963). *Four theories of the press*. Urbana: University of Illinois Press.

Stephen, J. F. (1993). *Liberty, equality, fraternity*. New York: Henry Holt.

Wiener, N. (1967). *The human use of human beings: Cybernetics and society*. New York: Houghton-Mifflin.

Zakaria, F. (2003). *The future of freedom*. New York: W.W. Norton.

4

POSTMODERNISM, UNCERTAINTY, AND JOURNALISM

Peter J. Gade, University of Oklahoma

The relative stability that characterized U.S. journalism—and other social institutions—for much of the twentieth century has been pushed aside by a tidal wave of change in recent decades. Modernity, with its emphasis on rationality, science, universal truths, and social order, although deeply ingrained, is challenged by new social phenomena and epistemological forms under the penumbral idea of *postmodernism*.

Postmodernism is associated with contemporary life patterns that are familiar in developed societies: a fast pace of life, technological innovation, constant change in social tastes and trends, consumerism, increasing reliance on media, globalization, multi-culturalism, relativity, and logical inconsistency (Malpas, 2005; Strinati, 2004; Webster, 2006). And it is more . . . or perhaps less. Strinati (2004) summarizes postmodernism as reflecting five societal shifts: the rejection of meta-narratives claiming truth; the instability of time and space; the breakdown of distinctions between high art and pop culture; the power of media to construct a sense of reality and social relations; and an emphasis on style, arbitrariness, and playfulness over substance and meaning. French philosopher Baudrillard (1984) calls postmodernity "the immense process of the destruction of meaning . . . Whoever lives by meaning, dies by meaning" (pp. 38–39).

Postmodern life is found in a networked world that breaks down traditional national borders and merges cultures. It reflects societies where most things are at our fingertips, where the security of tradition and community is not apparent, where consumerism replaces production. Context and history are of minor importance; personal impulse and subjectivity are arbiters of truth. Irony, ambiguity, and contingency are the basis of a world view (Rorty, 1989). The eclectic and complex nature of the postmodern world and the concepts that support it make defining postmodernism a difficult task, but this is exactly the point. The logic of identification, definition, and classification associated with modernity (and its embrace of rationality, science, and structure) is not what postmodernism is about. "Postmodernism, in contrast, seeks to grasp what escapes these processes of definition and celebrates what resists or disrupts them" (Malpas, 2005, p. 4).

Definitive is the contrast between modern and postmodern societies. The development of modern societies can be traced to the European Enlightenment, when scientific advances became the basis for a shift away from the authority of the church and a belief that humanity—through its exercise of reason—could uncover and explain the mysteries of the natural world. Wilson (1998) characterizes these seventeenth- and eighteenth-century thinkers:

> They were driven by the thrill of discovery. They agreed on the power of science to reveal an orderly, understandable universe and thereby lay an enduring base of free rational discourse. They thought the perfection of the celestial bodies discovered by astronomy and physics could serve as a model for human society. They believed in the unity of all knowledge, natural law, and indefinite human progress. (p. 44)

It was only a small leap, then, to think that if science could open the door to understanding the natural world, it could also be used as a method to understand the social world, to solve distinctly human problems, and to improve and perfect social institutions. The complexity of human problems could be mastered by rational, structured, systematic, and objective processes. At the end of the nineteenth century, this embrace was the source of optimism for "progressives," who saw it as correcting corruption in social institutions driven by capitalist greed and religious claims of moral authority (May, 1959; Steel, 1999).

Science, as a basis for the discovery of truth and the progress of humanity, became the core logic of the *modern* world. Science permeated social institutions, emerging as an essential element of education, the advancement of medicine, creation of new technologies, and the research and development of major corporations. It also became the organizing logic of how businesses structured and executed their work. Taylor's (1911) *scientific management* ideas were accepted as the best approach to efficient and quality production.

The Progressive Era is an important reference point because it is the period in which many of the values and practices of modern journalism emerged (Gans, 1979; Schudson, 1990). These values and practices reflect the broader ideologies of their times—an enthronement of rationality, science as *the* way of knowing, and systematic and orderly processes that ensured efficient production. Modern values have defined journalistic notions of truth and the practices used to reveal it, especially objectivity as a basis for credibility.

Taylor's ideas on scientific management also largely explain the way journalism work was organized for most of the twentieth century; news organizations adopted bureaucratic structures with hierarchical authority, specialization, and assembly modes of production. Finally, modern values guided the development of journalistic routines to support efficient news production, such as relying on official sources to provide the most valid versions of truth (Entman, 2004; Gans, 1979; Glasser, 1992).

Postmodernism helps to explain the extent to which modern ideals are challenged, and perhaps unsuited for the unstable, fast-shifting, and relative environment of contemporary life. Many scholars contend that postmodernism is not an extension of modernity; rather it is a *rejection* of it and its associated ideals (Baudrillard, 1983; Chen, 1987; Hassard, 1994; Lyotard, 1984; Malpas, 2005; Strinati, 1993, 2004). In this way, postmodernism represents a fundamental—*paradigmatic*—shift in epistemology, the nature of reality, truth, and social values.

Media play an essential role in this shift. Media have long been understood as important creators and shapers of reality. Media create pictures in our heads (Lippmann, 1922), shaping how we think and act (McLuhan, 1964), even suggesting how life should be lived (Postman, 1985). This part is not new. What comes to the fore in the postmodern shift is a rejection of media as a reflection—or mirror—of the world as it exists (Strinati, 1993), which calls into question the credibility of journalism. Beyond this, and just as important, digital media facilitate two opposing yet powerful forces in the postmodern world (Castells, 2009). They enhance individualism by allowing people to control the media they consume, to create their own media messages, to disseminate and share media messages, and to choose which media networks (or communities) they want to engage and interact with. Conversely, media also create new senses of communalism, no longer defined by time and space. People are collaborating across cultures in unprecedented ways, contributing to the development of a global culture, albeit one that is connected by networks of niches (Friedman, 2007). People use media to establish and maintain social relationships with others of similar interests, with little regard for geography. The news media's embrace of social networking sites (e.g., Facebook, Twitter, Digg) to tap into niche groups, tailor content for them, and allow audiences to comment and share content with others all reflect individual empowerment and new forms of community in the postmodern, digital world (Skoler, 2009).

This chapter takes on the task of understanding postmodernism and its relation to journalism and identifying postmodernism as a source of uncertainty. It begins with an overview of postmodernism as a social philosophy and epistemology. Then, the normative theories that define modern journalism, its values (primarily objectivity), and practices are explained, including critiques of these values that incorporate some elements of postmodern ideas. The chapter then turns to organizations and postmodern influences on their strategies and structures, and how these are apparent in news media organizations. Finally, the chapter discusses how postmodern concepts are impacting journalism as an institution, and its normative values and practices. In total, the chapter illustrates how postmodern influences are manifest at three levels—societal, normative, and organizational—in an attempt to identify how postmodernity is causing significant uncertainty in journalism.

Postmodernism: An Overview

The intellectual fabric that has become known as postmodernism is woven by scholars from several disciplines, primarily philosophy, sociology, political economy, cultural studies, and linguistics. Thus, the concepts that are linked to postmodern thought are diverse, abstract, and at times ambiguous (Hassard, 1994). In a broad sense, postmodernism addresses epistemological questions about the nature of knowledge, truth, and legitimacy (Baudrillard, 1994; Derrida, 1978; Lyotard, 1984; Rorty, 1989). Postmodernism is a radical departure from the dominant culture and socioeconomic organization of modernity (Jameson, 2008). More specifically, postmodernism questions the validity of science as the "meta-narrative" for creating knowledge, suggesting instead that most truths are elusive, human creations shaped by symbolic discourse, intuition, and subjectivity (Baudrillard, 1984; Lyotard, 1984; Rorty, 1989). Hassard (1994) notes that the "post" prefix is attached to at least 15 concepts—most common, post-industrialism and post-capitalism—that together identify a new historic period. "A theme associated with many of these 'post'-prefixed concepts is that the social and economic structures since the industrial revolution are now fragmenting into diverse networks held together by information technology and underpinned by . . . 'postmodernist sensibility'" (p. 305).

Postmodernism's rejection of science stems from a conviction that humans lack the ability to observe and describe the world objectively. The symbols humans use to think and express themselves are not capable of describing reality as it exists; rather they reflect the limitations of symbols, language, and the choices of the speaker (Baudrillard, 1984; Derrida, 1978; Lyotard, 1984; Rorty, 1989). Symbols are just that—symbols—and cannot be understood as objective representations of reality. This logic is extended to the relatively arbitrary (human-created) syntax for how the symbols are used, which gives form and structure to how humans think and craft expressions. To postmodernists, science is but one discourse, and it includes all the biases of any discourse: it imposes a set of processes and rules on how to see and define the world, and these processes shape thinking in ways that obscure seeing the world as it actually is. In this way, reality is distinct from how humans can describe it. Thus, science has no more validity for claims of creating knowledge or finding truths than any other form of discourse. Rorty (1989) explains:

Great scientists invent descriptions of the world which are useful for purposes of predicting and controlling what happens, just as poets and political
thinkers invent other descriptions of it for other purposes. But there is no
sense in which *any* of these descriptions is an accurate representation of
the way the world is in itself. . . . Truth cannot be out there—cannot exist
independently of the human mind—because sentences cannot so exist, or
be out there. The world is out there, but descriptions of the world are not.
(pp. 4–5; emphasis original)

Lyotard (1984) asserts that science acquired its legitimacy as a meta-
discourse because of its claims of truth in relation to social and economic
progress; science became accepted as a tool for humanity to exert control over
the environment, freeing people from mundane subsistence and opening the
possibilities for the creation of wealth. This "meta-discourse" was embraced
by Western cultures and created a relatively stable socioeconomic environment
in which science was the tool by which inputs and outputs could be regu-
lated and controlled (Hassard, 1994). However, postmodernism—as a form
of knowledge—rejects the stability prescribed by science, instead seeking to
explain a world in rapid change, one that is—ironically—the product of the
advances of science, technology, and dispersion of information. Postmodern
discourse, Lyotard (1984) writes, is the search for instabilities unexplained by
accepted epistemologies. Accordingly, the postmodern society is full of diverse
and conflicting discourses, each with its own logic and structure. No one discourse is assumed more privileged than others, and knowledge results from an
acceptance of a plurality of diverse discourses (Lyotard calls these discourses
"language games").

The postmodern era is resplendent with media, images, and symbolic representations of objects that have shaped perceptions of those objects and come
to replace them as reality. The simulation has become the reality (Baudrillard,
1994). The mediated simulations, and the codes or syntax within them, pre-
cede experience with reality, so reality is discerned from the representations
of it. "The territory no longer precedes the map, nor does it survive it. It is
nevertheless the map that preceded the territory . . . today it is the territory
whose shreds slowly rot across the extent of the map" (Baudrillard, 1994,
p. 1). Thus, the "simulacra"—the images and representations of objects and
events—have become real, and the "precession of simulacra" creates what
Baudrillard calls the hyper-real. In the modern industrial society, production (an objective, tangible output) was the foundation of organization, and
increasing its efficiency was equated with progress. In the postmodern society,
simulacra replace production, creating diverse forms and structures. Carried
a step further, in modern societies most forms of social organization were
characterized by specialization, differentiation, and hierarchical processes that
enhanced production; conversely, postmodern societies are consumption (or

consumer) oriented, which shifts the goal of social organization from productive efficiency to meeting the demands of diverse social groups and individuals whose interests change quickly (Strinati, 1993). Rapid change and uncertainty are accepted as part of the postmodern environment, calling into question the validity of modern social theories and forms of organization that supported efficient production in stable environments.

Postmodern culture is formed from "heaps of fragments"—a mosaic of recycled ideas and images that are inextricably interwoven with new and surprising cultural elements (Jameson, 1991). The mosaic reflects the unexpected and inconsistent images of the contemporary, mediated, and networked age. The simulacra in the postmodern world create the perception that everything has been done in one form or another. Accordingly, the lesson becomes that the world replicates itself again and again. Distinctions between production and reproduction, image and object, and high and low culture have little meaning. "There is a plethora of myths of origin and of signs of reality—a plethora of truth, of secondary objectivity and authenticity" (Baudrillard, 1994, p. 6). Culture is laden with artifacts of a fragmented and recycled past that have only a faint resemblance to contemporary reality. The importance of tradition and history is reduced (Huyssen, 1987).

Changing social structures and skepticism toward tradition impact individuals' relationships with social institutions. Individuals are empowered by technology to create and maintain social relationships in mediated environments. These relationships develop largely because of individual wants and needs, and create a different sense of community (Castells, 2009). Generalized to non-mediated life, individuals tend to see the world as a smaller place but also experience looser ties with social institutions; people tend to judge institutional value based on their individual—not collective—needs (Bauman, 2000; Deuze, 2007; Putnam, 2004).

Gitlin (1988) contends that postmodern fragmentation is particularly prevalent in the United States. Americans have embraced a form of global capitalism that requires high levels of consumption, which has led to a "ceaseless transformation in style, a connoisseurship of surface, an emphasis on packaging and reproducibility" (p. 35). What is considered "American eclecticism" is a distinctive lack of American culture, which can be understood by the sense that "anything goes."

In sum, this overview of postmodernism—although far from exhaustive—reveals postmodernism as a multi-disciplined approach to theorizing about the nature of reality, truth, and society. It assumes a distinction between objective reality and a human capacity to understand and communicate that reality. Truth is not demonstrable and objective; it is, rather, a reflection of those who create it. This assumption extends to a rejection of any forms of epistemology that claim greater validity than others, including a rejection of science as a meta-discourse for social progress. Traditional sources of authority (i.e., social institutions) are viewed skeptically in a rapidly changing world. New technologies have spawned new and multiple forms of social structures, each with its own set of processes and rules. Media are important in the creation and maintenance of social relations, and people engage in communities based on their individual needs more than the needs of the collective.

Journalism Norms: Freedom, Responsibility, and Objectivity

U.S. journalism norms are a product of the modern era, anchored by a synthesis of two philosophical ideals: freedom and social responsibility (Merrill, 1989). The ideals supporting freedom are Enlightenment constructs that took hold in the seventeenth and eighteenth centuries in Europe and were influential on the U.S. Founding Fathers and their seminal works on governance (e.g., Declaration of Independence and U.S. Constitution). Among the core ideas are that humans are rational, able to discern fact from fiction, and bestowed by their creator with natural rights that no human authority (i.e., church or government) can deny. Milton (1911 [1644]), in *Areopagitica*, asserted the existence of a *self-righting principle*—that truth was definite, demonstrable, and had unique powers to make itself evident to rational people. Locke (2003 [1689]), in *Two Treatises on Government*, urged a social contract based on natural rights, tolerance, and laws of reason. These ideals provided the basis for free expression, private ownership, and individual freedom (e.g., life, liberty, and the pursuit of happiness). They also form the rationale for a free press, one that is independent from government and other social institutions, and one that is privately owned. If the press is free *from* external constraint, it will—in theory—provide a plurality of views that will help individuals find truth (Merrill, 1974). The press, then, fosters democracy by providing a *"marketplace of ideas"* that puts people in a conversation with one another in which claims of truth compete and are sorted out (Schmuhl & Picard, 2005).

Scientific advancements spurred the belief that the processes and laws of nature were discoverable by humans through a systematic and logical approach (Siebert, 1956; Wilson, 1998). The idea that reality existed "out there" in the world, was universal, and could be discovered by humans became the basis for advancing science as a method for finding truth. By the mid-nineteenth century, people were tired of "preachers and sermons," wanting instead "objective facts" (Mindich, 1998, p. 95). Nineteenth-century scholars (e.g., Marx and Spencer) championed extending science into the social realm as a method for understanding sociology, economics, and politics.

Modern notions of journalistic objectivity that emerged in the late nineteenth century were directly tied to the application of science to journalism. The social and historical conditions leading to the Progressive Era saw an embrace of realism and scientific method across most social institutions, including management, literature, law, and journalism (Schudson, 1990). "Reporters in the 1890s saw themselves, in part, as scientists uncovering the economic and political facts of industrial life more boldly, more clearly, and more 'realistically' than anyone had done before. This was part of the broader Progressive drive to found political reform on 'fact'" (p. 167).

To be objective meant to apply the logic of science to journalism. In practice this meant to be detached, to control one's biases in order to let the facts speak for themselves, to be non-partisan, to rely on empiricism (what can be observed and measured), to seek multiple views and be fair and balanced in representation. If journalists adhere to objectivity, their reports should better reflect reality, be truthful, and provide the public with the information it needs to make decisions and participate in democracy (Kovach & Rosenstiel, 2007; Mindich, 1998; Schudson & Tifft, 2005). Of course, not all journalists in a free press would adhere to such standards, but the public was assumed—and trusted—to be able to sort out fact from fiction.

Initial modern critiques of press freedom and journalistic objectivity were primarily those of political economy. The profit-oriented media have their own agenda to make money and serve the interests of their owners, advertisers, and audiences. These goals can conflict with finding truths, creating a marketplace of ideas, and serving the broader goals of society and democracy. The Commission on Freedom of the Press (1947) (Hutchins Commission) assailed the post-World War II press as a powerful institution without sufficient oversight, irresponsible in the use of its freedoms, and pandering to a class-based set of values. The Commission asserted a new ethic of social responsibility that identified a positive freedom—a freedom *for* serving society:

> Freedom of the press means freedom from and freedom for. . . . This implies that the press must be held accountable to society for meeting the public need and for maintaining the rights of citizens and the almost forgotten rights of speakers who have no press. It must know that its faults and errors have ceased to be private vagaries and have become public dangers. (pp. 18–19)

It wasn't long before scholars uncovered how newsroom processes undercut the neutral and objective values journalists swore to uphold. Breed (1955) found that newsrooms abided by a "publisher policy" that was unstated but understood by journalists. Journalists were socialized to the policy in their news organizations, and the policy—which identified issues and ideas that were favored and taboo—undermined journalism values. Journalistic "routines," created to build efficiencies in news coverage, also tended to constrain journalism. Although routines (e.g., work flow, deadlines, story formats such as inverted pyramid) ensured journalists would fill space and time in media products, they also restricted journalists' ability to seek out multiple views and tell complete stories (Tuchman, 1973). But more important, they led to reliance on available and authoritative sources, meaning the truth in news often became what the powerful said it was, without dissenting or minority views (Gans, 1979). Boorstin (1978) asserted that news media are complicit with their sources in the creation of *pseudo-events*, which serve the media's interest in creating news and the sources' interests in advancing their views of truth. The technical and esthetic media packaging of pseudo-events makes them appealing, yet makes it harder for the public to sort out fact from fiction.

The development of cultural studies casts further skepticism over journalism as social science and an objective endeavor (Strinati, 1993; Zelizer, 2004). Postmodern thinking is apparent in cultural studies, which focuses on the "untidy and textured *materiel* of journalism—its symbols, ideologies, rituals, conventions and stories," and "sees the world of news as offering up a complex and multi-dimensional lattice of meanings for all those involved in journalism" (Zelizer, p. 101). Objectivity is an inherently conservative ideology, Glasser (1992) argues, that favors the status quo and is biased against journalists using independent thinking. News "sizes up situations, names their elements and names them in a way that contains an attitude toward them" and in doing so contributes to a culture's sense of itself (Carey, 1974, p. 245).

These inquiries concluded that journalism as practiced was less a social science than a human construction, and as such it fell victim to the same types of human biases and flaws as other social endeavors. In other words, the world "out there" (reality) could not be easily explained and communicated by objective practices. Science could not lay claims as the meta-narrative for finding truth; some facts may be indisputable, but their meaning is relative to social contexts and shaped by human interpretations and claims of morality. Whereas in modern times science's detachment from moral evaluation was the basis for its claims to finding truth, a growing body of thought suggested that the application of science in journalism—and its embrace of objectivity—was shoddy and obscured the distinctly moral dimensions of larger human truths (Carey, 1989; Gans, 1979; Glasser, 1992; Kovach & Rosenstiel, 2007; Zelizer, 2004).

In the late twentieth century, journalism was critiqued as a corporate endeavor with capital interests trumping democratic ones; an elitist practice disconnected from the relevant issues of most people's lives; a public spectacle that captured attention but revealed little substance or context about the world. The norms of a free and responsible press provided few opportunities for the public to understand or solve broader problems (Glasser, 1999; Rosen & Merritt, 1994). The basis of the critiques was that objectivity as a norm and practice actually stifled journalistic freedom and prevented the news media from being socially responsible.

The Organization: Modern to Postmodern

For most of the twentieth century the organizing logic of news media industries was similar to that of other modern manufacturing industries (Kanter, 1983, 2002). The modern organizational model was based on scientific and mechanical thinking that sought to create businesses that ran like smooth-running machines; the model followed ideas of early twentieth-century scholars (e.g., Taylor and Weber) and featured hierarchical division of labor, employees with specialized skills, and efficient systems that maximized production. Managers were the "thinkers" and labor the "doers" (Senge, 1990).

In recent times, the uncertainty associated with globalization, technological innovation, and the impact of these on business environments has forced many industries—including media—to reassess their business models and seek to innovate. The problem for most U.S. industries has been that they were organized for stability, not innovation; thus, the very structures that yielded efficient production became obstacles to innovation. The segmented, mechanical structure—the smooth-running machine—that was preferred during stable times created change-resistant organizational processes; when something went wrong, the response was to seek solutions that worked well in the past when the machine operated smoothly (Kanter, 1983).

Postmodern influences in organizational thinking are apparent in the call for a new metaphor—the "organic" organization (Clegg & Hardy, 1996)—which accounts for changing environments and provides greater flexibility. The organic organization is a move "from bureaucracy to fluidity"; it embraces "decentralization," and flattens the organizational hierarchy. Employees are recognized as sources of organizational competencies and knowledge; organizational interests collaborate, and authority is shared. Bergquist (1993) takes the organic metaphor a step further, suggesting that the postmodern organization is a "liquid," with fast-shifting and unpredictable boundaries. The liquid organization contains elements of stability and change, but most interesting are the shifting boundaries—the edges—because this is where innovation and organizational learning occur.

Globalization and technological innovation, characteristics of what Friedman (2007) calls a flat world, have forced U.S. firms to seek measures that ensure continuous organizational change. Drucker (1995) asserts postmodern themes in this assessment of post-industrial organizations, which "must be organized for the systematic abandonment of whatever is established, customary, familiar, and comfortable, whether that is a product, a service, or a process; a set of skills; human and social relationships; or the organization itself. In short, [they] must be organized for constant change" (p. 77).

Reorganizing for constant change means rethinking organizational structure (Grant, 1996; Huber, 2004; Kanter, 1983; Nooteboom, 2000). An organization's structure creates work patterns and authority relationships and determines organizational rules and behaviors, as well as patterns of decision-making and communication (Donaldson, 1996; Mintzberg, 1979). Structures that create *novel combinations* (Schumpeter, 1949) break up existing organizational boundaries and provide opportunities for exchanges of ideas. This *integrated* structure is essential for innovation (Kanter, 1983), as it decentralizes authority and permits organizations to leverage their existing knowledge, *wherever that knowledge resides*.

Integrated organizations avoid "overspecialization" and create a more collaborative, team-based organizational culture. A shift from production in modern times to information (driven by technological advancements) in postmodern times means the firm's core competency is not a specific product as much as its knowledge (Drucker, 2001). Organizational knowledge, and the creative capacity of the organization's employees, is the resource that allows the organization to respond to uncertainty associated with fast-changing environments. "If the strategically most important resource of the firm is knowledge, and if knowledge resides in a specialized form among individual organizational members, then the essence of organizational capability is the integration of the individuals' specialized knowledge" (Grant, 1996, p. 375).

The shift in organizational metaphors from machines to liquids reflects postmodern influences and concepts: fast and unpredictable change; the need to be flexible and quick to meet consumer wants; a restructuring that breaks down hierarchies, systems, and scientific approaches to management; and a sense that knowledge exists throughout the structure and its application is relative to the context (no one knowledge is preferred).

Reorganizing Journalism Work: Postmodern News Organizations

Until the past decade and widespread diffusion of digital technologies, news media operated in geographic markets, and their control over the creation and dissemination of news and information meant their core product—news—was a relatively scarce commodity. Competition existed, but entry barriers were high and most news media thrived in oligopoly markets that ensured high profit margins (Lacy & Blanchard, 2003; Martin, 1998; Picard, 1989). The environment was relatively stable, the need to innovate relatively low. Newsrooms were hierarchical in structure (e.g., from publisher to reporter, with many tiers in between), and distinct (segmented) from other units in the organization, for example, business and technology. The creation of news was much like an assembly line, with ideas and directives working their way first down, from editors to news gatherers, and then back up, from news gathers to editors, before information reached public view. News was what journalists decided it was, and most news focused on social institutions and the high-ranking officials within them. The "wall" between church and state—journalism and business—was deemed sacred, and the public was not a key player in the news creation process. Elements of modern systems, such as hierarchy, authority, specialization, segmentation, and mass production, dominated the organizing logic.

Then the digital age unleashed already present postmodern forces, creating a networked, subjective, interactive, and consumer-oriented era that destroyed the stability of the mass media (Castells, 2009; Deuze, 2007; Gade & Raviola, 2009; Gillmor, 2004; Kanter, 2002). News organizations were forced to reorder their priorities. Under the guise of change, news organizations began disassembling the assembly line, working in teams, and redefining their areas of coverage in ways that put journalism more in touch with news consumers (Gade, 2008). It is important to note that—paralleling the growth of postmodernism—all these efforts were well under way prior to the emergence of the Internet, a fact easily overlooked in the wave of twenty-first-century change.

Collaboration, inclusivity, and fluidity have replaced hierarchical, segmented, and one-best-way approaches. News organizations have become *integrated*, attempting to spur innovation and become more responsive to fast-changing environments and audience preferences. Integration extends into the news organization through interdepartmental teams and newsroom teams, and through processes that are open to the public; these are discussed briefly below.

Interdepartmental teams are composed of personnel from news/editorial, business/marketing, and information technology, charged with collaborating on product development, market strategies, and special projects (Gade & Raviola, 2009). Interdepartmental integration knocks down the "walls" that segmented the business and news/editorial departments, creating a lateral organizational structure that emphasizes internal coordination and communication. These teams give news organizations greater market orientation and sensibility, and can be assembled quickly to respond to market opportunities.

Restructuring newsrooms into self-directed topic coverage teams, especially in newspapers, moves coverage away from beats defined by social institutions (government, courts, education, business) toward reader-identified interests. Newsroom teams put information gatherers, editors, and presentation staff together, responsible for planning and coordinating their work (Gade & Perry, 2003). The teams decentralize authority by reducing the number of mid-level managers (Schierhorn, Endres, & Schierhorn, 2001; Woo, 2003). The restructuring generally eliminates the linear, assembly-line approach, changing the nature of news work from a largely individual process, in which journalists worked alone on specialized tasks, for example, news gathering, writing, editing, design, to a more fluid, collaborative environment. These changes—reducing hierarchical structures, decentralizing authority, eliminating systematic (linear) approaches, de-specializing work through increased collaboration—reflect the transition from modern to postmodern organizational thinking.

Multimedia journalism facilitates this transition. The American Press Institute, a professional training organization, emphasizes the essential role of teamwork in multimedia journalism (Buttry, 2008). Multimedia requires journalists to work together to gather, edit, and present stories in various formats. Journalists are encouraged to collaborate "early and often" because multimedia elements and continuous deadlines demand ongoing coverage decisions and coordination. Journalists have more tools at their disposal for gathering and disseminating information from the field, yet they also find themselves more tethered to each other to coordinate decisions (Deuze, 2008).

News organizations are integrating the public into their processes to utilize the interactive and networked mediated systems that now exist. Citizens are asked to pass on news tips, comment on stories, and report and create their own news (Byrne, 2008; King, 2008; Phillips, Singer, Vlad, & Becker, 2009). Journalists are also becoming avid consumers of citizen-based media; searching citizen-based and social media for story ideas and developments is a routine part of their daily work (Emmett, 2009; Messner & Watson DiStacio, 2008; Phillips et al., 2009). The benefits include a broader field of journalistic vision, as well as the opportunity to draw audiences to online news products in a competitive marketplace. However, news organizations see that citizen integration into journalism creates organizational challenges, as it rearranges journalists' work and requires fact-checking and verification, which expands the work of journalists who have other responsibilities (Hermida & Thurman, 2008; Phillips et al., 2009).

Overall, news organizations are reassessing their priorities and reorganizing work to be more flexible and market oriented. They are flattening organizational hierarchies, integrating work processes, and seeking to create more innovative cultures. These developments reflect unsettling postmodern forces that include changes in social values, technological advancements, nonbureaucratic approaches, and a focus on consumer interests.

Postmodernism and Journalistic Uncertainty

This chapter has explored postmodernism and its influences at three levels: societal, normative, and organizational. Societal influences at macro levels can be seen as rippling through normative and organizational levels. The task now is to connect the dots to illustrate how these ripples can be seen, and to better understand the uncertainties they create.

Postmodernism's rejection of meta-narratives calls into question the very notion of demonstrable broad-based truths. This has undeniable implications for journalism and its embrace of objectivity as a normative value. In a postmodern society, in which large segments do not believe that objectivity is an attainable goal—and even if it is it holds no greater authority than other forms of discourse—the journalistic rationale for objectivity as a core norm appears dubious. Perhaps the best journalism can do is tell many stories from diverse perspectives, creating a basis for better public understanding of the multiple perspectives on issues (Ettema & Glasser, 1994). This moves journalism to a public orientation that focuses less on the power and authority of officials and social institutions. Media critics, some scholars, and public/civic journalists have advocated such for several decades; however, this approach further diminishes distinctions between journalists and other mediated voices (e.g.. bloggers) and can lead to greater social fragmentation as people seek out media that reinforce their interests and values (Jones, 2009; Merrill, 2006). Bowden (2009) asserts that the chaos of online media defines a "post-journalistic" era in which a search for truth has been lost; the goal of most mediated voices is to advocate for one's views and values—*to win*. Partisan goals do not require accurate information, nor do they seek to persuade; they seek only power, leaving no room for debate or compromise.

This objectivity conundrum is at the heart of the ongoing debate about journalism professionalism. Journalists maintain objectivity as a norm and practice that ensures their credibility; it is part of their professional identities, a source of power for asserting occupational control (Glasser, 1992; Kovach & Rosenstiel, 2007; Schudson, 2001). A societal shift that devalues objectivity carries with it a threat to journalism's ability to define and control the values that support the craft. Faced with such challenges, there are pronouncements about the need for professionalization (accrediting journalists and journalism organizations by a set of standards for values and practices). Journalists' work would be identified and distinguished—by their objective approaches, and thus claims of authenticity and truth—from other voices in the Information Age (Merrill, 2006; Meyer, 2004). Professionalization would address uncertainty at the normative level, and move to reassert journalism's institutional authority, but given the postmodern zeitgeist this move appears dubious, as it further distances journalism from the networked and interactive public.

A more optimistic view is that journalism can use online media to enhance its voice in the postmodern sphere and exercise evolving norms of freedom *and* responsibility. The tweets, blogs, and interactivity that create egalitarian discourse online provide more existential formats that liberate journalism from the strict adherence to prescribed methods and formats. Credibility is not established primarily by journalistic objectivity; it is, rather, buttressed by the public through crowdsourcing and wiki-type forms of verification and transparency. In this way, the work of journalism becomes more responsive and responsible to its publics.

Postmodern impulses also mean that people have different relationships and expectations of social institutions. Networked society breeds an individualism in which social bonds are created and maintained increasingly by mediated relationships (Castells, 2009). Ideas and communication power move side to side and in multiple directions. These developments, too, erode the power of social institutions—including journalism—as definitive voices and places where people seek collective solutions to their problems (Bauman, 2000). These trends suggest a reversal of roles between individual journalists and their organizations. Institutional journalism appears in decline, whereas non-institutional journalism is gaining strength (Gillmor, 2004; Project for Excellence in Journalism, 2010). News organizations try to enhance their market position by having individual journalists develop a following online through blogs and social networks, and, in a reversal of fortune, attach the brand of the news organization to their individual "stars." Put another way, the era in which journalists gained their prestige through the organizations they worked for is being turned on its head; news organizations are hitching their name to the individual journalists who can attract a following.

The abundance of sources of information in the digital world, and the ways that information is now created, shared, and distributed, all work to the detriment of news organizations, which often get little credit for their original reporting and make no money from it. Baudrillard's (1984, 1994) ideas of simulacra are apparent in the commoditization of news, its aggregation, sharing, repackaging, and repurposing. The simulation replaces the reality; the representation trumps the original and becomes the hyper-real. But the important point here is that, for large segments of the audience, the original source of the information is not very important. It is the mixing and reproduction, much the way news aggregators are doing, and targeting various mixes at specialized niches (a form of gatekeeping) that appears to make the difference (Van Weezel, 2009). This development creates both uncertainty and opportunity for news media firms.

News organizations are now following the path that other post-industrial corporations walked in the closing decades of the twentieth century. They are restructuring for innovation; they are integrating their resources among departments, within the newsroom, and with the public. These initiatives create numerous challenges. Integrated news organizations experience conflicts over priorities. Journalists, business, marketing, and information technology personnel have different educations, skills, professional values, and goals in their work. Organizational decision-making results from negotiation, resulting in a fluid environment with departments having shifting levels of power and influence. Interdepartmental integration can reduce uncertainty in relation to audience and technology, but in doing so tends to pressure staff and create greater uncertainty in regard to journalism values and their organizational influence (Gade, 2008).

The restructuring of newsrooms from the beat system into team-based, multimedia coverage areas also has implications for journalism practices and norms. Teams require a broader base of technical skills (to contribute to information gathering, editing, and presentation tasks), and less specialized knowledge about specific beats, the workings of social institutions, and public officials. This shift tends to make news more planned in the newsroom, less spontaneous, and less the discovery of the reporter. It also means many journalists don't develop the expertise to cover specialized areas, which can frustrate sources (because journalists don't understand the subject matter) and result in superficial reporting (Gade, 2004). The newsroom culture changes from an emphasis on creative individual inputs to standardized outputs, from a creative to an administrative news culture (Witschage & Nygren, 2009). Others have called this a "de-skilling" of journalism (Picard, 2009). This trend contrasts with journalists as "knowledge workers," an essential rationale for restructuring, and contributes to greater uncertainty about the knowledge base required for journalism.

To conclude, postmodernism represents a fundamental shift away from modern times, which enthroned human rationality, science, and efficient systems approaches to maximize production. It is a subjective, relative, and eclectic philosophy that fits with the networked, fast-moving, impulsive cultures of developed nations. The ascendancy of postmodernism raises many questions about journalism as an institution, and its norms and practices. Journalism is moving to integrate postmodern ideals into its norms, and using online media as a way to do so. Journalism organizations are restructuring to adopt new practices that reflect changing social values and business environments, but nearly all these innovations create additional uncertainties, which add to the complexity of understanding the shifting environment in which journalism resides.

Thought Questions: Contemplating Change

1. To what extent do you perceive that society is becoming postmodern? How do postmodern ideas impact you, your friends, and social networks?
2. Postmodernism ushers in different ideas about press freedom and social responsibility. In what ways are news media more (or less) free and responsible in postmodern times?
3. Can journalists be objective in their information gathering and story-telling? Should they be? In what instances is objectivity an asset to journalism? Should journalism abandon objectivity as a norm?
4. How does journalism change in "integrated" news organizations? What ideas and values do journalists need to learn and articulate to ensure that journalism's influence remains strong in news organizations?

References

Baudrillard, J. (1983). *Simulations*. New York: Semiotext.

Baudrillard, J. (1984, Spring). On nihilism. *On the Beach, 6*, 38–39.

Baudrillard, J. (1994). *Simulacra and simulation*. Ann Arbor: University of Michigan Press.

Bauman, Z. (2000). *Liquid modernity*. Cambridge, UK: Polity Press.

Bergquist, W. (1993). *The postmodern organization: Mastering the art of irreversible change*. San Francisco: Jossey-Bass.

Boorstin, D. (1978). *The image: A guide to pseudo-events in America* (7th ed.). New York, Atheneum.

Bowden, M. (2009, October). The story behind the story. *The Atlantic*, 164–169.

Breed, W. (1955, May). Social control in the newsroom: A functional analysis. *Social Forces*, 326–335.

Buttry, S. (2008, January). *Multimedia storytelling and collaboration*. American Press Institute. Guidelines distributed at seminar for *The Oklahoman*/NewsOK.com, Oklahoma City, OK.

Byrne, J. (2008). Suggest a topic – and content flows to it. *Nieman Reports, 62*(4), 62–64.

Carey, J. (1974). Journalism and criticism: The case of an underdeveloped profession. *Review of Politics, 36*, 227–246.

Carey, J. (1989). *Communication as culture: Essays on media and society*. Boston, MA: Unwin Hyman.

Castells, M. (2009). *Communication power*. Oxford, UK: Oxford University Press.

Chen, K. H. (1987). The masses and the media: Baudrillard's implosive postmodernism. *Theory, Culture & Society, 4*, 71–88.

Clegg, S., & Hardy, C. (1996). Organizations, organization and organizing. In S. Clegg, C. Hardy, & W. Nord (Eds.), *Handbook of organizational studies* (pp. 1–28). London: Sage.

Commission on Freedom of the Press. (1947). *A free and responsible press*. Chicago: University of Chicago Press.

Derrida, J. (1978). *Writing and difference*. London: Routledge & Kegan Paul.

Deuze, M. (2007). *Media work*. Cambridge, UK: Polity Press.

Deuze, M. (2008). Understanding journalism as newswork: How it changes, and how it remains the same. *Westminster Papers in Communication & Culture, 5*(2), 1–23.

Donaldson, L. (1996). The normal science of structural contingency theory. In S. Clegg, C. Hardy, & W. Nord (Eds.), *Handbook of organizational studies* (pp. 57–76). London: Sage.

Drucker, P. (1995). *Managing in a time of great change*. New York: Truman Talley Books/ Dutton.

Drucker, P. (2001). *The essential Drucker*. New York: HarperCollins.

Emmett, A. (2009, December/January). Networking news. *American Journalism Review*. Retrieved May 30, 2009, from http://www.ajr.org/Article.asp?id=4646

Entman, R. (2004). *Projections of power: Framing news, public opinion and foreign policy*. Chicago: University of Chicago Press.

Ettema, J., & Glasser, T. (1994). The irony in – and of – journalism: A case study in the moral language of liberal democracy. *Journal of Communication, 44*(2), 5–28.

Friedman, T. (2007). *The world is flat: A brief history of the 21st century*. New York: Picador.

Gade, P. (2004). Newspapers and organizational development: Management and journalist perceptions of newsroom cultural change. *Journalism & Communication Monographs, 6*, 5–55.

Gade, P. (2008). Journalism guardians in a time of great change: News editors' perceived influence in integrated news organizations. *Journalism & Mass Communication Quarterly, 85*(2), 371–392.

Gade, P., and Perry, E. (2003). Changing the newsroom culture: A four-year case study of organizational development at the *St. Louis Post-Dispatch*. *Journalism & Mass Communication Quarterly, 80*, 327–347.

Gade, P., & Raviola, E. (2009). Integration of news and news of integration: A structural perspective on news media changes. *Journal of Media Business Studies, 6*(1), 87–111.

Gans, H. (1979). *Deciding what's news*. New York: Random House.

Gillmor, D. (2004). *We the media: Grassroots journalism by the people, for the people*. Cambridge, MA: O'Reilly.

Gitlin, T. (1988, November 6). Hip-deep in post-modernism. *The New York Times Book Review*, pp. 1, 35–36.

Glasser, T. (1992). Objectivity and news bias. In Cohen, E. (Ed.), *Philosophical issues in journalism* (pp. 176–183). New York: Oxford University Press.

Glasser, T. (Ed.). (1999). *The idea of public journalism*. New York: Guilford Press.

Grant, R. (1996). Prospering in dynamically-competitive environments: Organizational capability as knowledge integration. *Organization Science, 7*(4), 375–387.

Hassard, J. (1994). Postmodern organizational analysis: Toward a conceptual framework. *Journal of Management Studies, 31*(3), 303–324.

Hermida, A., & Thurman, N. (2008). A clash of cultures: The integration of user-generated content with professional journalistic frameworks at British newspaper websites. *Journalism Practice, 2*, 343–356.

Huber, G. (2004). *The necessary nature of future firms: Attributes of survivors in a changing world*. Thousand Oaks, CA: Sage.

Huyssen, A. (1987). *After the great divide*. Bloomington: Indiana University Press.

Jameson, F. (1991). *Postmodernism or the cultural logic of late capitalism*. Durham, NC: Duke University Press.

Jameson, F. (2008). *The ideologies of theory*. London: Verso.

Jones, A. (2009). *Losing the news: The future of the news that feeds democracy*. Oxford, UK: Oxford University Press.

Kanter, R. M. (1983). *The change masters: Innovation for productivity in the American corporation*. New York: Simon & Schuster.

Kanter, R. M. (2002, Summer). News innovation and leadership. *Nieman Reports, 56*, 30–34.

King, K. (2008). Journalism as conversation. *Nieman Reports, 62*(4), 11–13.

Kovach, B., & Rosenstiel, T. (2007). *The elements of journalism*. New York: Three Rivers Press.

Lacy, S., & Blanchard, A. (2003). The impact of public ownership, profits and competition on the number of newsroom employees and starting salaries in mid-sized daily newspapers. *Journalism & Mass Communication Quarterly, 80*(4), 949–968.

Lippmann, W. (1922). *Public opinion*. New York: Free Press.

Locke, J. (2003 [1689]). *Two treatises on government*. Shapiro, I. (Ed.). New Haven, CT: Yale University Press.

Lyotard, J.-F. (1984). *The postmodern condition: A report on knowledge*. Manchester, UK: Manchester University Press.

Malpas, S. (2005). *The postmodern: The new critical idiom*. London: Routledge.

Martin, H. J. (1998). Measuring newspaper profits: Developing a standard of comparison. *Journalism & Mass Communication Quarterly, 75*, 500–517.

May, H. (1959). *The end of American innocence: A study of the first years of our own time, 1912–1917*. Chicago: Quadrangle Books.

McLuhan, M. (1964). *Understanding media*. New York: McGraw-Hill.

Merrill, J. C. (1974). *The imperative of freedom: A philosophy of journalistic autonomy*. New York: Freedom House.

Merrill, J. C. (1989). *The dialectic in journalism: Toward a responsible use of press freedom*. Baton Rouge: Louisiana State University Press.

Merrill, J. C. (2006). *Media, mission and morality*. Spokane, WA: Marquette Books.

Messner, M., & Watson DiStacio, M. (2008). The source cycle: How traditional media and weblogs use each other as sources. *Journalism Studies, 9*, 447–463.

Meyer, P. (2004). *The vanishing newspaper: Saving journalism in the information age*. Columbia: University of Missouri Press.

Milton, J. (1911 [1644]). *Of education; Areopagitica; The Commonwealth*. Lockwood, L. (Ed.). Boston: Houghton Mifflin.

Mindich, D. T. Z. (1998). *Just the facts: How objectivity came to define American journalism*. New York: New York University Press.

Mintzberg, H. (1979). *The structuring of organizations*. Englewood Cliffs, NJ: Prentice Hall.

Nooteboom, B. (2000). *Learning and innovation in organizations and economies*. New York: Oxford University Press.

Phillips, A., Singer, J., Vlad, T., & Becker, L. (2009). Implications of technological change for journalists' tasks and skills. *Journal of Media Business Studies, 6*, 61–85.

Picard, R. G. (1989). *Media economics: Concepts and issues*. Thousand Oaks, CA: Sage.

Picard, R. G. (2009). Why journalists deserve low pay. *Christian Science Monitor*. Retrieved May 21, 2009, from http://www.csmonitor.com/2009/0519/p09s02-coop.html

Postman, N. (1985). *Amusing ourselves to death: Public discourse in the age of television*. New York: Viking.

Project for Excellence in Journalism. (2010). *State of the news media 2010: Overview*. Retrieved March 15, 2010, from http://www.stateofthemedia.org/2010/overview_intro.php

Putnam, R. (Ed.). (2004). *Democracies in flux: The evolution of social capital in contemporary society*. Oxford, UK: Oxford University Press.

Rorty, R. (1989). *Contingency, irony, and solidarity*. Cambridge, UK: Cambridge University Press.

Rosen, J., & Merritt, D. (1994). *Public journalism: Theory and practice*. Dayton, OH: Kettering Foundation.

Schierhorn, A., Endres, F., & Schierhorn, C. (2001). Newsroom teams enjoy rapid growth in the 1990s. *Newspaper Research Journal, 22*(3), 2–15.

Schmuhl, R., & Picard, R. (2005). The marketplace of ideas. In G. Overholser & K. Hall Jamieson (Eds.), *The press* (pp. 141–155). Oxford, UK: Oxford University Press.

Schudson, M. (1990). *Origins of the ideal of objectivity in the professions: American journalism and law, 1830 to 1940*. New York: Garland Publishing.

Schudson, M. (2001). The objectivity norm in American journalism. *Journalism, 2,* 149–170.

Schudson, M., & Tifft, S. (2005). American journalism in historical perspective. In G. Overholser & K. Hall Jamieson (Eds.), *The press* (pp. 17–47). Oxford, UK: Oxford University Press.

Schumpeter, J. (1949). *The theory of economic development.* Cambridge, MA: Harvard University Press.

Senge, P. (1990). *The fifth discipline: The art and practice of the learning organization.* New York: Doubleday/Currency.

Siebert, F. (1956). The libertarian theory of the press. In F. Siebert, T. Peterson, & W. Schramm (Eds.), *Four theories of the press* (pp. 39–71). Urbana: University of Illinois Press.

Skoler, M. (2009). Why the news media became irrelevant – and how social media can help. *Nieman Reports, 63*(3), 38–40.

Steel, R. (1999). *Walter Lippmann and the American century.* New Brunswick, NJ: Transaction Publishers.

Strinati, D. (1993). The big nothing? Contemporary culture and the emergence of post-modernism. *Innovation in Social Science Research, 6(3).* Retrieved September 9, 2009, from http://web.ebscohost.com/ehost/detail?vid=7&hid=106&sid=73dc2. . .gr11 1&bdat a=JnNpdGU9ZWhvc3QtbGl2ZZQ%3d%3d#db=aph&AN=9707202883

Strinati, D. (2004). *An introduction to theories of popular culture.* London: Routledge.

Taylor, F. (1911). *Principles of scientific management.* New York: Harper & Row.

Tuchman, G. (1973). Making news by doing work: Routinizing the unexpected. *American Journal of Sociology, 79,* 110–131.

Van Weezel, A. (2009). Organizational changes in newspaper firms and their relation to performance. *International Journal on Media Management, 11,* 144–152.

Webster, F. (2006). *Theories of the information society.* London: Routledge.

Wilson, E. O. (1998, March). Back from chaos. *The Atlantic Monthly,* 41–62.

Witschage, T., & Nygren, G. (2009). Journalistic work: A profession under pressure? *Journal of Media Business Studies, 6,* 37–59.

Woo, W. (2003, Fall). Journalism's "normal accidents." *Nieman Reports, 57*(3), 47–53.

Zelizer, B. (2004). When facts, truth and reality are God-terms: On journalism's uneasy place in cultural studies. *Communication and Critical/Cultural Studies, 1,* 100–119.

5

THE CALL AND CHALLENGE FOR DIVERSITY

George Sylvie, University of Texas

The two preceding chapters illustrated, first, how the notion of democracy has fostered journalistic ideals of freedom and responsibility; and, second, how "truth" born of the advent of modernity and progressivism has generated journalistic uncertainty. But no idea has more confused the soul of journalism than the notion of diversity.

The media diversity movement in the United States gained momentum shortly after World War II from the work of the Commission on Freedom of the Press (Hutchins Commission), which stated that not only should news media present truthful information and provide a place for the exchange of ideas, but also they should provide "a representative picture" of society's various groups (Commission on Freedom of the Press, 1947). The so-called "social responsibility" ideal implied that pluralism of content was desirable and lack thereof was "wrong" and the object of sanctioned change (Hausman, 1992). Such a critical assessment of the news media implied that the press had a duty to serve society's needs as well as its own.

This duty began to be more obvious as racial segregation called into question the validity of the America-as-melting-pot ideal (Glazer & Moynihan, 1964), women began to question gender disparities (Friedan, 2001), and the population of racial minorities began to grow. The U.S. government intervened, eventually passing the Federal Civil Rights Act of 1964, which made discrimination illegal, and enacting a series of stringent broadcast industry regulations regarding "fairness" and "equal time" that essentially encouraged multi-culturalism (Wilson, Gutiérrez, & Chao, 2003).

The federal Kerner Commission (1968), reviewing the causes of civil unrest in 1967 and 1968, boosted the appeal for parity and equality in the media by condemning mainstream media hiring practices that it claimed led to distorted media coverage of minority concerns. Scholars began to call for equal access to "the power to communicate ideas" (Barron, 1967, p. 1647), and the media eventually formally embraced the call; for example, when studies showed that minorities composed only 4 percent of newspaper employees in 1979, the American Society of Newspaper Editors pledged parity in newsroom racial composition by 2000 (ASNE, 2009). American journalism education followed suit in 1982 by establishing an accreditation standard mandating schools to try to recruit, advise, retain, and prepare minority students and minority and women faculty (Kern-Foxworth & Miller, 1993). The resulting multiculturalism emphasis—although considered a "positive way to encourage publication of certain information" (Merrill & Lowenstein, 1973, p. 209)—registered haphazard results, at best.

This chapter illustrates how uncertainty regarding diversity arose from those results. A dual approach, focusing on numeric and ideological aspects, shows how diversity interacts with journalism and how uncertainty subsequently developed. The chapter ends with a discussion of the implications of the fight for diversity on journalism, on the diversity of ideas, and on journalism organizations—and why this creates a critical dilemma for all involved parties.

Diversity by the Numbers

As with any innovation, the struggle for diversity encountered roadblocks. First, and foremost perhaps, were the resulting feelings Americans had for those long excluded from mainstream media coverage. As Wilson and colleagues (2003) noted, one of the first reactions as minorities gain more exposure is fear by the majority (p. 118), with stereotyping promoting much (if not most) of it (Gerbner, Gross, Signorielli, & Morgan, 1980). When Balon, Philport, and Beadle (1978) examined the effects of a television newscaster's sex and race on audience perceptions of credibility, their findings suggested that audiences judged African-American male newscasters as less qualified, more introverted, less cheerful, and more sympathetic than other newscasters. This sense of difference and conflict between the races continued (Entman & Rojecki, 2000), not so much in the traditional, overt bigotry but in more subtle terms of inadequacy, exaggeration, disruption, and victimization (pp. 205–211). Such mindsets also permeated the newsroom, where Merritt and Gross (1978) found male editors more likely to cover more male-oriented subjects as well as entertainment, recreation, and leisure; women tended to choose club and social news as well as women's movement issues.

Obviously, diversity would take time, especially at upper levels of newsroom management. Ogan and Weaver (1979) studied women in newspaper management and found not only that men dominated trainee positions (80 percent), but also that women managers tended to have more women working for them than men managers did (two-thirds vs. two-fifths) and were more likely to say they'd recommend a woman replace them (72 percent vs. 12 percent). Five years later, Ogan's (1984) follow-up found little major progress to speak of. Men on average directly supervised twice as many people as women. Female managers reported 5 men and 4 women as direct reports whereas male managers reported 16 and 1 respectively. More women tended to work for smaller newspapers. Men earned an average $46,000 yearly whereas women earned $27,000 and still were more likely to say they'd recommend a woman replace them (44 percent vs. 16 percent).

The industry's slow hiring rate of blacks aided this lack of progress (Bergmann & Krause, 1972): "What emerges very clearly, is that in the 1960s events were moving in the desired direction of greater (racial) integration but at a glacial rate" (p. 406). The authors predicted that, if rates changed for the better, the publishing industry would reach a 5.2 percent black employment rate for professional jobs in 1977 (p. 407). Instead, ASNE reported a 4.0 minority percent figure for that year (ASNE, 2005).

Progress did occur, especially at the highest levels. For example, by 1994 *The New York Times* had increased the number of female bylines, which correlated with an increased appearance of women in story references and photos and increased writing about women by male reporters (Dorsher, 1997). However, success stories were scarce because diverse people are, well, *different*. For example, in TV journalism there is the suggestion of age discrimination between genders; that is, men supposedly get more "distinguished looking" as they age, while women "lose their looks" as they age—meaning that older men can earn more. Nuance is also evident in how managers view pay levels: "When a staff has a high proportion of men, women could be seen as a comprising a small minority of the available labor pool, not as actually expanding that labor pool," and thus get paid more (Smith, Fredin, & Ferguson, 1988, p. 10), whereas "when staffs have a higher proportion of women, that could be seen as reflecting the general phenomenon of women expanding the labor pool," and women would get paid less (p. 11).

Such perplexity also applied to other aspects of the journalistic institution. The few minority journalists in mainstream media in the 1970s had difficult times in terms of acceptance and opportunity. For example, minorities filed a discrimination suit in 1972 against *The Washington Post*. And much anecdotal evidence revealed minority journalists' feelings of repression, lack of managerial support, and a sense of disloyalty toward the black community (Gilliam, 1972). Moreover, tension continued within newsrooms, with most concern focusing on newer, more cynical, "second generation" (Kotz, 1979, p. 24) issues such as "token" or symbolic hiring and coverage. This prompted one scholar (Mapp, 1979) to suggest that the "role orientation" of black journalists deserved more than "the focus on supply and demand" (p. 6) provided to that point. Mapp argued that this "identity crisis" (p. 12)—that is, being ideologically trapped between mainstream, institutional journalistic routine, the need to make white Americans sensitive to black America's needs, and the managerial assumption that black journalists were inferior except in covering black issues—mirrored dissatisfaction and a lagging sense of accomplishment among black journalists (pp. 10–15).

Not until the late 1980s did statistics fully reflect the severity of that dissatisfaction. The broadcast industry's total of black male employees dropped for the first time, and minorities started exiting the newsroom faster than they entered (Stone, 1988). In newspapers, a similar trend emerged: Among a sampling of newspaper journalists, minority journalists were more likely than whites to say they had known former co-workers who quit newspapering because of perceived or real obstacles to their career advancement (white journalists said they knew more whites who left, and minorities knew more women and minority journalists who left) (Pease, 1991). In a purposive sampling, blacks in particular—still the dominant minority group at the time—showed this discontent at about double the rate for other groups, and reported that prejudice still existed in newsrooms (Bramlett-Solomon, 1992). The feeling mainly stemmed from lack of advancement into and representation among management (Bramlett-Solomon, 1993).

Criticism of management resonated because subsequent studies of the country's best journalists showed that reporting wasn't consistently hitting the mark. For example, a study of 1987 network coverage (Ziegler & White, 1990) revealed "extremely low" story counts by white females and non-whites compared with their white male peers. And although coverage of issues important to blacks increased in four of the country's major newspapers in the 1970s, it decreased in the 1980s (Martindale, 1994). Finally, a study (Entman, 1994) of 1990 network news coverage showed a tendency toward more stereotypical coverage of blacks than of whites, as well as less varied and less positive portrayals. Not only did these studies point toward the need for more detailed coverage, they also invited subsequent studies suggesting rampant dissatisfaction and discrimination in the news industry, and a need for more contextual and nuanced interaction at work.

For example, in contrast to what is found in other professions, Liebler's (1994) telephone surveys with reporters at eight newspapers showed that, although minority journalists perceived autonomy nearly equal to that of non-minority journalists, minority men reported the least autonomy. And, in fact, as newsroom diversity increased, perceived autonomy decreased, especially for minority journalists. Liebler suggested that, as the work force diversifies, uncertainty in the newsroom regarding job assignments, capabilities, experience, and other similar factors may increase. Under such conditions an editor may be inclined to hold a tighter rein on all reporters. Furthermore, the idea that race may affect the nature of content seemed to conflict with the news value of objectivity. Thus, she reasoned, greater newsroom diversity may result in a perceived new threat of personal bias, meaning that editors may grant less autonomy if they feel they need to protect traditional notions of newsworthiness against a negative diversity-driven outcome (p. 127).

Colleagues and the work environment also could pose problems. For example, a survey of U.S. women journalists found that they felt discriminated against in pay, promotions, and assignments (Walsh-Childers & Chance, 1996). Those "from the most male-dominated newsrooms were least likely to agree that their male peers treat women as equals" (p. 83). Although news sources constituted the most frequent harassers (Walsh-Childers, Chance, & Herzog, 1996), more than one-fourth reported non-physical sexual harassment at least sometimes from supervisors or others in power (25.1 percent) and from peers at the same organizational level (29.1 percent), and nearly one-fourth reported harassment by subordinates (23.6 percent) or in other professional settings (22.5 percent) (p. 567). Not surprisingly, the authors called for better managerial policing of established harassment policies, in addition to further research into stress and turnover (p. 579). Ross (2001), meanwhile, surveyed a small sample of British TV women journalists and found other problems: for example, editors giving low priority to coverage of "women's" issues, and a male-ordered culture hostile to women with family responsibilities. Most women surveyed believed that more women in decision-making positions would have a positive impact on developing a more women-friendly news agenda, but significant ambiguities existed as to gender's salience in determining a specifically en-gendered journalistic practice (p. 531).

Organizational influences also constrain the impact of diversity in hiring. For example, newsroom acculturation and group interaction could lead to a job. Becker, Lauf, and Lowrey (1999) studied journalism school graduates from 1988 to 1996 and found race and ethnicity—but not gender—linked to lower levels of employment. But add an internship, good grades, and a school's accreditation status, and race disappeared as a factor. Although women fared slightly better than men in job hunting, the authors concluded that women and ethnic minorities most likely suffered from the newsroom tradition that grounded hiring decisions on whether—among other things—they had internships (an organizational encounter). Hollifield, Kosicki, and Becker (2001) somewhat reinforced this finding in a survey of newspaper editors and TV news directors, which revealed that these managers put greater emphasis than they did 20 years before on "organizational values" (as opposed to journalistic skills).

Still, as noted in the Liebler (1994) work above, one could not deny the influential role of news work's professional culture as a factor in diversity. Deuze (2008) suggests that journalists share traits and values in their routine work, applying them in many ways to confer meaning to work. This "dominant occupational ideology of journalism" (p. 18), or *modus operandi*, maintains operational closure and prevents influence from entities beyond—from outsiders, or from those who may want to join the group. At the opposite, more positive end of "operational closure," Becker, Vlad, Daniels, and Martin (2007) found that daily newspapers with an "extended internal labor market" would be more likely to hire minority journalists than other newspapers (presumably fostering a professional culture among minorities). Such markets facilitated the hiring of, investment in, and training of employees, thus allowing those newspapers to avoid some uncertainties of external labor markets, such as competition for, and scarcity of, talent. And Elmore's (2007) in-depth interviews with 15 former women journalists found a male-dominated newsroom culture that "applied exclusionary strategies, made news decisions on the basis of sex, encouraged assertiveness and toughness, . . . and where female editors adopted tough male characteristics to the detriment of rank and file female journalists" (p. 18).

In short, news media experienced what general organizational research began to find: Implementing diversity had issues. Although some felt that the theory of in-group/out-group dynamics (e.g., Tajfel, 1978) put the matter too simply, research on racial diversity in organizational groups intimated that those different from the majority may experience less positive responses, may be less likely to get positive supervisory evaluations, and may be more likely to leave the organization. Milliken and Martins (1996) said that lower levels of organizational attachment and lower performance ratings combine to drive out minorities more quickly than other employees. In fact, the Williams and O'Reilly (1998) landmark study of 40 years of literature could find no consistent main effects of diversity on organizational performance, suggesting the need for a more complex framework and conceptualization. A subsequent, four Fortune 500-company study (Kochan et al., 2003) found neither positive nor negative effects from racial or gender diversity. Companies should instead ask, the authors argued, "Under what conditions do work units that are diverse with respect to gender or race outperform or underperform work units that are more homogeneous? What conditions mitigate or exacerbate diversity's potential negative or positive effects?" (p. 18).

Jehn, Northcraft, and Neale (1999) tried to answer that question by studying 92 work groups and surveying members of three leading household goods companies. The survey produced a more toned finding: Whenever social-category diversity increased satisfaction and commitment to the company, it was mediated by group performance:

> [I]t may also be that value diversity (occurring when members vary as to how they perceive the group's objectives), which is often not immediately discernible, becomes more important as a predictor of group performance over time, while age and gender diversity, characteristics that are readily apparent, become less relevant over time. (p. 758)

In short, the authors argued, "diversity itself is not enough to ensure innovation; the nature of the team's diversity is critical" (p. 759). Other studies soon echoed these results (e.g., French, 2005; Homan et al., 2008; Mannix & Neale, 2005), suggesting several possible diversity management strategies.

Against that backdrop, hiring alone became inadequate. Liebler (1993) reviewed geographic and organizational predictors of newsroom minority employment and found that *where* you hired mattered; minority percentage of the local population strongly correlated with a newspaper's minority newsroom employment; so did the race of a city's mayor. Similar research on American broadcasting (Hollifield & Kimbro, 2008) showed that location, not organization, encourages workforce diversity. The strongest predictors included diversity of the surrounding population, a station's strategic positioning in a minority audience-targeted market, and the market's size; the data also suggested that minorities may be more likely to be hired by non-dominant organizations and by independent stations as opposed to network affiliates.

Still, old ideas died hard: Critics continued to push for a managerial solution (e.g., McGill, 2000; Terry, 1993). A survey of minority journalists (Rivas-Rodriguez, Subervi-Vélez, Bramlett-Solomon, & Heider, 2004) supported that push, suggesting strong rank-and-file belief that a minority manager "can make a difference in several key areas, including a news operation's sensitivity to racism and how it covers minority groups" (p. 39). However, contrary evidence began to accumulate. Lacy, Davenport, and Miller (1998) found that female newspaper newsroom managers had a negligible impact on the hiring of more women managers. Craft and Wanta (2004) studied the content of 30 newspapers' websites and found that they covered similar issues regardless of the number of women in management. They found similar results when comparing male and female reporters (similar issue agendas, but varying story categories—more politics coverage by men, more economics, business, and education stories by women). Male and female reporters at papers with lower totals of women managers did show a difference in the issues they covered. Even Everbach's (2006) ethnographic study of *The Sarasota Herald-Tribune* found that, although gender wasn't an issue at the women-led paper, the staff lacked racial and ethnic diversity and content "favored a male perspective" (p. 488). Zeldes, Fico, and Diddi (2007) analyzed the content of TV stories of a governor's race and found

> that women reporters were more likely than their male colleagues to use women and nonpartisan sources such as experts and ordinary citizens. But minority journalists were only slightly more likely to use minority sources and were less likely than non-minorities to use nonpartisan sources. (p. 345)

Finally, Beam and DiCicco's (2008) examination of content changes at 10 small dailies during the year after a woman replaced a man in a top newsroom editing job found coverage changed minimally, but style of news did change (especially in photos, sourcing strategies, and feature leads).

So, as the first generation of journalists who experienced newsroom diversity prepared to retire, "there were signs that no revolution was under way" (Weaver, Beam, Brownlee, Voakes, & Wilhoit, 2007, p. 182). Women were less likely than men to think they had influence on hiring and firing, especially women in broadcasting, and gender did not predict job satisfaction nor did it correlate strongly with beliefs about the roles and ethics of journalistic work. Although women made up the majority of U.S. college and journalism/mass communication graduates, they were not staying in journalism work at levels comparable to men; men made up three-fourths of those with 20 or more years of experience (pp. 182–196). The percentage of minority journalists still lagged well below the percentage of minorities in the general population (9.5 percent vs. 30.9 percent), and minorities made up only 5.1 percent of journalists with 20 years or more experience (furthermore, an inverse relationship exists between the percentage of minority journalists and experience; e.g., 16.9 percent of journalists with up to four years' experience are minorities, but only 7.8 percent of journalists with five to nine years' experience are minorities). Minorities were more likely to be female and an employee of a large group-owned journalism organization (averaging 153 news employees). There was wide variation among minority groups in terms of assessments of their work, yet minorities still were less likely to report hiring influence, more likely to report editing influence in broadcast, and less likely to report editing influence in newspapers. African-American journalists were more likely to say they hoped to be working somewhere else in the future (pp. 192–212).

Diversity by Ideas

In this context, then, diversity—in terms of a solely numerical approach—seemed, if not a failure, then at least somewhat misguided and incomplete. Particularly imposing is the popular notion of the marketplace of ideas—the faith that truth and/or good decisions occur from competition (see, for example, Schmuhl & Picard, 2005). This concept (originating in ancient Greece, furthered by Enlightenment scholars, and popularized by Justice Oliver Wendell Holmes) took a stronghold in libertarianism press theory, which believes that a free press operates to reveal and show the truth through many voices (Merrill & Lowenstein, 1973). Diversity, with its strong moral tones, should coincide with the marketplace notion that everyone should have a voice.

Still, shortly after it started, the diversity movement came under ideological challenge (Wilson et al., 2003, pp. 232–239): Questions arose about the qualifications of women and minorities, as some might expect; the politicization of race made it inevitable that some would argue that diversity fostered reverse discrimination, that is, that affirmative action had run amuck. Primary allegations included double standards of hiring, lowering of standards to accommodate unqualified minorities, and the abolition of meritocracy in the workplace. Entman and Rojecki (2000) explored the nuances of the social circumstances surrounding those standards, and applied the discussion to journalism. Indeed, at the turn of the century, the notion of news media diversity and multi-cultural content came under strong criticism; one particular work excellently illustrates that analysis.

Claiming that diversity has corrupted journalism, McGowan (2001) used several cases at leading American journalistic institutions—most notoriously how well-meaning, honest journalists get caught up in well-intentioned but ill-advised corporate efforts to implement diversity—to suggest that journalistic diversity created a litany of bad things. Primarily, McGowan said that the news media constitute defective channels for diverse news and news about diversity, arguing that journalists have adopted Democratic Party and academic dogma supporting diversity to the exclusion of common sense and fair play, as well as to the detriment of their own credibility (pp. 9–35). Specifically he said that this orientation resulted in lowered standards for minority journalists, dampening and tainting diversity-related stories, and promoting sexual orientation/racial/gender issues, the assignment of beats by race/gender/sexual orientation, the overlooking or omission of certain viewpoints in stories, the silencing (by fear, intimidation, and conformity) of differing views in the newsroom, the fear of editors to publicly acknowledge this bias, and the fear of journalists to discuss diversity because of the fear of being labeled racist, sexist, or homophobic. As a result, McGowan said, newsrooms became more "monocultural . . . defined by diversity that is in fact only skin deep" (p. 225), a hoped-for increase in multi-cultural audiences never materialized, and there was a migration of many middle-class whites to other news media—notably talk radio and Fox News (pp. 239–249).

Noted journalism guardians and reformers Kovach and Rosenstiel (2001) somewhat agreed. "Intellectual diversity is the real goal," and getting more minorities in the newsroom is a target or means—not a goal—of diversity, they contended in their seminal work *The Elements of Journalism* (p. 188). They described the "pursuit of a journalism of proportion" (p. 188) as meaningless if it results in group-think in the newsroom. Credibility, they reasoned, came from journalists with an individual awareness of ethics and responsibility (p. 181) and a duty to their sense of right and wrong (pp. 179–198). They warned of newsrooms that approach—through hiring, training, risk aversion, bureaucracy, journalistic routine, and efficiency—standardization (p. 189). Although not anti-diversity (they did argue for citizen access to the journalistic process), Kovach and Rosenstiel described diversity as practiced as imprudent, simplistic, and avoiding open debate and access (p. 190). Some have agreed that an emphasis on diversity has constrained it in the areas of ideological differences (Crouteau & Hoynes, 2001) and moral purpose (Ettema & Glasser, 1998), while others (Merrill & Lowenstein, 1973) have said that tying pluralism to libertarianism "tends to be directive and thereby restricts pluralism . . . But in so doing, press freedom is diminished" (p. 193).

Of course, organizations such as newsrooms do have elements of a monolithic or dominating culture. Nowhere have such elements become more evident as during the current move toward convergence, which continually compels newspapers to adapt to uncertainty and has resulted in "defensive" group cultures. Such groups typically lack self-confidence, evade conflict, unquestioningly obey rules, define jobs narrowly, intensely supervise subordinates (and highlight mistakes instead of rewarding desired behavior), or express heightened concern with status or territory (Readership Institute, 2000). Meanwhile, the Internet's increasing influence makes such "defensiveness" more likely (Hansen, Neuzil, & Ward, 1998; Russial, 1994; Singer, Tharp, & Haruta, 1999; Sylvie, Wicks, Hollifield, Lacy, & Sohn, 2008; Sylvie & Witherspoon, 2002). Numerical and value differences between cultures within the newsroom provide a sizeable obstacle to recruiting and retaining newer, more diverse cultures, as well as deterring the existing cultures' capacity to discover from each other (Gade, 1999, 2004; Gentry, 1997; Readership Institute, 2000; Sylvie, 1996; Sylvie et al., 2008). As a result, American newspapers began a campaign for change, not sparing newsroom culture (e.g., McLellan & Porter, 2007), in the move toward improving newspapers' declining popularity and influence.

The Janet Cooke and Jayson Blair incidents left an indelible mark on the news media and probably have more to do with uncertainty over diversity than any other occurrence or factor (Boehlert, 2003; Henry, 2003, 2007; Shapiro, 2006). The principals, who were African-American, perpetrated professional fraud and negligence, and worked for the country's paragons of journalism (*The Washington Post* and *The New York Times* respectively). In both instances, critics raised the specter of cultural support of affirmative action as an underlying factor that managed to not only prevent some of journalism's top managers and journalists from correctly doing their jobs but also enable a spiral of silence and lack of due diligence by those who should know better (Henry, 2007, pp. 13, 89).

That these two newspapers had and still have a long history of supporting diversity, and the Civil Rights Movement in particular (diversity's strong moral claim to conscience), certainly makes for double dramatic ironies and illustrates diversity's paradoxical nature. First, as earlier suggested, the movement unquestionably became synonymous with the drive for diversity, and the news industry took its Kerner Commission description as a kind of admonition to "do the right thing." However, as McGowan (2001) noted, this is a somewhat false perception. In fact, as noted earlier, the media received their original diversity prescription from the Commission on Freedom of the Press (1947); Udick (1993) observed that the so-called Hutchins Commission had recommended the media present a representative picture of all of society's constituencies.

Second, the connection to the Civil Rights Movement, as McGowan (2001) noted, gave diversity "an overly righteous, moralistic air" (p. 33), no doubt adding to diversity's appeal. That moralistic call gained traction from the general business community's attempt in the 1970s and 1980s to develop more positive corporate cultures to sustain successful growth of a diverse labor pool (Kochan et al., 2003). Such promotion came via training programs targeting appreciation of diversity, and encouraging attitudinal changes and more employee interaction—showing that "diversity" meant more than simply racial and gender differences (p. 4). The so-called "business case" for diversity evolved into an argument stating that diversity helped the bottom line and reflected customers' concerns.

So even arguments by Kovach and Rosenstiel (2001) and others that "real" diversity results from conscience and morality—not solely from conventional, numerical-based diversity initiatives—tapped the same sources of inspiration for authority: a sense of right and wrong! Following this line of thought—that is, that diversity is an expression of the urge to do right and to rectify wrongs— points to a basic paradox: Those who advocate the moral authority of diversity also advocate that diversity means there must be multiple views—including multiple views on the notion of diversity itself. Diversity, then, *is* and *isn't* a civil rights artifact. Diversity *is* and *isn't* a moral choice. Yes, the choice is an imperative, a matter of virtue, a matter of morality itself, but it also carries a non-sectarian flaw, saying, "No one view is right." Which is it? And who should determine the answer? Should we let the public in on the paradox and the game of playing journalism, with full access, and full moral authority? Or should we see diversity as the purview of a journalist, using his or her own conscience and deciding for everyone?

The Elements of Diversity

Recall that in the early days of diversity, minority journalists were torn between their desire to be mainstream journalists, their desire to serve the black community, and their desire to educate non-minorities about minorities. McGowan (2001) said that this situation devolved into minority journalists wanting to advocate for the black community's causes as opposed to being objective—a quality he said minority journalists ridiculed as out of date (p. 231).

The choice of whether to be objective, one can reasonably assume, is a matter of conscience for these journalists. So why is that kind of conscience— in the eyes of Kovach and Rosenstiel (2001) at least—so bad? Doesn't this fulfill the "personal obligation to differ with or challenge editors," to which Kovach and Rosenstiel refer (p. 181)? Perhaps, as Udick (1993) says, "resolving this paradox means using Gans' (1980) multi-perspectival news . . . a purposeful inclusion of diverse opinions in news reportage" (p. 155). Too bad he didn't say *how* to do so.

And yet, wouldn't Kovach and Rosenstiel's advocacy of objectivity and the steady building of truth really ring hollow if we ceased trying to diversify newsrooms? What good is "intellectual diversity," that is, the marketplace of ideas, if those creating it have no applicable experiences with women or persons of color or if they exclude certain groups? This seems to foolishly say to minorities, "Trust us. We know what's best." Such foolhardiness—some might call it arrogance—does less for journalistic credibility than failed recruitment.

Diversity invites such vagueness and circuitous logic because of the nature of uncertainty, and, more specifically, of doubt. A person doubts or hesitates in ambiguous situations because there is a lack of knowledge. By its nature, unplanned or unbridled diversity introduces a lack of knowledge (and thus control). Uncertainty is the search for meaning, and diversity inherently takes away all grounding, decontextualizes context, and opens up to debate what were once accepted as "facts." This is the basic argument that Kovach and Rosenstiel (2001) engage early on when—in the name of attempting to establish journalism's purpose—they try to define the truth. They initially and rightfully describe truth as "the first and most confusing principle" (p. 36), but eventually they settle on a functional, constantly growing variety of truth: truth with a small "t." You can't fault them, since their self-titled goal is public transparency and journalistic utility, and small "t" truth meets the conditions on both scores.

So, then, what is Truth? What does it signify for the uncertainty surrounding diversity? And what does it imply for the future of journalism? Truth is a dominating, overshadowing, universally accepted idea about someone or something. This chapter proves the truth about diversity: It's a work in progress, lacking an overarching universality of approach and mission. There is no Truth in numbers, or in demography, or in the surrounding ideological arguments as we know them today. As Mierzjewska and Hollifield (2006) concluded, slight attention has been given to framing media diversity research in a managerial context; so what we know is limited.

The resulting Uncertainty (as opposed to the "practical" uncertainty detailed thus far in this chapter) need not suggest failure of diversity nor hand-wringing for its future. Like the existential journalist in the continuous state of search for his/her authenticity (Merrill, 1977), diversity *is* a work in progress. Although this may sound more like "small u" uncertainty, the Truth is that all concepts evolve; that is, we don't know what we don't know about diversity. Just as we've realized it's not entirely about numbers, this chapter shows that neither is it entirely about diversity of ideas or moral high ground. The challenge is the challenge: Whatever its form, diversity requires open-mindedness—and that in itself will remain a challenge for humans everywhere.

That is because the presented dual diversity approach, focusing on numeric and ideological aspects, shows that, as diversity interacts with journalism, more uncertainty—rather than the hoped-for Truth (or "resolved uncertainty")—develops and carries troublesome implications. First, the marketplace of ideas, for all its good intentions, is an analog concept in a digital world. Not only do the Internet and other technologies make it a very crowded marketplace (to the point that no one filters or even hears the message), they make it possible for commercial firms to bypass the market, and even create their own (Schmuhl & Picard, 2005). So the marketplace has competition from other types of marketplaces—seriously damaging the potential for idea diversity in the public sphere, and opening the door for increased uncertainty.

Second, the Internet also threatens to fragment audiences to the point that no one is listening to Truth, but to smaller, individual truths that they find nestled among their desired "communities." The "long" or "heavy tail" statistical economic model developed by Anderson (2006) and Brynjolfsson, Hu, and Simester (2007) states that information technology—specifically the Internet—increases the share of niches in the distribution of a commodity. As Internet markets arm audience members with search capabilities, they also lower search costs and affect product and content usage (Brynjolfsson et al., 2007, p. 2). Sylvie (2008) suggested that, applied to the online newspaper industry, this "geographic long tail" (GLT) concept might suggest that usage may become less and less concentrated among "local" readers, that is, those within relatively close proximity to the newspaper, and more concentrated among long-distance users—with deep repercussions for online news product development strategy. This also could mean that minority voices will be drawn to minority-aimed (instead of mainstream-targeted) publications, leaving the "marketplace" missing these additional voices, thus producing less competition for non-minority ideas—eventually distorting the truth-development process and aggravating uncertainty.

Third, news organizations already find the pursuit of these two diversity foci especially uncertain, for economic reasons. The recession that started in 2008, coupled with the technological convergence movement, has forced many news outlets to effectively reconsider staffing formulas, cut back, and retrench (Edmonds, 2010). As staffing casualties increase, minority newsroom positions tend to suffer most (see National Association of Black Journalists, 2010; UNITY, 2009). As news becomes infused with audience participation and feedback, news media are caught between the economic drive to become more audience friendly (especially when the much-desired Internet demographic is white; see Project for Excellence in Journalism, 2010) and the push to increase minority newsroom representation, in particular when it's easier to lay off veteran, better-paid journalists (including those who are minority).

These dilemmas fail to satisfy the hunger of those seeking justice or fairness, especially as trends suggest more diversity trouble ahead for journalism. Sylvie and Gade (2009) warned that, in making "the business case" for diversity in newsrooms, managers will have to make some sense of diversity's pluses and minuses (pp. 129–132). The inherent tensions that come with diversity may themselves be a lesson and, thus, an important step toward greater certainty, because the question could be asked: Would greater certainty allow us to be open-minded to new possibilities? However, for the newsroom to succeed, diverse people will have to find a way to collaborate—that is, to overcome the differences in their values and methods and to generate the creativity that is the inevitable fruit of diversity. That also will mean democratizing and sharing decision-making power—power to do things but also power to set new rules and norms—and allowing their groups to dissolve and re-form anew. Gradually, such decentralization may require redefining news and the credentials it requires.

Diversity has proven uncontrollable; so if we seek control, we may eventually want to re-examine the issue of licensing or professional training, in light of technological ramifications regarding freedom *to* a press and the news media's relative lack of numerical diversity success. However, if unfettered enlightenment is the ultimate goal, we'll have to be satisfied with the trial-and-error approach, learning how to better accommodate diverse voices, people, and ideas. We'll have to do better; that's the only certainty.

Thought Questions: Contemplating Change

1. What are the implications of diversity for digital newsrooms? How should they incorporate teamwork? How can they facilitate trust? Will any of it make a difference in terms of diverse content?
2. If intellectual diversity is the goal, what should journalists (especially editors) under the supervision or watchful eye of non-journalists in their organizations say to show that "the business case" for diversity still is a viable goal for their company? Should they try to change anyone's mind in that regard? How would they go about it?
3. Using Karl Weick's concept of "sense-making" (see Weick, 1995), go through the steps that mainstream journalism has taken in its experiment with diversity. Now compare those with the adoption of innovation stages as outlined by Everett Rogers (see Rogers, 1995).
4. You run a diverse, contentious newsroom. You have reporters who believe objectivity is passé, others who think you have double standards and abandoned notions of meritocracy, others who are sexist, and still others who would like to see you fail (think one of your ambitious assistants). You have scheduled a staff meeting for next week: What would you say? What would your presentation include or illustrate? What would be your "Truth"?

References

Anderson, C. (2006). *The long tail: Why the future of business is selling less of more*. New York: Hyperion.

ASNE (2005). Table A. Reston, VA: American Society of Newspaper Editors. Retrieved December 6, 2009, from http://204.8.120.192/index.cfm?id=5646

ASNE (2009). More than three decades of commitment to diversity. Reston, VA: American Society of Newspaper Editors. Retrieved December 3, 2009, from http://asne.org/key_initiatives/diversity.aspx

Balon, R. E., Philport, J. C., & Beadle, C. F. (1978). How sex and race affect perceptions of newscasters. *Journalism Quarterly, 55*, 160–164.

Barron, J. A. (1967). Access to the press: A new First Amendment right. *Harvard Law Review, 80*, 1641–1678.

Beam, R. A., & DiCicco, D. T. (2008, August). *When women run the newsroom: Management chance, gender and the news*. Paper presented at the annual convention of the Association for Education in Journalism and Mass Communication, Chicago, IL.

Becker, L., Lauf, E., & Lowrey, W. (1999). Differential employment rates in the journalism and mass communication labor force based on gender, race, and ethnicity: Exploring the impact of affirmative action. *Journalism & Mass Communication Quarterly, 76*, 631–645.

Becker, L. B., Vlad, T., Daniels, G., & Martin, H. J. (2007). The impact of internal labor markets on newspaper industry personnel practices. *International Journal on Media Management, 9*, 59–69.

Bergmann, B. R., & Krause, W. R. (1972). Evaluating and forecasting progress in racial integration of employment. *Industrial and Labor Relations Review, 25*, 399–409.

Boehlert, E. (2003, May 15). The forbidden truth about Jayson Blair. *Salon*. Retrieved December 8, 2009, from http://dir.salon.com/story/news/feature/2003/05/15/nytimes/

Bramlett-Solomon, S. (1992). Predictors of job satisfaction among black journalists. *Journalism Quarterly, 69*, 703–712.

Bramlett-Solomon, S. (1993). Job satisfaction factors important to black journalists. *Newspaper Research Journal, 14*(3/4), 60–69.

Brynjolfsson, E., Hu, Y. J., & Simester, D. (2007, November). Goodbye Pareto principle, hello long tail: The effect of search costs on the concentration of product sales. Available at SSRN: http://ssrn.com/abstract=953587

Commission on Freedom of the Press. (1947). *A free and responsible press: A general report on mass communication: Newspapers, radio, motion pictures, magazines, and books*. Chicago: University of Chicago Press.

Craft, S., & Wanta, W. (2004). Women in the newsroom: influences of female editors and reporters on the news agenda. *Journalism & Mass Communication Quarterly, 81*, 124–138.

Crouteau, D., & Hoynes, W. (2001). *The business of media: Corporate media and the public interest*. Thousand Oaks, CA: Pine Forge Press.

Deuze, M. (2008). Understanding journalism as newswork: How it changes, and how it remains the same. *Westminster Papers in Communication and Culture, 5*(2), 4–23.

Dorsher, M. (1997, August). *Women and "All the news that's fit to print"? A quantitative content analysis*. Paper presented at the annual convention of the Association for Education in Journalism and Mass Communication, Chicago, IL.

Edmonds, R. (2010). *The state of the news media 2010: An annual report on American journalism. Newspapers summary essay.* Retrieved April 29, 2010, from http://www.stateofthemedia.org/2010/newspapers_summary_essay.php

Elmore, C. (2007). Recollections in hindsight from women who left: The gendered newsroom culture. *Women & Language, 30*(2), 18–27.

Entman, R. M. (1994). Representation and reality in the portrayal of blacks on network television news. *Journalism Quarterly, 71,* 509–520.

Entman, R. M., & Rojecki, A. (2000). *The black image in the white mind: Media and race in America.* Chicago: University of Chicago Press.

Ettema, J. S., & Glasser, T. L. (1998). *Custodians of conscience: Investigative journalism and public virtue.* New York: Columbia University Press.

Everbach, T. (2006). The culture of a women-led newspaper: an ethnographic study of *The Sarasota Herald-Tribune. Journalism & Mass Communication Quarterly, 83,* 477–493.

French, E. (2005). The importance of strategic change in achieving equity and diversity. *Strategic Change, 14*(1), 35–44.

Friedan, B. (2001). *The feminine mystique.* New York: Norton.

Gade, P. (1999). Turbulent times: A study of change in the newspaper industry [Doctoral dissertation, University of Missouri-Columbia]. *Dissertation Abstracts International, 60,* 3182.

Gade, P. J. (2004). Newspapers and organizational development: Management and journalist perceptions of newsroom cultural change. *Journalism & Communication Monographs, 6,* 5–55

Gans, H. (1980). *Deciding what's news.* New York: Vintage Books.

Gentry, J. K. (1997). Keys to success: Change survey results. In ASNE (Eds.), *Change: Living it, embracing it, measuring it* (p. 21). Reston, VA: American Society of Newspaper Editors Change Committee.

Gerbner, G., Gross, L., Signorielli, N., & Morgan, M. (1980). Aging with television: Images on television drama and conceptions of social reality. *Journal of Communication, 30,* 37–47.

Gilliam, D. (1972). What do black journalists want. *Columbia Journalism Review, 11*(1), 47–52.

Glazer, N., & Moynihan, D. P. (1964). *Beyond the melting pot.* Cambridge, MA: MIT Press.

Hansen, K. A., Neuzil, M., & Ward, J. (1998). Newsroom topic teams: Journalists' assessments of effects on news routines and newspaper quality. *Journalism & Mass Communication Quarterly, 75,* 803–821.

Hausman, C. (1992). *Crisis of conscience: Perspectives on journalism ethics.* New York: HarperCollins Publishers.

Henry, N. (2003, Fall). Racial reverberations in newsrooms after Jayson Blair. *Nieman Reports.* Retrieved December 8, 2009, from http://www.nieman.harvard.edu/reportsitem.aspx?id=100998

Henry, N. (2007). *American carnival: Journalism under siege in an age of new media.* Berkeley: University of California Press.

Hollifield, C. A., & Kimbro, C. (2008, August). *Understanding media diversity: Structural and organizational variables influencing personnel diversity in the television industry.* Paper presented at the annual convention of the Association for Education in Journalism and Mass Communication, Chicago, IL.

Hollifield, C. A., Kosicki, G. M., & Becker, L. B. (2001). Organizational vs. professional culture in the newsroom: Television news directors' and newspaper editors' hiring decisions. *Journal of Broadcasting and Electronic Media, 45*(1), 92–117.

Homan, A. C., Hollenbeck, J. R., Humphrey, S. E., Van Knippenberg, D., Ilgen, D. R., & Van Kleef, G. A. (2008). Facing differences with an open mind: Openness to experience, salience of intragroup differences, and performance of diverse work groups. *Academy of Management Journal, 51*, 1204–1222.

Jehn, K. A., Northcraft, G. B., & Neale, M. A. (1999). Why differences make a difference: A field study of diversity, conflict, and performance in workgroups. *Administrative Science Quarterly, 44*, 741–763.

Kerner Commission. (1968). *Report of the National Advisory Commission on Civil Disorders*. New York: Bantam.

Kern-Foxworth, M., & Miller, D. A. (1993). Multicultural journalism education revisited: 1982–1991. *Journalism Educator, 48*, 46–55.

Kochan, T., Bezrukova, K., Ely, R., Jackson, S., Joshi, A., Jehn, K., Leonard, J., Levine, D., & Thomas, D. (2003). The effects of diversity on business performance: Report of the diversity research network. *Human Resource Management, 42*(1), 3–21.

Kotz, N. (1979). The minority struggle for a place in the newsroom. *Columbia Journalism Review, 17*(6), 23–31.

Kovach, B., & Rosenstiel, T. (2001). *The elements of journalism: What newspeople should know and the public should expect*. New York: Three Rivers Press.

Lacy, S., Davenport, L., & Miller, C. (1998, March). Women in newspaper newsroom management: 1949 to 1979. *Web Journal of Mass Communication Research, 1*(2). Retrieved December 8, 2009, from http://www.scripps.ohiou.edu/wjmcr/vol01/1–2a-B.htm#discussion

Liebler, C. M. (1993). Geographic and organizational predictors of newsroom minority employment. *Mass Communication Review, 20*, 158–168.

Liebler, C. (1994). How race and gender affect journalists' autonomy. *Newspaper Research Journal, 15*(3), 122–130.

Mannix, E., & Neale, M. A. (2005). What differences make a difference? The promise and reality of diverse teams in organizations. *Psychological Science in the Public Interest, 6*(2), 31–55.

Mapp, T. F. (1979). Beyond the numbers: The role of the black journalist in the U.S. news media. *Journal of Communication Inquiry, 5*(1), 3–19.

Martindale, C. (1994). Significant silences: Newspaper coverage of problems facing black Americans. *Newspaper Research Journal, 15*(2), 102–115.

McGill, L. T. (2000). *Newsroom diversity: Meeting the challenge*. Arlington, VA: The Freedom Forum.

McGowan, W. (2001). *Coloring the news: How crusading for diversity has corrupted journalism*. San Francisco: Encounter Books.

McLellan, M., & Porter, T. (2007). *News, improved: How America's newsrooms are learning to change*. Washington, DC: CQ Press.

Merrill, J. C. (1977). *Existential journalism*. New York: Communication Arts Books.

Merrill, J. C., & Lowenstein, R. L. (1973). *Media, messages, and men*. New York: David McKay.

Merritt, S., & Gross, H. (1978). Women's page/lifestyle editors: Does sex make a difference? *Journalism Quarterly, 55*, 508–514.

Mierzjewska, B. I., & Hollifield, C. A. (2006). Theoretical approaches in media management research. In A. B. Albarran, S. M. Chan-Olmsted, & M. O. Wirth (Eds.), *Handbook of media management and economics* (pp. 37–66). Mahwah, NJ. Erlbaum.

Milliken, F. J., & Martins, L. L. (1996). Searching for common threads: Understanding the multiple effects of diversity in organizational groups. *Academy of Management Review, 21*, 402–433.

National Association of Black Journalists. (2010). *Newsrooms continue to cut black journalists from their ranks: More diverse nation fails to value diversity in print and online newsrooms.* Retrieved April 29, 2010, from http://nabj.org/newsroom/news_releases/2010/newsrel041310asne.php

Ogan, C. L. (1984). Life at the top for men and women newspaper managers: A five-year update of their characteristics. *Newspaper Research Journal, 5*(2), 57–68.

Ogan, C. L., & Weaver, D. H. (1979). Women in newspaper management: A contradiction in terms? *Newspaper Research Journal* (prototype edition), 42–53.

Pease, T. (1991). Blaming the boss. *Newspaper Research Journal, 12*(2), 2–21.

Project for Excellence in Journalism. (2010). *Online audience behavior.* Retrieved April 29, 2010, from http://www.stateofthemedia.org/2010/online_audience.php#online_whogetstheirnews

Readership Institute – Impact Study. (2000). *Culture report: A profile of the impact newspapers and their performance.* Evanston, IL: Author.

Rivas-Rodriguez, M., Subervi-Vélez, F. A., Bramlett-Solomon, S., & Heider, D. (2004). Minority journalists' perceptions of the impact of minority executives. *Howard Journal of Communication, 15*(1), 39–55.

Rogers, E.M. (1995). *Diffusion of innovations* (4th ed.). New York: Free Press.

Ross, K. (2001). Women at work: Journalism as en-gendered practice. *Journalism Studies, 2*(4), 531–544.

Russial, J. T. (1994). Pagination and the newsroom: A question of time. *Newspaper Research Journal, 15*(1), 91–101.

Schmuhl, R., & Picard, R. G. (2005). The marketplace of ideas. In G. Overholser & K. Hall Jamieson (Eds.), *The press* (pp. 141–155). New York: Oxford University Press.

Shapiro, I. (2006). Why they lie: Probing the explanations for journalistic cheating. *Canadian Journal of Communication, 31*, 261–266.

Singer, J. B., Tharp, M. P., & Haruta, A. (1999). Online staffers: Superstars or second-class citizens? *Newspaper Research Journal, 20*(3), 29–47.

Smith, C., Fredin, E. S., & Ferguson, C. A. (1988). Sex discrimination in earnings and story assignments among TV reporters. *Journalism Quarterly, 65*, 3–19.

Stone, V. A. (1988). Trends in the status of minorities and women in broadcast news. *Journalism Quarterly, 65*, 288–293.

Sylvie, G. (1996). Departmental influences on interdepartmental cooperation in daily newspapers. *Journalism & Mass Communication Quarterly, 73*, 230–241.

Sylvie, G. (2008, April). *Developing an online newspaper business model: Long distance meets the long tail.* Paper presented at the annual International Symposium on Online Journalism, Austin, TX.

Sylvie, G., & Gade, P. (2009). Changes in news work: Implications for newsroom managers. *Journal of Media Business Studies, 6*, 113–148.

Sylvie, G., Wicks, J. L., Hollifield, A., Lacy, S., & Sohn, A. B. (2008). *Media management: A casebook approach.* Mahwah, NJ: Erlbaum.

Sylvie, G., & Witherspoon, P. D. (2002). *Time, change, and the American newspaper.* Mahwah, NJ: Erlbaum.

Tajfel, H. (Ed.). (1978). *Differentiation between social groups: Studies in the social psychology of intergroup relations.* Oxford, UK: Academic Press.

Terry, C. (1993, November). The color(s) of power. *Presstime, 15*, 36–41.

Udick, R. (1993). The Hutchins paradox: Objectivity versus diversity. *Mass Communication Review, 20*, 148–157.

UNITY: Journalists of Color, Inc. (2009). UNITY calls on ASNE for new approach as diversity drops in newsrooms. Retrieved April 29, 2010, from http://unityjournalists.org/news/2010/news041210asne.php

Walsh-Childers, K., & Chance, J. (1996). Women journalists report discrimination in newsrooms. *Newspaper Research Journal, 17*(3/4), 68–87.

Walsh-Childers, K., Chance, J., & Herzog, K. (1996). Sexual harassment of women journalists. *Journalism & Mass Communication Quarterly, 73*, 559–581.

Weaver, D., Beam, R., Brownlee, B., Voakes, P. S., & Wilhoit, G. C. (2007). *The face and mind of the American journalist: 4th decennial survey finds an older, better paid, more professional workforce*. Bloomington, IN: Indiana University School of Journalism.

Weick, K. E. (1995). *Sensemaking in organizations*. Thousand Oaks, CA: Sage.

Williams, K. Y., & O'Reilly, C. A. (1998). Demography and diversity in organizations. In B. M. Staw, & R. M. Sutton (Eds.), *Research in organizational behavior: Vol. 20* (pp. 77–140). Stamford, CT: JAI Press.

Wilson, C. C. II, Gutiérrez, F., & Chao, L. M. (2003). *Racism, sexism, and the media: The rise of class communication in multicultural America*. Thousand Oaks, CA: Sage.

Zeldes, G. A., Fico, F., & Diddi, A. (2007). Race and gender: An analysis of the sources and reporters in local television coverage of the 2002 Michigan gubernatorial campaign. *Mass Communication and Society, 10*, 345–363.

Ziegler, D., & White, A. (1990). Women and minorities on network television news: An examination of correspondents and newsmakers. *Journal of Broadcasting & Electronic Media, 34*, 215–223.

6

COMMUNITIES, CULTURAL IDENTITY, AND THE NEWS

Maggie Rivas-Rodriguez, University of Texas

In the 1800s, as the covered wagons expanded what would become the United States, the local newspaper was considered an essential institution, the heart of a community. Notes Altschull (1990):

> The small-town paper was at the very center of the lives of the new settlements. Land was plentiful, and farms and ranches were far removed from the towns. Only through the pages of the newspaper could farmers and ranchers keep up with what was going on. The local newspaper became and remained a bulletin board for the community. Without the local paper there was in fact no community. (p. 214)

Those early newspapers not only served to inform readers, but also created a sense of identity, of unity, either on a national scale or, "especially in the case of the antebellum South, of sectional unity" (Altschull, 1990, p. 214).

In the mid-1800s, when some of those wagons would have traversed the continent, of the country's 23 million inhabitants, 84.3 percent were white and 1.9 percent were free blacks. There were no enumerations for slaves, or for other races or ethnic groups. The Census could not ascertain the numbers of "Indian (taxed) domesticated and absorbed in the population" (De Bow, 1854, p. 39). In fact, racial categories were stipulated in Article I, Section 2 of the Constitution. Slaves were counted as three-fifths of a person, "the notorious Three-Fifths Compromise" (Snipp, 2003, p. 565).[1]

Fast forward to the twenty-first century, when the concept of the "bulletin board of the community" is as vastly different as the make-up of the communities themselves. Today the local newspaper faces competition from all sides: radio, including satellite radio that beams down commercial-free radio programs without geographical impediments; cable television, providing a dizzying array of choices to viewers; and the Internet, with the potential to bring people with common interests together throughout the world. The Internet is even more revolutionary in that it allows virtually anyone with a computer and a modem, or with a cell phone, to become a "publisher" of information (Hampton, Sessions, Her, & Rainie, 2009).

If the delivery system of information on the "community bulletin board" has changed, the transformation in and uncertainty about who is part of that community are just as substantial. In the 1800s community newspaper editors in the United States most likely did not think to include information of interest to non-whites, but that has changed. In 2010, there is at least an acknowledgement that general interest news outlets have an obligation to address concerns of all racial groups. The complexion of America has darkened steadily and considerably toward a population that is 15 percent Hispanic, 12 percent black, 4 percent Asian, and 75 percent white (U.S. Census Bureau, 2008). The Hispanic category, an ethnic rather than a racial grouping, pushes the total to over 100 percent—a challenge for demographers. However, some Latinos find they don't fit neatly into the racial groupings that would require them to check off black, white, Asian, or American-Indian/Aleut/Eskimo. One Maryland hairdresser told *The New York Times* in 2005: "I'm not black and I'm not white; we don't define ourselves that way . . . So I would choose 'some other race' " (Swarns, 2004).

The Census Bureau estimates that 87.5 percent of the country's 301 million residents are native born, whereas 12.5 percent are foreign born (U.S. Census Bureau, 2008). However, whether or not all of those foreign born are counted in official figures is debatable and an enduring cipher for demographers, journalists, and anyone else hoping to understand the make-up of the country.

To add another layer of complexity, the federal government has finally recognized a fact that has been developing for some time: Americans no longer fit neatly into discrete categories of black, white, Latino, Native American, or Asian. The 2000 U.S. Census found that 6.8 million, or 2.4 percent, of the 281 million residents of the United States were of more than one race. It was the first time in the history of the Census that individuals have been allowed to claim more than one race (U.S. Census Bureau, 2008). And, as noted above, the issue of how Hispanics are counted remains problematic (Castillo, 2010).

The transformation of America's make-up is not universally embraced. There has been, in fact, considerable resistance to what has been called "the browning of America." Historian Arthur Schlesinger raised the ire of many in 1991 when he lashed out, attacking ethnic studies in colleges and universities, bilingual education, and immigrants who he believed refuse to learn English and adopt "American ways." Schlesinger (1991) credited a white Anglo-Saxon Protestant tradition with the success of the founding of the country:

Having cleared most of North America of their French, Spanish, and Dutch rivals, the British were free to set the mold. The language of the new nation, its laws, its institutions, its political ideas, its literature, its customs, its precepts, its prayers primarily derived from Britain. (p. 8)

Samuel Huntingon followed suit, raising many of the same questions, but he focused his ire on the Latino community: "Will the United States remain a country with a single national language and a core Anglo-Protestant culture? By ignoring this question, Americans acquiesce to their eventual transformation into two peoples with two cultures (Anglo and Hispanic) and two languages" (Huntington, 2004, p. 32).

To that, Raul Yzaguirre (2004), then-president of the National Council of La Raza, the country's largest Latino advocacy organization, wrote:

Tempted as I am to challenge Huntington's assertion that the United States was settled only by white Anglo Protestants [this would come as a surprise to my ancestors, Texans since the early eighteenth century], I will leave it to the academics to address the shoddy research, questionable analysis, and breath-taking leaps of logic in his piece. However, I grant Huntington this much: Hispanic-Americans do have an agenda for the future of this country, and organizations such as the National Council of La Raza [NCLR] are at the forefront of it. But here's where we differ from Huntington: We see our agenda as the United States' agenda. (p. 4)

The United States has a long history of nativism, going back to the founding of the country when some worried that Germans were refusing to adopt Anglo ways and the English language (Fishman, 1966). For these more recent nativists the greatest fear is the loss of the ideal of homogeneity, as it was for the original nativists. Schlesinger (1991) wrote:

The ethnic revolt against the melting pot has reached the point, in rhetoric at least, though not I think in reality, of a denial of the idea of a common culture and a single society. If large numbers of people really accept this, the republic would be in serious trouble. The question poses itself: how to restore the balance between *unum* and *pluribus*? (p. 80)

Leaving aside for the moment whether indeed there has ever been anything approaching any real *unum,* forging cohesion in the United States in the dawn of the twenty-first century is indeed daunting, and the news media are central to this challenge. However, it is a challenge that transcends ethnic and racial considerations. Journalists must consider how to provide news and information that is useful and relevant to a population that must share enough of a unified purpose that it will care to become informed about issues. To accomplish their goals, journalists must consciously overcome their own personal social limitations, becoming more aware and gaining a more complete understanding of the various parts of their society. They must do this despite the likelihood that they will encounter criticism from a small but vocal group that regards any attempt to cover all segments of society as "un-American." Finally, they must accomplish this more meaningful coverage with fewer resources, in an age of tremendous economic uncertainty for journalism outlets.

This chapter explores changes in, and uncertainty about, community identity and how this may shape professional practice and decision-making by journalists. It applies the conceptual framework of social responsibility, touching on participatory democracy and how the news media may affect policy and political outcomes. It raises issues that are not generally part of public discourse, issues that a handful of scholars have been wrestling with for dozens of years—most notably the possibility of "alien suffrage," or non-citizen voting.

Social Responsibility

The news media's role in communicating issues of concern and interest to its community is at the core of the mission of journalism, particularly in a democracy. In a system of self-governance, the news media's social responsibility is to inform the general community about itself and any problems and issues that may affect it (Peterson, 1963). One of the earliest written criticisms of the press came in 1923 from Harold I. Ickes, who inveighed against newspaper barons who seemed more concerned with the moneymaking aspect of the press than with the public service they were charged with. As more individuals raised concerns about how commercial aspects of the press might interfere with its public service mission, a group was formed in the mid-1940s to examine problems raised. The Commission on Freedom of the Press, commonly known as the Hutchins Commission, issued its 1947 findings and provided a foundation for what is now considered the social responsibility of the press. The Hutchins Commission's five requirements for a press in a free society have a direct bearing on how the press should relate to its community. The press should provide:

1 Truthful, comprehensive, and intelligent account of the day's events in a context which gives them meaning;
2 A forum for the exchange of comment and criticism;
3 A means of projecting the opinions and attitudes of the groups in the society to one another;
4 A method of presenting and clarifying the goals and values of society;
5 A way of reaching every member of the society by the currents of information, thought, and feeling which the press supplies. (Commission on Freedom of the Press, 1947, pp. 20–21)

Later, Peterson (1963) incorporated those functions into the "social responsibility of the press." Peterson's basic understanding: With freedom comes an obligation. "Social responsibility theory accepts the role of the press in servicing the political system, in enlightening the public, in safeguarding the liberties of the individual; but it represents the opinion that the press has been deficient in performing those tasks." The theory also holds that, although the press has an economic role, that role should be subservient to its primary function in "promoting the democratic processes or enlightening the public." In fact, some specific media should not have to be self-supporting. And although the media are expected to entertain their audience, "that entertainment should be 'good' entertainment" (p. 74).

Social responsibility theory has critics. Among them is John Nerone (1995), who wrote that, although it might be easy to dismiss the social responsibility theory as a "sterile intellectual exercise," it also may be argued that

> there is a serious intellectual battle being fought around the concept of responsibility. In this view, the adoption of social responsibility theory means a radical reconstruction of the relationship between individuals and communities, with an emphasis on the latter. Social responsibility thus represents the triumph of community over the lone individual. (p. 78)

In the twenty-first century, public concerns about the fracturing of the United States seem to revolve mostly around immigration issues. But in another time the fault line was racial: a hot summer in 1967 that saw 164 riots, 83 deaths, and millions of dollars in damage. The 11-person National Advisory Commission on Civil Disorders, more commonly known as the Kerner Commission for its chair, Illinois governor Otto Kerner, attributed this violence to a general hopelessness among urban black youth. However, the commission also called the mainstream news media to task, holding that they had not imparted a fair and accurate portrayal of the disturbances, thus creating the impression that they were more destructive, more widespread, and more racialized than they actually were. "We are deeply concerned that millions of other Americans, who must rely on the mass media, likewise formed incorrect impressions and judgments about what went on in many American cities last summer" (National Advisory Commission on Civil Disorders, 1968, p. 362).

The Kerner Commission admonished the mainstream media for viewing the world through a "white man's eyes":

> By and large, news organizations have failed to communicate to both their black and their white audiences a sense of the problems America faces and the sources of potential solutions. The media report and write from the standpoint of a white man's world. The ills of the ghetto, the difficulties of

life there, the Negro's burning sense of grievance, are seldom conveyed. Slights and indignities are part of the Negro's daily life. And many of them come from what he now calls 'the white press' – a press that repeatedly, if unconsciously, reflects the biases, the paternalism, the indifference of white America. This may be understandable, but it is not excusable in an institution that has the mission to inform and educate the whole of society. (p. 366)

Despite the recommendations of the Kerner Commission, problems in depiction of race continue to challenge the news media. To what degree do the contemporary news media similarly contribute to Americans forming "incorrect impressions" and judgments about the current demographic transformation of the country? In today's world, the transformation relates in particular to the case of Latino immigrants, who are often conflated with all Hispanics, but also concerns non-Hispanic black Americans. For example, research shows that welfare recipients and poor people are most often depicted as African-Americans, despite the fact that whites get public assistance more than blacks (Iyengar, 1996).

Most race-related academic research has focused on black–white relations. However, there are some notable exceptions that do examine Latinos in questions of race. McDonald (2001), for instance, found that whites in Florida judged blacks and Hispanics differently. The whites in this survey were more likely to use "lack of motivation" as the reason for blacks' inequality (46.4 percent) than they would for Hispanics (31.2 percent). There was less of a spread for those who believed "no chance for an education" was the reason for inequality. Older respondents were more likely to see "lack of motivation" as the cause of inequality, but the "why" of this perception hung in the air. Perhaps, McDonald said, "as people get older they become less tolerant of certain minorities or more susceptible to media reports—[or it could be] the outcome of historical changes in society that have affected white Floridians beliefs in equality" (McDonald, 2001, p. 570).

Gilens (1996) also holds the news media responsible for misconceptions:

The correspondence of public misunderstandings and media misrepresentations of poverty reflects the influence of each upon the other. On the one hand, the media are subject to many of the same biases and misperceptions that afflict American society at large and therefore reproduce those biases in their portrayals of American social conditions. On the other hand, Americans rely heavily on the mass media for information about the society in which they live, and the media shape Americans' social perceptions and political attitudes in important ways. Media distortions of social conditions are therefore likely to result in public misperceptions that reinforce existing biases and stereotypes. (p. 516)

In studying news magazine and television portrayal of American poverty, Gilens found that the media tend to portray most poor Americans as black, despite the fact that two out of three poor Americans are non-black:

> Whatever the processes that result in distorted images of poverty, the political consequences of these misrepresentations are clear. First, the poverty population shown in newsmagazines—primarily black, over-whelmingly unemployed, and almost completely nonelderly—is not likely to generate a great deal of support for government antipoverty programs among white Americans. Furthermore, public support for efforts to redress racial inequality is likely to be diminished by the portrait of poverty found in these newsmagazines. Not only do African-Americans as a whole suffer from the exaggerated association of race and poverty but poor African-Americans (who are often the intended beneficiaries of race-targeted policies) are portrayed in a particularly negative light. (p. 537)

Why do journalists over-represent African-Americans in news accounts of poverty? Gilens argues that it is the case of the convenience sample, in particular in the case of news magazines' choice of photographs, as news magazine bureaus are located in urban areas. Gilens concludes that photographers are drawn to urban areas with high concentrations of poor people, and, as African-Americans are more likely to live in homogeneous areas where poverty is high, a photographer would seek out those neighborhoods. "Social structures outside of the newsroom influence the availability of news content," Gilens concludes (p. 533).

Journalists striving for a more accurate understanding of poverty would do well to consider the poverty levels in the area in question and strive for a better understanding of poverty. Census figures down to the tract level are available online. Similar tools may be used to report other social issues, such as health problems, with greater precision.

Another possible structural reason for a lack of understanding by journalists is their relationship to sources: Journalists may be far removed from the people they are covering. For instance, the *Indianapolis Star* some years ago explored its own newsroom's racial attitudes by dispatching its reporters to visit places where they would be in the minority. Reporter Bill Theobold commented later, "My views about race have mostly been formed by thinking, by reading, or by talking to whites. Talking to blacks about the subject is uncomfortable. I don't know how to ask the questions; perhaps I am afraid of the answer" (Cose, 1994, p. 4).

The formation of opinions and views of African-Americans by talking to white people is in part related to the "bias of convenience," cited by Howard Rosenberg and Charles S. Feldman in their 2008 book *No Time to Think*. And this "bias of convenience" is directly tied to another reason journalists struggle to represent the country's demographics more fully and accurately: the more recent continuous demand for news, a demand created by the Web and 24-hour cable news channels. Journalists who must "feed the beast," or turn in stories on deadline, often engage in frenzied news production, without ample time to reflect, to explore more perspectives, or to challenge prevailing public opinion (Rosenberg & Feldman, 2008).

News operations may have the best intentions to cover varied communities by hiring reporters from these communities. However, whether or not an individual hire necessarily translates into more inclusive, accurate, and fairer coverage remains to be seen. If an individual reporter lacks an understanding or empathy with the local community, a disconnect may remain. Affinity and understanding of a community require recognition of hundreds of variables of class, culture, politics, education, and so on, factors that are not automatically conferred with ethnicity or skin color. So, the phenomenon of journalists "parachuting in" applies here.

Demographics and the New Nativism

In recent years, there has been what Roberto Suro (1998), a former journalist and former director of the Pew Hispanic Center, calls "a demographic storm." The number of immigrants who arrived in the United States in the 20-year period between 1975 and 1995 is 7 million more than in the 50 years from 1925 to 1975. Suro says the arrival of the largely non-white immigrants coincided with demands by Latino advocacy groups for more generous policies and led some whites to associate the immigrants with "minority group activism" and fed fears of "reverse discrimination" (pp. 23–24). Suro acknowledges that immigrants will continue to join those already here, and many will form "a new class of outsiders." He says it is not known "where these new people are supposed to fit into American society, and yet their story has become an American one" (p. 26).

He notes that immigrants are swelling the ranks of the working poor and so may help the United States reconsider its long-held assumptions about poverty—particularly because the "ambition and optimism of the Latino" clashes with the perception that poor people are "no more than an unsightly appendage to an affluent society. Instead they will be viewed as an integral part of the larger whole, one that must have opportunities to escape poverty in order for the whole to prosper" (Suro, 1998, p. 26).

The influx of Latino immigrants has been so remarkable, in fact, that it has sounded alarms for those concerned that the "American way of life" is being threatened—people such as Harvard professor Samuel Huntington, who says he thinks it is natural that a new "white nationalism" should emerge: "These new white nationalists do not advocate white racial supremacy but believe in racial self-preservation and affirm that culture is a product of race." He says that the changing demographics in the United States "foretell the replacement of white culture by black or brown cultures that are intellectually and morally inferior" (Huntington, 2004, p. 41).

Huntington upbraids and rejects the pronouncements of Lionel Sosa, a Texas-based Republican marketing and advertising executive, who, ironically, is one of the most vocal supporters of integration into U.S. society. Huntington (2004) writes:

> Sosa ends his [1998] book, *The Americano Dream*, with encouragement for aspiring Hispanic entrepreneurs. "The Americano dream?" he asks. "It exists, it is realistic, and it is there for all of us to share." Sosa is wrong. There is no Americano dream. There is only the American dream created by an Anglo-Protestant society. Mexican-Americans will share in that dream. (p. 45)

Interestingly, there is some agreement for that aspect of the nativist viewpoint among those who advocate maintaining various ethnic cultures. De la Garza, Falcon, and Garcia (1996), for instance, examined the notion that Mexicans and Mexican-Americans were less than accepting of "American" values such as individualism and patriotism. They traced the incorporation of immigrants into American society: First there is an adoption of the values and standards of the dominant society, then a "structural (educational and occupational), marital and identificational assimilation" (p. 337). They noted that, in some groups that have suffered discrimination and have recognized it, there is a likelihood of resentment of their plight, and in some countries there is a possibility of a separatist movement—the fear of some of the nativists. However, in the United States, that has not been the case; instead, the ethnic groups organize for greater group cohesion and to become more active in U.S. politics and society.

A central tenet of American identity is individualism and patriotism, beliefs underscored by writers from de Tocqueville to current times, and De la Garza and his colleagues set out to explore in a survey to what degree Mexican-Americans believed in those values. After controlling for demographic characteristics in a multiple regression analysis, the researchers found that Mexican-Americans at all levels of acculturation who are U.S. citizens showed greater patriotism than Anglos. Why? Perhaps it has to do with Anglos becoming more critical of their country. Alternatively, the study's authors muse, it may be owing to naturalized citizens undergoing a transformation with strong emotional overtones. There is also a substantial patriotic fervor and a history of military service among Mexican-Americans who perhaps feel they must "prove" their loyalty to their country. As to individualism, there is barely any statistical difference between Anglos and Mexican-Americans. The authors speculate that economic individualism is not a uniquely American value—that in Mexico, citizens are expected to help themselves, with little help from their government.

The authors lay at the door of the nativists this argument: Yes, Mexican-Americans are different from Anglos. However, "there is no theoretical reason . . . why such cultural distinctiveness would be linked to differences in political values." Mexican-Americans will undoubtedly pursue more political participation, and that participation will be "grounded in a commitment to fundamental American values . . . That does not mean that increased Mexican-American political involvement will not jar the system." Most likely, there will be increased demands for better opportunities in employment and education that would "seriously challenge the existing social arrangements. Such demands are completely compatible with the nation's core political values" (De la Garza, Falcon, & Garcia, 1996, p. 348).

Applying, then, the social responsibility concept as it relates to new, uncertain, and increasingly complex demographics, how well are the news media fulfilling their role? Are they in fact giving residents a truthful and comprehensive understanding of today's world, in a way that informs society more fully about itself, and its people about society's goals and values? Are they providing a forum for the exchange of comment and criticism, and do they provide a way to let the various groups within society gain a better understanding of themselves? Is it possible to reach every member of society?

The Community Gap and Local Content

News organizations have tried to address "the community gap"—the gap between journalists and their communities—in several ways. Will Bunch (2008), a Philadelphia journalist, notes that some of the most successful at bridging the gap are those who meet members of the community in person. However, he also recommends that journalists use the Internet to make connections with their communities. Bunch and others encourage journalists to embrace blogs and social media to forge links to members of their local community as well as to those who share common interests who may not be local.

Also, he brings up a long-standing problem: To what degree are journalists themselves incorporated into the community? Bunch notes that some journalists have strived to remain dispassionate observers to the point of refusing to vote in elections. Bunch also cites a reporter in Providence, RI, who noted the problem of language barriers between journalists and their communities. She said that students at the schools she covers are Latino, whereas the teachers and school administrators are largely white: "I don't speak Spanish and many of the parents don't speak English, so it's hard to reach out to families for their thoughts, comments and criticisms" (Bunch, 2008, p. 39).

Bunch points to a paradox: The journalists asked to create the "hyperlocal content" are not always equipped to do so. Larger newspapers often employ ambitious career journalists who are required to hop from newsroom to newsroom, looking for the larger market, the bigger paycheck, greater responsibility; these career journalists are expected to work long hours, and they generally spend their leisure time with one another (Bunch, 2008, p. 40).

The possibility of a "digital divide" in the larger community and its implications must be considered as well. A Pew Report in 2008 found that 37 percent of Hispanics had broadband at home, compared with 43 percent of African-Americans; those figures compared with an average of 56 percent of all Americans (Horrigan, 2009). Pew conducted the survey a year later, but only in English, and with vastly different results: When Spanish-speaking respondents were excluded, the percentage of Hispanics with broadband was 68 percent—31 percentage points higher. No explanation was provided as to why there was no Spanish-language option in the second survey. Applied to journalism, the survey suggests that by not providing non-English speakers the option of participating, either as an audience, or as creators of content, and by not having reporters able to speak to them in their own language, our understanding of the United States will be skewed.

It has been suggested before, in a broader context, that responsibility for deciding what is news should be shared with others outside of the newsroom. Herbert J. Gans (1980), for instance, argues that selection of news stories should not be the sole responsibility of journalists—that, in fact, the content should be shared with the powerless and the powerful. Gans says, "journalists are not detached, for their enduring values are political values, which imply the advocacy of one kind of social order." Moreover, he says, because there are political implications to news, and source power strongly shapes news selection, journalists "are unwittingly part of the political process" (p. 322).

To add yet another wrinkle, consider how the digital age has changed the definition of *community*. A news article in the *Los Angeles Times*, for instance, may be circulated throughout the country, and indeed the world, linking people of like interests. To what extent are the news media responsible to that larger, amplified audience?

Demographics and Politics

Whereas the nativists worry that immigrants are not assimilating into the country, or that they are settling in the United States and forming a permanent underclass, a few scholars offer a different possibility: Because non-citizen residents also constitute the community, they should be completely enfranchised. Tienda (2002) notes that the 14th amendment considers the Census the basis for congressional representatives: "Representatives shall be apportioned among the several states according to their respective numbers, counting the whole number of persons in each state, excluding Indians not taxed" (U.S. Constitution). Then, Tienda adds that, although mere residence determines representation, only citizens vote in national elections; this suggests "that the right to representation is more fundamental than the right to exercise the franchise" (p. 595). Although the Constitution prohibits non-citizens from voting in national elections, it provides no such strictures at the state and local levels. Schuck (1997), for one, notes that the disenfranchisement of non-citizens is premised on various assumptions:

> that aliens' political socialization is too fragmentary and embryonic to be trusted in matters of public choice; that confining political participation of this kind to citizens carries an important symbolic message about the value and significance of full membership; and that exclusion of aliens from such participation encourages them to naturalization as soon as possible. (p. 13)

However, Tienda and others argue that the value of representation is eroded to the extent that a growing number of "new Americans" have no voice in selecting who represents them. Tienda writes that, early on in our history, non-citizens were allowed to vote. However, after the War of 1812, those rights for foreigners were slowly eroded. The larger preoccupation was with suffrage for women and for African-Americans. Asian nationals and Native Americans living on reservations were enfranchised in the early to mid-1950s (Keyssar, 2000, pp. 254–255), and in many Southern states African-Americans were essentially disenfranchised until the Voting Rights of 1965 was fully enforced. Tienda (2002) advocates that non-citizen residents also be allowed to vote on matters that affect them, noting that they already have congressional representation, pay taxes, may serve in the military, and are required to adhere to the same laws as non-citizens.

Applying these ideas to journalism, news outlets should seek to make the immigrant population an integral part of the community—not only for immigration stories, but also for an overall understanding of the concerns and problems within the community in which the news outlets are found.

Implications

The radical changes in the country's demographics coincide with the economic upheaval of the news media: 5,900 newspaper jobs were lost from 2008 to 2009 (American Society of Newspapers Editors, 2009). How to cover the countless, complex stories about demographic changes with diminished news staffs and with fewer veteran reporters, who have been the victims of massive layoffs? And how important is it for the news media to employ journalists of color to cover communities of color? The "demographic storm," as Roberto Suro puts it, is one of the biggest stories of the century, requiring the closest attention of the news media. How to tackle it?

It has many angles and moving parts, some of which are failing to register with the news media, or the public. One development in the fall of 2009 made scarcely a blip on the radar: Republican senators Bob Bennett of Utah and David Vitter of Louisiana proposed that Census respondents be asked if they are citizens—a question that was dropped in 1950. Vitter said in a news release that counting non-citizens would "artificially increase the population count in certain states, and that will likely result in the loss of congressional seats for nine other states, including Louisiana" (Bowman, 2009).

As the country's make-up changes, offering new challenges, there are important opportunities for the news media to sharpen their skills and reinvent themselves to become more relevant and useful to the new community, locally as well as nationally (Rivas-Rodriguez, 2007). Among the possible steps:

1. Report at a higher level, being sure to include the historical context that makes sense of the story. A story about an ethnic festival may be turned into a major take-out on the pressing issues to that group.
2. Don't take the easy way. Well-heeled organizations will have slick news releases and news conferences to spoon feed journalists. Get voices in the coverage that may have less wherewithal, but important perspectives.
3. Take the various constituents of the community seriously. Non-profit community organizations and government offices that handle various community groups may be thoroughly investigated.
4. Be fair when reporting on relations between groups. Veteran activists often complain that the news media may pursue "divide and conquer" practices in stories on relations between ethnic groups.
5. Watch the language. Linguist Otto Santa Ana (2002) conducted a detailed content analysis of how the *Los Angeles Times* covered three statewide referenda that had special relevance to immigrants and/or Latinos: Proposition 187, Proposition 209, and Proposition 227. Proposition 187 outlawed providing any state services to undocumented workers. It passed, but was overturned later. Proposition 209 outlawed the use of affirmative action in state hiring and firing, and in college admissions. Proposition 227 would eliminate bilingual education in public schools. Santa Ana found that the news media and politicians, including California Governor Pete Wilson, freely used metaphors that effectively rendered immigrants subhuman: "California is awash in a brown tide," and undocumented immigrants are "invaders" (Santa Ana, 2002).

At the dawn of the twenty-first century, the responsibility of journalists to cover their communities has never been more crucial, challenging, or complex. However, the tools at the disposal of journalists are many, including a body of research to illuminate the way. For the willing and able, the rewards will be plentiful.

Thought Questions: Contemplating Change

As the United States' demographics change at a fast rate, journalists are well advised to cover both the story of those demographic changes, as well as how the demographics affect almost all aspects of American life. Other developing stories include the growth of populations that are insisting on greater participation, and resistance to that greater participation.

1. Look up the public school enrollment in your state and local community. What are the racial/ethnic breakdowns compared with 5, 10 years ago? How are those demographics affecting your state and local community, and what kinds of stories can you find within those numbers? What kind of coverage should journalists provide, and do you think most news outlets would provide it? Why or why not?
2. You are the letter editor for your local news organization. On Monday, a Southwestern state passes a repressive anti-Latino law. That same day you receive a flurry of letters, very similar to one another, supporting the repressive law. There are no letters opposing the law. Do you print all the letters, although there are no letters from opponents to counter-balance the supporting letters? Do you call opponents and urge them to submit letters? Why or why not?

Note

1 The practice of counting slaves was intended to establish wealth. Margo Anderson (1988) notes that Southern states would not include slaves in the count for legislative apportionment, but the writers of the amendment believed that slaves should be included for apportionments for taxes, otherwise slaveholders would have "an undue advantage." Anderson writes that "the apportionment rule built into the census a tradition of differentiating these three great elements of the population" (p. 12).

References

Altschull, J. H. (1990). *From Milton to McLuhan: The ideas behind American journalism.* New York: Longman.

American Society of Newspapers Editors (2009, April 16). *U.S. newsroom employment declines.* Retrieved November 23, 2010, from http://asne.org/article_view/smid/370/articleid/12/reftab/101.aspx

Anderson, M. J. (1988). *The American census: A social history.* New Haven: Yale University Press.

Bowman, L. (2009, November 1). *A question of citizenship.* Retrieved November 23, 2010, from http://tinyurl.com/2b9tx5b

Bunch, W. (2008). Disconnected. *American Journalism Review, 30*(4), 38–45.

Castillo, J. (2010, April 17). For some Latinos, census stymies with race question. *Austin American-Statesman.* Retrieved November 23, 2010, from http://tinyurl.com/29rgx3a

Commission on Freedom of the Press. (1947). *A free and responsible press: A general report on mass communication: Newspapers, radio, motion pictures, magazines, and books*. Chicago: University of Chicago Press.

Cose, E. (1994). Seething in silence: The news in black and white. *Media Studies Journal, 8*, 1–10.

De Bow, J. D. B. (1854). *Statistical view of the United States*. Washington: U.S. Department of the Census. Retrieved November 23, 2010, from http://www2.census.gov/prod2/decennial/documents/1850c-03.pdf

De la Garza, R. O., Falcon, A., & Garcia, F. C. (1996). Will the real Americans please stand up: Anglo and Mexican-American support of core American political values. *American Journal of Political Science, 42*, 335–351.

Fishman, J. A. (1966). *Language loyalty in the United States: The maintenance and perpetuation of non-English mother tongues by American ethnic and religious groups*. The Hague: Mouton.

Gans, H. J. (1980). *Deciding what's news: A study of CBS Evening News, NBC Evening News, Newsweek and Time*. New York: Vintage Books.

Gilens, M. (1996). Race and poverty in America: Public misperceptions and the American news media. *The Public Opinion Quarterly, 60*(4), 515–541.

Hampton, K., Sessions, L., Her, E. J., & Rainie, L. (2009). *Social isolation and new technology: How the Internet and mobile phones impact Americans' social networks*. Retrieved November 23, 2010, from http://tinyurl.com/yzzlk33

Horrigan, J. (2009). *Wireless Internet use. Pew Research Center's Internet & American Life Project*. Retrieved November 23, 2010, from http://tinyurl.com/lql939

Huntington, S. P. (2004). The Hispanic challenge. *Foreign Policy, 141*, 30–45.

Iyengar, S. (1996). Framing responsibility for political issues. *Annals of the American Academy of Political and Social Science, 546*, 59–70.

Keyssar, A. (2000). *The right to vote: The contested history of democracy in the United States*. New York: Basic Books.

McDonald, S. J. (2001). How whites explain black and Hispanic inequality. *Public Opinion Quarterly, 65*, 562–573.

National Advisory Commission on Civil Disorders. (1968). *Report of the national advisory commission on civil disorders*. New York: Dutton.

Nerone, J. (1995). *Last rights: Revisiting four theories of the press*. Urbana: University of Illinois Press.

Peterson, T. (1963). The social responsibility theory of the press. In F. S. Siebert, T. Peterson, & W. Schramm (Eds.), *Four theories of the press: The authoritarian, libertarian, social responsibility, and Soviet communist concepts of what the press should be and do* (pp. 73–104). Urbana: University of Illinois Press.

Rivas-Rodriguez, M. (2007). Coverage of Latinos in the news media: We're not there yet. In P. Poindexter, S. Meraz, and A. S. Weiss (Eds.), *Women, men, news: Divided and disconnected in the news media* (pp. 304–316) Mahwah, NJ: Lawrence Erlbaum.

Rosenberg, H., & Feldman, C. S. (2008). *No time to think: The menace of media speed and the 24-hour news cycle*. New York: Continuum.

Santa Ana, O. (2002). *Brown tide rising: Metaphors of Latinos in contemporary American public discourse*. Austin: University of Texas Press.

Schlesinger, A. M. (1991). *The disuniting of America: Reflections on a multicultural society*. New York: W. W. Norton.

Schuck, P. H. (1997). The re-evaluation of American citizenship. *Georgetown Immigration Law Review, 12*, 1–34.

Snipp, C. M. (2003). Racial measurement in the American census: Past practices and implications for the future. *Annual Review of Sociology, 29*, 563–588.

Suro, R. (1998). *Strangers among us: How Latino immigration is transforming America* (1st ed.). New York: Alfred A. Knopf.

Swarns, R. (2004, October 24). Hispanics resist racial grouping by census. *The New York Times*. Retrieved December 21, 2010, from http://www.nytimes.com/2004/10/24/national/24census.html

Tienda, M. (2002). Demography and the social contract. *Demography, 39*, 587–616.

U.S. Census Bureau (2008). *2006–2008 American community survey 3-year estimates. Selected characteristics of the native and foreign-born populations.*

Yzaguirre, R. (2004). Huntington and Hispanics. *Foreign Policy, 142*, 4.

7

CHANGES IN COMMUNITY POWER STRUCTURES

Douglas Blanks Hindman, Washington State University

Because media organizations, and news organizations in particular, depend on other groups for content and income, changes in the social environment force adjustments in the way media organizations operate. The change in the social environment that is particularly pertinent to news organizations is social differentiation, which is observed in the greater ethnic and racial diversity of the population and in the increasing diversity of occupational specialization. Differentiation through the division of labor and occupational specialization is "the peaceful solution to the struggle for survival" (Aron, 1989 [1967], p. 23). As society becomes more differentiated, the power structure becomes more differentiated as well (Tichenor, Donohue, & Olien, 1980). By power structure, I mean those individuals, groups, and institutions that have the resources, organization, and skills necessary to achieve goals in spite of opposition from others.[1]

Media organizations experience the increasingly differentiated social environment in a couple of ways, both of which create change and uncertainty. First, audience diversity is directly related to audience fragmentation, or the de-massification of mass audiences. Traditional mass media—newspapers, news magazines, broadcast network television—have lost readers and viewers to specialized media offering greater varieties of content and delivery options. Second, the rising diversity of the power structure means that news organizations have a wider range of potential news sources.

I will use theories developed in classical sociology, public opinion, and mass communication research to explain ways that media organizations and other social institutions have adjusted to these changes, and are likely to change in the future. The general theoretical argument is that media organizations and the social environment are interdependent, and that media organizations are best understood as both derived from, and supportive of, the broader social environment (Donohue, Tichenor, & Olien, 1973).

It is also important to point out that social actors are not powerless products of their social environment. Although all individuals have agency, or the ability to act independently of social constraints, some social actors can play a larger role than others in shaping and adjusting to the social environment. Hence, a media organization can adjust to the complex social forces of differentiation and diversity in ways that enable it to cope, or even thrive, in the new environment. Similarly, political institutions react to the diversity of the power structure in ways that preserve traditional institutions while attempting to incorporate the diversity of the political environment within existing institutions.

As I will show, both media organizations and political institutions have attempted to adjust to social differentiation through different types of organizational consolidation. Audience fragmentation has been countered by media consolidation, and the rise in the diversity of the power structure has been countered by political polarization. I will argue that media consolidation and political polarization constrain the news media's traditional role in the search for the truth—in other words, knowledge that citizens in a democracy can use to better govern themselves, to vote in ways that represent the best interests of themselves and their communities. News organizations have traditionally enacted this important role through a commitment to accuracy, fact-checking, multiple sourcing, and skepticism regarding other's truth claims. I suggest that news organizations can restore their roles in fostering democracy through a commitment to traditional journalistic practices such as a commitment to fact-checking and accuracy, and through the creation of opinion forums that privilege knowledge over ideology and that disclose the special interests that are often hidden behind partisan rhetoric.

The chapter includes a review of the inter-related trends of audience fragmentation, media consolidation, and political polarization; the challenges and uncertainties these trends pose to media organizations; and theoretical concepts of social differentiation and pluralism that shed light on potential media responses to these challenges and uncertainties.

Audience Fragmentation and Media Consolidation

Audience fragmentation is most vividly captured in the precipitous decline of the prime-time season-average audience shares for ABC, CBS, and NBC television networks from 1980 to the present, the declining circulation of big city newspapers, declining audiences for television network evening news, and the flight of advertising dollars from traditional to online and mobile media sources (Hindman & Wiegand, 2008; Project for Excellence in Journalism, 2010). Even local media face declining audiences as viewers bypass local newspapers and network affiliates by obtaining content online from non-local sources.

In 1980, the three networks commanded 90 percent of all viewers using television. In 2005, the Big Three's combined share was a meager 26 percent, with the remainder of the viewers divided among additional broadcast networks such as Fox Television Network and a multitude of cable networks such as ESPN, CNN, and Fox News (Hindman & Wiegand, 2008).

Echoing the proliferation of radio music formats following the exodus of network talent from radio to television in the 1950s and 1960s, television audiences have become fragmented in terms of both programming choices and preferences for delivery methods. Appointment-based television and newspaper subscriptions are challenged by consumer preference for on-time, any-place delivery of media content through mobile devices such as 3G and 4G cell phones and tablet computers.

Audience fragmentation, as evidenced by the Big Three broadcast networks' precipitous decline in shares of the prime time television audience, was countered through corporate consolidation—the purchase of competing media companies such as cable networks, online properties, production studios, and syndicator/distributors (Hindman & Wiegand, 2008). Similarly, corporate consolidation in the newspaper industry closely follows the degree of social differentiation in the nation as a whole (Demers, 1996).

Diversity of Power Structures and Political Consolidation

Whereas media consolidation is the corporate reaction to fractured mass audiences, political partisanship is the reaction to the greater diversity of power structures. Media consolidation is primarily driven by a concern for economic control; political consolidation through polarization and partisanship is driven by a concern for political control. Evidence of increasing partisanship and polarization includes a greater proportion of party-line votes in Congress, intensification of voter identification with parties, and widening gaps between the president's party and the opposition party in presidential approval (McCarty, Poole, & Rosenthal, 2006). As voters identify more closely with political parties, moderates tend to be driven out of the political process (Prior, 2007).

The consolidation of power into Democratic and Republican Parties is evident in the rise in partisanship and polarization among the executive, legislative, and judicial branches of government at the national and, increasingly, local levels. Conflicts that might involve a wide range of groups or span areas of agreement among conservatives and liberals are instead consolidated into the two-party political system. This process requires that both Democratic and Republican parties expand their platforms to include an increasingly broad range of issues, many of which do not have obvious ideological dimensions.

These attempts at political consolidation often over-reach and outlive their usefulness to each group, resulting in fractured coalitions and room for the emergence of third parties. However, the political environment from which third parties emerge is different in the present era of partisanship and polarization. In previous eras, third-party presidential candidates targeted the political center, including John Anderson in 1980 and Ross Perot in 1992 and 1996. However, in 2010, political factions emerged from within the Republican Party that drew the party further to the right. The success of Tea Party-endorsed candidates for Congressional and gubernatorial offices exacerbated partisanship and polarization between the parties.

The political system has not always been polarized. In a study of voters from the 1950s and early 1960s, Converse (1964) determined that the general population, as distinct from elite ideologues, had a lack of consistent ideological frames of reference. Instead, most voters were interested only in issues pertinent to their livelihoods or communities, while failing to see the ideological relevance of these personal and local issues. Daniel Bell (1960) saw evidence for a decline in ideologically based politics as education levels and living standards rose. Indeed, partisanship among the electorate, defined as identification with one political party and voting in ways consistent with that identification, reached a low point in the 1970s (Bartels, 2000).

Since then, however, partisanship has increased steadily, as seen in presidential voting (Bartels, 2000). Partisan differences in the approval of George W. Bush's performance ranged from the narrowest to the widest ever recorded for a president—yet the variation in approval ratings was nearly all accounted for by Democrats and Independents (Jacobson, 2008, pp. 4–6). The differences between Republicans' and Democrats' average approval ratings for Barack Obama's first year in office were the largest on record: 65 points, compared with 45 points during the first year of the George W. Bush administration, and 52 points during Bill Clinton's first year (Jones, 2010).

Studies of congressional roll-call voting have shown declining partisanship from the turn of the century until the 1970s (Poole & Rosenthal, 2007, p. 315). However, since the mid-1980s, Congress has become more polarized along party lines than it has since the politically violent era of intense income inequality before World War I.

The polarization of politics at the national level is mirrored in city councils and school boards across the nation. Candidates for formerly non-partisan races are now winning endorsements from state and national-level political parties, industry trade groups, and special interest groups, often signaling a change in policy that reflects Republican or Democratic agendas (Gerber & Hopkins, 2009). Notable examples include Alaska state Republican Party support for Sarah Palin's candidacy for the Mayor of Wasilla, AK, population 7,000 (Yardley, 2008), and both left-leaning and right-leaning political action committee support for competing city council candidates in Sioux City, IA

(Hayworth, 2009). In 2010, former governor and vice-presidential candidate Palin supplied endorsements in a number of Congressional races, siding with candidates who were to the right of candidates endorsed by local Republican organizations (Bruni, 2010).

National-level partisanship also affects the attitudes of local citizens toward each other. For example, Hopkins (2010) showed higher anti-immigration attitudes among communities with sudden demographic changes when national-level rhetoric politicizes the change. Similarly, local partisan environments shape perceptions about the causes of poverty (Hopkins, 2009). According to Hopkins (2009), the percentage of the local county that voted Republican in the last election predicted the tendency to attribute poverty to individual rather than system-wide problems.

Some argue that audience fragmentation has led to the rise in political partisanship (McPherson, 2008; Prior, 2007). Clearly, specialized cable news channels devoted to liberal or conservative audiences both reflect and reinforce audience fragmentation. I instead argue that the underlying process is social differentiation. Fox News cable network was started by Rupert Murdoch in 1996 to compete with CNN by providing a channel that combines an abundance of sharp, partisan opinions along with a smattering of news. The idea was to take advantage of cable's ability to deliver upscale audiences interested in news and conservative opinions (McDermott, 2010), thereby earning more profit. Murdoch is viewed more as a pragmatist than an ideologue (Goldman, 2007).

Similarly, local radio stations adopted the Rush Limbaugh-syndicated programs and the imitators to follow because the hosts produced large, ideologically homogeneous audiences in sufficient numbers to be of interest to advertisers. Although news audiences in general tend to be more educated and wealthier than viewers of other programs, Limbaugh's program also attracts predominantly male, churchgoing, conservative, and Southern audiences (Jamieson & Cappella, 2008).

The result is a political environment at local and national levels in which issues are consistently mapped to conservative versus liberal, or Republican versus Democratic, dimensions, in which sources of non-partisan authority are suddenly subject to partisan challenge, and in which knowledge itself, a mainstay of democratic functioning, has become relative.

Challenges Facing Media Organizations

These two main changes—fractured mass audiences and shifting power structures—and the two main reactions to these changes—media consolidation and the rise of political and ideological polarization—are all symptoms of social differentiation. How does this uncertain, differentiated environment affect decision-making by media organizations?

First, media organizations, and news organizations in particular, must determine who is in charge of the political and economic institutions on which their news workers depend for information. News organizations have reciprocal relationships with organized sources of social power: Reporters depend on public officials for content, and officials depend on news organizations for publicity that helps build support for policies or that challenges opponents' claims. Second, news organizations steering into the choppy and uncharted waters of the economic turmoil and political storms of the twenty-first century have to decide which journalistic values to preserve, and which to cast overboard like so much ballast.

I suggest that these changes can be best understood by employing conceptual frameworks from classical sociology, public opinion analyses, and studies of community newspapers. These frameworks are useful in that each illuminates distinct responses that news organizations may employ to adjust to these changes.

Who is in Charge?

News media may be viewed as an industrial system that converts the raw materials of public pronouncements and official actions into stories about the democratic functioning of the nation and community (Turk, 1986). The most reliable sources of these raw materials are public officials (Sigal, 1973).

In a polarized political environment, particularly in cases in which one party holds a slim majority in elected offices, political debates fall predictably into Republican versus Democratic frames. Narrow margins of political victories ensure that few issues will win bipartisan support. Nearly all public policy becomes subject to debate and challenge. However, because the debates generally fall along party lines, the journalist's job of finding balance in coverage of issues is simplified. Sources for and against issues tend to fall into predictable, gridlocked patterns.

In one respect, the job of a reporter becomes easier in a polarized political environment. However, on another level, the polarized environment produces uncertainty for news organizations. First, in a highly differentiated society, not all political debates are captured by the Democrat versus Republican frame. Religious conservatives, for example, who tend to be in lower income brackets, do not necessarily benefit from issues that benefit higher-income conservatives (Frank, 2004). Environmental concerns that a religious conservative views as consistent with a Christian principle of stewardship might be at odds with an economically conservative opposition to climate change treaties that threaten industrial sources of CO_2 emissions. Similarly, groups with expertise in a particular issue may be excluded once the issue enters the political sphere, as was the case with scientists in the global warming debate (McRight & Dunlap, 2000). The uncertainty facing journalists comes from excluding sources they

formerly defined as reliable in order to faithfully report the ongoing political debate. Uncertainty also develops within the audience, who face news
coverage of problems that seems hopelessly divided along partisan lines. The
net effect is that moderates are driven out of the political process as partisans
become more entrenched (Prior, 2007).

Second, when political elites are divided over nearly every issue, the lines
of authority are not clear. This creates uncertainty in society, and, by extension, uncertainty within news organizations (Donohue, Tichenor, & Olien,
1995). When individuals are elected to office by a slim majority, the opposition
party is never far from the reins of power. Members of the opposition challenge nearly all official pronouncements from elected officials. The minority
party, awaiting its chance to challenge the incumbents, makes itself available to
reporters in order to point out mistakes, to spin opponent victories as losses,
and to prepare its supporters for a comeback to the reins of power. Journalists
report the actions of the authorities but must also keep opposition groups "in
pocket" for comment on day-to-day issues, anticipating the day that the opposition regains power. Hence, the question of who is really in charge becomes
an ongoing concern for journalists. At the local level, issues that in the past
might have been decided quickly or with token opposition instead become
polarized along conservative–liberal lines.

Social differentiation, and the corresponding attempt to control through
consolidation, affects all aspects of society, not just politics and news organizations. Local retail organizations have been replaced by corporate chains; school
districts and metropolitan governments have been consolidated; state and federal agencies exert increasing control over local governmental offices; and local
affiliates of radio and television stations that broadcast emergency warnings are
owned by non-local corporations. All pose challenges: Reporters cannot find
a source to comment on plans to build a Wal-Mart in town, local media sales
account executives can find no one with authority to make decisions about
advertising a chain restaurant or appliance store, and local officials can find no
one at local stations owned by non-local groups to issue an emergency alert
regarding severe weather or local disasters (Klinenberg, 2007).

What Values Are Threatened?

Pressures to produce news economically, and to develop new modes of reaching consumers, challenge traditional notions of journalism: a commitment to
unbiased reporting, the separation of news from commentary, the separation of
editorial from advertising functions, the use of copy-editors and fact-checkers,
the use of reporters trained to write with accuracy and perspective, the use of
unbiased experts and unpaid sources, and a willingness to report news that
powerful groups do not want to hear. All of these techniques are not ends
in and of themselves, but are instead tools aimed at supporting the needs of

citizens in a democracy to know the truth. News organizations face questions relating to which journalistic values must be preserved, and which can be discarded in order to remain viable in the new environment.

News organizations that produce content serving exclusively conservative or liberal audiences have rejected contemporary Western journalistic values of unbiased reporting and the separation of news from commentary. These organizations have embraced economic and not contemporary Western journalistic values by serving an ideologically homogeneous audience with content that reinforces, rather than challenges, political predispositions. Similarly, organizations that favor balance over accuracy reproduce the simplistic and misleading pro-con or conservative–liberal dichotomy that dominates political debates and news coverage. The readers miss sources who are crowded out of the partisan debate and who have key information that does not fit easily into a conservative versus liberal frame. A "balanced" debate between ideological pugilists does not produce the knowledge and, more fundamentally, the truth upon which a democracy depends. In contrast, news organizations devoted to the time-honored journalistic values of accuracy, fact-checking, multiple sourcing, and basic copy-editing are less likely to be drawn into the political posturing that dominates public policy debates.

The unintended effect of conservative partisan media has been the creation of "echo chambers" in which citizens face a steady diet of consistent partisan beliefs. Audiences of conservative media have tended to distrust major news media such as television news, local newspapers, and news magazines more than audiences of these same major news media (Jamieson & Cappella, 2008, pp. 163–176; Morris, 2005). The "liberal media" argument, traced to elite conservative politicians' claims (Domke, Watts, Shah, & Fan, 1999), gained currency in media, to the extent that members of the so-called liberal CNN can be heard to repeat the "liberal media" reference on their own channels (Anderson Cooper 360 Degrees, 2009; CNN Newsroom, 2009). MSNBC enjoyed economic success after adopting the Fox News cable network's business model: small news staffs and a talk/commentary programming schedule that attracts ideologically homogeneous audiences and repels those with different views (McDermott, 2010). One-sided news channels from the right and the left are likely to contribute to the claim that all mainstream media are biased. The danger is in turning news consumers away from traditional day-to-day news reporting. This distrust of major news media pressures news organizations to abandon traditional journalism based on groups of editors, reporters, and publishers and to adopt instead the more profitable model of "news" dominated by pundits and producers.

Another threat posed by rising partisanship and media fragmentation is the disassociation of education from knowledge. The original knowledge gap hypothesis viewed mass media as exacerbating inequities in knowledge between higher- and lower-status segments of society, with education used as a proxy for status. As issues have become polarized, the link between education and knowledge of politically contested issues such as the role of human activity in causing global warming has become a link between ideology and beliefs (Hindman, 2009). Similarly, knowledge itself has become suspect, with the more politically malleable term "beliefs" becoming the preferred term. Hence, scientists have one set of beliefs, and affected industries, their political representatives, and partisan supporters have another set of beliefs. If knowledge is becoming merely beliefs, if facts are becoming ideologically biased perceptions, then the need to search for truth is even more pressing.

Traditional journalistic methods of reporting are time-honored tools for revealing the truths that would otherwise remain suppressed. However, as news staffs become more depleted, news organizations are employing news "subsidies" such as video news releases, citizen journalists equipped with camera phones, and expert guests who are on the payroll of industry or governmental agencies. These news subsidies challenge the traditional journalistic practices of separating news from commentary, editorial from advertising functions, and professional journalists from inexperienced and potentially biased observers. Similarly, strategies to reach consumers such as product placement, news linked to promotion of other content, and self-promotion that combines advertiser "partners" in pseudo-public service campaigns all represent a breakdown of traditional journalistic values. When news organizations cut staffs by eliminating copy-editors, fact-checkers, or professional reporters, and then instead employ subsidies and promotional content, the journalistic value of accuracy is compromised, giving support to those who claim mainstream journalism is no different from ideologically biased news/commentary.

The failure to produce news that challenges powerful parties is perhaps the biggest casualty of an environment characterized by media fragmentation and political polarization. Spiking stories that might offend powerful groups sacrifices journalistic commitment to the truth. It sacrifices the commitment to provide facts that citizens can use to make decisions that serve their own best interests, and occasionally that serve the interests of the community as a whole.

Social Fragmentation and Political Polarization: Conceptual Frameworks

A social environment of political polarization and media fragmentation demands responses on the part of the news media. Some of these responses are under way, and others can only be anticipated. I am seeking to shed light on how news organizations will respond to the uncertainty of "who is in charge" and what journalistic values are worth preserving, whatever the cost. Toward this end, conceptual frameworks can be useful if they explain in a simple way the complexity of a situation, while also providing educated guesses, or hypotheses, about the future.

Social Differentiation

A parsimonious explanation for the rising partisanship and media fragmentation is the sociological concept of social differentiation. Herbert Spencer (1891 [1860]) likened society to an organism that grows from small, single-celled, unspecialized structures to large, complex structures with interdependent organs, with regulatory systems coordinating all the parts. Spencer, who preceded Charles Darwin in coining the term "survival of the fittest," saw social structures evolve and grow in complexity until the systems serving a complex society no longer functioned within the environment, at which point they ceased to exist (Survival of the fittest, 2010). An example can be seen in the decline of the Big Three television networks' share of prime-time viewers. This phenomenon is commonly associated with the rise of cable television, but it more closely fits indicators of the degree of social differentiation in the nation: the percentage of ethnic minorities, the rise of educational levels, and the economic heterogeneity of the workforce (Hindman & Wiegand, 2008).

Accompanying social differentiation is the related concept of the division of labor, as articulated by Emile Durkheim (1933 [1893]). Durkheim and the economists who preceded him viewed the division of labor as a rational response to competition for scarce resources (Aron, 1989 [1967]). Rather than competing head to head with everyone for the same limited set of resources, a radio station, for example, programs a music format not currently available in a community, and which is likely to attract an audience that advertisers find attractive. Similarly, as music formats left AM radio for FM in the 1970s, AM stations turned to news, sports, and talk formats to draw older, more educated, and higher-income audiences. Just as FM radio stations became fragmented into increasingly specialized music formats, the majority of AM talk format stations further specialized by serving primarily conservative male audiences.

Public Opinion and Self-Interests

Political polarization does not represent an escalation of social conflict, however. If anything, the polarization of political elites and the electorate formalizes and controls conflicts into institutional settings. The challenge is separating from the partisan and ideological packaging the true motivation for all political battles: self-interests.

Walter Lippmann (1925) became disillusioned with the ability of the public to fulfill its democratic obligations of being omniscient observers of governmental functioning. Instead, he understood that self-interests, both individual and corporate, drove political involvement. The problem as he saw it was that political debate often obscured the true self-interests at stake in what might be staged as principled and ideological battles.

For Lippmann (1925) the solution was public discussion that did not "obscure and censor private interest" but instead helped it "to sail and make it sail under its own colors" (p. 112). As a result, individuals joining a partisan cause will be "somewhat less likely to mistake a party's purpose for the aim of mankind" (p. 114). In the current political environment, debates framed as liberal-versus-conservative fights over high-minded principles of free enterprise, intellectual property, and state's rights obscure actual interests, such as in maintaining profitable industries or propping up wasteful bureaucratic structures. The value of disclosing, through moderated debate, the self-interests at stake in a political debate is to ensure that citizens are best able to vote in their own best interests.

Political and Structural Pluralism

The conceptual model of political pluralism is an application to the political sphere of Spencer and Durkheim's notions of social differentiation and the division of labor. In a politically pluralistic society, all social groups flourish, and no one social group dominates the others. Conflicts over scarce resources do not reach disruptive levels because each individual is a member of multiple and competing interest groups, and these cross-cutting loyalties reduce the likelihood of excessive conflict (Coser, 1956). Political pluralism, in its ideal state, prevents debates from becoming divisive and violent (Erlich, 1982).

Cross-cutting loyalties result in the moderation of conflict. However, in an environment of political polarization, all debates become reframed along liberal–conservative lines, regardless of the complexities and inconsistencies in the interests that each debate represents. For example, a conservative principle of a lack of governmental intervention in business is challenged when a lack of governmental oversight leads to catastrophic oil spills or economic collapse. Liberal principles of governmental oversight for the good of all is inconsistent with policies that favor minorities over majorities.

Political polarization, by reducing complex debates into a single liberal–conservative dimension, pulls together coalitions of groups with often contradictory self-interests (Frank, 2004). These loose coalitions of economic and religious conservatives on the right and economic and social liberals on the left are themselves rife with potential conflict and disunion. Examples include Sarah Palin's advocacy of a Conservative Party candidate over a Republican candidate in a New York U.S. House race, the emergence of Republican Tea Party activists following the Obama election, and religious conservative adoption of environmental causes. These strains show that the polarization of all issues into Democratic versus Republican camps does not capture fully the diversity of the political concerns of the electorate.

Another conceptual framework useful for understanding the uncertainty facing news organizations is the structural pluralism model. This approach was developed over 30 years of study of Minnesota community newspapers and public opinion data by Tichenor, Donohue, and Olien (1980). The structural pluralism model goes beyond political pluralism, which suggests a perfect balancing of diverse interests and a self-regulation of special interests. Instead, the structural pluralism model notes the disproportionate power of those in elite positions to control their fates. Some institutions (economic and government) are more powerful than others (religious, family, education), and some organizations (financial and multi-national corporate organizations, executive and legislative branches of government) are more successful at maintaining their positions of power than others.

Hence, political polarization is one way of maintaining the balance of power among economic and governmental institutions; polarization efficiently controls the myriad of special interests that might emerge and begin to challenge the elite's control of scarce resources. Political elites, seeking to avoid competing with diverse groups of opponents, instead frame debates as liberal versus conservative, Republican versus Democratic arguments to ensure decisions are made within the existing political structure, thus maintaining the role of elected officials in mediating key decisions affecting their constituents. News organizations, dependent upon these powerful groups for both content and income from political advertising, help maintain the balance of power as they dutifully report the party line from both groups (Donohue et al., 1995).

A guiding principle of the structural pluralism model is that, to understand a local newspaper, one must first understand the community the newspaper serves. Similarly, to understand national media, one must understand the social, political, and economic climate in which those media operate. The idea is that media, both local and national, are both limited and enabled by the products of the external social systems in which the media exist. This model suggests that media organizations reflect the larger social climate of political polarization and social fragmentation.

News organizations reflect the community through dependence on powerful groups for news content. In larger, more complex communities, there are more potential sources of organized social power, and more sources of advertising dollars. Hence, newspapers in larger communities contain more reports of conflict than do newspapers in small towns, which often contain small groups of leaders who make the majority of decisions affecting the community. In larger communities, the power structure is more complex as a result of the greater number of organized interest groups, larger news staffs, and more formal means of airing grievances and raising challenges. As a result, big city newspapers have more conflicts to cover than do small town papers.

The structural pluralism model is reminiscent of Durkheim's mechanical–organic solidarity ideal types. Small towns represent mechanical solidarity, which is social cohesion based on the homogeneity of community members' ethnic and familial backgrounds, and big cities represent organic solidarity, social cohesion based on interdependencies resulting from specialization, diversity of the population, and the division of labor (Hindman, Littlefield, Preston, & Neumann, 1999).

The structural pluralism model suggests that more complex societies or communities have greater potential sources of organized social power, and hence greater potential for conflict, than do smaller, less complex societies or communities. News media reflect these changes over time and across communities (Hindman, 1996). Hence, small town media operate differently from big city media, and media in a politically partisan environment operate differently from media in a non-partisan environment.

The structural pluralism model conceptualizes communities as social systems containing institutions (economic, governmental, religious, family, and education) that maintain and reproduce the community. In this model, news organizations serve supporting roles in communities by communicating across institutions and reinforcing institutional values. News organizations reflect the size and complexity of their communities, as do all local institutions.

The partisan environment in which incumbents are challenged by members of the opposition who are lying in wait for missteps and politically advantageous situations is reflected faithfully by news media. Rather than weighing the evidence for claims and counter-claims, the news media dutifully represent the statements from easily obtainable representatives of opposing factions— which, not coincidentally, generally include Republicans versus Democrats. Although the bitter debates among partisan opponents are faithfully reported in news media, the substance of the debate is not examined because news organizations are better equipped to report what sources say than to investigate the value of those statements.

Conclusions

Who Is in Charge?

Political elites have, in effect, collapsed a wide range of concerns emerging from a plethora of potential sources of organized power into a simple, unidimensional Republican versus Democratic frame—or, more accurately, a conservative versus liberal frame. As a result, news organizations have ready-made sources for nearly any story that reaches the level of organized politics (Poole & Rosenthal, 2007). Elected officials and agency heads increasingly use news media to conduct their work of building support for initiatives, pressuring opponents to react to challenges, and informing constituents of progress toward political solutions (Cook, 1998). Reporters can generally find willing sources eager to be interviewed about projects relevant to the sources' purposes.

News organizations facing declining budgets and depleted reporting staffs rely on increasingly restricted sets of sources, often reinforcing the conservative versus liberal framing of issues. The same groups line up on one side or the other for issues at the national, state, and, increasingly, even local levels. Incumbents and challengers, majority and minority caucuses form the lion's share of news sources, in spite of the potentially complex sources of organized social power in a differentiating society. Citizens seeking to learn about the issues of the day that affect their self-interests are not well served by a political system that frames all debates on this conservative–liberal dimension.

The responses to social differentiation—media consolidation and political polarization—both contain the seeds of their own destruction. Both tend to drive away readers and sources. Representatives of interest groups seeking news coverage will find it increasingly difficult to get the attention of traditional news media, and instead will likely bypass mainstream media altogether, seeking audiences directly via blogs, social networking sites, podcasts, text messaging, and e-mail updates to supporters. Similarly, readers are abandoning paid media in favor of free online news sources and media that fit their own political predispositions. In other scenarios, interest groups may be given direct access to the pages of a small town newspaper in order to promote upcoming events, to write opinion pieces, or even to get their press releases printed in the paper's news sections.

When news media give unedited access to advocates of one side or the other of political controversies, the medium becomes something foreign to the professional news organization it formerly represented. The local newspaper becomes a common carrier, exerting little or no editorial judgment, and relying on readers by way of online remarks or letters to the editor to correct blatant errors, scurrilous charges, and errors of taste and style. When newspapers open their opinion pages to unedited attacks by representatives of opposing factions, the community becomes more deeply divided and the newspaper appears to be nothing more than a bulletin board. In such a situation, journalists fail to resolve uncertainty in an effective way. They prove unwilling and unable to exercise editorial judgment for fear of alienating one or more factions within the community. What is lost is a sense of the greater good, of seeking solutions to problems facing the community as a whole.

At its best, a news medium would publish editorial debates that disclose the special interests of parties involved in the debate rather than cloaking the arguments in vague ideological platitudes (Lippmann, 1925). Moderated debates in print or online allow statements to be challenged and motives to be revealed.

The structural pluralism model explains the link between economic interests and editorial interests during times of economic stress (Donohue, Olien, & Tichenor, 1989). No employee is immune from concern about the stability of an organization facing increasing demands for profits from shareholders, and declining levels of advertising support from retailers. When editorial and business decisions merge, the willingness to offend readers is offloaded to newspaper contributors. Similarly, editorial decisions about which events to promote or which letters to publish are simply abrogated so that everything gets in. Small community newspapers have been following a model similar to this for decades (Donohue et al., 1989). And it is expected that this failure to exercise editorial judgment will extend further up the food chain, to larger newspapers, TV stations, and online news media.

The consequence of cable networks showcasing political pundits rather than honest debate, of local newspapers opening their pages to partisans who speak only to their own followers, is that traditional journalism becomes a force for its own demise. In the common carrier model of journalism, unedited, unverified, and unsubstantiated opinions are delivered to homes along with the tacit stamp of legitimacy that the media provide.

What Values Must Be Preserved?

In spite of pressures to reflect powerful groups within the nation and within communities, news organizations must find ways to reflect in their content the diversity of special interests that exist in an increasingly complex world. Diverse interests transcend liberal versus conservative dimensions. Groups that are counted as part of liberal or conservative coalitions are not well represented by Democratic or Republican elected officials, who take them for granted, and debates that resort to ideological platitudes tend to hide the special interests behind the debates. News organizations that reveal the special interests behind political debates will help citizens identify for themselves which group reflects their own best interests, and the best interests of the community.

Citizens will value news organizations that reassert editorial control by refusing to print ad hominem attacks and scurrilous charges, by revealing special interests behind partisan bickering, by representing the diversity of knowledge rather than the divisiveness of opinion, and by demanding that commentary reflect high standards of evidence and argument. Similarly, news organizations that are committed to the search for truth through traditional journalistic practices and by providing a forum for the free and open discussion of ideas will stand apart from those that do not reflect those values. By privileging knowledge over beliefs, accuracy over ideology, and inclusiveness over partisanship, news organizations can dispel, rather than reinforce, the myth that everything is relative, even the truth.

Thought Questions: Contemplating Change

College Town, population 25,000, is located in a picturesque and isolated region within a conservative state. Outdoor enthusiasts can choose from among millions of nearby acres of national forests and wilderness areas. The nearest city with a population over 100,000 is 70 miles away. The community is outwardly peaceful, but bitterly divided. Division runs along multiple dimensions: religious, occupational, and ideological. The community hosts an annual Hempfest that celebrates the many uses of marijuana, as well as an annual festival bringing together conservative home-schoolers from across the nation. The city council includes both pro-business and "sustainability" advocates who fight over questions such as tax breaks for big-box stores. Churches that publicly denounce homosexuality clash with those that help sponsor the annual gay pride parade.

The local newspaper editor is committed to representing the diversity of opinion within the community. However, the columnists tend to use opinion pieces to cast each issue as a clash between liberals and conservatives, and to disparage and stereotype opponents' arguments rather than appealing to the common interests of the community. A reader feedback feature on the paper website had to be restricted after responses degenerated to profanity and name calling.

How can the editor use media (whether print, online, mobile, etc.) to:

1. represent the diversity of the community without falling into simplistic liberal–conservative framing;
2. reveal the self-interests, and community interests, represented by each contributor;
3. maintain a civil discourse that shows respect for all parties and beliefs; and
4. create an environment in which the truth, or at least the best ideas, can rise to the top in a free and open debate?

Note

1 Local power structures can be formal or informal. Formal power structures comprise elected or appointed officials such as mayors and school superintendents. Informal power structures comprise individuals with a reputation for "getting things done" in the community, such as local developers or prominent philanthropists with deep roots in the community (Powers, 1965).

References

Anderson Cooper 360 Degrees (2009, November 9). *GOP wins Virginia, New Jersey gubernatorial races*. Retrieved April 30, 2010, from Lexis-Nexis Academic Database.

Aron, R. (1989 [1967]). *Maincurrents of sociological thought: Durkheim, Pareto, Weber*. New York: Anchor Books.

Bartels, L. (2000). Partisanship and voting behavior, 1952–1996. *American Journal of Political Science, 44*, 35–50.

Bell, D. (1960). *The end of ideology: On the exhaustion of political ideas in the fifties*. Glencoe, IL: Free Press.

Bruni, F. (2010, May 31). Carly Fiorina means business. *The New York Times Magazine*. Retrieved June 8, 2010, from http://www.nytimes.com/2010/06/06/magazine/06Fiorina-t.html

CNN Newsroom (2009, September 26). *Floods again threaten Southeast: Inspecting Iran's secret plant: N.Y. Rep. Maloney's husband dies: State of our nation: Chemicals and bombs in new terror plots: Marines with breast cancer*. Retrieved April 30, 2010, from Lexis-Nexis Academic Database.

Converse, P. E. (1964). The nature of belief systems in mass publics. In D. E. Apter (Ed.), *Ideology and discontent*. New York: Free Press.

Cook, T. E. (1998). *Governing with the news: The news media as a political institution*. Chicago: University of Chicago Press.

Coser, L. A. (1956). *The functions of social conflict*. New York: Free Press.

Demers, D. (1996). *The menace of the corporate newspaper: Fact or fiction?* Ames: Iowa State University Press.

Domke, D., Watts, M., Shah, D., & Fan, D. (1999). The politics of conservative elites and the "liberal media" argument. *Journal of Communication, 49*, 35–58.

Donohue, G., Olien, C., & Tichenor, P. (1989). Structure and constraints on community newspaper gatekeepers. *Journalism Quarterly, 66*, 807–812, 845.

Donohue, G., Tichenor, P., & Olien, C. (1973). Mass media functions, knowledge and social control. *Journalism Quarterly, 50*, 652–659.

Donohue, G. A., Tichenor, P. J., & Olien, C. N. (1995). A guard dog perspective on the role of media. *Journal of Communication, 45*, 115–132.

Durkheim, E. (1933 [1893]). *The division of labor in society*. New York: Free Press.

Erlich, S. (1982). *Pluralism on and off course*. Oxford, UK: Pergamon Press.

Frank, T. (2004). *What's the matter with Kansas: How conservatives won the heart of America*. New York: Henry Holt.

Gerber, E., & Hopkins, D. (2009, April). *When mayors matter: Estimating the impact of mayoral partisanship on city policy*. Paper presented at the annual meeting of the Midwest Political Science Association, Chicago, IL.

Goldman, A. (2007, August 1). Murdoch cuts wide swath through NYC. *USA Today*. Retrieved April 29, 2010, from http://www.usatoday.com/money/economy/2007-08-01-2544448810_x.htm

Hayworth, B. (2009, October 25). City elections: Partisan politics' growing influence worries candidates; observers say PACs, loaded language likely here to stay. *Sioux City (Iowa) Journal*. Retrieved April 23, 2010, from http://www.siouxcityjournal.com

Hindman, D. B. (1996). Community newspapers, community structural pluralism, and local conflict with nonlocal groups. *Journalism Quarterly, 73*, 708–721.

Hindman, D. (2009). Mass media flow and the differential distribution of politically disputed beliefs: The belief gap hypothesis. *Journalism & Mass Communication Quarterly, 86*, 790–808.

Hindman, D., Littlefield, R., Preston, A., & Neumann, D. (1999). Structural pluralism, ethnic pluralism, and community newspapers. *Journalism & Mass Communication Quarterly, 76*, 250–263.

Hindman, D., & Wiegand, K. (2008). The Big Three's prime time decline: A social and technological context. *Journal of Broadcasting and Electronic Media, 52*, 119–135.

Hopkins, D. (2009). Partisan reinforcement and the poor: The impact of context on explanations for poverty. *Social Science Quarterly, 90*, 744–764.

Hopkins, D. (2010). Politicized places: Explaining where and when immigrants provoke local opposition. *American Political Science Review, 104*, 40–60.

Jacobson, G. (2008). *A divider, not a uniter: George W. Bush and the American people*. New York: Pearson Longman.

Jamieson, K., & Cappella, J. (2008). *Echo chamber: Rush Limbaugh and the conservative media establishment*. New York: Oxford University Press.

Jones, J. (2010). Obama's approval most polarized for first-year president. *Gallup politics*. Retrieved April 29, 2010, from http://www.gallup.com/poll/125345/Obama-Approval-Polarized-First-Year-President.aspx

Klinenberg, E. (2007). *Fighting for air: The battle to control America's media*. New York: Metropolitan Books.

Lippmann, W. (1925). *The phantom public*. New York: Harcourt Brace.

McCarty, N., Poole, K., & Rosenthal, H. (2006). *Polarized America: The dance of ideology and unequal riches*. Cambridge, MA: MIT Press.

McDermott, T. (2010, March/April). Dumb like a Fox. *Columbia Journalism Review*. Retrieved June 10, 2010, from http://www.cjr.org/cover_story/dumb_like_a_fox.php?page=all

McPherson, J. (2008). *The conservative resurgence and the press: The media's role in the rise of the right*. Evanston, IL: Northwestern Press.

McRight, A., & Dunlap, R. (2000). Challenging global warming as a social problem: An analysis of the conservative movement's counter-claims. *Social Problems, 47*, 499–522.

Morris, J. (2005). The Fox News factor. *Harvard International Journal of Press/Politics, 10*, 56–79.

Poole, K., & Rosenthal, H. (2007). *Ideology and Congress*. New Brunswick, NJ: Transaction Publishers.

Powers, R. (1965). *Identifying the community power structure*. North Central Regional Extension Publication No.19. Retrieved June 7, 2010, from http://www.soc.iastate.edu/extension/presentations/publications/comm/NCR19.pdf

Prior, M. (2007). *Post-broadcast democracy: How media choice increases inequality in political involvement and polarizes elections*. Cambridge, UK: Cambridge University Press.

Project for Excellence in Journalism (2010). *Network TV: Audience*. Retrieved November 30, 2009, from http://www.stateofthemedia.org/2009/narrative_networktv_audience.php?media=6&cat=2

Sigal, L. (1973). *Reporters and officials: The organization and politics of newsmaking*. Lexington, MA: D. C. Heath.

Spencer, H. (1891 [1860]). The social organism. Reprinted in *Essays: Scientific, political, & speculative*. London: Williams & Norgate. Retrieved November 16, 2006, from http://oll.libertyfund.org/Home3/HTML.php?recordID=0620.01#LF-BK0620–01pt01ch008

Survival of the fittest. (2010). In *Encyclopædia Britannica*. Retrieved April 30, 2010, from http://www.britannica.com/EBchecked/topic/575460/survival-of-the-fittest

Tichenor, P. J., Donohue, G. A., & Olien, C. N. (1980). *Community conflict and the press*. Beverly Hills, CA: Sage.

Turk, J. (1986). Information subsidies and media content: A study of public relations influence on the news. *Journalism Monographs, 100*.

Yardley, W. (2008, September 3). Palin's start in Alaska: Not politics as usual. *The New York Times*. Retrieved April 23, 2010, from Lexis-Nexis Academic Database.

8

NEWS: ONCE AND FUTURE INSTITUTION?

Wilson Lowrey, University of Alabama

Bringing in the newspaper, and reading it, and tuning in to the nightly newscast were once as natural and taken-for-granted as turning on a faucet. The news was ready and accessible, and accessing it was habit. Or we might consider it ritual rather than utility. The recurring act of news consumption has been communal, informed by deeper shared significance.

Either depiction recalls journalism's fundamental legitimacy in twentieth-century America. From the Progressive Era through late modernism, news media were thought to connect with the norms, values, and expectations of the American cultural majority (Kaplan, 2006; Schudson, 1978). Journalism has been a national institution as well as a commercial business (McQuail, 2010), and even journalism's business model mostly meshed with the nation's social and cultural expectations. However, recent decades have seen a widening gap between the public and news professionals. Skepticism, even cynicism, about journalists' intentions and competence has grown (e.g., American Society of Newspaper Editors, 1999; Pew Research Center, 2002). A recent Pew survey revealed that, by the U.S. public's estimation, news media accuracy had hit a two-decade low, and media bias was at an all-time high (Pew Research Center, 2009). Drops in circulation and ratings for traditional media have been well documented (e.g., Project for Excellence in Journalism, 2010a). Industry professionals and journalism scholars have worried over these patterns and the uncertainty they suggest, calling for journalists to connect again with everyday citizens. After years of losing touch with specialized communities while pursuing economy of scale, news organizations face audience patterns that are ever more complex and fragmented, as well as shifting norms, values, and expectations.

Although audience attention and preferences seemed more focused and straightforward decades ago (Pew Research Center, 2009), the content consumed was also more focused, originating from a media that were largely oligarchical, and institutionally secure. The content they produced was intended to travel one direction, to a mass. And media use by this mass was relatively habitual. Within such institutional arrangements, organizations are less likely to assess customer/client needs strategically, or to base decisions on assessment (DiMaggio & Powell, 1991). Both producers and customer/clients are more likely to follow comfortable, widely understood routines and conventions, remaining blind to alternatives.

This is not to argue that audience needs never change, or that the news media never assess and address these changes. In fact, the current uncertainties and changes that are rocking institutional foundations may be nudging the news media toward a level of wide-awake, rational assessment not seen before. Nevertheless, this chapter argues that rational-choice, strategic behavior on the part of news producers and audiences has been only part of the story. Journalism's institutional status, its taken-for-granted legitimacy, and the socially shared understanding about journalism's practices and forms have been at least as important to journalism's success to date as any instrumental, informational purposes that news has served in the everyday lives of citizens and consumers.

The chapter embraces social theorist and economist Max Weber's (1947) position that authority and efficacy depend not only on economic fit and well-being, but also on legitimacy. As sociologist Richard Scott (2008) argues, "organizations exhibiting culturally approved norms and activities . . . , receiving support from normative authorities, and having approval from legal bodies are more likely to survive . . . [and] [l]egitimacy exerts an influence on organizational viability independent of its performance" (p. 157). Sources of journalism's institutional legitimacy are explored, as well as the benefits and problems of maintaining legitimacy and stability when facing environmental uncertainty and a need for change. Drawing on institutional approaches from sociology, the chapter discusses ways journalists and news organizations may reposition themselves within society's new, complex network structures, so they may both secure legitimacy and reconnect with citizens—two goals that would seem to dovetail naturally, but can be at odds.

Journalism and Legitimacy

Legitimacy is a complex idea. Scholars have identified several types, and two are at issue here. "Normative legitimacy" implies conscious moral choice, and it is granted when there is accord with widely accepted cultural and social norms and values. "Cognitive legitimacy" suggests that behaviors follow unquestioned habit and unexamined premises. These run deeper than rational moral judgment. The practices and forms that result take on socially shared meanings, and they become taken for granted and routine (Aldrich & Ruef, 2007; Scott, 2008; Suchman, 1995).

The cognitive and normative legitimacy that underlie journalism's authority are rooted in the resources and relationships that journalists and news organizations have grown over time. However, the roots now seem brittle in a shifting, uncertain landscape that is proving precarious for all institutions (Bruns, 2008; Castells, 2000; Deuze, 2007). This shifting was evident decades ago, even before the advent of the Internet, as a credibility divide between journalists and audiences emerged in the 1980s. Since, our society and culture have become increasingly postmodern, as discussed in Chapter 4 of this book. Fragmented perspectives are splintering once-dominant institutions. The market that had sustained generalist "big journalism" is also fragmenting, providing inadequate revenue (Hindman & Wiegand, 2008). New technologies, low barriers to entry, and the disconnect between traditional news outlets and audiences are encouraging niche areas in the margins for non-journalists, from citizen news sites and blogs to websites by PR practitioners. Network structures appear to be on the rise, while traditional hierarchies and interdependencies are weakening or becoming financially unsustainable. Dire economic forecasts for an industry already burdened by debt have put owners and managers in a reactionary position, scrambling to find anything that might float, financially. And concerns about the impact on journalism's control over work, knowledge base, ethics, and professional mission are being shoved to the back.

These responses are understandable. Who has time to shore up long-term legitimacy and credibility when storms are raging right now, and the ship is taking on water? Still, in embracing change based purely on immediate market realities, do managers and owners risk delegitimizing journalism? This is a cause for concern at multiple levels. March (1991) warns of this risk at the level of the individual organization: Organizations must take care not to over-explore (pursue too much change) and not to over-exploit (rely too strongly on tried and true processes and resources). Though radical change seems called for, such change may invite a "liability of newness." Organizations that start afresh with new products in new markets become new organizations in a sense, complete with all the burdensome trappings of newness—unproven track records, weak knowledge domains, tenuous external relationships, and unreliable resource flow (Aldrich & Ruef, 2007; Baum, 2001). We have seen evidence of this danger at the corporate level as well, with financial woes brought on by attempts to diversify into unfamiliar media businesses (Jung & Chan-Olmsted, 2005), a response to media fragmentation. Journalism scholars have warned of similar dangers at the more macro level of the institution—of the news industry squandering long-earned legitimacy, trust, and brand recognition by oversteering when encountering short-term challenges (Meyer, 2004). So some middle path between institutionalism and a hasty response to markets may be in order. As this chapter suggests, institutional legitimacy and hierarchical structures may be persistent, in spite of predictions of a post-bureaucratic world (e.g., Castells, 2000).

News as an Institution: Benefits and Dysfunctions

Much of the literature on news media production has emphasized the impact of structures and contexts on individual decision-making, at organizational, community, market, institutional, and cultural levels (e.g., Dimmick & Coit, 1982; Peterson & Anand, 2004; Shoemaker & Vos, 2009; Sigal, 1973; Tichenor, Donohue, & Olien, 1980; Tuchman, 1978). The emphasis on higher-order causes stems partly from concerns over corporate and public ownership and increasing attention to markets, and partly from the news media's traditionally strong connections with governmental and political institutions. As Schudson (2002) has said, "the story of journalism on a day-to-day basis is the story of the interaction of reporters and bureaucrats" (p. 255). Journalists "index" the news according to the diversity of views held by officials (Bennett, 1990), and pluralism and diversity among the powerful in a community can lead to greater diversity of views in the news (Pollock, 2007; Tichenor et al., 1980). Some scholars taking institutional approaches see journalism as a sort of governmental appendage, deftly used by bureaucrats and politicians to communicate to publics and to one another, and receiving governmental support such as reduced taxes and postal subsidies, as well as information subsidies (e.g., Cook, 2005).

Scholars have also emphasized journalism's cultural contexts. Some similarity in norms and values across news systems suggests the existence of a journalism professional culture across news media systems (e.g., Deuze, 2005; Laitila, 1995). However, news media also gain legitimacy by not straying far from particular norms and values of their geographically based cultures, helping to account for variation in journalism ethics systems. The traditional norms and values of the U.S. news system are grounded in a Progressive Era technocratic culture, with its emphasis on facts, expert knowledge, and detached science (Cook, 2005; Kaplan, 2006; Patterson & Seib, 2005), which are themselves grounded in Enlightenment Era thinking. The idea that democracy depends on the existence of an informed public is deeply ingrained, even naturalized. This helps give the U.S. news system cognitive legitimacy and institutional status.

Uncertainty about the rules of engagement and the "grammar" of interaction among journalists, audiences, and other institutions has led to conventional agreements among these groups. As Bennett (2005) says, "The curious fact of seeking a common reality has led to the most standardized news in the world" (p. 181). News routines have persisted despite recent changes. For example, journalists have shown reluctance to fully embrace interactive and multimedia features of online news, preferring instead to protect traditional norms and practices (e.g., Domingo, 2008; Garcia, 2008; Russial, 2009; Sheffer & Schultz, 2009; Singer, 2010).

The fact that routines can be found across news organizations suggests that routines serve a macro-level institutional purpose in addition to the more obvious organizational purpose of making work more efficient in the face of resource and time pressures (Ryfe, 2006). Both news sources and publics have had an understanding of journalistic routines, have relied on them, and have even helped act them out. Cook (2005) cites former House Speaker Newt Gingrich's answer to a question by *USA Today's* editorial staff about why he uses colorful language: "Because you all [the media] will pick it up . . . I've simply tried to learn my half of your language" (p. 114).

A number of perspectives on media production explain the role media routines play for the entire social network that shapes news production, and not just within the media outlet's walls. In their book *Media Logic*, Altheide and Snow (1979) portray media as having a dominant, accepted logic to which other institutions and the rest of society conform. The way the world is presented through media is taken as legitimate, and "[t]he legitimizing function of media is the essence of media influence" (p. 237). Altheide and Snow's media logic was a forerunner to the more recent "mediatization" thesis, which proposes that media play a formative role in the lives of everyday people, saturating the environment within which people construct identities, make sense of social arrangements, and interpret their surroundings. According to this idea, culture is increasingly dependent on media (Lundby, 2009).

This influence works the other way as well, as society legitimizes, and gives meaning to, media and its processes. According to this "production of culture" approach, symbols in the media "are shaped by the systems within which they are created, distributed, evaluated, taught, and preserved" (Peterson & Anand, 2004, p. 311). Howie Becker's *Art Worlds* (1982) is a good example of this approach. Becker's study focuses on art production, but his ideas fit the production of news, and in fact he looks into journalistic tasks such as editing and photography. Art production is a collective activity that extends far beyond just the individual media producer, to include suppliers of raw material, schools that train, professional associations, audiences, and critics who help craft norms. We may substitute the word "news" for "art" in the paragraph below:

> Art worlds consist of all the people whose activities are necessary to the production of the characteristic works which that world, and perhaps others as well, define as art. Members of art worlds coordinate the activities by which work is produced by referring to a body of conventional understandings embodied in common practice and in frequently used artifacts. (p. 34)

Becker focuses on the importance of agreed-upon conventions for specific areas or "worlds" of media work, and these worlds have contested boundaries. As in journalism, changes in art worlds do not come easily. Individuals and organizations have developed stakes in agreed-upon and legitimized conventions, routines, and grammars. "Mavericks" who defy conventions are often banished to the hinterlands. When change does come, it often comes through almost accidental "drift," through a "series of almost imperceptible shifts"—or because producers "enlarge [the] vocabulary" of their crafts to accept practices and forms that were previously illegitimate (p. 303). Any substantial and sustainable change requires the support of a network, an observation also made by scholars of organizational innovation (Cohen & Levinthal, 1990).

Becker's "drift" calls to mind the effects of mimicry by organizations, a phenomenon studied by scholars of institutionalism in organizations (e.g., DiMaggio & Powell, 1983). Mimicry of forms and practices of other organizations can initially invite subtle variations on a theme, but largely it encourages sameness across a field. Mimicry and isomorphism have been evident in the production of news and other media. They have been encouraged by environmental uncertainty, vague internal criteria for success, and weak evaluation of staff and production (Cook, 2005; Lowrey, 2005; Ryan & Peterson, 1982). These encourage reporters to check accounts by other news organizations to ensure their own accounts don't differ dramatically (Bennett, 2005; Dunwoody, 1997), and the Web makes this practice more likely (Boczkowski, 2009). Mimicry helps news organizations keep up legitimized appearances with other like organizations, helps them maintain accord with the expectations society has of journalism, and helps them avoid claims of negligence. All of this can bring resources, while keeping substantive innovation at arm's length (Cook, 2005; Lowrey, 2005).

During uncertain times, organizations may also try to avoid external disruption in order to avoid evident change—change that could undermine accord with societal norms and so jeopardize public legitimacy. Organizations may "loosely couple" themselves with turbulent surroundings, buffering external influences from organizational output, buffering internal divisions from one another, and largely ignoring feedback from clients, consumers, and the public (Meyer & Rowan, 1977). Traditionally, journalists have put distance between themselves and their audiences (Gans, 1979; Sumpter, 2000), perhaps contributing to the widening credibility gap in the 1980s. The industry and the profession tried to breach the gap in a number of ways, from the civic and public journalism movements of the 1990s to newsroom reorganization later in that decade (Gade, 2004), and, more recently, by inviting user-generated content and tracking audience statistics. Still, journalists tend to construct images of the audience that have little basis in audience feedback (McQuail, 2010; Shoemaker & Vos, 2009). Also, within the newsroom journalists have traditionally received limited overt feedback or evaluation on their work from supervisors (Beaupre, 1991; Curran, 2000). If these external and internal buffering tendencies persist, they may prove hazardous in the face of extreme turbulence in journalism's environment, which would seem to demand some bending to the winds.

Institutional Erosion and Network Structures

Journalism has been infamously slow to change, especially for those who champion substantive innovation in an era of uncertainty and disruption. As mentioned in this book's introductory chapter, efforts to innovate have at times been sluggish and temporary, or even just ceremonial. And this is not surprising, given the identities and meanings grounded in institutionalized forms and practices.

Yet finally, it appears journalists and news organizations are pushing for substantial change. Many do this for economic reasons: News organizations must change or face extinction. Media markets are unstable and unpredictable (Chyi, 2009). Others see cultural and social change driving media change. According to these views, we live in a post-industrial, postmodern age (Castells, 2000; Deuze, 2007; Wall, 2005), and the organizing elements of our society and culture are becoming "liquid" and precarious. Conditions under which society's members act change so fast that routines, habits, and conventions cannot keep up. Social organizations and institutions fragment. New technologies and forms appear and wither without taking root, and tasks, roles, and job positions are in constant flux.

Network Structures and Their Benefits

The dominant organizing structure for such a post-bureaucratic work environment is the social network. Networks consist of "relationships that are negotiated in an ongoing communicative process, and which [rely] on neither market nor hierarchical mechanisms of control" (Phillips, Lawrence, & Hardy, 2000, cited in Swan & Scarbrough, 2005, p. 916). Networks are human-centric rather than market-centric. Communication connections among individuals within and outside of organizational structures become at least as relevant as the structures themselves. The constant change of network structures discourages (but does not entirely prevent) the development of cognitive legitimacy and the formation of stable routines and conventions. Individuals and organizations with deeper experience and involvement in networks learn more from them (Swan & Scarbrough, 2005). Deep involvement in networks tends to foster innovation (Powell, Koput & Smith-Doerr, 1996), especially true for far-flung networks with unfamiliar "weak ties" (Granovetter, 1973).

Network structures are not new to journalism. Reporters' connections with sources and with one another have offered opportunities for social change, with reporters connecting disparate social groups and individuals through their stories (Bro, 2010). However, these structures have tended toward conventionality, with officials dominating source lists (Cook, 2005). Flexible, online networks challenge the dominance and stability of these traditional networks, as non-journalists, from everyday citizens to elite experts to corporate PR wings, are easily able to report, opinionate, and publish.

News users are increasingly active and engaged in online news networks (Bruns, 2008). According to a 2010 Pew survey (Pew Internet and American Life Project, 2010), three-quarters of online news consumers in the United States said they received news from social networking sites (e.g., Facebook), and nearly a quarter of social networking site users said they followed news organizations or journalists on these sites. Around 37 percent of Internet users said they had "contributed to the creation of news, commentary about it, or dissemination of news" in some fashion, mostly through commenting or through linking via social media. Just less than 10 percent said they had generated original news or opinion content. Engagement in networks enables further involvement: The most frequent and participatory online news users are 300 percent more likely than the average online news consumer to visit blogs.

Journalists themselves say they tend to follow local bloggers, discussion comments, and online traffic statistics, and they frequently communicate what they learn in news meetings (Lowrey & Mackay, 2008; Lowrey & Woo, 2010). Journalists also report they are using blogs and social networking sites for source information (Lariscy, Avery, Sweetser, & Howes, 2009; Lowrey & Mackay, 2008). Efforts to include non-journalists in reporting and to include user-generated content through social networking are mounting, though some journalists voice concern that user-generated content threatens professional norms and practices (Singer, 2010). Recent research also shows that PR practitioners are becoming avid users of social media (Curtis et al., 2010), and bloggers predict that their use of PR news release information via social media will grow (Steyn, Salehi-Sangari, Pitt, Parent, & Berthond, 2010).

Enthusiasts for networked online journalism say it will encourage diversity of viewpoints, giving voice to marginalized groups. And they see networked forms—online crowdsourcing and crowdfunding efforts, social media groups and communities, hybrid partnerships between news organizations and citizen sites—as offering a vast, rich knowledge environment that even the world's largest news organizations could not hope to generate through only their own resources (Gillmor, 2004).

Dysfunctions of Networks

Networks introduce problems as well, most notably complexity and confusion, fragmentation, and the potential for diminished legitimacy and credibility. According to a 2010 survey of U.S. audiences (Pew Internet and American Life Project, 2010), 70 percent said they find today's vast, diverse array of media sources to be "overwhelming." This echoes findings from experiments on cognitive effects of new digital media formats—these can cause cognitive overload (Moreno, 2004), or lead to a selective scanning of information (Eveland &

Dunwoody, 2002), both of which may limit learning. The vast interconnectedness of the online networked environment challenges the news/information hierarchy. News users need a way to engage with networks that brings some order to the bewildering multiplicity and flatness.

A number of efforts to encourage online news users to initiate and participate in news reporting—for example, crowdsourcing and pro-am efforts—have shown promise but have proved tough to manage. These participatory efforts, in which journalists are linked with a broad array of non-journalists, have tended to fall apart from a lack of centralized control and from volunteers' waning enthusiasm for reporting and writing traditional news stories (Potts, 2007; Rosen, 2007). Where they have managed to sustain crowd interest and activity, they have done so by widening the definition of news content to include personal ruminations, creative works, and blog commentary (what Becker would call "enlarging the vocabulary"). A possible solution is for professional journalists to assert greater authority in these efforts (Potts, 2007; Rosen, 2007), but crowdsourcing advocates have balked at top-down approaches in projects that are supposed to encourage democratic participation (e.g., Muthukumaraswamy, 2010).

If order does not come from journalists, others may fill the vacuum. Political, corporate, and governmental source organizations seem happy to wade into the murkiness and assert truth claims (Curtis et al., 2010; Rosenwald, 2010). Past studies of democratically structured organizations tell us something about the role of power in these efforts (Tolbert & Hiatt, 2009). In his classic study of the Tennessee Valley Authority in the 1930s, Selznick (1966) found that efforts to foster constituents' democratic participation paved the way for co-optation by wealthy farmers. Recently, we see many examples of commercial interests doing an end-run around mainstream journalism: Bloggers are paid for commercial products they review (Rosenwald, 2010), and corporations, political groups, and government agencies are disseminating messages directly through social media, and creating pseudo-news events in hopes that video from them will go viral.

Online networks also tend to encourage the formation of subcommunities (Granovetter, 1973)—these are not necessarily dysfunctional, but they may have troubling consequences. Recent research by sociologist Robert Putnam (2007) reveals a tendency toward social splintering in times of uncertainty. Communities tend to run to the familiar, to turn in on themselves—what he calls "turtling." Yet he says this fragmentation may be overcome through "new, cross-cutting forms of social solidarity and more encompassing identities" (p. 137).

This fragmentation is evident in the unruly, even abusive nature of online discussion, with its polarizing "jerk swarms" (Palser, 2006) and "barroom brawls," discouraging thoughtful discussion (Perez-Pena, 2010). There is anecdotal evidence that such comments may drive away already hesitant news sources who are shocked to find readers' angry comments flaming them at the ends of stories (Davenport, 2010). Journalists still hesitate to incorporate user-generated content in the core product (Domingo, 2008) for fear that content deemed biased, offensive, and unprofessional will erode credibility or bring lawsuits (Singer, 2010).

Despite concerns, news organizations are intensifying their engagement with social networks and increasing their scrutiny of marketing data. Editors regularly meet with advertising/marketing personnel (Gade, 2008; Lowrey & Woo, 2010), and journalists avidly track website traffic data to learn about audience behavior (Farhi, 2010; Lowrey & Woo, 2010; MacGregor, 2007). According to a recent survey study of U.S. newspaper editors, just over 60 percent said they monitored statistical feedback from online audiences on a daily basis, nearly 50 percent said they monitored discussion forums daily, and around 55 percent said they discussed findings from traffic data at least "often" in news meetings (Lowrey & Woo, 2010). News managers are chasing readers via social media, pursuing ad revenue on mobile devices and iPhone apps, and pursuing "hybrid" approaches that tap non-journalism sources of revenue. These responses to uncertainty are understandable, given that managers are likely to monitor their environments during uncertain times in order to make resource flow more predictable (Beam, 1996). However, it's not clear what impact this intense marketing orientation will have on long-earned legitimacy, brand, and credibility. Devoting substantial resources to marketing, chasing social media users (via digital networks and geopositioning technology), and pursuing non-news products and services might pay financial dividends in the short term, though whether or not they add much economic value is questionable (Picard, 2009). However, moving such activity to the core puts news organizations at the level of everyone else pursuing these strategies, inviting long-term liabilities that face any new organization in a budding market or industry (Aldrich & Ruef, 2007; Baum, 2001).

Strong institutionalism has its dysfunctions, as described earlier—mindless mimicry and buffering from external realities are among them. However, we now face a scattering centrifugal tendency, leading to splintering, confusion, eroded legitimacy, and potential abuse by the powerful in a field with weak journalistic control. It's not even clear that "liquid," egalitarian network structures offer media workers greater freedom. Though institutional rules and routines certainly constrain, uncertain indeterminacy can lead to a kind of paralysis. Emile Durkheim (1961 [1925]) calls this "drowning in a dissolving sense of limitlessness" (p. 40). A similar sentiment may be found in the words of a TV screen writer: "Setting limits increases creativity . . . if you take a creative person and give him [sic] nothing to fight against, nothing to bump up against, . . . he gets flabby" (Ettema, 1982, p. 104). And so journalists and audiences both confront paralyzing bewilderment, as the rules and conventions relied on to produce legitimized journalism within our "news world" are being fundamentally questioned.

Enduring Institutions?

Advocates for new participatory, egalitarian forms of journalism say fleeting individual connections, experimentation, and temporary agreements are the order of the day (Castells, 2000; Deuze, 2007; Gillmor, 2004). Others argue that formal organizational and institutional forms and routines will persist (Perrow, 1986) and will continue to evolve (e.g., Aldrich & Ruef, 2007; Carroll & Hannan, 1995). A 2010 Pew study (Pew Internet and American Life Project, 2010) found that engaged online news readers typically turn to only a handful of sources in their daily reading: "While people are hunting for what they are interested in, they are not hunting everywhere. They are hunting among a landscape of sources they know and are familiar with." This suggests attempts to create boundaries in the face of limitlessness, and some need for legitimacy and a shared logic about media forms and practices in order to make sense of complex environments.

Study of collectivist social movement organizations has shown that intentionally flat organizational structures, intended for open democratic participation, often shift toward centralized, hierarchical structures (e.g., Clemens & Minkoff, 2004). Pickard (2006) and Eliasoph (1997) reached similar conclusions in their research on democratically structured alternative news media: Organizational processes became unwieldy, and members begin to centralize and adopt rules and routines. More recently, several high-profile crowdsourcing efforts have struggled from the burden of complex coordination and weak administration (Adams, 2008; Potts, 2007; Rosen, 2007). It is not clear that these idealistic participatory structures can work without some degree of hierarchy and centralization.

There are a number of explanations for this tendency to drift toward centralized structures, one of which is Robert Michels' (1962 [1911]) iron law of oligarchy. Michels was a pupil of Weber, and traces of Weber's ideas about the development of bureaucracy are found in his work. According to Michels, organizational growth leads to greater complexity and a split between the interests and vision of managers and staff. Problems of internal coordination mount, and bureaucratic mechanisms are adopted to bring control. Eventually a few long-time leaders accrue internal control, as only they have the knowledge and expertise to negotiate the organization's increasing complexity. Organizations gain external clout and connections, and leaders begin to value connections with their institutional environment more than they value the organization's initial goals, a phenomenon scholars later labeled "goal displacement" (Tolbert & Hiatt, 2009).

The author's research on the structure of citizen news blogs lends some support to these predictions (Lowrey, Parrott, & Meade, 2011). Under certain conditions, these citizen blogs—traditionally known for their independence and irreverence toward mainstream media—develop organizational form, including evidence of formalized rules and policies, division of labor, pursuit of revenue, and increased formality in postings. In the study, over half of a sample of 151 blogs (A-list or near A-list blogs) offered terms of service and legal terms, and nearly 70 percent gave formal instructions on how to register. Around 30 percent had staff with designated roles. Further, this tightening of organizational structure and pursuit of advertising correlated with a tendency by bloggers to be more balanced, more fact based, less opinionated, and more formal in their writing—evidence of goal displacement, and of pursuit of external legitimacy. Similarly, a recent study of U.S. citizen news sites found that more than half were pursuing advertising (Project for Excellence in Journalism, 2010b), suggesting a move toward institutional connections in this new genre.

Social network theory and theory on organizational ecology also offer some explanation for flat structures moving toward hierarchy. "Nodes" (network connecting points) that have longevity will attract more and more traffic. This happens partly because it is efficient: The well-connected offer more connections than the poorly connected. Dense interconnectedness goes hand in hand with level of incoming resources, and so the rich get richer (Tremayne, Zheng, Lee, & Jeong, 2006). Also, those experienced at making connections in networks become better at it, gain a reputation, and attract links (Powell et al., 1996), an idea consistent with Michels' observation that external connections bring clout. Again, we see public legitimacy at issue.

This process is similar to the evolution of organizations across long periods of time, according to organizational ecology research. Organizations gain resources and legitimacy over time, and other organizations seek connections with such organizations. Older organizations have lower failure rates than younger organizations, which tend to have few and weaker connections and lower levels of capital and legitimacy (Baum, 2001; Carroll & Hannan, 1995).

Repositioning for Legitimacy

This chapter's argument has taken a few twists and turns, and so it would help to chart the course so far. The chapter has discussed journalism's connections and accord with its cultural, social, political, and economic environments, and journalism's traditional institutional status and legitimacy. The advent of networked, participatory communication structures has undermined these connections and legitimacy. The field is now more leveled, giving voice to a diverse array of non-journalists, while undermining journalists' control over work and making things more complex and uncertain for audiences and journalists. The field is also more fragmented, and the media logic less clear, and previously taken-for-granted routines and conventions—the stuff of cognitive legitimacy—are being challenged. However, it appears journalists and audiences feel a need to wring some order from confusion and uncertainty. It may be that participatory, flat, media structures will begin to centralize and formalize, and seek greater legitimacy.

But how to gain and maintain legitimacy in this topsy-turvy environment? Journalism must reposition itself so it is grounded in today's fluid, networked environment, while also establishing a widely understood "media logic" that signals legitimacy. Some have called for news organizations to make wholesale change by, for example, abandoning print—to "burn the boats . . . and commit" as Netscape inventor Marc Andressen has urged (Mutter, 2010). Maybe, but disruption of long-earned relationships and competencies is a leading indicator of organizational decline. Starting afresh in new fields and taking on new tasks and roles risks the liability of newness (Baum, 2001; Tolbert & Hall, 2009). This is not an argument against innovation. The industry and profession is finally engaged in a desperately needed reassessment of taken-for-granted practices, forms, and relationships, which have too often obscured journalism's deeper purposes, and which now may be turning off audiences. Rather this is an argument against blindly throwing over core competencies and connections. Though too much stability and control can suffocate creativity and autonomy, too much change and too little stability can confuse and paralyze. Although routines and conventions can obstruct needed change and limit diversity of viewpoints, they can also discourage careless and possibly destructive adaptation to mere "noise" in the environment. It makes sense for news organizations and journalists to reposition somewhere between order and disorder, between exploration and exploitation (March, 1991).

A number of macro-level theoretical perspectives focus on ways professional entities reposition themselves to secure legitimacy, control, and resources, and on factors that shape repositioning. Three such approaches—the systems of professions approach, Pierre Bourdieu's field theory, and neo-institutionalist approaches—are briefly sketched here at the chapter's end. They hold promise for framing future research on repositioning institutions, occupations, and organizations within shifting environments.

The systems of professions approach focuses on control over professional work, and for journalists this means primarily the work of providing news and information for publics. "Jurisdictional claims" (Abbott, 1988, p. 2), or the links of control between occupations and expert tasks, are reshaped and sometimes broken by both "objective" and "subjective" qualities of the professional process. Objective qualities include economic, technological, legal, political, and cultural changes, and threats from rival occupational groups, all of which journalism has experienced. In the face of objective challenges, occupational members may adjust internal "subjective qualities" to maintain jurisdiction, including definitions of client needs, professional goals, and criteria for solving problems (Abbott, 1988; Anderson & Lowrey, 2007; Dooley, 1999; Zetka, 2001). The success of a jurisdictional claim enhances legitimacy, and vice versa, and success comes to occupations with a knowledge base that is abstract enough to aid repositioning.

Field theorists also see a landscape within which occupations and other social collectives jockey for control. Individuals within an occupation have agency, but their efforts are structured within "fields," which are arenas of struggle within which individuals and organizations may acquire economic and cultural capital. In journalism, economic capital derives largely from ratings and ad revenue, and cultural capital relates to practices and forms that enhance reputation—journalism awards, for example (Bourdieu, 2005). Individuals and organizations seek to "valorize" these forms of capital to improve their position within various fields. Too much economic capital at the expense of cultural capital can erode cultural standing, whereas the opposite may result in a lack of tangible resources. Individuals and organizations with authority in a field are those who can "successfully convert one form into the other" (Benson & Neveu, 2005, p. 4), thereby gaining networks of clients and resources, as well as legitimacy (Benson & Neveu, 2005; Bourdieu, 2005).

New institutionalism shares characteristics of systems and field theory. Again, we have a shifting landscape within which individuals and organizations may position themselves to gain economic capital as well as legitimacy through accord with norms of the wider culture. Some organizations are institutional in nature, placing high emphasis on accord with wider institutional values, norms, and expectations. They are likely to mimic trends adopted by other organizations, adopting and discarding them with little actual evaluation, and they may buffer their operations and their legitimized image from the uncertain caprice of external economic realities (DiMaggio & Powell, 1991; Meyer & Rowan, 1977).

All three approaches suggest that journalism, as an occupation, institution, or organization, will try to reposition itself relative to the changing social and economic fields it inhabits in order to secure legitimacy. Journalists may need to "enlarge their vocabulary," as Howie Becker (1982, p. 303) put it, by embracing some new practices and forms as legitimate, while maintaining legitimacy and shared understandings in their relationships with other organizations and institutions. This requires looking beyond routines, tapping into the profession's abstract knowledge base, and adjusting "subjective qualities" of the profession, as Abbott (1988) suggests.

What new subjective qualities might journalism embrace? How can journalism gain capital deriving from network traffic, while holding on to core competencies and professional mission, and gaining legitimized "cultural capital"? A good starting point may be the widely perceived need for cohesiveness and sense-making. The discussion in this chapter suggests that some degree of both is needed, given the complexity and lack of hierarchy in the networked environment. Hierarchy of meaning will likely come in some form, and so it would seem that professional journalism and the news industry should play a role in developing it, at both institutional and symbolic levels. Institutional cohesiveness provides the legitimacy needed to seek some order in a chaotic, splintered digital world. Jay Rosen (2007) concluded from his Project Zero crowdsourcing experiment that participatory news projects are more likely to succeed if they possess the cohesiveness of "[e]xisting communities, people in already-formed networks, [which are] strong on coordination and mobilization." Similarly, Becker (1982) says that sustained change requires "capturing existing cooperative networks or developing new ones" (p. 301). So we can see the need for some structure and order, grounded in public legitimacy.

However, the fact that these efforts tend to work best in specialized, tight-knit communities suggests the potential for fragmentation and polarization across society. This reminds us of Putnam's (2007) call for "cross-cutting forms of social solidarity" across "turtling" discrete groups. Here is where journalism must "enlarge its vocabulary" and reposition itself into a new role—a role of fostering intelligent interaction, sense-making, and clarity across disparate, networked, and specialized individuals and groups. Journalists must look for patterns and themes, suggesting thought-provoking questions, urging cohesiveness on scattered fragments of discussion, and discouraging group-think complacency. This may be a hybrid process, involving both news staff and those outside news organizations. And it is important that this sense-making role be grounded in journalists' traditional core roles as diligent, autonomous watchdogs, verifiers of public information, and seekers of diverse viewpoints and broad truths.

By rethinking the "subjective elements" of their profession, journalists may embrace the flat, pluralistic communication structures of social media while maintaining journalistic core competencies, norms, values, and connections. Journalists may strengthen their ability to work toward accounts of public life that are more widely reflective and meaningful, while continuing to check facts, check the powerful, and facilitate public discussion. They may listen widely but also lead, encouraging discussion and helping to draw connections across specialized, participatory communities, wringing sense from uncertainty and complexity. In this way, journalism maintains institutional legitimacy even as it interacts—with a humble indispensability—among the myriad nodes in the wider network.

Thought Questions: Contemplating Change

This chapter has discussed journalism's traditional institutional legitimacy and relationships and the ways networked, participatory media forms and practices are challenging these. The field is now more egalitarian but also more complex for journalists, news organizations, and non-journalists/audiences. The industry and its markets are splintered, and it is not clear what the pervasive media logic should be. However, it appears journalists and audiences desire sense-making in this fragmented environment.

1. This chapter argues that journalism must maintain some core competencies and relationships but still adjust to change. Do you think it is possible and/or beneficial for journalists to straddle tradition and change? Why or why not?

2. This chapter proposes that flat, fluid networked communication structures will bend toward hierarchy—that some entity *must* have greater power and control. Do you agree? Why or why not, and what are the consequences for democratic society?

3. How important is it for journalists to embrace a mission of "sense-making" as a professional goal, in the context of other traditional journalistic goals?

References

Abbott, A. (1988). *The system of professions: An essay on the division of expert labor.* Chicago: University of Chicago Press.

Adams, R. (2008, June 4). Big daily's "hyperlocal" flop: Loudounextra.com fails to give lift to Washington Post. *The Washington Post,* p. B1.

Aldrich, H. E., & Ruef, M. (2007). *Organizations evolving.* Los Angeles: Sage.

Altheide, D. L., & Snow, R. P. (1979). *Media logic.* Beverly Hills, CA: Sage.

American Society of Newspaper Editors. (1999). *Examining our credibility: Perspectives of the public and the press.* Retrieved November 23, 2010, from http://204.8.120.192/index.cfm?id=2632

Anderson, W. A., & Lowrey, W. (2007). What factors influence control over work in the journalism/public relations dynamic? An application of theory from the sociology of occupations. *Mass Communication and Society, 10,* 385–402.

Baum, J. A. C. (2001). Organizational ecology. In S. Clegg, C. Hardy, & W. R. Nord (Eds.), *Handbook of organization studies* (pp. 77–114). London: Sage.

Beaupre, L. K. (1991). Rating the performance of newsroom professionals. *Newspaper Research Journal, 12*(2), 22–27.

Beam, R. (1996). How perceived environmental uncertainty influences marketing orientation of U.S. daily newspapers. *Journalism & Mass Communication Quarterly, 73,* 285–303.

Becker, H. (1982). *Art worlds.* Berkeley: University of California Press.

Bennett W. L. (1990). Toward a theory of press-state relations in the United States. *Journal of Communication, 40,* 103–125.

Bennett, W. L. (2005). *News: The politics of illusion.* New York: Pearson.

Benson, R., & Neveu, E. (2005). Introduction: Field theory as a work in progress. In R. Benson & E. Neveu (Eds.), *Bourdieu and the journalistic field* (pp. 1–25). Cambridge, UK: Polity Press.

Boczkowski, P. J. (2009). Materiality and mimicry in the journalism field. In B. Zelizer (Ed.), *The changing faces of journalism: Tabloidization, technology and truthiness* (pp. 56–67). London: Routledge.

Bourdieu, P. (2005). The political field, the social science field and the journalistic field. In R. Benson & E. Neveu (Eds.), *Bourdieu and the journalistic field* (pp. 29–47). Cambridge, UK: Cambridge University Press.

Bro, P. (2010). When newsmen use networks. *Journalism Practice, 4,* 17–32.

Bruns, A. (2008). The active audience: Transforming journalism from gatekeeping to gatewatching. In C. Paterson & D. Domingo (Eds.), *Making online news: The ethnography of new media production* (pp. 171–184). New York: Peter Lang.

Carroll, G. R., & Hannan, M. T. (1995). *Organizations in industry: Strategies, structure and selection*. New York: Oxford University Press.

Castells, M. (2000). *The rise of the networked society* (2nd ed.). Oxford: Blackwell.

Chyi, H. I. (2009). Information surplus in the digital age: Impact and implications. In Z. Papacharissi (Ed.), *Journalism and citizenship: New agendas in communication* (pp. 91–107). New York: Routledge.

Clemens, E. S., & Minkoff, D. C. (2004). Beyond the iron law: Rethinking the place of organizations in social movement research. In D. A. Snow, S. A. Soule, & H. Kriesi (Eds.), *The Blackwell companion to social movements* (pp. 155–170). Maldwell, MA: Blackwell.

Cohen, W. M., & Levinthal, D. A. (1990). Absorptive capacity: A new perspective on learning and innovation. *Administrative Science Quarterly, 35*, 128–152.

Cook, T. (2005). *Governing the news: The news media as political institution*. Chicago: University of Chicago Press.

Curran, J. (Ed.). (2000). *Media organizations in society*. Oxford: Oxford University Press.

Curtis, L., Edwards, C., Fraser, K. L., Gudelsky, S., Holmquist, J., Thornton, K., & Sweetser, K. D. (2010). Adoption of social media for public relations by nonprofit organizations. *Public Relations Review, 36*, 90–92.

Davenport, C. (2010, March 4). Blowback: Do comments scare off sources? *The Washington Post*. Retrieved November 23, 2010, from http://tinyurl.com/y8twbue

Deuze, M. (2005). What is journalism? Professional identity and ideology of journalists reconsidered. *Journalism; Theory, Practice and Criticism, 6*, 442–464.

Deuze, M. (2007). *MediaWork*. Cambridge, UK: Polity Press.

DiMaggio, P. J., & Powell, W. W. (1983). The iron cage revisited: Institutional isomorphism and collective rationality in organizational fields. *American Sociological Review, 48*, 147–160.

DiMaggio, P. J., & Powell, W. W. (1991). Introduction. In DiMaggio, P. J. & Powell, W. W. (Eds.), *The new institutionalism in organizational analysis* (pp. 1–40). Chicago: University of Chicago Press.

Dimmick, J., & Coit, P. (1982). Levels of analysis in mass media decision-making. *Communication Research, 9*, 3–32.

Domingo, D. (2008). Interactivity in the daily routines of online newsrooms: Dealing with an uncomfortable myth. *Journal of Computer-Mediated Communication, 13*(3), 680–704.

Dooley, P. L. (1999). Journalistic occupational development and discourses of power. In D. Demers and K. Viswanath (Eds.), *Mass media, social control and social change* (pp. 333–358). Ames: Iowa State University Press.

Dunwoody, S. (1997). Science writers at work. In D. Berkowitz (Ed.), *Social meanings of news* (pp. 155–167). Thousand Oaks, CA: Sage.

Durkheim, E. (1961 [1925]). *Moral education: A study in the theory and application of the sociology of education* (Everett K. Wilson, Ed.). New York: Free Press of Glencoe.

Eliasoph, N. (1997). Routines and the making of oppositional news. In D. Berkowitz (Ed.), *Social meaning of news* (pp. 230–254). London: Sage.

Ettema, J. S. (1982). The organizational context of creativity: A case study from public television. In J. S. Ettema & D. C. Whitney (Eds.), *Individuals in mass media organizations: Creativity and constraint* (pp. 91–106). Beverly Hills, CA: Sage.

Eveland, W. P., & Dunwoody, S. (2002). An investigation of elaboration and selective scanning as mediators of learning from the Web versus print. *Journal of Broadcasting & Electronic Media, 46*, 34–53.

Farhi, P. (2010, Fall). Traffic problems. *American Journalism Review, 32*, 46–51.

Gade, P. (2004). Newspapers and organizational development: Management and journalist perceptions of newsroom cultural change. *Journalism and Communication Monographs, 6*, 3–55.

Gade, P. (2008). Journalism guardians in a time of great change: Newspaper editors' perceived influence in integrated news organizations. *Journalism & Mass Communication Quarterly, 85*, 371–392.

Gans, H. J. (1979). *Deciding what's news*. New York: Pantheon Books.

Garcia, E. P. (2008). Print and online newsrooms in Argentinian media: Autonomy and professional identity. In C. Paterson & D. Domingo (Eds.), *Making online news: The ethnography of new media production* (pp. 61–76). New York: Peter Lang.

Gillmor, D. (2004). *We the media: Grassroots journalism by the people, for the people*. Cambridge, MA: O'Reilly.

Granovetter, M. S. (1973). The strength of weak ties. *American Journal of Sociology, 78*, 1360–1380.

Hindman, D., & Wiegand, K. (2008). The Big Three's prime time decline: A social and technological context. *Journal of Broadcasting and Electronic Media, 52*, 119–135.

Jung, J., & Chan-Olmsted, S. (2005). Impacts of media companies' dual diversification on financial performance. *Journal of Media Economics, 18*, 183–202.

Kaplan, R. L. (2006). The news about new institutionalism: Journalism's ethic of objectivity and its political origins. *Political Communication, 23*, 173–185.

Lariscy, R. W., Avery, E. J. Sweetser, K. D., & Howes, P. (2009). An examination of the role of online social media in journalists' source mix. *Public Relations Review, 35*, 314–316.

Laitila, T. (1995). Journalistic codes of ethics in Europe. *European Journal of Communication, 10*, 527–544.

Lowrey, W. (2005). Commitment to newspaper–TV partnering: A test of the impact of institutional isomorphism. *Journalism & Mass Communication Quarterly, 82*, 495–514.

Lowrey, W., & Mackay, J. (2008). Journalism and blogging: A test of a model of occupational competition. *Journalism Practice, 2*, 64–81.

Lowrey, W., Parrott, S., & Meade, T. (2011). When blogs become organizations. *Journalism: Theory, Practice and Criticism, 11*, 1–17.

Lowrey, W., & Woo, C. W. (2010). The news organization in uncertain times: Business or institution? *Journalism & Mass Communication Quarterly, 87*, 41–61.

Lundby, K. (2009). Introduction: Mediatization as key. In K. Lundby (Ed.), *Mediatization: Concept, changes, consequences* (pp. 1–18). New York: Peter Lang.

MacGregor, P. (2007). Tracking the online audience: Metric data start a subtle revolution. *Journalism Studies, 8*, 280–298.

March, J. G. (1991). Exploration and exploitation in organizational learning. *Organization Science, 2*, 71–87.

McQuail, D. (2010). *McQuail's mass communication theory* (6th ed.). London: Sage.

Meyer, P. (2004). *The vanishing newspaper*. Columbia, MO: University of Missouri Press.

Meyer, J., & Rowan, B. (1977). Institutionalized organizations: Formal structure as myth and ceremony. *American Journal of Sociology, 83*, 340–363.

Michels, R. (1962 [1911]). *Political parties: A sociological study of the oligarchical tendencies of modern democracy*. New York: Collier Books.

Muthukumaraswamy, K. (2010). When the media meet crowds of wisdom. *Journalism Practice, 4*, 48–65.

Mutter, A. (2010, March 11). Andreessen's not-so-hot idea for publishers. Reflections of a newsosaur. Retrieved November 25, 2010, from http://newsosaur.blogspot.com/search?q=netscape

Moreno, R. (2004). Decreasing cognitive load in novice students: Effects of explanatory versus corrective feedback in discovery-based multimedia. *Instructional Science, 32*, 99–113.

Palser, B. (2006, April/May). Coping with jerk swarms. *American Journalism Review, 28*, 70.

Patterson, T., & Seib, P. (2005). Informing the public. In G. Overholser & K. H. Jamieson (Eds.), *The press* (pp. 189–202). Oxford, UK: Oxford University Press.

Perez-Pena, R. (2010, April 11). News sites rethink anonymous online comments. *The New York Times*. Retrieved April 18, 2010, from http://tinyurl.com/yah5jde

Perrow, C. (1986). *Complex organizations: A critical essay*. New York: McGraw-Hill.

Peterson, R. A., & Anand, N. (2004). The production of culture perspective. *Annual Review of Sociology, 30*, 311–334.

Pew Internet and American Life Project. (2010, March 1). *The new news landscape: Rise of the internet*. Retrieved November 23, 2010, from http://tinyurl.com/ycje3n5

Pew Research Center for the People and the Press. (2002, August 4). *News media's improved image proves short-lived*. Retrieved November, 23, 2010, from http://tinyurl.com/2fhryh9

Pew Research Center for the People and the Press. (2009, September 13). *Press accuracy rating hits two decade low: Public evaluations of the news media: 1985–2009*. Retrieved November 23, 2010, from http://people-press.org/report/543/

Phillips, N., Lawrence, T. B., & Hardy, C. (2000). Inter-organizational collaboration and the dynamics of institutional fields. *Journal of Management Studies, 37*, 23–43.

Picard, R. (2009, May 19). Why journalists deserve low pay. *Christian Science Monitor*. Retrieved November 23, 2010, from http://www.csmonitor.com/2009/0519/p09s02-coop.html

Pickard, V. W. (2006). United yet autonomous: Indymedia and the struggle to sustain a radical democratic network. *Media Culture & Society, 28*, 315–336.

Pollock, J. (2007). *Tilted mirrors: Media alignment with political and social change – a community structure approach*. Cresskill, NJ: Hampton Press.

Potts, M. (2007, July 15). Backfence: Lessons learned. *Recovering Journalist*. Retrieved November, 23, 2010, from http://tinyurl.com/25u6on

Powell, W. W., Koput, K., & Smith-Doerr, L. (1996). Interorganizational collaboration and the locus of innovation: Networks of learning in biotechnology. *Administrative Science Quarterly, 42*, 116–145.

Project for Excellence in Journalism. (2010a). *Overview: The state of the news media 2010*. Retrieved July 20, 2010, from http://www.stateofthemedia.org/2010/overview_intro.php

Project for Excellence in Journalism. (2010b). *PEJ report on online community journalism sites—phase II*. Retrieved November 25, 2010, from http://tinyurl.com/3xshu3z

Putnam, R. (2007). E pluribus unum: Diversity and community in the twenty-first century: *Scandinavian Political Studies, 30*, 137–174.

Rosen, J. (2007, October 9). *What I learned from Assignment Zero*. PressThink. Retrieved August 9, 2010, from http://tinyurl.com/396jdv

Rosenwald, M. S. (2010, March 29). Reputations at stake, companies try to alter word of mouth online. *The Washington Post*. Retrieved November 25, 2010, from http://tinyurl.com/ylqyhwp

Russial, J. (2009). Growth of multimedia not extensive at newspapers. *Newspaper Research Journal, 30*(3), 58–74.

Ryan, J., & Peterson, R. A. (1982). The product image: The fate of creativity in country music songwriting. In J. S. Ettema & D. C. Whitney (Eds.), *Individuals in mass media organizations: Creativity and constraint* (pp. 11–32). Beverly Hills, CA: Sage.

Ryfe, D. M. (2006). Guest editor's introduction: New institutionalism and the news. *Political Communication, 23*, 135–144.

Schudson, M. (1978). *Discovering the news*. New York: Basic Books.

Schudson, M. (2002). The news media as political institutions. *Annual Review of Political Science, 5*, 249–269.

Scott, W. R. (2008). *Organizations: Rational, natural, and open systems* (5th ed.). Upper Saddle River, NJ: Prentice Hall.

Selznick, P. (1966). *TVA and the grass roots*. New York: Harper and Row.

Sheffer, M. L., & Schultz, B. (2009). Blogging from the management perspective: A follow-up study. *International Journal of Media Management, 11*, 9–17.

Shoemaker, P. J., & Vos, T. P. (2009). *Gatekeeping theory*. New York: Routledge.

Sigal, L. (1973). *Reporters and officials*. Lexington, MA: D. C. Heath.

Singer, J. B. (2010). Quality control: Perceived effects of user-generated content on newsroom norms, values and routines. *Journalism Practice, 4*, 127–142.

Steyn, P., Salehi-Sangari, E., Pitt, L., Parent, M., & Berthond, P. (2010). The Social Media Release as a public relations tool: Intentions to use among B2B bloggers. *Public Relations Review, 36*, 87–89.

Suchman, M. C. (1995). Managing legitimacy: Strategic and institutional approaches. *Academy of Management Review, 20*, 571–610.

Sumpter, R. (2000). Daily newspaper editors' audience construction routines: A case study. *Critical Studies in Mass Communication, 17*(3), 334–336.

Swan, J., & Scarbrough, H. (2005). The politics of networked innovation. *Human Relations, 58*, 913–943.

Tichenor, P. J., Donohue, G. A., & Olien, C. N. (1980). *Community conflict and the press*. Beverly Hills, CA: Sage.

Tolbert, P. S., & Hall, R. H. (2009). *Organizations: Structures, processes and outcomes* (10th ed.). Upper Saddle River, NJ: Pearson.

Tolbert, P. S., & Hiatt, S. R. (2009). On organizations and oligarchies: Michels in the twenty-first century. In P. S. Adler (Ed.), *The Oxford handbook of sociology and organization studies* (pp. 174–199). Oxford, UK: Oxford University Press.

Tremayne, M., Zheng, N., Lee, J. K., & Jeong, J. (2006). Issue publics on the web: Applying network theory to the war blogosphere. *Journal of Computer-Mediated Communication, 12*. Retrieved November 25, 2010, from http://jcmc.indiana.edu/vol12/issue1/tremayne.html

Tuchman, G. (1978). *Making the news: A study in the construction of reality*. New York: Free Press.

Wall, M. (2005). Blogs of war: Weblogs as news. *Journalism: Theory, Practice and Criticism, 6*, 153–172.

Weber, M. (1947). *The theory of social and economic organization* (A. M. Henderson & T. Parsons, Trans.). New York: Oxford University Press.

Zetka, J. R., Jr. (2001). Occupational divisions of labor and their technology politics: The case of surgical scopes and gastrointestinal medicine. *Social Forces, 79*, 1495–1520.

PART III

MARKETS, ORGANIZATIONS, AND PROFESSION

9

MARKET JOURNALISM

Stephen Lacy, Michigan State University, and Ardyth Broadrick Sohn, University of Nevada-Las Vegas

The term "market journalism" has taken on a variety of connotations during the past three decades. Some people define it as the pursuit of profits at the cost of quality journalism. This definition suggests that news organizations in markets will automatically produce entertainment-oriented information at the expense of serious news and that reacting to market conditions will force news organizations to integrate advertising and news departments to a greater degree (McManus, 1994, pp. 1–3). A slightly more benign definition argues that market journalism places the priority on profits but with a secondary concern for journalism. Both seem to carry an implicit assumption that markets, by definition, result in lower-quality journalism.

However, not all research has supported this assumption. Beam (2003) found that newspapers with strong market orientation continued to produce high levels of public affairs reporting and even produced more special reports and investigations than did the weak market-oriented newspapers. At the heart of the concerns about commercial journalism are questions about whether poor journalism is an inherent condition of markets, the result of failures in the market, or the result of some other factors that influence markets. Does the market, or do the players in the market, or both determine the relationship between profit and journalism? How has the growth of digital delivery affected this relationship? How is this growth affecting uncertainty in the market, and what are the risks that face news organizations in the markets?

To address these questions, the nature and processes of news media markets will be defined using economic theory about how markets operate and by discussing organizational goals and how they determine the strategies that news organizations pursue. Second, the role of uncertainty and risk in the markets needs to be examined. All firms face uncertainty and assume risks when they operate in a market. The degree of both affects the process and outcome of managers' decisions. Third, the impact on journalism markets of the increasing digital delivery of news requires discussion. Fourth, the implications of current trends for the future of news markets will be considered. Finally, the ongoing changes at the *Las Vegas Sun* will be examined at the end of the chapter to illustrate how these trends are affecting strategies at an award-winning news organization.

What Is the Nature of Uncertainty and Risk?

The terms "risk" and "uncertainty" are often used almost interchangeably, but this analysis of markets uses the distinction made by Sylvie, Wicks, Hollifield, Lacy, and Sohn (2008). Risk is the potential loss or gain from a decision, whereas uncertainty is the subjective probability of a decision resulting in the preferred outcome of a decision.

If a news organization hires six journalists to create an online investigative unit with the expressed goal of increasing Web visits, the organization's maximum risk equals the salary of the journalists and any potential cost from not using those journalists in other ways (opportunity costs). The subjective probability reflects the manager's perceived probability that the expected increase in Web visits will actually occur. The term "subjective probability" is used because all estimates of probability involve assumptions about future conditions. The future cannot be predicted with 100 percent accuracy, which results in a variable level of subjectivity with any prediction.

Why distinguish between uncertainty and risk? Although the two are correlated, the correlation is not perfect. Uncertainty reflects the influence that managers have over an outcome. A news organization could act to gain revenue in ways that have high uncertainty with little risk (e.g., adding a new blog on local government), or in ways that have low uncertainty and high risk (e.g., cutting newsroom staff to reduce cost, which might lower content quality). Risk and uncertainty can affect organizational strategy in different ways.

Markets

The Nature of News Markets

At its simplest level, a market involves the exchange between a seller and a buyer. With media consumers, this exchange involves the seller providing content in exchange for the buyer's money, potential attention to advertising, or both. This content is available within a geographic market area, which is determined by the geographic orientation of the content and the nature of the distribution system. In addition to the geographic market, media content exists in a product market, where media products compete for consumers' time and money. If a significant number of consumers consider two news products to be substitutes, they exist in the same product market.

The nature of the content (product market) in relation to the geographic market determines who demands the media product. In the United States, most newspapers produce and emphasize news and information content that concerns a limited geographic area—town, county, or metro area. The availability of the paper version of a newspaper is usually limited to those local areas that receive news coverage, even though the website is available to the entire world. The international availability of news through the Internet does not alter the demand to a great degree because the unique content in the news products usually concerns local areas and issues. Most visitors to the news site live in the geographic area that the newspaper covers. If one wants to know about events in Greenville, MI, one reads the *Greenville News*, but only a few people outside of the Greenville area read the *News'* website.

Digital distribution shapes news products because it affects a newspaper's ability to create and deliver the content. Newspapers have traditionally been bundles of news and information often divided into discrete sections. Readers received a variety of news from various geographic areas—sports from close to home and around the world, local and international entertainment information, features, advice, opinion, and many other topics. This bundling increased the likelihood that the paper would have something to please multiple people in a household. Digital delivery has unbundled news and information. Specialty websites allow people who want to know about Big Ten basketball to do so without subscribing to the rest of the news and information in the newspaper bundle. For example, many newspaper readers have read the Associated Press stories online the day before they appear in the printed newspaper. The unbundling has increased the uncertainty that a print newspaper can adequately serve the information needs and wants of all the people in a household.

Some newspaper organizations have reacted by introducing specialty print and Web products. These aim to attract smaller segments of the market with more targeted news and information. This multiple product line is a way of decreasing uncertainty and spreading the risk across these products.

Digitizing news and distributing it by Internet and wireless has affected the very nature of newspaper news products. Digital distribution of news products does four things better than traditional print distribution. It increases the speed of delivery. With the advent of radio, newspapers fell behind in the breaking news business. Digital delivery levels the playing field for newspapers and broadcast and cable news with regard to speed of delivery. Second, digital distribution allows for a depth of information and news at a fraction of the cost of print production and distribution. Electrons are much cheaper than ink and paper, and storage of digital information for future access is easier and less expensive. Third, digital creation and distribution allows newspapers to produce multimedia packages of information. This presents an entirely new way of conveying the stories that newspapers cover. Fourth, digital distribution allows interactivity. One of the ways to reduce uncertainty with regard to customers is to find out what they need and want. Interactivity is a way of doing this, and it allows citizens to participate more in the exchange of information and opinion about community issues.

Digital distribution and production also affect barriers to entry, as illustrated by the thousands of commercial and citizen journalism websites that have appeared on the Web. It costs very little to create a site, although generating independent, factual journalism is not cheap. However, as more alternative websites develop, readers are likely to stop reading newspapers and visiting these sites. The result is more management uncertainty about the marketplace.

Within the structure of a market, a news manager must develop a strategy to meet the demand of consumers. Such a strategy starts with an assumption about what the consumers want from the news organization. Understanding consumer demand for news is a highly uncertain process because the meaning of news is a function of the individual's perception as well as the symbols used in the content. As a market becomes more diverse, understanding demand becomes more difficult. Lacy (1993) called media markets "fuzzy" because of the uncertainty caused by complex and increasingly diversifying demand.

The Nature of Advertising Markets

News organizations exist as joint or dual products (Lacy & Simon, 1993; Picard, 1989) because they produce news and information content for consumers and they juxtapose advertising with this content to serve advertisers. Businesses pay for the advertising space because they assume at least some of the consumers will pay attention to their ads.

Consumers eagerly seek some advertising (e.g., price-reducing coupons), but in other situations consumers find the advertising a nuisance. In some markets, consumers pay money for news and information content, such as subscriptions for most daily newspapers, but in other cases, people do not pay money for content (e.g., free weeklies and local TV news programming).

Because the production of news products serves two economic markets and provides an important societal function, scholars and critics are concerned about the impact of the advertising market on the news and information. These concerns reflect the possibility that advertisers might directly influence the news, or that news managers will self-censor to avoid making advertisers angry enough that they will withdraw their advertising (McManus, 1994). The fact that the vast majority of newspaper revenues comes from the advertising market exacerbates the potential problem.

All market demand is uncertain because news organizations change their products on a regular basis and because demand itself shifts over time with the introduction of new products and media. However, having to evaluate demand in two markets and the relationship between demand in those two markets also increases the overall uncertainty about news decisions. Managers may be fairly sure that consumers want a story about how to buy automobiles more cheaply, but such a story would increase the uncertainty of whether a given automobile dealership would want to buy advertising in that newspaper. Car dealers may object to the newspaper helping car buyers to bargain for a lower price. This sort of dilemma illustrates the potential conflict between customers in the dual markets.

Competition

Two news products compete if a consumer of one will stop reading or watching it to read or watch the other. This competition affects news outlets when managers decide that a large number of consumers will substitute one or more news products for their similar product. However, competition does not have to be a one-for-one substitution because many people have a media mix that involves several media outlets to fulfill their information needs. These people attend to multiple media products and that mix can vary from person to person and across time and still provide the same level of utility (Lacy, 2000). Indirect substitution exists when a person stops using one news product (e.g., a newspaper) and replaces it with two or more other information sources (e.g., the National Public Radio station and a local television station) in his or her media mix.

Types of market structures for news vary. Small cities with news outlets covering local events typically qualify as monopolies (one-firm markets) or oligopolies (a small number of firms in a geographic market). Increasingly, larger cities fall within a market structure called monopolistic competition (Chamberlin, 1962), in which news products function as imperfect substitutes. Niche websites, such as sports and political blogs, have developed to challenge the market influence held by traditional media outlets. These niche sites compete for the attention of consumers and advertisers in subsegments of the local markets. They may not compete for all the consumers and advertisers that use traditional media, but they compete for enough to affect managers' strategic decisions.

Reacting to this competition, managers develop strategies that will differentiate their product from the substitutes. The differentiation could involve a variety of product attributes, such as more investigative reports, high-profile columnists, and higher levels of sports coverage. The goal of differentiation strategies is for a product to be similar enough to a competing product so it remains a substitute but different enough that consumers will prefer the differentiated product. However, competition creates more uncertainty about strategy for news content because consumers have choice.

The fact that consumers have imperfect but acceptable substitutes for news products also increases the risk of failed market strategies. If the differentiation strategies don't work, consumers can simply move to the substitute, and, if enough move, the survival of the news organization will be threatened. The restructuring of local markets to increase competition started in the 1980s with the growth of cable channels and their ability to sell local advertising, and it has grown with the expansion of the Web to include more local sites. Even if cable channels and websites are imperfect substitutes, they take time away from traditional journalism products, and all sites, including local entertainment outlets, compete for advertising with traditional news outlets.

Beam's (1996) study of 78 daily newspapers found that competition, defined as the presence of two or more daily newspapers in the home county, was correlated with managerial uncertainty. Managerial uncertainty was correlated with the use of reader research. Use of such research is aimed at reducing uncertainty.

Organizational Goals

How a news organization confronts the uncertainty and risk of a market depends in part on the goals of the organization. These goals determine performance expectations and dictate market strategy. All commercial news organizations have financial goals, but some may have other goals, such as community improvement, quality journalism, and political influence. However, with multiple goals, companies must prioritize those goals, and the priority shapes the strategies.

In all organizations, owners, or their representatives, determine the organization's goals. Ownership structure, therefore, plays a crucial role in how news organizations react to uncertainty and risk. Ownership structure for news organizations can be classified into three types: private single ownership, private group ownership, and public group ownership. Private single ownership occurs when a person or group of people control all the stock of one newspaper, television station, or some other news outlet. Private group ownership involves all of the stock of a company with two or more news outlets being owned by a person or group or people and not being available to the public. Public ownership occurs when stock is available for purchase by the general public. A publicly owned group of news organizations occurs when the company holds two or more news outlets—often more than one type of news medium. Public ownership of newspaper groups boomed during the 1980s and 1990s as companies raised capital to expand the size of their corporations.

The distinction between private and public ownership is crucial to determining organizational goals. Owners of a private company can pursue whatever goals they like. Even though this usually involves returning a profit, the level of profit may or may not be the maximum possible. Private owners can invest in their communities to the degree they wish. The owners are the managers of private companies unless they want to hire someone to manage the company for them. On the other hand, the managers who run publicly held corporations are often not the owners. They are hired by a board of directors who are elected by the stockholders of the corporation. Of course, if a single stockholder or a group of stockholders control a significant proportion of the corporation's stock, he, she, or they can manage the corporation or appoint the managers. Regardless of the distribution of stock, the primary goal of publicly owned news corporations is to generate high consistent profits (Martin, 1998). High consistent profits usually keep demand for the company's stock high, which in turn keeps stock prices high.

When markets are uncertain, the only way high profit margins can be met consistently is through cost controls. When advertising revenues decline, news organizations tend to control costs by laying off employees. Of course, this is a short-run strategy with potentially negative long-term consequences. A reduction of newsroom employees can lower the quality of the news product, which in turn can reduce the number of customers (Lacy & Martin, 2004) and increase the uncertainty of retaining readers, viewers, and listeners. Research indicates that, as outside control (stock owned by people who are not on the board or in management) of stock increases in publicly held news media corporations, the profit margins increase, and newsroom investment declines (Blankenburg & Ozanich, 1993; Chang & Zeldes, 2002; Lacy & Blanchard, 2003; Lacy, Shaver, & St. Cyr, 1996).

In 2010, as public news corporations, such as Gannett, saw increases in profits after a year of losses, there was no indication whether they would begin to use the profits to reinvest in newsrooms. This strategic decision will affect their ability to retain and attract new consumers to their news products.

In contrast to publicly held corporations, private companies have more control over how much they spend on their products. This commitment to invest in long-run audience building allows them, if they choose, to reduce market uncertainty because they have the flexibility to better serve their audience.

Recent Market Strategy and Behavior—Risk and Uncertainty

The ability to translate all news content into digital form has reshaped the news industry. In addition to the changes in the nature of news products mentioned above (interactivity, depth, speed of communication, and multimedia), digital distribution creates the ability to segment audiences, and it lowers the costs of production and distribution. Creating online news content does not require large printing plants and the network of carriers that deliver hard copies of newspapers to houses. Although not free, once Internet news content is created, the per-unit costs of distribution are much smaller than the per-unit costs of printed newspapers. Adding large amounts of capacity to news sites can require additional hardware and software to handle higher traffic, but the cost of these additions is considerably lower than the cost of printing facilities.

By reducing costs, a company can lower the risk associated with news products. If a new product fails, it loses less money. However, the lowered costs from digital distribution do not necessarily compensate for the growth of competition and the corresponding increase in market uncertainty that comes with more news outlets, which result from low barriers to entry. The lower barriers allow easier entry, while the increased uncertainty from more competition creates easier exit.

In the advertising market, news organizations are confronting competition from news and non-news sites. The impact of competition from non-news sites is similar to total market coverage and shoppers that have competed with newspapers for decades. Perhaps more challenging to newspapers is the ability of businesses and individuals to sell directly to consumers without the help of news websites. As a result, historically lucrative real estate agencies and auto dealerships do not necessarily need newspapers to attract buyers. Craigslist and other free advertising sites have had an equally strong impact by siphoning off classified ads from newspapers.

Faced with increasing declines in readership and advertising revenues brought on by the growing movement online, many newspaper managers responded to the short-run uncertainty by actually increasing long-run uncertainty. One of the trends that developed as a result of newspaper companies going public was the need for high and consistent profit margins (Martin, 1998). Two strategies for accomplishing the consistent profits during the 1990s and early 2000s were clustering and cutting circulation in geographic areas with high costs. Cutting high-cost circulation areas involved eliminating circulation in areas with small numbers of subscribers who were further from the central market. Not only were these areas expensive to serve, but, because they were often on the market's fringe, the readers were not as attractive to advertisers.

In addition, newspaper companies bought up newspapers in the same and adjoining counties (clustering). This allowed them to gerrymander the circulation areas so that competition disappeared in fringe market areas (Lacy & Simon, 1997). Two dailies in the same county or even in adjoining counties often compete if owned by separate companies, but they cease to compete when owned by the same company. In addition to reducing cost by eliminating circulation, this allowed newspaper companies to reduce newsroom expenditures when they eliminated areas of competition (Fu, 2000; Martin, 2001, 2003). Intense competition for readers usually results in increased newsroom investment (Lacy & Simon, 1993).

These two strategies reduced costs and allowed the maintenance of high profit margins, but they contributed to circulation decline. This purposeful circulation elimination plus the declines due to the growing use of the Internet caused the perception of an industry in distress to spread even faster. Such a perception can influence readers and advertisers to look elsewhere for information and audiences. Observers of the news industry do not always question the origins of their perceptions. Certainly, the deepest recession in 70 years affected the loss of readers and advertising in the news industry from 2008 to 2010, as did the self-imposed circulation decline. As the economy began to rebound in early 2010, news companies returned to profitability. As the economy improves, it should become clearer to what degree the industry's struggles from 2007 to 2010 were caused by declines in advertising support and poor strategic decisions and to what degree they were caused by basic structural changes brought about by digital news distribution.

The efforts to cut labor costs during the early 2000s occurred against a background of the rising expense of borrowing money as news corporations expanded in size. During this period, companies continued to see newspapers as good investments. After all, newspapers had the largest local newsrooms and generated more content than radio and television stations. For example, the McClatchy Company aggressively acquired newspapers during the late 1990s and early 2000s. In 1998, McClatchy bought Cowles Media Company, which owned the *Minneapolis Star-Tribune*, for $1.4 billion, which left McClatchy $1.5 billion in debt (Fiedler, 1998). In 2006, McClatchy acquired Knight Ridder, then the second largest newspaper group in the country, for $6.5 billion. McClatchy borrowed $3.75 billion from banks to help finance the deal (McClatchy Company, 2006). The debt was lowered by the sale of 12 Knight Ridder newspapers (Rubinkam, 2006), but in 2009 McClatchy continued to have debts of almost $2 billion (McClatchy Company, 2009).

McClatchy was not alone as the world financial system edged toward disaster in late 2008. At least five newspaper companies with heavy debt were having trouble meeting their interest payments (Jesdanun, 2008). As a result, some argued that the heavy borrowing between 2005 and 2007 combined with the recession of 2008–2010 and the growth of the Internet as an advertising competitor have led the newspaper industry to the point of collapse (McMillan & Li, 2008; Mutter, 2008; Perez-Pena, 2008). Companies took on too much risk because they underestimated the uncertainty.

In late 2010, the newspaper industry, along with all news media, found itself confronting a more risky and uncertain future. Some of the risk and uncertainty resulted from corporate and market strategies that saw self-imposed circulation declines, but the risk and uncertainty also reflect the changing nature of digital media, the 2008–2010 recession, and problems in the world financial markets. Whatever the cause, the news industry of the future will continue to endure high risk and uncertainty. Newspapers will never see the levels of advertising revenue that existed before the growth of cable (Lacy, 1992) and before the arrival of the Internet. News organizations need to figure out how much and how many people will pay for news content to compensate for the loss of advertising revenue.

Living with Risk and Uncertainty

Given the changing industry landscape, managers of newspapers and other news organizations will have to adjust to living with market uncertainty and higher company risk. To survive the risk and uncertainty of the evolving news business, reporters and managers will need to experiment with new forms of products and new methods of distribution. At the same time, they must continue to meet consumers' needs and wants and serve the social and political functions that led to the creation of the First Amendment.

Although experimentation is essential, it is not the only way of coping with uncertainty and risk. The following observations are not meant as a map for the news industry, but could serve as a compass to provide direction in dealing with uncertainty.

Reducing Uncertainty and Risk

In the news and information market, a great source of uncertainty comes from a lack of knowledge about consumers' needs and wants. Currently, some of the decline in circulation reflects the increasing detachment of news organizations from their communities and the failure to invest in high-quality research about consumers' demands. Without knowing their customers, news organizations will struggle to produce content that their customers value. Reducing this uncertainty will require better research in a variety of forms and the use of Web interactivity to connect with the community. Basic research about why and how people use news can create a foundation for using the data that interactivity creates.

Perhaps the biggest risk news organizations face is the inability to control their content online. The monopoly power that local newspapers once enjoyed in the consumer market derived from their ability to control the physical manifestation of their content. Even if a newspaper generates high-quality content that no other news organization in its market can match, bloggers, news aggregators, and other news sites can easily copy and distribute that content. Of course, a news organization owns the copyright on the material it produces, but questions of legality have not stopped managers of some websites from using content without permission. A 2009 study found that, in one month, 75,000 websites were reusing news content without being licensed (Fitzgerald, 2009). In some cases, aggregators may pay for news. For example, Google, Yahoo, and other sites pay to use Associated Press (Fox News, 2006) and Agence-France Presse (Sutel, 2007) content, but most news content produced in the United States is produced by news organizations themselves and not news services.

The news industry began efforts in 2009 to assert its content ownership with talk about charging online consumers and limiting access to the content.

The American Press Institute (API) issued a report recommending that newspapers charge for their content and offering recommendations on how (Edmonds, 2009a). Rupert Murdoch, CEO of News Corp., announced in late 2009 that he might seek an exclusive arrangement with Bing, Microsoft's search engine, for his company's content and block Google's access to that content (Edmonds, 2009b). It is not clear whether the steps suggested by API or Murdoch will ultimately help the industry, but the reduction of risk in the news and information market will require greater control of content.

Reducing uncertainty and risk in the advertising markets will likely be more difficult because creating a Web vehicle for distributing advertisements costs potential competitors considerably less money than creating news content. As a result, websites aiming to sell advertising are growing quickly. A 2007 study of citizen journalism sites found that 55 percent carried advertising (Lacy, Riffe, Thorson, & Duffy, 2009). With the growing number of local websites offering to sell advertising, the ability of traditional news organizations to move print advertisers to their websites continues to be problematic. However, the ability to deliver advertising online is not the same as actually selling space and time on the Web. Potential advertisers remain uncertain about the processes and returns of online advertising, and traditional media remain uncertain about how to price online advertising.

This growth of websites that sell advertising has been a primary basis of predictions that the newspaper industry would cease to exist. The risk, however, may not be as great as some perceive, as demonstrated by the segmentation of broadcast television by cable during the 1980s and 1990s. Products that assemble the largest audiences relative to other products within a market can ask premium prices even as their audience declines in absolute terms. Even if local news organizations lose audience, they may continue to be the largest assembled audience within their market, which will make them attractive to some advertisers.

Demand is King

The long-run history of technological development is one of shifting control over content from suppliers to consumers primarily by creating choice and generating competition. From the development of the faster presses that helped create the Penny Press to the multiple channels available through cable and satellite, technology development has allowed more news outlets to enter markets. This competition allows consumers to influence content through their collective demand. Historical periods when companies dominated markets were ones in which regulation and producers' tacit collusion created monopoly power for a limited number of firms (Lacy, 2004). Currently, as the United States continues to become more diverse with regard to ethnic backgrounds and lifestyle choices of its citizens, and options for information expand online, news and other media organizations must adjust to serve the growing diversity.

Serving an increasingly diverse market likely will require multiple sites and publications. It is highly unlikely that news organizations can re-aggregate segmented markets, but the lower production and distribution costs of digital content will allow news companies to create specialized websites to serve the diversity of demand. Of course, separate sites should be cross-promoted because consumers have a variety of interests. Advertising can be run on multiple sites as well. Cross-promotion would allow a community to share a larger amount of knowledge about itself, which could generate a more cohesive public.

Investing in a Variety of Digital Technologies

Once content has been digitized, it can be distributed over the Internet or wireless and displayed in a variety of forms—desktops, laptops, personal devices such as iPhones and BlackBerrys, and even digital tablets such as the iPad, Kindle, and Plastic Logic.

Though this may create higher distribution costs in the short run, those costs should decline with standardization, and maintaining a relationship with customers would be worth the costs. News organizations will need to produce content that people want and need and distribute it in the form in which people want to receive it. Serious news consumers likely will access news in multiple forms.

As a corollary of this suggestion, news organizations that generate a large amount of text might consider investing in the development of digital tablets (Skowronski, 2009). Such tablets have more similarity to the conveniences of reading paper than do laptops because they are portable and easier to read. If the price of the tablets is reduced significantly, news organizations might give them away or sell them at large discounts with a long-term subscription—much as cell phones are today.

Interactivity and Community

In the late twentieth century, larger communities had multiple daily and weekly newspapers because they segmented the geographic area by demographics such as ethnicity, national origin, class, religion, income, and political leaning. This type of strategy served the readers, but it was inefficient for advertisers. As a result, newspapers began to consolidate because it was in the financial interest of the advertisers and newspaper owners to do so. This consolidation expanded the size of the readership base and led to newspapers serving more than one community within cities. As cities expanded in population and geographic size, metropolitan daily newspapers began to lose touch with their readers and communities, which in turn resulted in a loss of understanding about the nature of their readers. As long as consumers had few choices because of local monopoly power, losing touch did not mean increasing short-run uncertainty. However, when competition arrives, not understanding readers can send them elsewhere.

The Internet's interactivity allows individuals to create communities of their own choosing, and these communities range in size from small local forums and chatrooms to global communities on Facebook and MySpace. The ability to separate a community from geographic constraints has become an advantage of the online world, but the ability to do this does not mean geographically based communities no longer exist. The impact of governments within the United States at all levels is still geographically based, and, given this, governments continue to define some communities.

News organizations have the potential to help create and sustain online communities, especially when they have an offline geographic basis. Successfully creating such online communities requires that the community members participate in that creation and sustenance. This inclusion can take a variety of forms—some use online communication whereas others are a combination of online and offline gathering. News organizations that succeed in the creation of online communities should start by talking with their readers. Any such activities will work only if the goal is to serve community members rather than exploit them. Such services work better with journalists and managers who have a commitment to the community rather than with journalists and managers who work at companies that move them around every few years.

The twentieth century was a period that saw newspapers within markets consolidate to serve advertisers. These consolidations created monopolies that eliminated the need to understand and react to the needs and wants of readers. It was the lack of competition that allowed newspaper managers to produce lower-quality journalism, yet retain enough readers to make high profits (Lacy, 1989). The Internet is breaking up those monopolies, but it also gives news organizations the tools for better understanding their readers and for creating communities that value news. However, the process for doing this is uncertain and carries risks because of the need to rethink how journalism organizations meet news demand. Despite the uncertainty and risk, or perhaps because of it, the next two decades hold the potential of being a period when journalists take advantage of their new digital tools and improve their journalism. However, this will depend on how the news managers react to the current uncertainty and risk. At a minimum, news managers will need to pursue strategies that rededicate them to understanding and serving their communities and readers and which expand their definition of what constitutes journalism.

Some news organizations have already undertaken such strategies and are experimenting with ways of better serving their customers. The chapter's final section explores the changes at one of those news organizations.

Building on Risk and Uncertainty at the Las Vegas Sun

The *Las Vegas Sun* is a 60-year-old daily newspaper that has emerged as an example of how a news organization can adjust to the current digital transition of news and to the deep economic downturn of 2008–2010. While adjusting to its changing environment, its journalism has grown in quality. The *Sun* won the 2009 Pulitzer Prize for Public Service, and in the same year its innovative website (LasVegasSun.com) won the Best Overall Newspaper-Affiliated Web Site in its class from *Editor & Publisher* and *Mediaweek Magazine*.

The *Sun*'s transition started in 2005 when Brian Greenspun, editor and publisher and overseer for Greenspun Media, replaced the afternoon edition of the *Sun* with an eight-page insert with no advertising that is the third section in each morning's *Review Journal* (RJ). The *Sun* and RJ have been involved in a joint operating agreement since 1989. The *Sun* does not carry breaking news; it runs investigative and interpretive articles that explore issues more deeply.

Shortly after unveiling the new version of the *Sun*, Greenspun started work on LasVegasSun.com for breaking news as well as comprehensive coverage of sports and entertainment. In late 2007, Greenspun recruited Rob Curley from *The Washington Post* to build his new product. Curley is as strong a believer in community journalism as Greenspun.

The transition of the *Sun* is remarkable because its hometown has experienced the worst of the economic downturn that started in 2008. By November 2009 unemployment was the second highest in the nation. However, the *Sun* has benefited from two characteristics. First, it is family owned. Greenspun does not have to please a board of directors or stock analysts. The family can invest as it sees fit. Second, the Greenspun family owns multiple media operations. In addition to the *Sun* and LasVegasSun.com, Greenspun Media owns Vegas.com (a marketing website) and Home News, a group of suburban newspapers that serve the greater Las Vegas area. These papers have helped the website address local news in the Las Vegas area.

Starting in 2008, Greenspun Media responded to the changing market by experimenting with a variety of news and information products. These do not always work, but a company facing uncertainty must try new products knowing that some will fail. Using the Web reduces this uncertainty to a degree because the *Sun* management uses Web traffic metrics to constantly monitor use of the various online content. For Curley, one of his biggest disappointments was losing 702 TV, which was to be a television news program delivered over the Internet (R. Curley, personal communication, November 6, 2009). The idea for 702 hinged on big video-on-demand deals with major cable players throughout the country. When those fell through, Curley was already far along in building a show that was supposed to work as well in Idaho as it did in Las Vegas. In addition, Greenspun Media had to drop four editions of the

Home Town newspapers because of a drastic decline in advertising revenue that resulted from the recession.

Despite the losses, the *Sun* is concentrating on building audience in a variety of ways so that the company will be competitive as advertising money returns to its market. For example, the site has invested heavily in sports coverage. Curley says its audience continues to grow. The overall traffic on the website has increased tremendously, going from 2 million page views in 2007 to 12 million page views by the end of 2009.

In discussing the future, he said, "We all know that mobile is the key . . . so we are building a local product that will launch first on the web, but it won't take anyone five seconds to figure out we really built it for mobile," adding that his staff is geocoding every element of content that he collects: "we made a very conscientious decision to not do it as an iPhone app . . . part of the reason for that is we wanted to work on more than just an iPhone . . . we feel these products have to be mobile, but they have to be mobile-browser-based . . . that's the play here . . . Are we there yet? No . . . but we're laying the groundwork for that" (R. Curley, personal communication, November 6, 2009).

Although optimistic, Curley worries that there is a general disconnect on understanding the role of his website. "Very few people realize that the *Las Vegas Sun*'s website is not a newspaper online . . . it's an online newspaper . . . and when you see that difference and realize it, you can understand what's really going on" (R. Curley, personal communication, November 6, 2009).

Thought Questions: Contemplating Change

1. Discuss the relationship between uncertainty in the advertising market and uncertainty in the news and information markets. How does being a dual product affect the journalism process? Does uncertainty in one of the two markets affect news organizations more than uncertainty in the other? Does declining demand in the advertising market create a greater risk to news organizations than declining demand for news and information?

2. Some argue that news organizations produce lesser-quality journalism because they seek profits in commercial markets. What is quality journalism? Does being a commercial enterprise guarantee lesser-quality news products? What better system is there for generating journalism than a market system?

3. Greenspun Media Group has been experimenting with a variety of news and information products, both on and off the Web. What types of experiments should news organizations be conducting now? Are some of these experiments more risky and uncertain than others? Why? How might a news organization conducting experiments reduce the uncertainty due to market forces?

References

Beam, R. A. (1996). How perceived environmental uncertainty influences the marketing orientation of U.S. daily newspapers. *Journalism & Mass Communication Quarterly, 73*, 285–303.

Beam, R. A. (2003). Content differences between daily newspapers with strong and weak market orientation. *Journalism & Mass Communication Quarterly, 80*, 368–390.

Blankenburg, W. B., & Ozanich, G. W. (1993). The effects of public ownership on the financial performance of newspaper corporations. *Journalism & Mass Communication Quarterly, 70*, 68–75.

Chamberlin, E. H. (1962). *The theory of monopolistic competition* (8th ed.). Cambridge, MA: Harvard University Press.

Chang, K. K., & Zeldes, G. A. (2002). How ownership, competition affect newspaper financial performance. *Newspaper Research Journal, 23*(4), 101–107.

Edmonds, R. (2009a, June 4). *API report to exec summit: Paid content is the future for news websites.* Poynter Online. Retrieved November 26, 2009, from http://www.poynter.org/column.asp?id=123&aid=164522

Edmonds, R (2009b, November 18). *Murdoch and Microsoft's Bing: A media marriage made in heaven?* Poynter Online. Retrieved November 26, 2009, from http://www.poynter.org/content/content_print.asp?id=173678&format=handheld

Fiedler, T. (1998, March 19). McClatchy completes acquisition of Cowles. *Star Tribune.* Retrieved November 26, 2009, from http://www.startribune.com/templates/Print_This_Story?sid=11209056

Fitzgerald, M. (2009, December 1). 75,000 copycats a month: Study reveals extensive copying of U.S. newspaper content. *Editor & Publisher.* Retrieved December 5, 2009, from http://www.editorandpublisher.com/eandp/news/article_display.jsp?vnu_content_id=1004049842

Fox News. (2006, August 4). *Google paying Associated Press for stories, photographs.* Retrieved November 26, 2009, from http://www.foxnews.com/story/0,2933,207105,00.html

Fu, W. J. (2000). *Three essays on the economics of networked and traditional information services.* Unpublished doctoral dissertation, Northwestern University, IL.

Jesdanun, A. (2008, October 13). Newspapers mired in debt even before economic crisis. *Editor & Publisher.* Retrieved November 26, 2009, from http://www.editorandpublisher.com/eandp/news/article_display.jsp?vnu_content_id=1003873380&imw=Y

Lacy, S. (1989). A model of demand for news: Understanding the impact of competition on daily newspaper content. *Journalism Quarterly, 66*, 40–48, 128.

Lacy, S (1992). Commentary: Basic ideas for prospering in changing newspaper markets. *Newspaper Research Journal, 13*(3), 85–94.

Lacy, S. (1993). Understanding and serving newspaper readers: The problem of fuzzy market structure. *Newspaper Research Journal, 14*(2), 55–67.

Lacy, S. (2000). Commitment of financial resources as a measure of quality. In R. G. Picard (Ed.), *Measuring media content, quality and diversity: Approaches and issues in content research* (pp. 25–50). Turku, Finland: Media Group, Business and Research Development Centre, Turku School of Economics and Business Administration.

Lacy, S. (2004). Fuzzy market structure and differentiation: One size does not fit all. In R. G. Picard (Ed.), *Strategic responses to media market changes* (pp. 83–95). Jönköping, Sweden: Jönköping International Business School.

Lacy, S., & Blanchard, A. (2003). The impact of public ownership, profits and competition on the number of newsroom employees and starting salaries in mid-sized daily newspapers. *Journalism & Mass Communication Quarterly, 80,* 949–968.

Lacy, S., & Martin, H. J. (2004). Circulation and advertising competition: Implications of research. *Newspaper Research Journal, 25*(1), 18–39.

Lacy, S., Riffe, R., Thorson, E., & Duffy, M. (2009). Examining the features, policies, and resources of citizen journalism: Citizen news sites and blogs. *Web Journal of Mass Communication Research, 15.* Retrieved November 26, 2009, from http://www.scripps.ohiou.edu:16080/wjmcr/vol15/

Lacy, S., Shaver, M. A., & St. Cyr, C. (1996). The effects of public ownership and newspaper competition on the financial performance of newspaper corporations: A replication and extension. *Journalism & Mass Communication Quarterly, 73,* 332–341.

Lacy, S., & Simon, T. F. (1993). *The economics and regulation of United States newspapers.* Norwood, NJ: Ablex Publishing.

Lacy, S., & Simon, T. F. (1997). Intercounty group ownership of daily newspapers and the decline of competition for readers. *Journalism & Mass Communication Quarterly, 74,* 814–824.

Martin, H. J. (1998). Measuring newspaper profits: Developing a standard of comparison. *Journalism & Mass Communication Quarterly, 75,* 500–517.

Martin, H. J. (2001). *A study of how a strategy creating clusters of commonly owner newspapers affects prices, quality and profits.* Unpublished doctoral dissertation, Michigan State University.

Martin, H. J. (2003). Clustered newspapers operate more efficiently. *Newspaper Research Journal, 24*(4), 6–21.

McClatchy Company. (2006, June 26). *McClatchy to acquire Knight Ridder: Becomes country's second largest newspaper publisher: $6.5 billion deal unites two historic franchises focused on great journalism: McClatchy will serve 30 markets growing 50% faster than U.S. average.* Press release. Retrieved November 2, 2009, from http://www.mcclatchy.com/press-releases/story/1596.html

McClatchy Company. (2009, October 15). *McClatchy reports third quarter 2009 earnings.* Press release. Retrieved November 26, 2009, from http://finance.yahoo.com/news/McClatchy-Reports-Third-prnews-1903805041.html?x=0&.v=1

McMillan, R., & Li, K. (2008, April 3). *Tribune Co faces default threat in '09.* Reuters. Retrieved November 26, 2009, from http://www.reuters.com/article/ousiv/idUSN0317292520080404?sp=true

McManus, J. H. (1994). *Market-driven journalism: Let the citizen beware?* Thousand Oaks, CA: Sage.

Mutter, A. (2008, December 21). *How debt did in American newspapers: Reflections of a Newsosaur.* Retrieved November 26, 2009, from http://newsosaur.blogspot.com/2008/12/how-debt-did-in-americas-newspapers.html

Perez-Pena, R. (2008, December 10). The newspaper bubble, too, has burst. *Dealbook, The New York Times.* Retrieved November 26, 2009, from http://dealbook.blogs.nytimes.com/2008/12/10/the-newspaper-bubble-too-has-burst/

Picard, R. G. (1989). *Media economics: Concepts and issues.* Thousand Oaks, CA: Sage.

Rubinkam, M. (2006, June 26). *McClatchy finishes divesting Knight Ridder newspapers.* SFGate.Com. Retrieved November 26, 2009, from http://www.sfgate.com/cgi-bin/article.cgi?f=/n/a/2006/06/26/financial/f090422D31.DTL&type=printable

Skowronski, W. (2009, June/July). Circulation boost? Newspapers explore delivery via electronic reader. *American Journalism Review*. Retrieved December 5, 2009, from http://www.ajr.org/Article.asp?id=4768

Sutel, S. (2007, April 6). *Agence France-Presse, Google settle suit*. SFGate.com. Retrieved November 26, 2009, from http://www.sfgate.com/cgi-bin/article.cgi?f=/n/a/2007/04/06/financial/f074054D18.DTL&type=printable

Sylvie, G., Wicks, J. L., Hollifield, C. A., Lacy, S., & Sohn, A. B. (2008). *Media management: A casebook approach* (4th ed.). New York: Taylor & Francis.

10

THE FRAGMENTING MASS MEDIA MARKETPLACE

John Dimmick, Ohio State, Angela Powers, Kansas State, Sam Mwangi, Kansas State, and Elizabeth Stoycheff, Ohio State

"Drop in newspaper circulation accelerates." "Cable wars are killing objectivity." "Google sees surge in iPhone traffic." "Broadcast networks battling uphill for profit and audience." "Skip the newspaper, save the planet." "Big radio makes a grab for Internet listeners." "New media breaks in, but tradition lives on."

The News Consumer: Gratification Opportunities

These contemporary headlines reflect the rapid change currently afflicting the news media in the United States. From the point of view of the firm, these rapid changes represent uncertainty—uncertainty concerning the behavior of news consumers and advertisers who provide the resources that allow media services such as news to survive and prosper. However, from the point of view of the audience, the rise of Internet news and the inception of mobile devices represent additional gratification opportunities, opportunities to consume news anytime, anywhere, in any modality—audio, video, graphics, or text. This chapter will deal with the changes in the news media from the perspectives of audience gratification opportunities and firm behavior that attempts to exploit these gratification opportunities.

Behind the headlines quoted in the first paragraph of this chapter lies the process of competition. Competition, currently from the Internet, is changing the economics of the traditional media industries, including the economics of news services. However, neither competition among media industries nor the effects of that competition are unique to the contemporary era. Figure 10.1 is one way of portraying the long-term effects of competition among media industries.

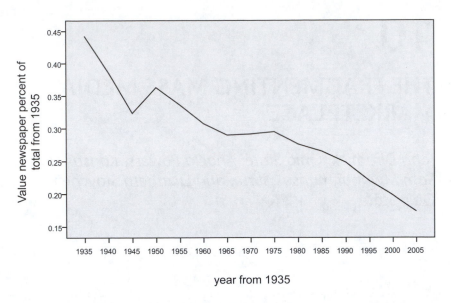

FIGURE 10.1 Newspaper Share (Proportion) of All Advertising: 1935–2006. *Source*: Robert Coen, Universal-McCann.

The figure displays the newspaper industry's proportional share of advertising for five-year intervals between 1935 and 2005. Newspapers' share declines from nearly half of all advertising in the 1930s to the teens in the past decade.

The marked and continuous decline in newspapers' advertising share is due to competition. The gain in shares by a series of "new" media beginning with radio in the late 1920s, followed by broadcast television, cable television, and the Internet, combined with mobile devices, has reduced newspapers' share of advertising by more than half. Each "new" medium in this serial competition was able to form a niche in the news industry domain by establishing competitive superiority over the newspaper and other formerly "new" media, usually over some set of audience needs or some segment of time and space.

The decline of newspapers' advertising share can be explained by concepts drawn from the theory of the niche (Dimmick, 2003). When a new medium invades an environment already populated by older media the new medium will, if resources such as advertising dollars do not increase, compete with the established media. If the new medium can establish competitive superiority over extant media, it will displace or take away resources from existing media or, at the extreme, competition will result in extinction.

However, in the competitive interaction between newer and older media, the older media may not be inactive or passively acquiesce to the displacement. The existing media may attempt to adapt to the altering environment. For example, radio, when outcompeted by television for audience time and advertiser dollars, altered its operations to adjust to changing circumstances. New technology in the form of the transistor, which made possible portable radio sets, emerged at about the same time as the inception of TV in the late 1940s. Television pre-empted radio's role as the family medium ensconced in the American living room. As Head (1972) observed, television

> drove radio out of the living room and into the kitchen, the bedroom, the study, the car. Radio became *personal* and *mobile*, following individual listeners about the house, along the superhighway, to the picnic, onto the beach, over the water, into the streets. (p. 219; emphasis original)

The radio industry adapted to the new-found mobility and shorter listener attention span by instituting shorter program units such as the five-minute newscast. Currently, news firms are attempting to adapt to an altered environment and these efforts are chronicled in the second half of this chapter.

The first competitor in the series of competitive interactions underlying the decline in newspaper shares shown in Figure 10.1, radio was able to report events such as those presaging World War II much faster than the newspaper, which required both a time-consuming printing process and transportation to the reader before it could be consumed. Radio's competitive superiority lay in its immediacy.

Television, like radio, was faster than the newspaper and, in addition, could provide moving images of news events. Competition from television moved the dominant consumption space for radio news from the household to the automobile, where it established itself as the news medium of choice in the morning and evening "drive time" for the commuter. Although TV dominated certain time periods, it was restricted largely to the early morning news programs such as *Today* or the early evening network newscasts. The competitive superiority of TV news was probably responsible, in part, for the demise of many evening newspapers.

Beginning in the early 1980s CNN, the first cable news channel, established its superiority as the ultimate in immediacy, providing news 24 hours a day. As cable diffused and became a mass medium it continued the erosion of advertising from newspapers.

By the 1990s, the Internet hosted a variety of news services ranging from the aggregators such as Yahoo to news sites owned by the once-dominant newspapers such as *The New York Times*. The Internet, as will be shown later in this chapter, has given office workers with their computers further opportunities to access news, either on the desktop computer or on the laptop. More recently, mobile devices such as the iPhone make it possible to access news sites on demand, anytime or anywhere.

The history of the news media in the past decades is replete with the drama of the growth of new media and the decline of older media such as newspapers and network TV news. These dramatic changes are an example of ecological succession (Ricklefs & Miller, 2000) in which once-dominant forms are now succeeded by newer competitors. The key to understanding this ecological succession in the news industry lies in the concept of gratification opportunities (Dimmick, 2003). Gratification opportunities are defined by three elements: (1) the choices of content available to the consumer; (2) the variety of time periods in which the content is available; and (3) the number of spatial locations in which content is accessible. As each new medium diffused, it succeeded, in part, because it was superior to its competitors in supplying information and news at the times and places and in the formats compatible with consumer needs. For example, cable news was available at any time, albeit only via a suitably equipped and wired TV set, and could gratify consumer needs for news better than the network TV news shows that were available at limited times. The Internet and the web-capable mobile device currently provide the ultimate in gratification opportunities as they make news available in a wide variety of times, places, and formats. This ecological succession in the news industries underlies the deterioration of newspaper advertising shares shown in Figure 10.1.

Data collected by Dimmick, Feaster, and Hoplamazian (2010) indicate that news consumption patterns have emerged by medium. Participants in the study were recruited through a private survey firm that had access to a national population. People were invited to take part in the study if they (1) used a mobile device for news; (2) had at least some college education; and (3) were not a full-time college student. Of the 2,131 people who responded to a screening questionnaire, 746 fitted the criteria and were invited to participate in the study. A total of 208 completed the study for a 27.9 percent response rate. Study participants recorded their news use sessions in a time–space diary for a randomly assigned 24-hour period. A session was defined as an uninterrupted period of time using a single medium that might involve access to one or more types of content (e.g., news and weather) from a content source such as a website or radio station. The study was supported by a grant from the Knight Foundation and the Harvard Center for the Press and Public Policy.

The study indicates that each medium occupies a unique niche in space and time, allowing multiple media to thrive in a competitive environment. These niches serve different gratification opportunities, varying by the needs and location of the user and media characteristics.

By tracking individuals' media consumption and location with time–space diaries, Dimmick, Feaster, and Hoplamazian (2010) found that a good deal of news consumption now takes place outside the home. Their data indicate that only 58 percent of news use occurred inside a residence, a substantial shift from times past when technology mandated that nearly all news consumption take place within a home. The television niche and the newspaper niche account for most in-residence news use. Individuals use newspapers in the early morning and television in the evening for general news content, weather, and sports.

Out-of-residence news use has diffused into spaces that were once improbable settings for news consumption and now accounts for 42 percent of all news use. These places, such as work environments and restaurants, and people on the go during transit and exercise, account for the majority of news consumption outside the home, as shown in Table 10.1a. Several niches explain this new trend: cell phones and mobile devices, radio, and desktop and laptop computers. Cell phones and mobile devices fill a transitory niche throughout the workday, and radio fills the transit niche on the way to and from work. The desktop and laptop computer niche allows news consumption to occur at work throughout the day.

This trend toward out-of-residence news use is a clear departure from past eras when media consumption was tied to the home. The Dimmick and colleagues study is the first of its kind to examine news use in both time and space, and so unfortunately empirical evidence documenting the locales and times of news use in previous eras does not exist. However, because of the stationary nature of past media, it is safe to assume that comparatively little news consumption occurred outside the home before the rise of mobile technologies.

These new environments for news consumption influence the time of day when individuals receive news. Traditionally, the vast majority of news use occurred in the morning and in the evening, accommodating most Americans' eight-hour workdays. However, as more consumption takes place outside the residence, news consumption no longer needs to be confined to just the times of day when most individuals are at home. Table 10.1b indicates that

TABLE 10.1 News Use by Space, Time, and Medium ($n = 1,843$ sessions)

a Percentage of News Use by Space (Sessions)

Residence	Work	Restaurant	Transit/Exercise	Other
57.83	21.29	2.46	18.13	0.27

b Percentage of News Use by Time (Sessions)

6 a.m. – 11 a.m.	11 a.m. – 1 p.m.	1 p.m. – 6 p.m.	6 p.m. – 6 a.m.
22.44	16.32	28.05	33.19

c Percentage of News Use by Medium (Sessions)

Newspaper	Radio	TV	Mobile	Computer	Other
9.17	9.1	28.9	11.99	38.63	2.22

over one-fourth of all news use occurs during the afternoon—a time when most Americans are at work or school. Likewise, Table 10.1b also indicates that 16.32 percent of news use occurs mid-day, another non-traditional time for news consumption. Out-of-residence news use has enabled individuals to deviate from the standard morning and evening news broadcasts.

These significant changes in news consumption have been possible with the development of the Internet and digital mobile media. These two developments have freed news audiences from predominantly in-residence use. Table 10.1c indicates that half of those surveyed use a computer or a mobile device to access news content. The use of these technologies accounts for news consumption at work, in transit, and during exercise. Recent trends of media, especially television, appearing as fixtures in doctors' offices, restaurants, and other public spaces may supplement media use outside the home; however, the use of mobile technologies accounts for the vast majority of news consumption on the go.

Figure 10.2 shows the frequencies of use or number of sessions devoted to various sources of news by the diarists in the study. The curve in the figure is clearly in the form of the letter J. J-shaped curves are a nearly ubiquitous phenomenon in the sciences. J-curves appear in fields as diverse as medicine and economics. Not surprisingly, the content of the curve is field dependent.

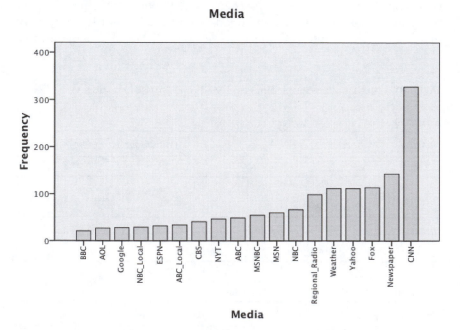

FIGURE 10.2 J-Curve of Websites Accessed with Mobile Media Devices.

In economics, for example, the curve is related to the balance of trade in relation to currency devaluation (i.e., as balance of trade improves, currency values appreciate) (Bahmani-Oskooee & Ratha, 2004). However, the sense in which the curve is used in this chapter is what Allport (1934) called a "telic continuum" or a curve representing categories of purposeful behavior. Specifically, in this paper the J-curve will denote what McPhee (1963, pp. 140–141) called the popularity problem, the "rank by frequencies of human choice or action." A recent popular work by Anderson (2006) uses a J-curve to represent the popularity of various media products such as song tracks and book titles. However, this author calls the J-curve a demand curve despite the fact that the traditional demand curve in economics is defined by two variables, price and quantity. As McPhee points out, the J-curve has often been found to occur in popularity data such as the news sources in Figure 10.2.

The J-curve in Figure 10.2 is anchored on the right-hand side by a strong vertical bar representing CNN, the cable news channel, one of the oldest of the national cable channels and the most venerable of the cable news services. The number of sessions devoted to other news sources declines rapidly until, rather quickly, the curve flattens as only a few sessions are devoted to each of the other news services utilized by the diarists. Indeed, the left-hand side of the curve would be much longer if the authors had not deleted news sources with sessions totaling less than 1 percent of the total in the interest of ease of visual display. Yet it is the long tail of the curve, including the missing portion, that is perhaps most significant. The long tail of the curve represents part of the movement toward "any news, any time, anywhere" that is now possible with the Internet and mobile devices such as the iPhone. This long tail, to the left of the bar denoting newspapers, accounts for 76.6 percent of the total sessions. Most of the news sessions graphed in Figure 10.2 involve the use of established media, and the small percentage of sessions in the "missing tail" (not shown in the figure) entails the use of non-traditional news outlets or outlets that could not be widely accessed prior to the Internet. For example, the "missing tail" accounts for only 7.38 percent of the total news sessions and is split among news outlets such as the Real Cities Regional Web, AccuWeather, and websites for *The Wall Street Journal*, Reuters, and *The Washington Post*. Nevertheless, the long tail of the curve represents substantial gratification opportunities. The "channel capacity" of the Web has made possible news services that are narrowly targeted in ways not possible in the era of three TV networks and monopoly newspapers.

Although the advent of the Internet has widened the opportunities for audiences to gratify their needs for news and information, it has also posed problems for firms engaged in news production and dissemination. News organizations have responded to the uncertainties associated with the advent of the Internet by engaging in innovation. The next sections focus on the theory of organizational innovation as a basis for understanding legacy media convergence in the first decade of this century, and how recent innovations have become routine parts of work in one news organization, the *Lawrence* (Kansas) *Journal World* (LJW).

Benefits of Innovation for Newsrooms and Consumers

In order to provide extended gratification opportunities and seize new markets, news organizations have had to change their operations. They have sought to create new products online, and create greater opportunities for audience interaction through their Web products and social media. To do so, they have had to innovate. Rogers' (1964) theory of organizational innovation identified five stages in the innovation process that organizations have undergone or will undergo as they address change: agenda setting, matching, redefining/restructuring, clarifying, and routinizing. Each stage affords newsmakers and consumers with challenges and benefits. The early stage of mass media innovations outlined in the first half of this chapter took place when media industries became aware of particular challenges and trends in consumer usage including more mobility, more news usage outside of the home, and more windows for news. This is the agenda-setting stage, when media recognized the need to innovate and began processes to respond to challenges by reconsidering their priorities (creating a new agenda).

The second stage of innovation, matching, involved creating opportunities to exploit changing environments and technology. This matching process can be observed in the race toward convergence in the early 2000s, as television stations and newspapers pooled their resources to create new online products (websites) that served emerging niche markets and extended audience gratification opportunities to online media. Meginnis (2003), one of the first local broadcast news directors to create a partnership with a competing newspaper, believed that local news was the competency of both television and newspaper organizations. However, local news operations faced increased online competition from national/international media. Convergence in initial stages allowed the locals to compete with media conglomerates by combining forces to create depth in local news. Each traditional medium's strengths complemented the other. Television's perspective was immediate and visual. Newspaper provided background and detailed information. Social media were not yet utilized in news.

Successful media convergence, according to Meginnis, required building relationships at various levels. Television and newspaper newsrooms needed to be committed to the process, and new relationships would be built with online audiences. Ultimately, convergence efforts enhanced traditional media's ability to bring rich and comprehensive local coverage to viewers or readers. According to Meginnis, consumers benefitted from convergence partnerships because media provided more coverage of greater depth in multiple platforms and formats.

Huang, Radenmakers, Fayemiwo, and Dunlap (2003) researched how media convergence in Tampa, FL, related to the quality of journalism. Newspaper and television journalists noticed a change in the dynamic of the newsroom after convergence, in the form of constant deadlines and a new outlook on stories. They also noticed that the newspaper staff was forced to see stories from a visual perspective, making the paper more visually appealing and succinct. They concluded that converging media platforms had the potential to create a powerful form of journalism. For the *Tampa Tribune*, convergence broadened perspectives and facilitated collaboration among other media, creating more in-depth stories. The findings indicated that the quality of news at the *Tampa Tribune* did not deteriorate because of convergence, and news organizations were more capable of meeting audiences' preferences through multiple formats and media niches.

As Frost (2002) stated, news organizations also benefited in the following ways by practicing media convergence:

- *Increased visibility.* Newspapers seek exposure on local TV stations because the audience for TV news is larger than that for print. Appearing on broadcasts means wider recognition for print reporters and their publications.
- *Shared reporting resources.* Newspapers typically have larger reporting staffs than local television stations. A TV station in a medium-size market usually has 10 or 15 reporters. A newspaper in the same community may have 100 reporters. Media convergence allows television news operations to take advantage of print operations' comprehensive news-gathering staff.
- *Credibility.* The presence of established television and newspaper journalists can help establish a website as a legitimate news outlet.
- *Cross-marketing.* Because TV, radio, and newspapers reach different audiences, convergence allows for media to extend their brands.

The third stage of organizational innovations involved redefining and restructuring work processes among converged media—processes that had occurred in fits and starts since the beginning of the decade. Despite shared facilities and common websites emerging in this stage, news staffs often remained separate, and journalists did not always agree that print and broadcasters were in the same business. As Singer (2003) found, most journalists were not overly enthusiastic about convergence. Although most journalists believed that their company was on the right track in converging newsrooms, the idea of convergence clashed with newsroom values. Print and broadcast journalists viewed each other skeptically, believing that often what makes a good print story makes a poor television story and vice versa. Another disparity came in the area of professional skills. Newspaper journalists were seen as more experienced, contributing more to the journalistic process. Salaries caused further disparities, with television journalists often earning more than print journalists in large markets, whereas television journalists were at the bottom of the pay scale in smaller markets.

Fostering a more positive environment by including journalists and consumers in the decision-making process appeared to be key in moving forward. Powers (2006) looked at the role of leadership in attaining convergence goals and job satisfaction in print and broadcast newsrooms. She found management supportive of convergence, news products were cross-promoted, and journalists indicated that they were producing multimedia, occasionally joining each other's staffs for planning meetings, and having a multimedia director as part of the management team. However, few organizations were found to have actually provided training for media convergence, and even fewer were providing monetary bonuses for additional responsibilities. Nevertheless, one variable that seemed to make a difference in furthering a convergence partnership was the leadership behavior of news managers. Newsrooms where managers had relationship-orientated leadership styles were more often practicing convergence activities. As relationship behavior increased, so did level of convergence.

Planning and decision-making in stage three also appeared to be at the heart of making convergence work in small and large news organizations. Media companies became more focused on the needs of audiences, providing expanded gratification opportunities through new and emerging technology and the development of new products. Companies also repositioned their missions to extend gratification opportunities for audiences. Mission statements such as the *Tribune*'s, "Build businesses that inform and entertain our customers in the ways, places and the times they want" (http://www.tribune.com/about/mission.html), were user oriented and reflected the growth of mobile media. Likewise, Google emphasizes consumers in its mission statement: "Focus on the user and all else will follow" (http://www.google.com/corporate/tenthings.html).

Stage four involved clarification and easing of the technical hurdles evident in converged newsrooms—critical given the importance of training to convergence success. Centers such as IFRA Newsplex have joined established professional development organizations (e.g., Poynter Institute and American Press Institute) to provide training for multimedia skills. Poynter, for example, equips journalists with new tools and ideas to handle the challenges of producing quality news reports, programs, and publications. The institute also provides journalists with new ways of thinking about their work and encourages them to take risks. Seminars include "Essential Skills for Digital Journalists," "Multimedia Tools," and "Customizing Google Maps" (http://www.poynter.org). Likewise, Newsplex was created to help news organizations adapt to news and information in different formats and across platforms. Workshops explore topics such as cross-platform advertising. They are particularly interested in training journalists to be more interactive.

The multiple uses of mobile media have media companies seeking new ways to both package and disseminate their information. Brainard (2010) contends that in 10 years e-readers will have become like televisions and cell phones, available and affordable in all varieties. Five media giants—Conde Nast, News Corporation, Hearst, Meredith, and Time Inc.—have created a project called Next Issue Media, setting up a clearinghouse for digital newspaper and magazine content where publishers and consumers may distribute and purchase content for smartphones, e-readers, tablets, netbooks, desktops, and laptops. The emphasis is on hand-held mobile devices because these media provide emerging opportunities to extend audience gratification opportunities.

The final stage of organizational innovations is the routinization of innovations. Although few organizations are operating comfortably at this stage, the *Lawrence Journal World* has made great strides working together across the company's media, addressing the needs of audiences in terms of more mobility and interactivity. The *Lawrence Journal World* is one of the most converged news operations in the United States, with multimedia operations across Kansas. The LJW owns a newspaper, magazine, broadcast station, and cable station, among other media entities in Northeast Kansas. Although many traditional newsroom routines (e.g., deadlines) have disappeared, the LJW blends accepted journalism practices and products with enhanced online audience opportunities for content creation and interactivity. For example, readers are able to create their own blogs. On any given day, there are at least three to five active local reader blogs, with topics including climate change, music, economics, life inspirations, and photography. The most popular blogs appeared to be those that asked fellow readers simple questions—about favorite songs associated with musicals, for example. Readers respond to the blogs by providing favorite songs as well as links to performances on YouTube.

The LJW also allows readers to comment on every story published on its newspaper website. Table 10.2 identifies 10 categories of news that have received the most comments. In a constructed week sample of the LJW home pages in December 2009, readers commented on local hard and soft news, state news, national news, science, and health stories, as well as stories on sports and weather. Reader comments were also common for editorials, blogs, and polls. On Wednesday of the sample, for example, the most commented-on news story concerned the weather, because of school closings. Interestingly, although blogs and polls generated a great deal of reader comments, local and state news were just as likely to engage readers. This is encouraging because it speaks to local websites' abilities to attract readers.

The interactivity (e.g, through comment sections and blogs) has created greater demands on journalists, who must stay connected with stories longer and monitor comments. Readers also have greater responsibilities. Users contributing comments, photo galleries, or any other feature must agree to

TABLE 10.2 Most Discussed Online News Stories (Percent), *Lawrence Journal World*, December 2009

Topic	Sun	Mon	Tues	Wed	Thurs	Fri	Sat
Local hard news	13.4	8.7	38.6		36.7	20.5	
Local soft news	1.5	5.1	7.6	5.5	14.1	9.8	
State news			6.0	15.1	11.1		
International/ national news	2.4		11.1	15.1			29
Science/health				17.6		25.1	
Weather				28.7			
Blogs	14.8	13.3	3.8	3.5	4.5	8.2	7.8
Polls		7.6	7.0	9.3	2.5	29.3	9.5
Sports	30.7	35.6	25.9	5.2		7.1	36.2
Letter to editor/ editorials	37	29.5			31.1		17.5
Total	100	100	100	100	100	100	100
$n =$	714	803	602	345	673	379	359

abide by the terms of a lengthy agreement and followgeneral "good manners" that are expected when interacting on the LJW website. Use of inappropriate language, potentially slanderous or libelous comments, and attacks on fellow commenters, people mentioned in stories, contributors, or any employee of the LJW or The World Company may be removed. Although it is possible for people from a variety of viewpoints to discuss issues in a civil manner, the company reserves the right, but assumes no obligation, to remove comments and ban accounts of users that foster incivility. They say this clarification of new media usage is important as it encourages media organizations and consumers to act responsibly in the new media landscape.

Within the newsroom, evidence that new practices are becoming routine is everywhere. According to Jane Stevens (2009), LJW multimedia director, the motto of the press corps is that there is a deadline every minute. Everything is multimedia. Reporters use their cell phones as notebooks. The staff views Facebook as a news site for information gathering and dissemination. Journalists work together to create new niche forms of reporting (Stevens, 2009). The newspaper is eliminating a separate section for multimedia because all sections now involve multimedia. LJW journalists are innovating their work processes and products, and keeping an eye on other successful innovators such as Westseattleblog.com, a news blog aggregator that has 800,000 page views per month and is profitable through advertising.

Newsroom personnel also share stories across platforms. For example, in fall 2009 the LJW found that there were effective, interactive ways online to share community-based stories about the H1N1 virus. A reporter moderated an online chat in which she brought in experts and took questions about the virus, also called swine flu. She had over 50 questions online. This compared with a town hall meeting that same reporter organized on H1N1 to which only three people came. The reporter also covered a swine flu clinic from where she called in with updates and posted on Twitter all day. Reporters at the *Lawrence Journal World* are finding that people are much more likely to engage with and share information when stories are conducted online. They advocate, however, that, although anyone can chat online, it is only the professional reporters who have the resources, time, and energy, and access to the most reliable information. As the *Lawrence Journal World* progresses, it is using social media to tell and find stories and connect with the community and with each other, and all journalists are expected to put these new tools to use. Changing routines are reflected in an outline of a typical workday:

1. Staff members discuss ideas in morning meeting; each reporter pitches at least five stories.
2. Reporters make phone calls or hit streets. They put up at least a paragraph online about what will be covered.
3. On their own, reporters shoot, interview, etc.
4. Reporters serve as one-person bands, community correspondents. They are engrossed in local community, always tweeting, always producing online.
5. Reporters must produce blogs offering a personal voice.
6. Music, culture, and arts reporters cover music scene in local community. They use Flip cameras; they strive to be social and engrossed in the community.

According to Stevens (2009), newspaper reporters are often introverted and afraid to extend their personalities into the community, but, she says, these fears can be overcome. The company looks for enterprising individuals who can come up with their own stories and in some cases even their own advertising. For example, the LJW plans to launch a Manhattan, KS, community site. One journalist will live and work in the Manhattan community and create the LJW brand with an emphasis on hyperlocalism. The correspondent will be a one-person band, thoroughly involved in the community. This journalist will sell advertising, report news, constantly be online, and be a community mobilizer, trying to turn the Manhattan site into a popular community hub. The LJW has similar plans for other communities, having bought newspapers in small regions in Eastern Kansas that it will transition from print to Web, changing formats to something similar to that of Westseattleblog.com. Moving away from the "we talk you listen" model, the company believes newspapers exist to help solve problems and be the watchdog of a community, and ask what "we as a community can do to solve problems." Stevens says she seeks multimedia journalists who have the ability to operate independently, to be adaptable, to listen well, to work quickly, to have an online presence, and perhaps most importantly to be fearless.

Satisfying the newsrooms' need to increase markets, as well as customers' need for information that is relevant, websites of news organizations such as the LJW are becoming highly specialized. Some newspapers call them channels, similar to the proliferation of niche channels available on satellite television. The LJW provides the aggregate of its channels in a product called "Marketplace," available for purchase by other online news organizations. Stevens says their version of the Marketplace provides a community with an online and easily searchable listing service for all local businesses. It also provides each local business with a free listing page and mobile alerts for customers. Each business's basic page includes the business name, address, phone number, website link, automatically updated hours of operation, accepted forms of payment, map, and a photo. Businesses pay to add more information: coupons, videos, more photos, etc. Marketplace offers numerous new revenue opportunities, from selling enhanced business listings, to selling premium sponsorships and banner ads. More importantly, Stevens says, Marketplace has helped traditional sales organizations reinvent their sales approaches and business models for local ad sales. According to Stevens, as people continue to research and shop online and rely less on print directories, sites such as Marketplace will help media organizations compete by becoming experts on local communities—for consumers at home or out in the community. Such highlights will include coupon tracking for local businesses, self-service publishing tools for local businesses, Web analytics reports, rating and event-sharing tools for consumers, and mobile-ready capability (Marketplace, 2010).

These innovations at the LJW illustrate how a legacy medium is attempting to solidify new practices into its work routines to embrace digital media and extend interactivity and gratification opportunities for its audiences. These efforts can be seen as a news organization's attempts to utilize technological innovation to reduce uncertainty.

Conclusion

The major thesis of this chapter has been that gratification opportunities guide consumer choices of news content and that the process of convergence in technology and content is providing the firm with new means of creating gratification opportunities for the consumer. The brief historical review provided at the beginning of the chapter outlined the process of change from a media landscape dominated by the newspaper to a landscape characterized by multiple media offering news and information and thus providing expanded gratification opportunities to the consumer. Technology that was once feared in most newsrooms and thought of as detrimental to newspapers is emerging into the creation of more usable forms of journalism that better meet the needs of new and younger consumers. The Internet is providing opportunities to reform outdated journalism techniques and build confidence in the news media once again.

This chapter began with the observation that the media in the United States, including news firms, are in a state of rapid change. This rapid change has engendered a number of uncertainties that include changes in the behavior of news consumers, the monetary decisions of advertisers, and the organization and structure of news firms. The chapter has focused on the first and third of these uncertainties. Part one of the chapter posited that gratification opportunities are an important motivation guiding the behavior of news consumers. However, the choices of content and the time and place of news consumption also mean, from the point of view of the news organization, that fragmenting audiences pose uncertainties for the firm. The second part of the chapter utilized Rogers' theory of organizational innovation to illustrate how news organizations attempt to cope with the uncertainties of the new technologies, different audience gratifications, and a fragmenting marketplace. News organizations such as the *Lawrence Journal World* are attempting to cope with uncertainty by using tools of technological convergence—digital video, audio, text, and graphics—to furnish the gratification opportunities formerly provided separately by distinct radio, TV, cable, and print media outlets. The digital revolution has made it possible for one organization to do the work formerly accomplished by several media organizations operating in traditionally discrete industries. Finally, the chapter offers some guidelines for initiating and managing converged newsrooms. Such guidelines are critical for journalists as they seek to manage uncertainties inherent in these emerging processes—uncertainties that open the door to new gratification opportunities for community residents to consume news "anytime, anywhere."

Thought Questions: Contemplating Change

1. Identify the three elements that define audience gratification opportunities and discuss media examples for each element.
2. Compare and contrast news media usage in terms of in-residence versus out-of-home usage. What are the advantages and disadvantages of various platforms?
3. What are the advantages and disadvantages of TV, radio, and newspaper organizations in one market combining forces to cover news, from the perspectives of management, staff, and the community?

4. How are journalists at the *Lawrence Journal World* working differently to increase gratification opportunities for news consumers? What uncertainties might such new processes present to journalists and to news consumers, and with what effects?

References

Allport, F. H. (1934). The J-curve hypothesis of conforming behavior. *Journal of Social Psychology, 5*, 141–183.

Anderson, C. (2006). *The longer long tail.* New York: Hyperion.

Bahmani-Oskooee, M., & Ratha, A. (2004). The J-curve: A literature review. *Applied Economics, 36*, 13, 1377–1398.

Brainard, C. (2010, July/August). Strong press, strong democracy: A second chance. *Columbia Journalism Review.* Retrieved July 21, 2010, from http://www.cjr.org/cover_story/a_second_chance.php?page=all

Dimmick, J. (2003). *Media competition and co-existence: The theory of the niche.* Mahwah, NJ: Lawrence Erlbaum.

Dimmick, J., Feaster, J. C., & Hoplamazian, G. J. (2010). News in the interstices: The niches of mobile media in space and time. *New Media & Society.* Retrieved May 18, 2010, at http://nms.sagepub.com/

Frost, M. (2002). Media organizations converge online. *MHRA News.* Retrieved January 15, 2004, from http://www.goletapublishing.com/mc.htm

Head, S. W. (1972). *Broadcasting in America: A survey of television and radio.* Boston, MA: Houghton Mifflin.

Huang, E., Radenmakers, L., Fayemiwo, M., & Dunlap, L. (2003). *Uncovering the quality of converged journalism: A case study of the* Tampa Tribune News *stories.* Retrieved November 11, 2009, from http://www.poynter.org/resource/69008/USF_study1.pdf

Marketplace. (2010). *Lawrence Journal World.* Retrieved April 25, 2010, from http://www2.ljworld.com/marketplace/

McPhee, W. N. (1963). *Formal theories of mass behavior.* New York: Free Press of Glencoe.

Meginnis, M. (2003, April). Convergence. Speech presented at the Illinois News Broadcasters Association, Moline, IL.

Powers, A. (2006). An exploratory study of the impact of leadership behavior on levels of news convergence and job satisfaction. In L. Kung (Ed.), *Leaders in the media industry: changing contexts, emerging challenges.* Jönköping, Sweden: Media Management & Transformation Centre, Jonkoping International Business School.

Ricklefs, R. E., & Miller, G. L. (2000). *Ecology* (4th ed.). New York: W. H. Freeman.

Rogers, E. M. (1964). *Diffusion of technologies.* New York: Free Press.

Singer, J. B. (2003). Who are these guys? The online challenge to the notion of journalistic professionalism. *Journalism, 4*, 139–163.

Stevens, J. (2009, November). Journos. Speech presented at Kansas State University, Manhattan, KS.

11

CHANGING PERCEPTIONS OF ORGANIZATIONS

Ann Hollifield, University of Georgia

In recent decades, technological change has so disrupted established media markets that the long-term survival of many traditional news media companies is seriously in doubt. Audience attention to news has steadily eroded over the past 50 years, particularly among young people. The advent of low-cost consumer-oriented digital production technologies has allowed audience members to become content producers in their own right, while the Internet offers them global distribution at the touch of a button. As the audience has fragmented across these new content options, so too have advertisers, making it increasingly difficult for media organizations to pull together enough advertising revenue to cover the costs of quality journalism. Thus, traditional news organizations are fighting a three-front war: increased competition in information production and distribution, combined with declining demand for news content and disappearing revenue sources.

In the face of the extreme uncertainty these changes have created, media executives are seeking new strategies for reducing costs and increasing revenues. Over the past two decades, organizational structure has become a key weapon in their strategic arsenal.

Organizational research has long since established that organizational structure plays a central role in organizational performance. In management literature, "organizational structure" tends to be a broadly applied concept that includes such elements as type of organizational ownership, organizational size, organizational complexity including complexity of subsidiary structures and product portfolios, leadership authority and hierarchy, decision authority, reporting lines, communication lines and relationships, organizational rules, and the working proximity of different organizational and professional cultures within organizational units. Organizational structures have been found to be related to different elements of organizational performance including equity value, revenue stability, financial efficiency, profit, market share, organizational and professional culture, work processes, employee satisfaction and retention, employee diversity, organizational creativity and innovation, and, in media organizations specifically, content quality.

So strong is the link between structure and performance that, until relatively recently, many management theorists believed that for each organization there was an optimal structure that would maximize performance. Research suggested the optimal structure was dictated by an organization's market environment (Donaldson, 2001). The key factors believed by scholars to influence the nature of an organization's optimal structure were the degree of uncertainty in the organization's internal production processes and external market environment, and its reliance on technology and innovation. The higher the uncertainty and the greater the need for innovation, the more decentralized, complex, and flexible the optimal structure would need to be. Management scholars believed organizations that failed to discover their own perfect structure would underperform or fail. Within this view, known as structural contingency theory, the organizational structure as a concept was grounded in assumptions of economic rationality and, therefore, fell near the structural end of the structure–agency continuum in management theory.

More recent research has suggested a different view, however: that there are numerous structural options for each organization and that optimal performance requires structural flexibility in response to changing environmental conditions (McGrath, 2006). Consequently, management theorists now concede a greater role for human agency in the development of organizational structures. Indeed, human networks, strategic networks, the leveraging of interdependencies, and the co-evolution of firms with their environments are all conceived of as critical components of organizational structures for the twenty-first century. However, recognition of the strong link between organizational structure and performance remains unchanged, as does the central role uncertainty plays in shaping effective organizational structures. Research continues to suggest that the higher the level of uncertainty an organization faces, the more critical structural flexibility and continuous evolution become to organizational survival. As a result, decisions about organizational structure have become critical elements in organizational strategy.

Given the increasing uncertainties in news markets, it is hardly surprising that both the macro- and micro-level structures of news organizations have changed dramatically in the past several decades, becoming increasingly fluid (Gade & Raviola, 2009; Phillips, Singer, Vlad, & Becker, 2009). At the macro level, ownership and subsidiary structures have been transformed as managers have experimented with various combinations of product portfolios in their attempts to maintain market share and stabilize revenues and profits. As a result of those changes and the general financial stress at the corporate level, media companies also have significantly restructured at the micro or organizational level. At the organization level, formal and informal structures have flattened as surviving employees have been forced to accept multiple responsibilities, digital technologies have reduced distinctions between TV, radio, and print news production, and audiences have become creators as well as consumers of news, softening the distinction between "professional" journalists and the rest of the world.

Although organizational structures are critically important to survival in times of market uncertainty, examining the relationship between organizational structure and performance is challenging because modern organizations are complex organisms and operate through multiple layers of structure. The structure established at each layer influences the structures of other layers, and influences the performance of organizational units both individually and collectively. Consequently, it is necessary to consider organizational structure as a factor in organizational performance and strategy differentially, depending on the level of the organizational unit being examined. Complicating the process even more in the media industry is the fact that media organizations are experimenting with new organizational structures as a result of the disruption of media markets in recent years.

Structure at the Macro-Organizational Level of Media Corporations

Ownership Structures

Over the past half century, most research on media organizational structures has focused on the impact of macro-organizational structures on performance—especially on ownership structures and their effects on media content (Mierzejewska & Hollifield, 2006). In the 1970s and 1980s, accelerating consolidation in the newspaper industry set off a wave of research on the effects of corporate or chain ownership compared with independent family ownership on newspaper content. The assumptions behind the research were that, as the number of newspaper chains grew, the number of points of view available to the public would fall and the vigor of reporting would be reduced as competition in media markets was reduced (Bagdikian, 1992). Findings generally supported those assumptions. A few studies, however, found either no effects or that chain-owned newspapers produced higher-quality content (Becker, Beam, & Russial, 1978) and were less subject to direct ownership influences on content (Demers, 1996, 1997a, 1997b).

As research on the importance of ownership structures in media was extended, scholars came to believe that the relationship between ownership structures and journalism was more complex than initially thought. Some argued that the effects attributed to ownership type were in fact effects of organizational size. Others suggested that the effects researchers attributed to chain ownership were really effects of a different type of ownership structure: public ownership (Cranberg, Bezanson, & Soloski, 2001).

By the late 1980s, many major media corporations around the world had become publicly held corporations, that is, companies in which the public could buy stock. Media owners found it advantageous to sell stock in their companies both to fund the acquisition of new media properties and, in the United States, to avoid the inheritance taxes that caused major succession problems for privately owned media. As Albarran (1996) noted, however, the transformation of a media company from a privately held to a publicly held corporation also changed it from a company operating in a dual-product market into one operating in a triple-product market. Media managers no longer had to manage just the two markets of audiences and advertising, they also had to manage the capital market. Public ownership forced media executives to monitor constantly the effects their strategies had on their company's stock price. Indeed, many media executives' pay was tied directly to stock-price performance, incentivizing them to focus on short-term financial performance over journalistic performance as measured by news quality, public service, professional reputation, and the company's ability to win and keep audiences and advertisers.

In recent years, scholars have added still another layer of complexity to the understanding of ownership structures and media performance. Picard and Van Weezel (2008) suggested ownership structures may have less effect on content quality than do other less obvious management priorities. Specifically, they argued that factors such as the separation between ownership and control, asymmetry of information between owners and managers, ability to acquire capital, profit incentives, and similar management priorities were more likely to account for differences in newspaper performance than ownership structures alone. Similarly, newspapers owned and managed by journalists through Employee Stock Ownership Plans (ESOPs) have been found to be just as profit driven as (and no more content driven than) corporately owned newspapers (Fedler & Pennington, 2003).

This is not to say that *ownership* does not affect media content and quality. There is considerable research (Akhavan-Majid, Rife, & Gopinath, 1991; Gaziano, 1989; Hollifield, 1999; Pratte & Whiting, 1986; Rystrom, 1987; Wackman, Gillmor, Gaziano, & Dennis, 1975) and anecdotal evidence that media owners and executives sometimes directly and indirectly influence the news content that reaches the public, as they pursue personal and corporate agendas. What has become less certain is whether ownership *structures* produce predictable effects on media performance independent of the conscious acts of the owners or managers themselves. Research has even questioned whether the increased ideological slanting of news seen in the United States in recent

years is an effect of media ownership or a strategic response to excessive competition in news markets, as media organizations try to capture niche audiences
(Becker, Hollifield, Jacobsson, Jacobsson, & Vlad, 2009; Hollifield, 2006).

Despite the growing uncertainty among scholars about the nature of the
relationship between media ownership structures and media performance,
the question took on new life within the U.S. journalism community at the
end of the first decade of the twenty-first century. So-called "legacy" media
companies found themselves struggling for survival in the face of disappearing audiences and advertisers and a global economic recession. In many cases,
their responses to these challenges had significant effects on news organizations' formal and informal structures. Thousands of journalists were laid off
industry-wide, while individual media organizations shared content between
subsidiaries and with competitors, spun off non-core assets, outsourced
processes such as printing and distribution, and increasingly filled time and
space with cheap-to-produce fluff stories and free audience-submitted user-
generated content (UGC). Despite these cost-saving measures, a number of
media organizations filed for bankruptcy anyway, particularly in the newspaper
industry. Experts began questioning whether journalism could survive as a for-
profit industry in the twenty-first century.

In 2009, the idea that non-profit ownership structures might be necessary
to rescue quality journalism from the ravages of the competitive marketplace
began to gain traction in public debate (Swensen & Schmidt, 2009). The Knight
Foundation issued a report arguing that quality journalism serving the public
interest could survive only through media innovation and if higher education, community, and non-profit institutions increased their involvement in
journalism (Kurz, 2009). Despite these proposals, it's not clear a non-profit
model would work. Maguire's (2009) study of non-profits in the magazine
sector led him to conclude that non-profits may be at least as vulnerable to
business cycles as for-profit publications. Similarly, Mutter (2010) concluded
that it would take one-third of the more than $300 billion donated to charity
in the United States in 2008 to fund the current weakened level of reporting
being done by existing for-profit media in the United States.

Nevertheless, more than a few news organizations are now trying the
non-profit model. Small non-profit investigative and community news
organizations have sprung up in recent years. Many have been launched by
experienced news professionals who have been laid off or forced into early
retirement by downsizing news corporations. Most are supported at least in
part by grants or donations from foundations and individuals. Although a
number of these innovative operations have been recognized for outstanding journalism, the question remains whether they are sustainable. Although
foundations and state and federal grants may be available to start projects,
they rarely, if ever, can be relied upon to fund operating costs indefinitely.

Eventually, a reliable source of revenue that covers operating expenses must be found, whether through subscription, advertising, direct sales and merchandising, user donations, or some other model.

In a sense, over a period of 50 years, the issues of ownership structure and journalistic performance have come full circle. In the 1960s, journalists and scholars questioned whether the profit motives and absentee ownership of corporate media groups would generate the high-quality journalism needed to serve communities, the public, and democracy. Today, considerable uncertainty exists as to whether the legacy media's shrinking profit margins and declining work force can support anything more than lapdog journalism and feature reporting. If the answer is "no," then the role of the legacy media in supporting the development of civil society will be greatly diminished. If that happens, the question becomes whether non-profit organizations and volunteer journalists will be able to fill the role of watchdog journalist for society and, if not, what organizational forms will emerge to sustain open and transparent government and the flow of critical information to citizens. Uncertainty surrounds this issue, which may well prove to be one of journalism's critical issues in the twenty-first century.

Organizational Structure as Strategy

The consolidation of media companies in the last quarter of the twentieth century opened the door to another macro-structural approach to management among media companies: the strategic creation of product portfolios through the acquisition or development of subsidiaries.

There are six primary approaches to product portfolio development that result from industry consolidation and affect macro-organizational structures: horizontal integration, or the acquisition of subsidiaries in the same line of business; vertical integration, the acquisition of subsidiaries in the production–distribution supply chain; diagonal or lateral integration, the acquisition of subsidiaries in related but different lines of business, such as television stations and newspapers; clustering, the acquisition of subsidiaries geographically close to one another; conglomeration, the acquisition of companies in wholly unrelated businesses; and globalization, the acquisition of subsidiaries in other countries. These macro-structural approaches to product portfolio development are designed to provide strategic benefits including increased market share, revenue growth, new revenue streams, cost control, control of supply and distribution, reduced competition, and smoother revenue flows by reducing the impact of business-cycle fluctuations in any single market sector.

The use of complex consolidated and integrated organizational structures is not new, but their adoption by the media industry accelerated as the result of the emergence of digital technologies. Digital technologies lowered the cost

of content reproduction and distribution, making it easy and cheap to reproduce successful content across multiple media platforms and distribute those
products worldwide. Additionally, increased competition created by the digital
revolution slashed media profits, forcing media corporations to cut production
costs and try to expand market share.

However, although corporate size and complex product portfolios were
expected to buffer media profits from market disruptions, there is little evidence
they have done so. Kolo and Vogt (2003) found that neither organizational size
nor diversification, nor a combination of the two, was related to improved
media financial performance. Only for radio was corporate size positively
related to performance, whereas in the entertainment sector—film, music, and
games—company size was inversely related to financial performance. These
findings may result from the fact that, prior to the Telecommunications Act
of 1996, many U.S. radio stations were in financial trouble as they lost market
share to television and new technologies. The consolidation and clustering
made possible by the Act helped return the radio industry to profitability.
Conversely, in the entertainment sector, which is dependent on blockbuster
hits and unpredictable consumer tastes, small companies may be more flexible, creative, and efficient.

Other analyses have shown that diversification into related media sectors
improved media companies' financial efficiency. However, companies that
restructured to acquire subsidiaries in media sectors less related to the organization's core media products saw decreased financial efficiency (Jung, 2003; Jung
& Chan-Olmsted, 2005). International diversification produced a curvilinear
relationship in media financial performance: Financial efficiency improved
initially with international diversification but decreased after a point (Jung &
Chan-Olmsted, 2005). These findings suggest companies incur greater coordination costs as they expand geographically, reducing the benefits of doing so.
Moreover, media content is a culture-based product. Thus, as media content
is distributed in more countries, cultural relevance is likely to become more of
an issue, further reducing overall profit margins (Priest, 1994).

These findings should have come as no surprise to media executives. Other
industries discovered after the merger and acquisition orgies of the 1980s that
relatively few such investments returned the anticipated benefits (Hollifield,
2003). Indeed, Copeland, Koller, and Murrin (1991) found that acquisitions,
integration, and diversification often had a net negative effect on corporate
profits and overall company value. Such cautionary experiences were, however, largely ignored by media executives after deregulation in the 1990s.

Unfortunately, efforts at media empire building in the 1990s and early part
of the millennial decade left many media corporations with high levels of debt.
When acquisitions failed to return the expected benefits after a few years, some
media executives began selling off non-core and underperforming subsidiaries
(Berg, 2005). Research showed that this process, known as "deconsolidation"

or divestiture, often resulted in material and economic gains through reduced debt and increased stock prices (Alexander & Owers, 2009). The divestiture trend was by no means universal among media, however. With the onset of the worldwide "Great Recession" of 2008, more than a few media corporations found themselves unable to keep up their payments on the debt they had acquired with their acquisitions, and they were forced into bankruptcy.

Although Wall Street and media executives are primarily concerned with how organizational structures and product portfolios affect corporate financial performance, an equally, if not more, important question is how organizational structures and portfolios impact journalistic performance. There is a clear connection. Research suggests that as financial performance, that is, profit margins, declines, media companies invest less in producing high-quality journalism (Becker et al., 2009; Hollifield, 2006; Lacy & Riffe, 1994). Staff sizes are cut, leaving the remaining journalists less time to produce original, balanced, in-depth stories based on multiple sources of information. Instead, media organizations fill time and space with content that is inexpensive to produce, such as scandal, sensationalism, sex, celebrity, sports, and controversial opinions, but which is likely to attract non-news-oriented audiences.

Thus, if complex integrated organizational structures erode media profitability, they may have a negative impact on journalistic quality. In those cases in which consolidation strengthens a corporation's financial performance, integrated corporate structures could improve journalistic quality, as long as they do not result in monopolistic local news markets,[1] and the owner or senior executives do not use their consolidated news operations to push a particular ideological agenda on the public.

Other elements of consolidated and integrated structures also appear to affect journalism quality. Martin (2003b) found that 52 percent of the daily newspapers in the United States that ceased publication between 1988 and 1998 were shuttered after being incorporated into a regional cluster. Martin argued that newspaper companies were closing selected newspapers within clusters in order to consolidate production and circulation and gain economies of scale. He noted the strategy increased short-term profits but contributed to the long-term decline of the industry. His research also showed clustered newspapers tended to have fewer editorial staff members than comparable newspapers operating outside of clusters and were more likely to share content and other resources (Martin, 2003a).

Similar trends have been noted in clustered broadcast operations. Some television groups have selectively shut down newsrooms in a station cluster, using those stations to rebroadcast the news produced by nearby sister stations. Other TV companies have started centralcasting blocks of the evening news—such as sports and weather—from a single hub, rather than hiring reporters at each station to cover those subjects. Thus, clustering may reduce the volume and depth of local community news coverage.

Globalization as a corporate structure also has been criticized for its potential impact on news content and quality, although relatively little research has tested the arguments. Critics argue that globalization of news media leads to homogenized news content and increases the impact of dominant points of view originating from powerful nations and global corporations (Demers, 1999). Many nations, including the United States, still limit foreign ownership of media out of concern that foreign owners may manipulate content in times of national crisis (Hollifield, 1999). However, research also suggests that, in countries where media have limited resources or where governments exercise direct control over the media, foreign ownership may provide additional resources and protections to journalists (Beachboard & Beachboard, 2006; Demers, 1999). Thus, the issues of global media structures' impact on news quality remain highly controversial. So far scholars have contributed much insight but little empirical evidence to the debate.

Structure at the Firm Level of News Media Companies

Although macro-organizational structures have been the primary concern of media scholars, regulators, and senior media executives, firm-level organizational structures arguably have the most immediate impact on journalistic quality. Moreover, they are the structures of greatest concern to front-line journalists and the ones most directly affected by the digital revolution.

Firm-level structures take the form of both formal and informal structures. Formal structures include such elements as departmental structures, reporting lines, decision authority, physical layout of office space, and line managers' spans of control or responsibilities. Informal structures include managers' leadership styles, the organizational culture, the strength of the professional cultures within the organization and their relationship to the organizational culture, communication networks within and between work groups, and the distribution of power among individuals and work groups based on such things as expertise, charisma, perceived importance to the organization, and personal connections.

Formal Organizational Structures

The relationship between organizational structures and organizational performance is well established although there is still much to be learned about how different structural elements specifically influence different aspects of performance. In general, the evidence indicates that the more vertical, formal, and hierarchical an organization's formal structure, the better that organization will be at dealing with time pressure, crises, and potentially dangerous situations. Conversely, however, formal hierarchal structures tend to make an organization less innovative, creative, and entrepreneurial. Horizontal structures in which reporting lines are less formal and power is shared through all levels of the organization are more effective at encouraging flexible, innovative thinking among employees. Such structures also are a necessary condition for creativity and, therefore, are critical to the success of media organizations producing creative content.

Traditionally, large and medium-sized news organizations have had a more or less hybrid formal structure, particularly in the newsroom.[2] Journalists reported to editors and producers and had their stories evaluated by those higher-ups. However, as professionals, journalists retained a fair degree of autonomy in their work and at least some control over the content they produced. In short, newsroom structures evolved to be efficient, responding to time pressures of daily deadlines and breaking news, while still providing their professional class of employees the autonomy required to produce unique, high-quality content. Also, in furtherance of the goal of maximum efficiency and quality, newsrooms evolved fairly high levels of task specialization.

In the face of the disruptions the past few decades have brought to the news industry, traditional organizational structures have started to crumble (Gade, 2004; Gade & Raviola, 2009; Witschge & Nygren, 2009). Newsroom jobs in newspapers fell almost 25 percent between 2000 and 2010, and broadcast newsrooms had similar cuts. The loss of staff left many news organizations struggling simply to produce enough news to fill time and space. Task specialization has become a luxury, and many newsrooms have adopted the "one-man band" model in which the reporter does everything: research, report, write, shoot photos or video as needed, and edit copy and visuals. Editing jobs have been slashed, severely reducing fact and quality checking of content. Departmental walls between journalists and the technical production specialists who supported them also are coming down. Some news organizations have folded the production department into the newsroom, requiring technicians to help with reporting, shooting, and editing during off-peak production hours, and reporters to help with production during the deadline rush (news executive, personal communication, November 10, 2009).

This merging of departmental functions also requires a compromise on professional standards of "quality." As individual staff members are required to perform an increasing number of tasks, and job specialization declines, so too does the expertise brought to each task (Phillips et al., 2009; Witschge & Nygren, 2009). As overall quality drops, the imperative to produce quality does as well. Even major media corporations are reportedly filling space by buying news stories from new types of wire services that get their content almost entirely from freelancers, paying them as little as $5 per story (Siegel, 2010). News organizations also are buying cheaper production equipment, such as video cameras, and sending equipment home with staff members. Sacrificing some of the visual quality of a newscast or newspaper seems a good decision in an age when the lower-quality home videos on YouTube have become a major competitor for audience attention.

Another way that news organizations are attempting to restructure and blend job functions is in bringing down the so-called "Chinese Wall" between the editorial and advertising departments (Witschge & Nygren, 2009). The "Chinese Wall" refers to the idea that employees in newsrooms and sales departments should work independently of each other in news media companies. Separation protects the news organization's credibility by buffering reporters from the pressure to slant coverage to please or protect advertisers. However, research suggests that, as uncertainty increases in media markets, media managers increase their market orientation as part of their uncertainty reduction strategies (Beam, 2001). In terms of organizational structures, increased market orientation often takes the form of closer cooperation with the business department of the organization.

In recent years, more than a few publishers and general managers have argued that such cooperation between the two departments is in everyone's best interest. By pleasing advertisers, profits will improve and editorial jobs will be protected. In some cases, the wall appears to have been largely reconfigured, if not breached. In late 2009, the *Dallas Morning News* announced that news editors for certain sections such as travel, entertainment, automobiles, and real estate would now "report directly" to managers of the sales department (Mong, 2009).

Not all journalists object to this change. In a national survey of newspaper editors, Gade (2008) found that many believed closer collaboration with other departments helped them spread journalistic values throughout the organization—even as they claimed success in keeping other departments' profit orientation from infiltrating the newsroom. Whether the editors were correct in their perception that the values transmission was largely one way, the trend toward closer collaboration between news and sales seems likely to continue as long as industry margins are under pressure. Close collaborations between news and sales departments might improve media revenues and profits in the short term, although some research suggests it does not necessarily result in circulation gains (Beam, 2001).

Regardless, the potential long-term effects are even less clear. As audiences for bloggers and citizen journalists have grown, news professionals have argued that society needs the legacy media because traditional media provide high-quality information that is independent of outside influences and agendas. However, if news–sales collaborations such as the one announced by the *Dallas Morning News* taint editorial independence, audiences will no longer have any reason to pay traditional news organizations for their product. Endless amounts of information of doubtful origin and influence are available for free on the Internet.

Informal Organizational Structures

The formal structures appearing on organizational charts notwithstanding, an organization's informal structures can be almost, if not fully, as powerful in influencing actual performance (Perrow, 1986). A manager's leadership style—authoritarian, mentoring, or completely laissez-faire—has tremendous influence on the organizational climate and performance of subordinates in much the same way that formal structures do. The organizational culture—encouraging or discouraging of risk; change oriented or change averse—also affects organizational initiatives and outcomes. Routines, organizational politics, institutional memory, all are part of the informal structures within organizations that shape, enable, and sometimes constrain organizational decisions and actions. One of the key elements of informal structures in news organizations is the strength of the traditional professional culture of journalism, which research suggests has become a critical factor in news organizations' ability to adapt to the uncertainties of their changing market conditions.

Culture is an invisible sociological structure that is historically and socially constructed and includes shared knowledge, values, and practices that govern behavior within a group (Bantz, 1997; Bloor & Dawson, 1994; Linton, 1945; Ott, 1989; Schein, 1992). Organizational culture emerges from the influence of the national and regional cultures surrounding an organization, the formal and informal structures established by the organization's founder and those of its current leadership, the staff of the organization, and the market and industry environment in which the organization operates (Ott, 1989). Professional cultures, such as journalism, are characterized by specific professional knowledge, the professional's delivery of a critical service that requires the application of professional knowledge, an established code of ethics, professional education, a certain degree of independence and discretion in the work process, and orientation toward other members of the profession as the primary reference group (Bloor & Dawson, 1994; Bourdieu, 1988; Forsyth & Danisiewicz, 1985; Martin & Frost, 1996; Ott, 1989; Toren, 1969).

Previous research on news organizations has established the critically important role that organizational and professional cultures play in shaping news content (Breed, 1955; Eliasoph, 1997; Ettema, Whitney, & Wackman, 1987; Gieber, 1964; Hirsch, 1977; Molotch & Lester, 1974; Shoemaker & Reese, 1991; Tuchman, 1973; Turow, 1992; Zelizer, 1997). The research indicates that, when organizational and professional cultures conflict in news organizations, journalists tend to adapt to the demands of organizational culture rather than insisting on the prerogatives of their professional culture (Altschull, 1997; Bagdikian, 1992; Breed, 1955; Gieber, 1964; Underwood, 1993). However, meeting the standards of the journalistic professional culture by producing what journalists perceive to be a quality news product is one of the strongest predictors of journalists' job satisfaction (Bergen & Weaver, 1988; Daniels & Hollifield, 2002; Pollard, 1995; Stamm & Underwood, 1993).

More recent research and debates suggest that the traditional professional culture of journalism is proving both a blessing and a curse in terms of the ability of news organizations to rapidly adapt to changing market and techno-logical conditions. On the positive side, the professional culture's traditional focus on news quality and public service may encourage journalists to produce higher-quality journalism than would be expected given the resources their news organizations provide (Hollifield, 2006). On the negative side, research shows journalists have resisted, resented, or struggled with many of the changes in structures, technologies, and processes introduced in newsrooms in the past decade (Daniels & Hollifield, 2002; Deuze, Bruns, & Neuberger, 2007; Lowrey, 2006; O'Sullivan & Heinonen, 2008; Schultz & Sheffer, 2008, 2009; Singer, 2003, 2004, 2009). Journalists' resistance to these tides of change stem from numerous sources. Some study findings show strongly felt percep-tions that management had excluded journalists from decisions involved in recent innovations, failed to provide the resources needed to support the new endeavors, or mismanaged the change process altogether (Daniels & Hollifield, 2002; Gade, 2004; Schultz & Sheffer, 2008, 2009). Other studies have cited the demand that converged journalists overcome the long-established rival-ries between print and broadcast reporting (Singer, 2004) or the clash of professional cultures between traditional journalists and their computer industry-oriented online counterparts (Singer, 2003). Where citizen journal-ism and user-generated content are concerned, journalists have been found to have deeply held convictions about their professional prerogatives and the superiority of the content they produce compared with that submitted by citi-zen journalists (Deuze et al., 2007; Lowrey, 2006; Singer, 2009). Regardless of the source of the resistance, the power of such informal structures within news organizations appears to play a major role in shaping the industry's response to the current environment of uncertainty. As Perrow (1986) noted:

> The explanation for organizational behavior is not primarily in the formal structure of the organization . . . it lies largely in the myriad subterranean processes of informal groups, conflicts between groups, recruitment poli-cies, dependencies on outside groups and constituencies, the striving for prestige, community values, the local community power structure, and legal institutions. (p. 159)

Although some frontline journalists continue to have doubts about the value of new models of journalism, a growing number are convinced that nothing less than a radical restructuring of news organizations is required for survival. This restructuring is likely to take a number of forms and to evolve over time through trial and error. If, however, no one is yet sure of the exact recipe, several things are certain: In the face of increased competition from free Internet content, declining revenues, and the audience's changing values, news organizations are going to be forced to radically cut costs, find new forms of content that reconnect audiences to news, and serve the public interest while serving the public's interests.

Already, a number of new formal and informal structures are emerging in news organizations. Managers in some media companies are developing a new perspective on citizen journalism. Skyrocketing demand for YouTube and other UGC on the Internet has convinced them that UGC has to be a part of the news bundle they offer to twenty-first-century audiences. It allows news organizations to tap the popular power of peer-to-peer communication, provides an opportunity to engage people with the news by encouraging them to contribute, and expands the news organization's reporting resources. One news executive called UGC "one of the most empowering developments in local and national media, ever" (news executive, personal communication, November 10, 2009). However, incorporating UGC into the news product requires journalists to redefine news "quality." News professionals must accept material produced by non-professionals, valuing such contributions for their content rather than their production values. Such a shift represents a major challenge to journalists' professional culture and their view of their own superiority as content producers.

Equally disruptive to news organizations' informal structures is the growing impossibility of defining journalism according to a particular distribution technology. As newspapers and television both migrate toward online and mobile platforms, the technological—and professional—distinctions between print and broadcast journalists are fading. For more than a decade, news managers have discussed the need for multimedia-capable journalists, although journalists themselves have been less than enthusiastic about the change (O'Sullivan & Heinonen, 2008; Schultz & Sheffer, 2008). Now, however, many news organizations consider it an imperative, not an option, that journalists be able to work competently across all formats and platforms.

Summary and Conclusion

Organizational theory has evolved in recent years to recognize that human agency plays a much greater role in organizational performance than scholars once believed. Today, even the concept of organizational structure itself is recognized as a product of human agency rather than economic rationality as was previously assumed. Recent research suggests the high-performance organization is innovative, flexible, constantly evolving in response to internal and external changes to its environment, and actively participating in both human and industry networks, gathering information and leveraging interdependencies (McGrath, 2006).

In news media organizations, macro-organizational structures have become more fluid over the past few decades. Public ownership, increased competition, declining news audiences, and a fragmenting advertiser market have forced media companies to shift focus from journalistic performance to financial performance. Deregulation in the 1980s and 1990s set off a cycle of media mergers and divestitures as executives sought to capture scale economies and develop strategically advantageous product portfolios. Research on the effects of these strategic structural reorganizations suggests, however, that they were mostly ineffective. For most media companies, the merger and acquisition activity did not return the anticipated benefits and, in some cases, actually proved harmful to the news organization as the result of increased debt loads, reduced financial efficiency, and, in a few cases, completely failed acquisitions.

As a result of the financial stress at the corporate level, media companies are significantly restructuring at the organizational level. Barriers that separated editorial and sales departments and protected news content from outside pressure are being chipped away by media owners and executives seeking improved profits. Financial pressure has forced many organizations to significantly cut the resources they devote to news gathering. Reduced resources, combined with the opportunities created by digital networks, have resulted in major changes in the formal and informal structures of news organizations. Staff reductions and technological changes have opened newsrooms to citizen journalists and computer specialists, have forced journalists to use multiple media in their reporting, and have blurred the historical distinctions between print, broadcast, and online journalists. Standards for what represents "quality" news content are falling as content is accepted from non-professional producers, newsroom task specialization dissipates, lower-quality production technologies are adopted, and content receives less scrutiny and editing before being released to the public.

On the positive side, these changes have made newsroom structures flatter and less hierarchical, which should encourage innovation and creativity. They also open the traditionally closed news-construction process to new ideas, new voices, new perspectives, and, hopefully, a more audience-centered focus. On the other hand, the increased workload and range of tasks required of journalists give news professionals little time to develop new ideas or do in-depth reporting. Additionally, the changes occurring in the formal and informal structures of news organizations raise serious questions about the quality, independence, and accuracy of the news and information audiences will receive in the future from legacy news media.

In the final analysis, one of the greatest challenges of the next few decades may be developing new organizational structures that can sustain the production of the quality journalism necessary to an open, democratic, transparent, and informed society. Indeed, understanding the nature of the optimal organizational structures for the tumultuous twenty-first-century news market may be one of the greatest uncertainties facing journalism.

Thought Questions: Contemplating Change

1. What is the difference between a formal and an informal organizational structure? Give examples.
2. What does research tell us about the relationship between media organizational structures and financial and journalistic performance?
3. Since the mid-1990s, organizational scholars have radically changed their views about the relationship between organizational structure and organizational performance. How and why have those views changed?

Notes

1 Research suggests moderate levels of competition among news media in a given market improves journalism quality as news organizations invest resources in strengthening their news product (Coulson & Lacy, 1996, 2003; Lacy, Coulson, & St. Cyr, 1999). However, when competition becomes excessive relative to the size of the available audience and advertiser markets, causing profit margins to fall sharply or disappear altogether, journalism quality suffers (Becker et al., 2009; Hollifield, 2006; Open Society Institute, 2005).
2 Smaller community news organizations such as weekly newspapers have tended to have relatively few employees. Traditionally, therefore, formal organizational structures in small news organizations have tended to be non-hierarchical.

References

Akhavan-Majid, R., Rife, A., & Gopinath, S. (1991). Chain ownership and editorial independence: A case study of Gannett Newspapers. *Journalism Quarterly, 68,* 59–66.

Albarran, A. B. (1996). *Media economics: Understanding markets, industries, and concepts.* Ames: Iowa University Press.

Alexander, A., & Owers, J. (2009). Divestiture restructuring in the media industries: A financial market case analysis. *International Journal on Media Management, 11,* 102–114.

Altschull, J. H. (1997). Boundaries of journalistic autonomy. In D. Berkowitz (Ed.), *Social meaning of news: A text reader* (pp. 259–285). Thousand Oaks, CA: Sage.

Bagdikian, B. H. (1992). *The media monopoly* (4th ed.). Boston: Beacon Press.

Bantz, C. R. (1997). News organizations: Conflict as a crafted cultural norm. In D. Berkowitz (Ed.), *Social meaning of news: A text reader* (pp. 123–137). Thousand Oaks, CA: Sage.

Beachboard, M. R., & Beachboard, J. C. (2006). Implications of foreign ownership on journalistic quality in a post-communist society: The case of finance. *Informing Science Journal, 6,* 144–161. Retrieved November 25, 2010, from http://inform.nu/Articles/Vol9/v9p143–162Beachboard83.pdf

Beam, R. A. (2001). Does it pay to be a market-oriented daily newspaper? *Journalism & Mass Communication Quarterly, 78,* 466–483.

Becker, L. B., Beam, R., & Russial, J. (1978). Correlates of daily newspaper performance in New England. *Journalism Quarterly*, 100–108.

Becker, L. B., Hollifield, C. A., Jacobsson, A., Jacobsson, E. M., & Vlad, T. (2009). Is more always better? Examining the adverse effects of competition on media performance. *Journalism Studies, 10*, 368–385.

Berg, C. (2005). *Myths of the corporate media. Institute of Public Affairs Review*. Retrieved November 25, 2010, from http://ipa.org.au/library/57-2-mythcorporatemedia.pdf

Bergen, L. A., & Weaver, D. (1988). Job satisfaction of daily newspaper journalists and organization size. *Newspaper Research Journal, 9*(2), 1–13.

Bloor, G., & Dawson, P. (1994). Understanding professional culture in organizational context. *Organization Studies, 15*, 275–295.

Bourdieu, P. (1988). *Homo academicus* (P. Collier, Trans.). Stanford, CA: Stanford University Press.

Breed, W. (1955). Social control in the newsroom: A functional analysis. *Social Forces, 33*, 326–335.

Copeland, T., Koller, T., & Murrin, J. (1991). *Valuation: Measuring and managing the value of companies*. New York: McKinsey.

Coulson, D. C., & Lacy, S. (1996). Journalists' perceptions of how newspaper and broadcast news competition affects newspaper content. *Journalism & Mass Communication Quarterly, 73*, 354–363.

Coulson, D. C., & Lacy, S. (2003). Television reporters' perceptions of how television and newspaper competition affects City Hall coverage. *Mass Communication and Society, 6*, 161–174.

Cranberg, G., Bezanson, R. P., & Soloski, J. (2001). *Taking stock: Journalism and the publicly traded newspaper company*. Ames: Iowa State University Press.

Daniels, G., & Hollifield, C. A. (2002). Times of turmoil: Short- and long-term effects of organizational change on newsroom employees. *Journalism & Mass Communication Quarterly, 79*, 661–680.

Demers, D. (1996). Corporate newspaper structure, profits and organizational goals. *Journal of Media Economics, 9*, 1–23.

Demers, D. (1997a, August). *Corporate news structure and news source perceptions: Another test of the editorial vigor hypothesis*. Paper presented at the annual convention of the Association for Education in Journalism and Mass Communication, Chicago, IL.

Demers, D. (1997b, August). *Revisiting corporate newspaper structure and profit-making: Was I wrong?* Paper presented at the annual convention of the Association for Education in Journalism and Mass Communication, Chicago, IL.

Demers, D. (1999). *Global media: Menace or messiah?* Cresskill, NJ: Hampton Press.

Deuze, M., Bruns, A., & Neuberger, C. (2007). Preparing for an age of participatory news. *Journalism Practice, 1*, 322–228.

Donaldson, L. (2001). The normal science of structural contingency theory. In S. R. Clegg, C. Hardy, & W. Nord (Eds.), *Handbook of organization studies* (pp. 57–76). Thousand Oaks, CA: Sage.

Eliasoph, N. (1997). Routines and the making of oppositional news. In D. Berkowitz (Ed.), *Social meaning of news: A text reader* (pp. 230–253). Thousand Oaks, CA: Sage.

Ettema, J. S., Whitney, D. C., & Wackman, D. B. (1987). Professional mass communicators. In C. R. Berger & S. H. Chaffee (Eds.), *Handbook of communication science* (pp. 747–780). Newbury Park, NJ: Sage.

Fedler, F., & Pennington, R. (2003). Employee-owned dailies: The triumph of economic self interest over journalistic ideals. *International Journal on Media Management, 5,* 262–274.

Forsyth, P. B., & Danisiewicz, T. J. (1985). Toward a theory of professionalization. *Work and Occupations, 12,* 59–76.

Gaziano, C. (1989). Chain newspaper homogeneity and presidential endorsements, 1972–1988. *Journalism Quarterly, 66,* 836–845.

Gade, P. J. (2004). Newspapers and organizational development: Management and journalist perception of newsroom cultural change. *Journalism & Communication Monographs, 6,* 3–55.

Gade, P. J. (2008). Journalism guardians in a time of great change: Newspaper editors' perceived influence in integrated news organizations. *Journalism & Mass Communication Quarterly, 85,* 371–392.

Gade, P. J., & Raviola, E. (2009). Integration of the news and the news of integration: A structural perspective on news media changes. *Journal of Media Business Studies, 6,* 87–111.

Gieber, W. (1964). News is what newspapermen make it. In L. A. Dexter, & D. M. White (Eds.), *People, society and mass communication* (pp. 173–182). New York: Free Press.

Hirsch, P. M. (1977). Occupational, organizational and institutional models in mass media research: Toward an integrated framework. In P. M. Hirsch, P. V. Miller, & F. G. Kline (Eds.), *Strategies for communication research* (pp. 13–42). Beverly Hills, CA: Sage.

Hollifield, C. A. (1999). The effects of foreign ownership on media content: Thomson's U.S. newspapers' coverage of the Quebec independence vote. *Newspaper Research Journal, 20*(1), 65–82.

Hollifield, C. A. (2003). The impact of financial markets on media management practices. *International Journal on Media Management, 5,* 224–226.

Hollifield, C. A. (2006). News media performance in hyper-competitive markets: An extended model of effects. *International Journal on Media Management, 8,* 60–69.

Jung, J. (2003). The bigger, the better? Measuring the financial health of media firms. The impact of financial markets on media management practices. *International Journal on Media Management, 5,* 237–250.

Jung, J., & Chan-Olmsted, S. (2005). Impacts of media companies' dual diversification on financial performance. *Journal of Media Economics, 18,* 183–202.

Kolo, C., & Vogt, P. (2003). Strategies for growth in the media and communication industry: Does size really matter? *International Journal on Media Management, 5,* 251–261.

Kurz, H. (2009, October 2). Access to news wildly unequal in U.S., study says. *The Washington Post.* Retrieved October 3, 2009, from http://www.washingtonpost.com/wp-dyn/content/article/2009/10/01/AR2009100104938.html

Lacy, S., Coulson, D., & St. Cyr, C. (1999). The impact of beat competition on City Hall coverage. *Journalism & Mass Communication Quarterly, 76,* 325–340.

Lacy, S., & Riffe, D. (1994). The impact of competition and group ownership on radio news. *Journalism & Mass Communication Quarterly, 71,* 583–593.

Linton, R. (1945). *The cultural background of personality.* New York: D. Appleton-Century.

Lowrey, W. (2006). Mapping the journalism–blogging relationship. *Journalism, 7*(4), 477–500.

Maguire, M. (2009). The nonprofit business model: Empirical evidence from the magazine industry. *Journal of Media Economics, 22,* 119–133.

Martin, H. (2003a). Clustered newspapers operate more efficiently. *Newspaper Research Journal, 24*(4), 6–21.

Martin, H. (2003b, August). *Some effects from horizontal integration of daily newspapers on markets, prices, and competition.* Paper presented at the Association for Education in Journalism and Mass Communication, Kansas City.

Martin, J., & Frost, P. (1996). The organizational culture war games: A struggle for intellectual dominance. In S. R. Clegg, C. Hardy, & W. R. Nord (Eds.), *Handbook of organization studies* (pp. 599–621). London: Sage.

McGrath, R. G. (2006). Beyond contingency: From structure to structuring in the designer of the contemporary organization. In S. R. Clegg, C. Hardy, T. B. Lawrence, & W. R. Nord (Eds.), *The Sage handbook of organization studies* (pp. 577–597). London: Sage.

Mierzejewska, I., & Hollifield, C. A. (2006). Media management theory. In A. Albarran, S. Chan-Olmsted, & M. O. Wirth (Eds.), *Handbook of media economics and management* (pp. 37–66). Mahwah, NJ: Lawrence Erlbaum.

Molotch, H., & Lester, M. (1974). News as purposive behavior: On the strategic use of routine events, accidents and scandals. *American Sociological Review, 39,* 101–112.

Mong, B. (2009, December 2). Memo from Bob Mong and Cyndy Carr, *The Dallas Morning News.* Retrieved April 22, 2010, from http://blogs.dallasobserver.com/unfairpark/2009/12/at_the_dallas_news_the_latest.php

Mutter, A. (2010, March 10). Non-profits can't possibly save the news. *Reflections of a Newsosaur.* Retrieved March 10, 2010, from http://newsosaur.blogspot.com/2010/03/non-profits-cant-possibly-save-news.html

Open Society Institute. (2005). *Television across Europe: Regulation, policy and independence: An overview.* Retrieved September 3, 2005, from/www.soros.org/initiatives/media/articles_publications/publications/eurotv_20051011

O'Sullivan, J., & Heinonen, A. (2008). Old values, new media. *Journalism Practice, 2,* 357–371.

Ott, S. (1989). *The organizational culture perspective.* Chicago: Dorsey Press.

Perrow, C. (1986). *Complex organizations: A critical essay* (3rd ed.). New York: McGraw-Hill.

Phillips, A., Singer, J. B., Vlad, T., & Becker, L. B. (2009). Implications of technological change for journalists' tasks and skills. *Journal of Media Business Studies, 6,* 61–86.

Picard, R. F., & Van Weezel, A. (2008). Capital and control: Consequences of different forms of newspaper ownership. *International Journal on Media Management, 10,* 22–31.

Pollard, G. (1995). Job satisfaction among news workers: The influence of professionalism, perceptions of organizational structure, and social attributes. *Journalism & Mass Communication Quarterly, 72,* 682–697.

Pratte, A., & Whiting, G. (1986). What newspaper editorials have said about deregulation of broadcasting. *Journalism Quarterly, 63,* 497–502.

Priest, C. (1994). *An information framework for the planning and design of "information highways."* Retrieved December 14, 2003, from http://www.eff.org/Groups/CITS/Reports/cits_nii_framework_ota.report

Rystrom, K. (1987). Apparent impact of endorsements by group and independent newspapers. *Journalism Quarterly, 64,* 836–845.

Schein, E. H. (1992). *Organizational culture and leadership* (2nd ed.). San Francisco: Jossey-Bass.

Schultz, B., & Sheffer, M. L. (2008). Blogging from a labor perspective: Lessons for media managers. *International Journal on Media Management, 10*, 1–9.

Schultz, B., & Sheffer, M. L. (2009). Blogging from a management perspective: A follow-up study. *International Journal on Media Management, 11*, 9–17.

Shoemaker, P. J., & Reese, S. D. (1991). *Mediating the message: Theories of influences on mass media content.* New York: Longman.

Siegel, F. (2010, April 28). More publishers outsourcing news. *MediaDailyNews.* Retrieved April 30, 2010, from http://adage.com/mediaworks/article?article_id=143565

Singer, J. (2003). Who are these guys? The online challenge to the notion of journalism. *Journalism, 4*, 139–163.

Singer, J. (2004). More than ink-stained wretches: The resocialization of print journalists in converged newsrooms. *Journalism & Mass Communication Quarterly, 81*, 831–856.

Singer, J. (2009). "Comment is free, but facts are sacred": User generated content and ethical constructs at the *Guardian. Journal of Mass Media Ethics, 24*, 3–21.

Stamm, K., & Underwood, D. (1993). The relationship of job satisfaction to newsroom policy changes. *Journalism Quarterly, 79*, 528–541.

Swensen, D., & Schmidt, M. (2009, January 27). News you can endow. *The New York Times.* Retrieved October 3, 2009, from http://www.nytimes.com/2009/01/28/opinion/28swensen.html?pagewanted=1&_r=1&partner=rss&emc=rss

Toren, N. (1969). Semi-professionalism and social work: A theoretical perspective. In A. Etzioni (Ed.), *The semi-professions and their organization* (pp. 141–195). New York: Free Press.

Tuchman, G. (1973). Making news by doing work: Routinizing the unexpected. *American Journal of Sociology, 79*, 110–131.

Turow, J. (1992). *Media systems in society: Understanding industries, strategies, and power.* New York: Longman.

Underwood, D. (1993). *When MBAs rule the newsroom.* New York: Columbia University Press.

Wackman, D., Gillmor, D., Gaziano, C., & Dennis, E. (1975). Chain newspaper autonomy as reflected in presidential campaign endorsements. *Journalism Quarterly, 52*, 411–420.

Witschge, T., & Nygren, G. (2009). Journalistic work: A profession under pressure? *Journal of Media Business Studies, 6*, 37–60.

Zelizer, B. (1997). Journalists as interpretive communities. In D. Berkowitz (Ed.), *Social meaning of news: A text reader* (pp. 401–419). Thousand Oaks, CA: Sage.

12

JOURNALISM AND DIGITAL TECHNOLOGIES

Jane B. Singer, University of Iowa

Not so very long ago, when I was working on my dissertation in the mid-1990s, I talked with dozens of journalists about what was then a newsroom novelty: the Internet. Few of them had ever actually used it. If they wanted to find something online, they filed a request with the newsroom librarian to conduct a search for them. If they wanted to communicate with a source, they picked up the telephone; if they wanted to communicate with readers . . . well, to be honest, they didn't really want to or see any particular reason why they should. And although a growing number of newspapers—around 1,500 worldwide by 1996, according to stats from trade magazine *Editor & Publisher*—offered some information through a computer in one form or another, my interviewees were highly unlikely to have played any part in putting it there.

Despite this lack of familiarity with the medium, everyone I spoke with had an opinion about it. Many journalists were wary; some were enthusiastic. Most acknowledged the Internet's potential, as best they could envision and articulate it at the time, but remained strongly convinced of the fundamental value of their own occupational role as information gatherers and interpreters (Singer, 1997b). And nearly everyone volunteered two disclaimers. The first was "I am not a geek." Computer technology was a tool, used with varying degrees of skill or relish, but it was emphatically not central to what they did as journalists. And what they did as journalists was what ultimately mattered. "It wasn't the printing press that changed the world, it was good journalism," one editor said. "The same goes for high tech" (Singer, 1997a, p. 9).

The other common disclaimer was "Newspapers may be doomed, but they won't die on my watch." Journalists at all stages of their careers were certain they would outrun any tidal wave of change, if just barely. "There will always be newspapers—for at least the next 25 years," one journalist said. Print may go away, said another, "but after I'm, I hope, retired on the beach and not worrying about it." A third envisioned that "by the time of, not my kids, but my children's children, newspapers will probably be gone" (Singer, 1997b, pp. 77–78).

Plus ça change, plus c'est la même chose, as the French say. The intervening years have dramatically expanded the capabilities of communication technology and journalists' use of—indeed, reliance on—their digital tools. The Internet has become integral to their jobs, and those jobs now incorporate technologically enabled practices not yet imagined in the early days of the Web, from creating video packages to engaging in online conversations with readers. Yet journalists' attitudes and self-perceptions have proven strikingly resilient.

At the same time, however, the uncertainties of today's news environment introduce new concerns for practitioners. They remain convinced of the fundamental value of journalism and journalists, but many are less confident that a media industry with steadily leaking revenue can stay afloat for the foreseeable future (Pew Research Center, 2010; Project for Excellence, 2008). And there is a growing recognition that any number of devils may lurk in the details of just how journalists go about doing their work and fulfilling their social roles as the media continue to evolve at breakneck speed.

This chapter highlights some of the seismic shifts in the occupation of journalism in recent years, exploring practitioners' reactions in a media environment that looks less familiar and more precarious than it did only a short time ago. Focusing on cultural norms and practices of journalists, the chapter examines pressures for (and challenges to) change in three inter-related areas: control over information, news production practices, and relationships with audiences.

Shifting Control

One of the most profound changes associated with the exponential growth of the Internet since the 1990s has been the creation of a world in which everyone can be a publisher. But that does not mean, journalists are adamant in insisting, that everyone can be a journalist. Technological developments and their accompanying social transformations have pushed journalists to ask the sort of existential questions they did not have to face before: Who is a journalist? What, exactly, does a journalist do that other people do not? Do journalists serve a unique social role, and, if so, what is it?

The answers they have come up with highlight occupational roles, discussed further below, but viewed largely from a normative perspective. Journalists see themselves as providing a public service, a hallmark of professionalism (Larson, 1977), which has been news workers' strongest claim to professional status over the past century (Dennis, 1996). If public service is what you believe you are about, and the provision of information is your vehicle for delivering that service, then the quality of the information matters—and you must identify and express ways of safeguarding it. Ethical guidelines fill that need, providing a framework for distinguishing between high-quality information that is a service to the public, and low-quality information that may be a disservice—and, by extension, also distinguishing the providers of the former from the providers of the latter.

High-quality information must be credible, so journalists highlight ethical principles such as truth-telling, normative stances such as independence, and newsroom practices such as verification. The providers of that information also must be credible, requiring journalistic adherence to such normative goals as accuracy—and accountability for inaccuracy (Gup, 1999; Kovach & Rosenstiel, 2007; Singer & Ashman, 2009). True, such lofty ethical precepts may too often be closer to the ideal than to the reality, but they nevertheless are fundamental to most journalists' definitions of themselves and their role in democratic society.

Those definitions have taken on something of a defensive tinge over the past decade and more, as the Internet has eroded alternative articulations of who is—and, crucially, who is not—a journalist. A journalist can no longer be defined by access to the means of disseminating information; technology puts that capability at everyone's fingertips. A journalist can no longer be defined by access to sources of data for the same reason. Employment status has always been a dubious criterion, as freelance journalists can attest. The ability to communicate cogently and effectively remains important, but it is an ability shared by a great many people who clearly are not journalists. The normative stances, however, are more useful in setting boundaries around the entity of journalism and the enterprises of those who practice it: Those within the ethical parameters are journalists, or at least are engaged in journalistic work, and those outside them are not. In short, the norms form occupational turf markers for journalists (Lowrey, 2006), and those markers are simultaneously less tangible and more durable than the ones the Internet is obliterating.

In particular, journalists have drawn on those normative claims to reconfigure their self-perceptions as gatekeepers in terms of the quality of information reaching the public rather than its quantity, which would be virtually impossible to limit in a global, open network. It is, in a way, their attempt to assert occupational control over the uncontrollable, to reclaim the authority that vanished in the transition from an environment in which journalists were central to the flow of information to one in which there is no center at all (Lowrey & Anderson, 2005; Robinson, 2007; Singer, 2007). Adapting the perception of exactly what it means to be an information gatekeeper so it rests on normative judgments and ethical enactment of those judgments allows journalists to reshape the definition of their role to fit the new information ecology, as well as to re-establish limits on admission to that role in an unlimited media space.

This attempt to adjust to shifts in control over information can be seen especially clearly in studies documenting journalists' reactions to "user-generated content" (UGC), material contributed to media websites by readers of those sites. As early as 2005, Thurman uncovered widespread concern about the effects of UGC on professional norms and values, including standards of spelling and punctuation, accuracy, and balance. Despite high resource costs for moderation, journalists at the British national media outlets in his study felt they needed to edit user contributions in order to ensure balance and decency (Thurman, 2008).

Subsequent studies have suggested that this perceived need to control not only journalists' own information output but also the output of their audiences is widespread. Journalists at national newspapers throughout Europe and North America moderate public contributions to limit the potential for ethical abuse and legal transgressions (Singer et al., 2011). In Britain, where the BBC and several national newspapers have been pioneers in making space available for user material, there are persistent concerns not just about legal liability but also about issues of reputation and trust (Hermida & Thurman, 2008). At *The Guardian*, for example, journalists worried about the potentially detrimental effect of "nasty comments, which can undermine the brand," and they saw what one editor called a crucial role for "the expert journalist who can interrogate and understand and all of those sorts of things in a way that the citizen reporter just can't" (Singer & Ashman, 2009, pp. 13–14). British journalists at local newspapers also strongly felt the need to oversee the quality of user contributions despite shrinking newsroom resources; for example, one described the value of UGC as "disproportionate to the excessive amount of management time which is taken up with trying to ensure it is accurate, balanced, honest, fair and—most importantly—legally safe to publish" (Singer, 2010b, p. 134).

Changes in the ways that online information can (or cannot) be controlled, then, have prompted journalists to differentiate themselves from other social actors largely in normative terms. In doing so, they have reconceptualized the nature of their gatekeeping role and reasserted its social value in a no-holds-barred media environment; they now are in the process of extending that role to oversight not only of their own actions but also those of their audiences. Along the way, they are incorporating new practices into long-standing newsroom work routines.

Shifting Practices

Journalists continue to see themselves as "not geeks," but proficiency with computer technology nonetheless has become central to the ability to do their jobs. A few journalists who came of age when the clatter of typewriters (and a lot of cigarette smoke) filled the newsroom are now hunting and pecking their way into retirement; larger numbers who learned to write, file, and perhaps paginate their copy using desktop computers still have a decade or two to go. However, as media structures and news-making processes have adapted to the continuous emergence of new technical capabilities (Boczkowski, 2005), life in the twenty-first-century newsroom has become far more technologically complex. The journalist's job now involves the use of multiple tools to produce multiple types of content for multiple delivery platforms.

The first decade of the 2000s was marked by ongoing evolution in work practices, accompanied by evolution in the jargon describing them. Among the first up was "backpack journalist," greeted largely with fear and loathing when it was bandied about in the early 2000s, as news organizations began to get serious about using their websites as something other than a repository for stories from the newspaper or (less commonly) television news show. The backpack journalist was seen, with considerable trepidation, as a "multiple media multitasker capable of operating a video camera, performing a TV stand-up, telling a print story, writing a broadcast script, creating a Flash animation, compiling a photo gallery, grabbing an audio clip and muckraking masterfully" (Stone, 2002). The predicted result: "a mush of mediocrity." Some journalists might be able to effectively juggle such a variety of tasks, Stone warned, but most would continue to be good at some aspects of the job—and bad at others.

The idea of newsrooms filled with people who could produce stories for print, television, and the Internet appealed to many media managers, however, especially those who ran companies that owned all three types of outlets in a single market. "Newsroom convergence" was the next buzzword to spread around the industry in the first half of the 2000s. The converged newsroom looked different in different places, but it involved some combination of news staffs, technologies, products, and geography from previously distinct media. Although its boosters hailed convergence as a sweeping industry phenomenon, and hundreds of U.S. news outlets eventually claimed to have some sort of converged arrangement for producing news (Lowrey, 2005), the reality on the ground was generally underwhelming. "Media convergence is like teenage sex," one Danish editor remarked in the early 2000s. "Everybody thinks everybody else is doing it. The few who are actually doing it aren't very good at it" (Dailey, Demo, & Spillman 2005, p. 151).

The most widely publicized U.S. example was in Tampa, where Media General built a $40 million "temple of convergence" (Colon, 2000, p. 26) for its *Tampa Tribune* newspaper, NBC television affiliate, and TBO.com website. Some (though far from all or even most) journalists significantly changed their work practices to accommodate additional outlets—for instance, assignment editors at least tried to coordinate with cross-media counterparts, and a handful of newspaper reporters did TV stand-ups—but many carried on much as they always had. There were reported shifts in self-perceptions (away from a medium-specific identity) and perceptions of colleagues (away from derogatory stereotypes), but by and large, newsroom culture at each media outlet proved stubbornly change resistant (Dupagne & Garrison, 2006; Lawson-Borders, 2003; Singer, 2004).

Regardless of the medium, however, gathering information and turning it into a story is central to newsroom culture, not just in the normative terms already described but in very practical ones: Those tasks are the day-to-day work of the journalist. Particularly since the mid-2000s, new technological capabilities have made that work simultaneously easier and harder.

It is easier because the tools have become smaller, simpler, and suppler. If the "backpack journalists" were barely visible beneath the staggering array of audio and video equipment they toted, the "MoJos"—yet another buzzword, this time for "mobile journalists"—who succeeded them travel relatively light. Most if not all of the bulky kit has been reduced to a size that fits cozily in a jacket pocket. Mobile and smartphones, digital voice recorders, personal digital assistants, and other similar devices offer compact versatility in capturing, organizing, and transmitting information of various kinds, from text to sounds to images, both still and moving.

However, a lighter physical load has not translated to a lighter workload for journalists. News practitioners today do, in fact, precisely fit the definition of the backpack journalist above; the only thing missing is the backpack. Telling stories across multiple formats is, put plainly, more and harder work. And there are fewer people to do it, as the size of newsroom budgets has shrunk almost as much as the size of video cameras. Meanwhile, the Internet, so peripheral that it was nearly invisible to journalists a generation ago, has become far more central to the news operation and far more voracious in its appetite for fresh information in a multiplying number of formats. Whether the combination adds up to a stronger public service or the predicted "mush of mediocrity" remains an open question (Martyn, 2009; Stone, 2002). Indeed, concerns about the ability to maintain standards of accuracy and verifiability seem to be growing along with the pressure to produce rapidly updated information (Pew Research Center, 2010). In general, it seems undeniable that the journalist's job has become harder because the information that proverbially doesn't grow on trees is no longer disseminated on them either.

And that's not all. As the backpack journalist has given way to the MoJo, the idea that convergence is primarily about media platforms has been overtaken by the view that it is more about the nature of the stories carried on those platforms. For example, journalists covering a breaking news event can (and increasingly are expected to) produce one version of the story as a continually updated online report, another based on images or quotes from the scene, and a third for the next day's newspaper. There are fewer distinct "online journalists"; aside from a handful of specialized areas, such as database construction, everyone does everything. The view of online content and the people who produce it as "separate and unequal," prevalent in newsrooms in the 1990s, has largely vanished. Converged newsrooms meant they were no longer physically separate; by 2010, "they" simply equaled "us."

But that's still not all. The final, most recent change in journalistic practice associated with technological development is perhaps the most profound cultural shift of the lot. It took journalists more than a decade to adjust their practices to the fact that the Internet is a digital medium and, as such, is endlessly flexible in the formats it can accommodate—again, from text to sound to images of various sorts. They now are adjusting to the fact that it is also a network. The give and take of an interactive medium raises issues of control, as discussed above, and of interpersonal relationships, which we'll come to soon. It also has brought about whole new narrative structures for journalistic storytelling.

Consider the "j-blog," the last bit of jargon for now. Beginning around the middle of the decade and rapidly becoming commonplace on media websites (Lowrey & Mackay, 2008), blogs have been adopted by journalists as an optimal place to display short-form reporting, short-form analysis, and short-form writing (Robinson, 2006). With the advent of tools such as Twitter, "live blogs" direct from the scene of a story have joined the mix as a way to reduce what was already mini to micro: immediate, informal, even impressionistic information, conveyed in tiny bursts of 140 characters or less and, perhaps, an image or two.

In addition to placing primary value on rapid-fire delivery, these new and evolving story forms also move journalistic writing styles much closer to those of content contributors from outside the newsroom. For example, journalists advised all their working lives to keep their personal views and voice out of their writing suddenly find themselves with a vehicle that encourages them to showcase both, much as other bloggers do. J-blogs are nearly the complete opposite in narrative structure to the traditional "objective" news story. In tone, the best are conversational, candid, even cheeky. They talk about "I" and "you" rather than that other, more distant "third person" who fills the paragraphs of most newspaper stories. They convey what the journalist thinks—both reflection on the world and self-reflection on the process of turning parts of that world into a news product (Singer, 2010a). Journalists, then, have adopted and adapted a narrative voice very different from the one that has been "theirs" since the maintenance of professional distance—call it objectivity—became the norm a century ago (Mindich, 1998). In doing so, they are joining, perhaps belatedly, the shift from a modern to a postmodern view of how reality is constructed and conveyed.

Also, crucially, these j-blogs and other more conversational journalistic formats invite input and responses from outside the newsroom—to which journalists, in turn, respond.

Shifting Relationships

Along with changes in control over content and in the practice of constructing a news narrative, life in a network brings changes in the nature of the relationship between those inside and those outside the newsroom. As suggested above, this shift to an inherently collaborative journalistic culture may be the hardest one of all for journalists.

Almost from the moment the Internet emerged from the scientific community and burst onto the public radar, it was hailed as a democratizing force across all phases of civic life. The potential of a platform enabling people to both obtain and provide information—instantaneous, interconnected, and completely unbounded information—was immediately obvious. The medium was seen as inherently empowering from all sorts of perspectives: political actor, social agent, goods or services consumer . . . or, of course, media audience member.

In fact, of all those roles, that of "media audience member" is perhaps the most clearly mutable (Gillmor, 2006; Rosen, 2006). As outlined above, the active role of producer and the more passive one of consumer of information, including the kind we might all agree is "news," are interchangeable. In a network open to universal participation, everyone has the potential to be both. Countless media practitioners and observers have pointed out the rules-changing implications for existing and new relationships between those who work in a newsroom and those who do not.

Among the propositions offered over the past decade for what these new relationships might look like are:

> News media organizations are actually story instigators. They track down important stories and relay them to the world. Once they are released, stories transform and can take a life of their own beyond the control of the news organization. The Internet community (and other media) appropriates the stories, retells them, comments on them, adds additional information or overlooked angles, and reworks them as part of a broad-based web of ideas and information. That's not only a good thing, it's essential. If it's not happening, it means your reporting has little value to your audience. (Bowman & Willis, 2003)

> Tomorrow's news reporting and production will be more of a conversation, or a seminar. The lines will blur between producers and consumers, changing the role of both in ways we're only beginning to grasp now. The communication network itself will be a medium for everyone's voice . . . This evolution—from journalism as lecture to journalism as a conversation or seminar—will oblige the various communities of interest to adapt.

Everyone, from journalists to the people we cover, to our sources and the former audience, must change their ways. (Gillmor, 2006, p. xxiv)

Gatewatching complements or, in some cases, entirely supplants traditional journalistic gate*keeping* practices . . . . The balance shifts from a publishing of newsworthy information to a *publicizing* of whatever relevant content is available anywhere on the Web (and beyond), and a subsequent evaluation of such material. This limits or eliminates the need for journalistically trained staff and opens the door to direct participation by audience members as information gatherers (that is, as gatewatchers), reporters, and evaluators—users become *produsers*. In effect, therefore, this model can be described as participatory journalism, and—due to the wide range of views commonly expressed by participating audience members—may lead to a multifaceted, multiperspectival coverage of news events. (Bruns, 2005, p. 2; emphases original)

The journalist as instigator, as conversationalist, maybe even as little more than bystander to "multi-perspectival" news coverage—these all diverge radically from traditional concepts of occupational roles and relationships based on providing information to a more or less passive audience. They affect not only the practice of journalism but its epistemological underpinnings, most notably notions of how truth claims—central to practitioners' self-perception, as discussed above—are best established and explored (Romano, 2009).

Well before the Internet became so popular, a twentieth-century modernist outlook that had nurtured the professionalization of newsroom culture and created the "god-terms" of journalism—facts, truth, reality—had already been shaken by newer views of relativity, subjectivity, and construction (Zelizer, 2004). Online, such esoteric notions are translated into an unending stream of plain-spoken, and often outspoken, language by millions of people all over the world. The journalist defines truth as the result of an occupational process: pre-publication verification—with the journalist doing the verifying. The online zeitgeist flips that idea on its head. Publication is the first, not the last, step in the process of verification because only after an idea is published can it be, collectively, vetted. In other words, truth emerges as a result of discourse rather than as a prerequisite to it (Matheson, 2004; Singer, 2007).

That is a very big shift indeed. In addition to shaking up occupational claims to control over information, as already discussed, it rocks the entire journalistic world view. It also wreaks havoc with such long-standing philosophical frameworks as objectivity, already touched on above. For journalists in the United States in particular, objectivity is the "moral norm" by which they live their professional lives; it is a means of social control and social identity, and the most legitimate grounds for parceling out both praise and blame. Objective journalists, at least in theory, report something called "news" without commenting on it, slanting it, or otherwise shaping it; the norm separates "real" journalists from both overt and covert partisans (Schudson, 2001, pp. 150, 167).

Essentially, claims of objectivity are claims to trustworthiness. Because in a traditional media system, audience members see only the end result of the journalistic activity—the "truth" as vetted by journalists and presented in the form of a packaged news report—they cannot know what went into producing it. By professing to have followed a particular procedure in confronting, organizing, and interpreting an invariably messy reality, journalists ask audiences to trust their accounting of that reality. The relationship is built on a request that readers or viewers put their faith in a set of intangibles: the past reputation, current integrity, and future accountability of both the individual practitioner and the news organization. This faith thus is not entirely blind, but the field of vision it offers is limited, defined by the journalist's overt behavior and the expectations it creates.

Objectivity, then, is the stance of someone engaged in a monologue aimed at audience members rather than a dialogue with them (Soffer, 2009); it is about exclusion and professional distance, not inclusion and collaborative news construction (Deuze, Bruns, & Neuberger, 2007). In a world in which the pursuit of truth is seen instead as a more collaborative enterprise, objectivity loses a considerable portion of its ostensible value. In fact, some observers have suggested that it is being replaced by a relationship norm much better suited to the networked world: transparency. Transparency entails communicating as much as possible about what has gone into a story—a story that is not complete once the journalist has written it but rather is part of an ongoing and more broadly shared process (Karlsson, 2008). Trustworthiness, in this view, is demonstrated rather than simply demanded. Or so goes the theory.

That journalists are even remotely on board with this fundamental shift in what they are about and how they build and maintain relationships is not a little amazing. Yet evidence is emerging that they are—to a point. "The official classical discourse that we were taught in college is no longer valid," said a Spanish editor. "Today, the receiver is a producer as well, and they may be much wiser than us all . . . That is wonderful" (Vujnovic et al., 2010, p. 291). Nearly 95 percent of the journalists in a study of local British papers agreed with the statement that "facilitating debate about local issues through comments is something we should be doing" (Singer, 2010b, p. 138); their national counterparts at *The Guardian* also valued new relationships, saying public input creates a more balanced website thanks to contributors who are, for the most part, "eloquent, intelligent, and able to add to the debate" (Singer & Ashman, 2009, p. 16). A broader European study found that nearly two-thirds of the journalists across a range of countries thought the ability to connect with the audience was an important benefit for online journalism (O'Sullivan & Heinonen, 2008).

It would be a major exaggeration, however, to say that, in the stark light of overhead fluorescents, the adjustment within the newsroom to new relationships with people outside it is proving anything less than extremely difficult. A raft of research since the mid-2000s, much of it already highlighted above, has indicated that making those relationships work is a struggle for many, if not most, journalists. For every expression of support in principle for the benefits of transparency, open discourse, and "multiperspectival news," there is a chorus of real-life concerns. It turns out that most people are not actually interested in talking about the news, at least not on media websites, and those who are interested too often make contributions that are abusive, inane, or just plain wrong. The mechanisms for optimizing the value of participatory journalism are cumbersome, the time to nurture online relationships is hard to find, and the rules of engagement are being written on the fly, if they are being written at all. More transparency seems, to many, to translate to less authority (Lowrey & Anderson, 2005), which most journalists rather like feeling that they have. In general, what one online journalist described as the "slip from professional discourse into a more personal discourse" is one for which journalists are generally unprepared and not a little ambivalent (Singer & Ashman, 2009, p. 17). Yet the transition is happening fast, and cope they must.

Conclusion

Back in the 1990s, when those journalists with whom I began this chapter looked into a future that has now become the past, they saw a world that looked essentially like the one they knew. It was a world in which their role as information providers to a relatively captive and passive audience was something they viewed with a considerable degree of certainty. The role, they felt, would remain central even as the world around it underwent technological change.

Yet the changes that those journalists confidently predicted would have little to do with them have shaken their professional world—and their world view—far more than they envisioned. Multi-faceted new tools and platforms have become integral to their working lives, boundaries between journalists and audiences have been breached, and the future of newspapers themselves is in considerable doubt. Indeed, dealing daily with change and with the uncertainty it introduces has become a core aspect of being a journalist.

The three specific categories of change described here—in the exercise of control, in journalistic practices, and in relationship structures—are, of course, inextricably connected. New relationships mean a reconsideration of how, and whether, to exercise control over information. New narrative structures invite transparency and the give and take of idea exchange, but it is unclear how those fit into either practical work routines or overarching normative frameworks. Publication of instantaneous, multimedia information raises concerns about the foundational principle of accuracy; feeding material from outside the newsroom into the mix adds more complications, not least for claims of journalistic authority.

Inside and outside the media industry, many who try to peer into a murky future are pessimistic about the impact of these changes, as well as others described throughout this book, on journalists' ability to carry out their civic role as well as (from practitioners' perspective) or better than (from the perspective of their critics) they have in the past (Christians, Glasser, McQuail, Nordenstreng, & White, 2009; Pew Research Center, 2010). The prevailing view seems to swing between celebrating the diminished authority of the "mainstream media" and bemoaning the loss of coherence provided by that same once-authoritative entity. For practitioners, the certainty of predicted stability has been replaced by the uncertainty of real-life flux, raising new sorts of existential questions about who journalists are and what they do.

Yet if the contemporary environment has brought such questions to the surface, it has not produced answers that are essentially any different from what they were 20, 50, or 100 years ago, from the time when journalists first began to frame their newly defined profession as a public trust and themselves as public trustees (Williams, 1914). Over the years, journalists have done different things, and they have done differently the things they did before. But throughout a century of profound transformation in the implementation of something called "journalism," their underlying conceptions about their role in society have held remarkably steady.

In 1971, journalists responding to a national survey saw a watchdog function—investigating government claims—as their most important social role, followed by analyzing complex problems and getting information to the public quickly. In 2002, those three, along with "avoid stories with unverified content," still were seen by a majority of journalists as extremely important (Weaver, Beam, Brownlee, Voakes, & Wilhoit, 2007). The 30-plus years in between brought the advent of cable television, an explosion in niche magazines, and, of course, the meteoric rise of the Internet; indeed, many of the respondents work in those media. Yet across the occupation, the core sense of "what we do" has remained firm.

So, too, have understandings of the appropriate ethical principles undergirding that work. Journalists' concerns about user-generated content, described above, stem in large part from this adherence to a very deep-seated sense of what journalism *should* be about. Professionals adopt these shared normative understandings as part of their socialization to newsroom work; research dating back to the 1980s shows that newsroom learning is the strongest source of influence on practitioner ethics, consistently cited by more than four of five journalists (Weaver et al., 2007). Also, as discussed above, the norms that each new journalist absorbs quickly become occupational turf markers (Lowrey,

2006), useful for drawing defining lines around the entity of journalism and the conduct of its practitioners.

Amid all the changes, then, journalists remain relatively certain of their contribution to democratic society and the normative precepts that support and define that contribution. They are, however, far more willing to admit they need to change *how* they do what they do: their work practices and the resulting products. Those are the areas now permeated by uncertainty.

So most journalists remain committed to their central role, but unsure how to go about maintaining its centrality or even its relevance for a society made up of individuals increasingly comfortable constructing their own mediated reality. They remain convinced that only credible information has real value, but unsure how to ascertain credibility in the face of demands for a continuous information flow. They remain attached to their self-perception as public servants but unsure how a "public" that co-produces as well as consumes news—and, moreover, is ambivalent about whether there is any need to be served by media institutions at all—fits into the picture, and even more unsure how to engage with such people.

The questions are difficult indeed, but the biggest obstacle to finding the answers is an unwillingness to look for them. For a decade and more, most journalists metaphorically squeezed their eyes tightly shut and hoped the whole Internet thing would go away. It didn't, and it won't. Ignoring the transformations described in this chapter is no longer an option, even for the most entrenched of the newsroom curmudgeons (should they happen to remain employed). News organizations around the nation and the world are now actively exploring how they can change, some out of desperation but others, increasingly, out of honest desire. A few have even declared at least limited victories in their newsroom culture wars (Pew Research Center, 2010; Williams, 2007).

I have no recipe for success to offer. I am intrigued by a variety of recent experiments, including efforts to make journalism more credible through collaboration, more trustworthy through transparency, and more engaging through the effective use of digital storytelling tools. As more "digital natives" enter the newsroom, uniting their knowledge of the medium with older colleagues' knowledge of the craft, answers to the "how" questions that seem so challenging will have more opportunities to emerge.

Questions of "who," "what," and "how," though, do not address the "why." With so much information at our fingertips and so many people willing and able to provide more, why does journalism matter at all?

Journalists take a lot of criticism for failing to meet the expectations and needs of a rapidly changing media world. Some of it comes from observers who point out that the reality too often falls far short of the admittedly glorified self-perception. Fair enough, and even notoriously thin-skinned practitioners would agree with at least some of those charges (particularly if directed at their competitors). Other criticism points to problems in economic and management structures, focusing on issues addressed in other chapters. However, much of the "they just don't get it" criticism comes from an assertion that our networked, information-rich, and technologically savvy society no longer wants or needs the services of its journalists.

That's just wrong. When everyone can be a publisher, anyone can be a spin merchant; we need the watchdog. When everyone can (and, it seems, does) publicly express an opinion about the latest bits of information trending on Twitter, someone needs to gather those bits, scrutinize them, and create a coherent narrative from the ones that pass muster; that someone is called a reporter (Downie & Schudson, 2009). When any event anywhere reverberates around the globe in a matter of seconds, we need the trustworthy analyst, the interpreter, the sense-maker—the journalist. We need to know that information is "true" in some sense that corresponds with reality before we act, and we need to know it quickly so that our actions will not come too late.

Of course, journalists should continue to change to accommodate changes in the society they serve. They must adapt to new media technologies, capabilities, and responsibilities, as well as to new participants in the enterprise of both defining and producing news. If they do not make these quite difficult adjustments, to their occupational culture as well as to their daily practices, journalists will inevitably lose the ability to be effective in the vital roles they have staked out. As today's practitioners have grown to realize, the roles and norms will hold durable value only as long as journalists remain flexible in enacting them.

Thought Questions: Contemplating Change

This chapter has argued that as the Internet has become an increasingly dominant information source, journalists have gone through significant changes in at least three areas: their self-perceptions as information gatekeepers, largely because of a loss of control over information; their work practices and newsroom environments; and their relationships with audiences. The occupational tasks and roles of the journalist are fundamentally the same as they were a generation ago, but the way those tasks and roles are enacted has evolved, and must continue to evolve, along with the technology.

1. To what extent do you think technology drives the process of change in the practice of journalism and in the journalistic product? What other factors are important, and how do they interact?
2. What will be the next big change affecting journalism, and what adaptations will journalists need to make to accommodate it? What will the challenges be? How might those challenges be overcome?

3. This chapter has focused on news workers rather than on other "stakeholders" in the quality of journalism, including but not limited to news sources, media owners, and the public. What are the effects of the three changes discussed here on those outside the newsroom? In what ways do their actions and reactions feed back into what happens in the newsroom? Where are the most fruitful areas for collaboration, and where will different needs or goals create conflict?

4. Most journalists are convinced that they continue to have a unique social role and to be uniquely, or at least optimally, capable of filling it. They agree that they need to change their practices and products but remain committed to what they see as their core function. Is that sort of incremental change sufficient? If so, how might they best go about it? Or would you redefine the journalist's role to fit today's media environment . . . and, if so, what would your revised definition include?

References

Bivings Group (December 18, 2008). *The use of the Internet by America's newspapers*. Retrieved November 17, 2009, from http://www.bivings.com/thelab/presentations/2008study.pdf

Boczkowski, P. J. (2005). *Digitizing the news: Innovation in online newspapers*. Cambridge, MA: MIT Press.

Bowman, S., & Willis, C. (2003). *We media: How audiences are shaping the future of news and information*. The Media Center at the American Press Institute. Retrieved November 18, 2009, from http://www.hypergene.net/wemedia/weblog.php?id=P34

Bruns, A. (2005). *Gatewatching: Collaborative online news production*. New York: Peter Lang.

Christians, C. G., Glasser, T. L., McQuail, D., Nordenstreng, K., & White, R. A. (2009). *Normative theories of the media: Journalism in democratic societies*. Urbana: University of Illinois Press.

Colon, A. (May/June, 2000). The multimedia newsroom. *Columbia Journalism Review*, 24–27.

Dailey, L., Demo, L., & Spillman, M. (2005). The convergence continuum: A model for studying collaboration between media newsrooms. *Atlantic Journal of Communication, 13*, 150–168.

Dennis, E. E. (1996). Dennis: Journalism is a profession. In E. E. Dennis & J. C. Merrill (Eds.), *Media debates: Issues in mass communication* (2nd ed., pp. 212–215). White Plains, NY: Longman.

Deuze, M., Bruns, A., & Neuberger, C. (2007). Preparing for an age of participatory news. *Journalism Practice, 1*, 322–338.

Downie, L., & Schudson, M. (October 19, 2009). The reconstruction of American journalism. *Columbia Journalism Review*. Retrieved April 30, 2010, from http://www.cjr.org/reconstruction/the_reconstruction_of_american.php?page=all

Dupagne, M., & Garrison, B. (2006). The meaning and influence of convergence: A qualitative case study of newsroom work at the Tampa News Center. *Journalism Studies, 7*(2), 237–255.

Gillmor, D. (2006). *We the media: Grassroots journalism by the people, for the people.* Sebastopol, CA: O'Reilly Media.

Gup, T. (1999). Who's a journalist – I. *Media Studies Journal, 13*(2), 34–37.

Hermida, A., & Thurman, N. (2008). A clash of cultures: The integration of user-generated content within professional journalistic frameworks at British newspaper websites. *Journalism Practice, 2,* 343–356.

Karlsson, M. (2008, May). *Visibility of journalistic processes and the undermining of objectivity.* Paper presented at the International Communication Association, Montreal.

Kovach, B., & Rosenstiel, T. (2007). *The elements of journalism: What newspeople should know and the public should expect.* New York: Crown.

Larson, M. S. (1977). *The rise of professionalism: A sociological analysis.* Berkeley: University of California Press.

Lawson-Borders, G. (2003). Integrating new media and old media: Seven observations of convergence as a strategy for best practices in media organizations. *International Journal on Media Management, 5,* 91–99.

Lowrey, W. (2005). Commitment to newspaper–TV partnering: A test of the impact of institutional isomorphism. *Journalism & Mass Communication Quarterly, 82,* 495–515.

Lowrey, W. (2006). Mapping the journalism–blogging relationship. *Journalism, 7,* 477–500.

Lowrey, W., & Anderson, W. (2005). The journalist behind the curtain: Participatory functions of the internet and their impact on perceptions of the work of journalism. *Journal of Computer-Mediated Communication, 10*(3). Retrieved November 19, 2009, from http://jcmc.indiana.edu/vol10/issue3/lowrey.html

Lowrey, W., & Mackay, J. B. (2008). Journalism and blogging: A test of a model of occupational competition. *Journalism Practice, 2,* 64–81.

Martyn, P. H. (2009). The mojo in the third millennium: Is multimedia journalism affecting the news we see? *Journalism Practice, 3,* 196–215.

Matheson, D. (2004). Weblogs and the epistemology of the news: Some trends in online journalism. *New Media & Society, 6,* 443–468.

Mindich, D. (1998). *Just the facts: How "objectivity" came to define American journalism.* New York: NYU Press.

O'Sullivan, J., & Heinonen, A. (2008). Old values, new media: Journalism role perceptions in a changing world. *Journalism Practice, 2,* 357–371.

Pew Research Center's Project for Excellence in Journalism. (April 12, 2010). *News leaders and the future: News executives, skeptical of government subsidies, see opportunity in technology but are unsure about revenue and the future.* Retrieved April 30, 2010, from http://www.journalism.org/node/20072

Project for Excellence in Journalism. (2008). *State of the news media 2008: Journalist survey.* Retrieved April 30, 2010, from http://www.stateofthemedia.org/2008/journalist_survey.php?cat=0&media=3

Robinson, S. (2006). The mission of the j-blog: Recapturing journalistic authority online. *Journalism, 7,* 65–83.

Robinson, S. (2007). "Someone's gotta be in control here": The institutionalization of online news and the creation of a shared journalistic authority. *Journalism Practice, 1*(3), 305–321.

Romano, C. (November 20, 2009). We need "philosophy of journalism." *Chronicle of Higher Education,* pp. B4–B5.

Rosen, J. (2006). The people formerly known as the audience. *PressThink*. Retrieved November 18, 2009, from http://journalism.nyu.edu/pubzone/weblogs/press-think/2006/06/27/ppl_frmr.html

Schudson, M. (2001). The objectivity norm in American journalism. *Journalism, 2*, 149–170.

Singer, J. B. (1997a). Changes and consistencies: Newspaper journalists contemplate online future. *Newspaper Research Journal, 18*(1/2), 2–18.

Singer, J. B. (1997b). Still guarding the gate? The newspaper journalist's role in an on-line world. *Convergence: The International Journal of Research into New Media Technologies, 3*(1), 72–89.

Singer, J. B. (2004). More than ink-stained wretches: The resocialization of print journalists in converged newsrooms. *Journalism & Mass Communication Quarterly, 81*, 838–856.

Singer, J. B. (2007). Contested autonomy: Professional and popular claims on journal-istic norms. *Journalism Studies, 8*, 79–85.

Singer, J. B. (2010a). Journalism ethics and structural change. *Daedalus: Journal of the American Academy of Arts and Sciences, 139*(2), 89–99.

Singer, J. B. (2010b). Quality control: Perceived effects of user-generated content on newsroom norms, values and routines. *Journalism Practice, 4*, 127–142.

Singer, J. B., & Ashman, I. (2009). "Comment is free, but facts are sacred": User-generated content and ethical constructs at the *Guardian*. *Journal of Mass Media Ethics, 24*, 3–21.

Singer, J. B., Hermida, A., Domingo, D., Heinonen, A., Paulussen, S., Quandt, T., Reich, Z., & Vujnovic, M. (2011). *Participatory journalism: Guarding open gates at online newspapers*. Malden, MA: Wiley-Blackwell.

Soffer, O. (2009). The competing ideals of objectivity and dialogue in American jour-nalism. *Journalism, 10*, 473–491.

Stone, M. (April 2, 2002). The backpack journalist is a "mush of mediocrity." *Online Journalism Review*. Retrieved November 13, 2009, from http://www.ojr.org/ojr/workplace/1017771634.php

Thurman, N. (2008). Forums for citizen journalists? Adoption of user generated con-tent initiatives by online news media. *New Media & Society, 10*, 1–30.

Vujnovic, M., Singer, J. B., Paulussen, S., Heinonen, A., Reich, Z., Quandt, T., Hermida, A., & Domingo, D. (2010). Exploring the political-economic factors of participatory journalism: Views of online journalists in ten countries. *Journalism Practice, 4*, 285–296.

Weaver, D. H., Beam, R. A., Brownlee, B. J., Voakes, P. S., & Wilhoit, G. C. (2007). *The American journalist in the 21st century: U.S. news people at the dawn of a new millennium*. New York: Routledge.

Williams, V. (2007). *All eyes forward: How to help your newsroom get where it wants to go faster*. Reston, VA: Learning Newsroom at the American Press Institute. Retrieved May 1, 2010, from http://www.learningnewsroom.org/alleyesforward.pdf

Williams, W. (1914). *The journalist's creed*. Retrieved April 30, 2010, from http://journal-ism.missouri.edu/about/creed.html

Zelizer, B. (2004). When facts, truth and reality are god-terms: On journalism's uneasy place in cultural studies. *Communication and Critical/Cultural Studies, 1*, 100–119.

13

"SO MANY STORIES, SO LITTLE TIME"

Economics, Technology, and the Changing Professional Environment for News Work

Randal A. Beam and Lindsey Meeks, University of Washington

A decade ago, most U.S. journalists were following what they believed would be safe, predictable career paths at newspapers, magazines, TV stations, and radio stations. Their employers were among the most reliable of moneymakers. The techniques they used to tell stories were well established and well understood. Today, economics and technology are conspiring to reshape the environment in which journalists make news. Red ink has replaced black ink on the balance sheets of journalists' employers (Mutter, 2009). News staffs have been slashed (Project for Excellence in Journalism, 2010). Traditional mass media such as newspapers and broadcast TV stations are transforming themselves into "platform-agnostic news organizations" that want their journalists to understand how to communicate with print, audio, video, photography, and animation—often in the same story (Wilson, 2008).

In the face of these changes, journalists are struggling to adapt. They are unnerved by the new technologies in their newsrooms, they are anxious about job security, and they are increasingly uncertain about the future of their profession (Beam, Weaver, & Brownlee, 2009; Mauro & Dindino, 2007; McNair, 2005; Wilson, 2008). That uncertainty is, in turn, affecting the practice and culture of U.S. journalism. This chapter examines three of the ways that economics and technology are reshaping American journalism:

- *News work is being redefined.* Digital communication technologies such as the Web and mobile devices are requiring journalists to master new tasks and skills. These technologies allow the audience to get news more quickly and more conveniently than ever before. Also, they allow news workers to experiment with new ways to tell stories. However, for many journalists, tasks are becoming more complicated even as their workloads are becoming heavier. And their relationship with their audience is changing as digital technologies make it easier for readers, viewers, and listeners to create and distribute their own content.

- *Journalism's public service mission may be at risk.* Journalists have traditionally embraced a commitment to serving the public, and evidence suggests journalists continue to care deeply about public service. However, profit pressures have led to staff cuts and encouraged U.S. news organizations to become more market driven. That, in the view of media critics, could undermine the profession's ability to serve the public.
- *Professional autonomy is threatened.* Professional autonomy—the ability to control the terms of one's work—is critical for journalists. It allows them to pursue stories that they believe need to be told. It helps them resist efforts by powerful outsiders to unduly influence coverage. However, smaller staffs, heavier workloads, stronger market pressures, and greater attention to the bottom line all are seen as eroding journalists' discretion to do their work as they see fit.

Normative theories of the press accord journalists a central role in a democracy (Christians, Glasser, McQuail, Nordenstreng, & White, 2009; Papacharissi, 2009). That role is to provide citizens with critical information about the world in which they live—information that presumably allows a self-governing nation to thrive. However, the changing environment in which journalists make the news is creating uncertainties about how effectively they can continue to fulfill that role. This chapter draws from a 400-person panel survey of journalists and from other sources to explore those uncertainties. The panel, completed in late 2007, is part of the American Journalist series of studies.[1] These studies have tracked the characteristics, attitudes, values, and working conditions of U.S. journalists since 1971.

The 2007 panel study found that, in some ways, journalists remained surprisingly resilient even as hard times set in at their news organizations. For example, more than 80 percent continued to be satisfied with their jobs even though layoffs or buyouts were taking place in newsrooms. However, the panel study also pointed to troubling uncertainties about the nature of journalistic work, public service, and professional autonomy. These uncertainties, in turn, raise this question: In the future, will journalists be making news that nourishes democracy or that allows it to starve?

Redefinition of News Work

For more than 150 years, technological innovations have been influencing news work. The telegraph supplanted the postal service as the main way of getting dispatches from distant reporters, making the news more timely. Film was replaced by video, which was easier to edit. Telephone, microwave, and satellite communication allowed radio and TV journalists to escape the studio and broadcast live from news events, real or staged. Newspaper and magazine editors who once sketched rough page designs with paper and pencil now create detailed layouts on computers (Dennis & DeFleur, 2010; Straubhaar, LaRose, & Davenport, 2010). All these have been important changes in the way news is produced. None, however, has transformed news work as profoundly as the Web.

The interactive, multimedia capabilities of the Web are forcing changes in what journalists do and in how they think about their professional roles. In *Digitizing the News*, Boczkowski (2004, pp. 64–65) outlined fundamental differences between traditional analog media such as newspapers and interactive online news products. Legacy media—newspapers, magazines, television, and radio—provide fairly uniform, non-customized content to large mass audiences. Their capacity to carry information is finite. They tend to be distributed in specific geographic areas. They have fixed production cycles and use a limited number of content forms—print, audio, video, still images—to convey information. Finally, the roles of the journalists and the audience members are distinct: Journalists create the content, and audience members consume it.

When legacy news media moved online, the rules changed (Boczkowski, 2004). On the Web, information can be customized to satisfy a consumer's preferences. The scarcity of space or broadcast time is no longer a constraint. Distribution is, potentially, worldwide. The deadline-driven production cycle gives way to continuous publication, updating, and revision. The toolkit used to make the news is bigger, and the tools in it are more complicated. Multimedia content production requires mastering not only the intellectual rigors of journalistic storytelling but also the sophisticated equipment and software used to weave together video vignettes, interactive maps, straight text, and the like. News organizations can easily juxtapose content made by trained professionals and amateur "citizen journalists." For journalists, a work environment that traditionally has had a relatively stable set of understandings about professional practice has become unsettled and uncertain (Phillips, Singer, Vlad, & Becker, 2009). The title of a recent advice column in *Quill*, the magazine of the Society of Professional Journalists, confronts the angst that many journalists have been feeling about their work: "Change Happens: Deal With It" (Kimbrough-Robinson, 2008).

One of the most visible changes is job enlargement. Many journalists are taking on a wider range of tasks and responsibilities that are often associated with creating content for the Web and mobile media such as cell phones or iPads. Producing multimedia content requires skills that are technically more complicated than those needed in the past (Cottle, 2003; Wallace, 2009). Recent studies have documented that both workloads and anxiety are increasing in the multimedia newsroom. One study found that about two-thirds of 975 print, broadcast, and online journalists were anxious about their employers' expectations that they learn new digital technologies (Wilson, 2008). Data from the 2007 American Journalist panel study also pointed to job enlargement and its consequences. About two-thirds of the 400 journalists in the study reported that their day-to-day tasks had changed "some" or "a lot" in the year before the study was carried out. When asked what had led to those changes, technology often figured in the answer. "We're doing more work to report news as it's happening for our website while also reworking these reports for the next day's print edition," one journalist explained. "We're adding blogs and even video presentations of the news."

The panel study documented other ways the Web was contributing to job enlargement. The study's 315 reporters were asked about a series of tasks that didn't exist in newsrooms until the Web became a common tool for distributing news.[2] In their responses, almost 60 percent of reporters said they filed breaking news stories for their organization's website. About 30 percent captured audio for the site, and almost 20 percent wrote blogs. Roughly 10 percent created podcasts or took part in live Web Q&A sessions. The panel study also found that it was common for reporters to shoot video (15 percent) or take photos (48 percent). Overall, the reporters estimated spending an average of 30 percent of their time creating or editing content specifically for the Web (though individual estimates varied widely). It seems likely that these percentages would be even higher today, if only because so many news executives see the Web and other digital communication tools as central to their organizations' futures (Project for Excellence in Journalism, 2010).

The expansion of Web tasks is linked to heavier workloads. That came through in both open-ended comments that the panel journalists made about their work lives and in their answers to the fixed-response survey questions. When asked about recent changes in the job, one respondent cited the "increased emphasis on Web production, and Web contributions; increased demand for videos on the Web; [and] a move to more hybrid positions, where someone who has considered themselves [sic] a reporter or an editor in the past is now doing elements of both jobs." Another journalist talked about increased demands because of technological change. "I have a podcast now that I didn't have a year ago," the respondent said. "Within the past year we've gone from once-a-day updating the Web to constantly updating the Web." All in all, about two-thirds of all the 2007 panel respondents reported that their workloads had increased in the previous year. Those reporting higher workloads tended to spend more time on multimedia or Web work than did those whose workloads hadn't grown (Table 13.1).

As the Web and other interactive tools for delivering news and information have become more central to the economic health of news organizations, the insinuation of the Internet into reporting and editing routines has been affecting news work in other ways as well. Several studies show dramatic growth in the amount of time journalists spend doing work online (Hermans, Vergeer, &

TABLE 13.1 Percentage doing Multimedia and Web Tasks by Workload Change

Journalists Who . . .	Workload Decreased or Same	Workload Increased
Write a blog for news organization	10	21
Shoot video for news organization	11	16
File breaking news for website of news organization	56	60
Capture audio for website of news organization	25	28
Create podcasts for news organization	6	13
Take part in live Q&A on news organization's website	8	7

Notes. Workload question asked respondents, "All in all, has your workload within the last year or so increased, decreased or stayed about the same?" $n = 400$ (varies slightly by item).

Pleijter, 2009; Machill & Beiler, 2009). The American Journalist studies have found evidence of this too. In 2002, news workers were asked about eight ways they might use the Web as a reporting or editing tool, such as checking names and addresses or conducting e-mail interviews. The journalists in the panel study were asked again in 2007 about those same tasks, and the percentage using the Web "daily" grew for all eight of them (Table 13.2). With one exception—conducting interviews by e-mail—only 5 percent or fewer of the journalists reported never using the Web for these tasks.

The impact of economic and technological change on news work is likely to become only more intense. "Liquid work" is how Deuze (2007) describes the evolving nature of media labor. The phrase evokes the idea that work in a networked society is less bounded. It's more contingent. It's more temporary. It's less organizationally based. It's more fluid. One cannot do justice to the concept of liquid work in a few sentences, but it includes two important implications for the future of news work.

The first is that the structural settings for news work will change, almost certainly leading to changes in the production of news itself. Increasingly, journalists and other media workers will be organized into temporary teams that solve a problem and are then disbanded. Much of their work will be accomplished outside of the formal organizational settings with which journalists have become so familiar. Those news organizations that remain will be outsourcing more tasks or forging alliances with firms that were once fierce competitors. That's a point that Gade and Raviola (2009) have made

TABLE 13.2 Percentage using Web "Daily" for Reporting, Editing Tasks

Daily Use of the Web . . .	2002	2007
To find names, addresses of sources	20	30
To conduct e-mail interviews	3	8
To get background information for stories	40	47
To search for story ideas	19	26
To check facts in a story	30	43
To search for, receive press releases	60	71
To communicate by e-mail with audience	37	48
To download raw data from computer databases	10	15

Notes. Respondents were asked, "How often do you use the Web . . ." Response options were "daily," "several times a week," "weekly," "less often than that," and "don't do this at all." Tabled figures show only "daily" responses. *n* = 400 (varies slightly by item).

in discussing what they characterized as a core challenge for the news media today: the seeming paradox of needing to change their organizational structures to make it possible to become more competitive *and* collaborative at the same time. No doubt the path to greater cooperation and outsourcing will be both beneficial and bumpy. On the one hand, collaboration and outsourcing mean that the audiences of legacy media will have access to a wider range of content than might have been available from the downsized staffs of these traditional news organizations. On the other hand, outsourcing means that the newsrooms sacrifice some control over the production of their content.

A second implication of work becoming more "liquid" is that the autonomy of media professionals could both shrink and expand (Deuze, 2007). Even now, some journalists are demanding more control over their work lives and making sacrifices to get it. Freelance work and temporary jobs allow them to avoid long-term commitments to a single employer. Flextime and part-time employment provide more control over their schedules. At the same time, the value of news work may become linked more strongly to its commercial potential. Content that can command a premium in the marketplace will be prized, and that could act as a constraint on professional autonomy. If the market values content that is simplistic and formulaic, freelance media workers will be expected to make content that is simplistic and formulaic. To be sure, many traditional journalistic skills—the capability to gather information accurately, the ability to tell compelling stories—will continue to have value. However, mastery of these skills alone will not guarantee survival in the increasingly uncertain environment in which news work is being redefined.

Challenges to Public Service Journalism

A commitment to public service has long been a core value of professions generally and journalism specifically (Becker et al., 2005; Hallin, 2000). Hardt (2000) describes public service as an element of the utopian vision of journalism. That vision, he argues, is becoming a victim of technological change and commercial pressures. As the environment in which news is produced has become more uncertain, so has confidence that journalists and the organizations for which they work can make good on a commitment to public service (Jones, 2009). Partly, this doubt reflects changes in news work. An emphasis on the technical skills needed to produce content is overwhelming attention to substantive or service dimensions of journalism (Hardt, 2000). However, blame also falls on the economics of journalism today. In the idealized vision of journalism, news organizations simultaneously do good work for society and make good profits for their owners. In reality, Hardt says, "the desirable balance between responsible journalism and profitable business is rarely accomplished" (p. 219).

During the last generation, media scholars and critics have identified various potential threats to journalism's public service mission (Beam, Brownlee, Weaver, & DiCicco, 2009). Perhaps the most fundamental threat arises from the fact that news making in the United States is mostly a commercial enterprise. Hallin (2000) has suggested that there is inherent tension between a news organization's commercial and professional goals, creating a persistent challenge to journalism's public service mission. That public service mission is always under threat to some degree because what is in the best interest of the public may not be in the best economic interest of the organization. Serving the public interest, for example, may mean skewering an important advertiser or local business. That makes it tough for news organizations to fully pursue commercial self-interests without harming public service (Picard, 2005).

The market-oriented editorial strategies of news organizations also have been criticized as a threat to public service journalism (McManus, 1994, pp. 1–3). A strong market orientation implies giving readers or viewers the content that they want, not necessarily the content they might need to be well-informed citizens in a democracy. Logically, a strong market orientation wouldn't necessarily lead to a weaker public service commitment. However, critics of market-oriented journalism argue that it tends to do so because, they say, substantive coverage of public affairs is rarely as appealing to the audience as crime, celebrities, and scandal (Beam, 2003; Beam, Brownlee, et al., 2009). As a result, popular news trumps important news.

Trends in ownership pose yet another threat to the public service mission. Political economists have persistently criticized government policies that have allowed the growth of large, publicly held "media conglomerates" (Baker, 2007; McChesney, 1999). The assumption is that these news organizations are too focused on producing high profits (Lacy and Blanchard, 2003; Meyer, 2004). Critics of "big media" suggest that an obsession with profit maximization crowds out expensive public service journalism (Cranberg, Bezanson, & Soloski, 2001; McChesney, 1999).

Most recently, the serious financial challenges facing news organizations have been cited as a threat to journalism's public service role. As profits have shriveled, U.S. newspapers and television stations have cut tens of thousands of jobs (Kaufman, 2009; Project for Excellence in Journalism, 2010). That means fewer journalists to cover the communities that the news organizations serve (Kennedy, 2008). Domestic and foreign news bureaus have been closed, and expensive enterprise reporting has been scaled back (Jones, 2009; Mutter, 2009). Clay Shirky, a scholar and commentator who specializes in understanding the implications of interactive journalism, argues that the rapidly unraveling economic model for legacy news organizations in the United States has put "accountability journalism" at risk (*Accountability Journalism*, 2009).

These threats have a common denominator: economics. The assumption is that economic uncertainty is leading news organizations to tip the balance between professional and commercial goals in favor of the latter. Poor economic conditions are encouraging these organizations to strengthen their market focus. Cost cutting—staff cutting—prevails as the way to manage newsrooms because increasing revenues is difficult. As resources become scarcer, the threat to public interest journalism presumably grows. Nonetheless, findings from the American Journalist studies suggest that public service remains an important professional value for many news workers. Even as business conditions worsened over the last few years, journalists continued to believe their news organizations were doing a good job of informing the public—an important indicator of public service. In the aggregate, these "informing the public" ratings for the panel journalists changed little over the five years of the study. About two-thirds rated their news organization either as "very good" or "outstanding." That's the good news. However, the bad news is that other information gathered in the 2007 panel study and from additional sources suggests that preserving a strong commitment to public service journalism could become more challenging in the future.

One hint of trouble arises out of questions about staffing. About half of the journalists in the 2007 panel reported that the size of their news staffs had shrunk during the previous year. As might be expected, the 2007 study found that journalists at news organizations that had experienced staff reductions gave significantly lower "grades" to their efforts to inform the public. About 59 percent of the journalists whose staff size had declined said their news organization was doing a "very good" or "outstanding" job of informing the public. That compared with 73 percent for those whose staff size had stayed the same or grown. Since the 2007 survey, the jobs of tens of thousands of journalists have been eliminated (Project for Excellence in Journalism, 2010). If journalists were asked today how well their news organization was inform-ing the public, it seems reasonable to assume that their assessment would be more pessimistic.

Another indication of trouble comes from four new questions in the 2007 survey that focused specifically on journalism that serves the public interest. Two of those questions asked respondents how important they thought it was for the news media generally to produce journalism that serves the public interest and to serve all the socioeconomic groups in their community. Those questions sought to get a sense of the journalists' general level of commitment to public service. The findings suggest that journalists remain strongly committed to that professional value. About 94 percent said that producing journalism that serves the public interest was either "quite important" or "extremely important." And about 85 percent said it was "quite important" or "extremely important" to serve all socioeconomic groups in the community. But the hint of trouble comes from responses to two companion questions. Those questions asked the journalists to assess the commitment of the owners or senior managers of their news organizations to public service journalism, and those assessments were more tepid. About 75 percent thought that serving the public interest was "quite important" or "extremely important" to the managers or owners of their news organization. That's about 19 percentage points below the question assessing the broader professional commitment. And only about 55 percent thought that serving all socioeconomic groups in the community was "quite important" or "extremely important" to the owners and top managers. That's about 30 points lower than the comparable question about the news media generally.

The results can be summarized this way: Journalists say they remain strongly committed to serving the public interest as a professional value; but they are much less certain that the people who run their news organizations share this commitment. If their perceptions are accurate, that's worrisome because the owners and managers control newsroom budgets and set organizational goals. Even if the journalists' perceptions are too pessimistic, their responses could suggest that news workers are becoming disillusioned about their organiza-tions' willingness to make public interest journalism a priority.

Threats to Autonomy

Autonomy has long been a central concept in the study of journalism and other professional work (Beam, 1990; Becker et al., 2005; Freidson, 1994). It can be a problematic concept because the label describes different social phenomena at the occupational, organizational, and individual levels of analysis. Occupations vary in the degree to which they have collectively gained authority to control their work, which is a way to think about professional autonomy at an occupational level of analysis (Abbott, 1988; Beam, 1990; Johnson, 1972). Like occupations, organizations can vary in the extent to which their news-making processes are insulated from powerful outside actors, such as advertisers or business leaders (Beam, 1990). That's autonomy at the organizational level. Finally, individual journalists vary in the amount of discretion that they have to decide what stories to cover and how to cover them (Weaver, Beam, Brownlee, Voakes, & Wilhoit, 2007). At the individual level, then, professional autonomy varies according to the latitude a professional employee has to execute his or her tasks.

The turbulent environment for the news media is affecting professional autonomy at all three levels. At the occupational level, journalists' jurisdiction over the production of news is being challenged. As an occupation group, journalists have never established as much jurisdiction over the terms of their work as have members of classic professions such as law and medicine (Abbott, 1988). Still, news workers have created some of the trappings of classic professions. Journalists have organized into professional associations that advocate on behalf of members and that promulgate ethics guidelines to shape professional behavior. Colleges and universities offer specialized training for individuals who want to become journalists. And many in the occupation group embrace, to greater or lesser degrees, common professional values such as a commitment to objectivity or public service (Schudson & Anderson, 2009; Tumber & Prentoulis, 2005; Weaver et al., 2007). The striking similarity of content across different traditional media organizations testifies to the power of journalism's institutionalized professional culture to shape news (Cook, 1998, pp. 76–78).

Recent evidence suggests that journalists may be starting to disengage from some aspects of their professional culture. Here's one example: The 2007 American Journalist panel study found that membership in professional associations has been dropping (Beam, Brownlee, et al., 2009). In 2002, about 47 percent of the journalists reported belonging to one or more professional associations; by 2007, that figure had dropped by 8 percentage points. Career commitment also appears to be waning. Among the panel journalists, the percentage who said that they hoped to be working outside the news media in five years rose about 6 points, to 21 percent, between 2002 and 2007.

The Web also is affecting the limited control that the profession has been able to achieve over the terms of its work. The definition of "legitimate news" is no longer the sole domain of so-called professional journalists (Rosen, 2005). Bloggers now break stories that prestigious news organizations feel compelled to follow (Walsh, n.d.). Readers and viewers with little or no journalistic experience are supplying content to TV and newspaper websites as "citizen journalists" (Riggio, n.d.). Rosen argues that the Web's interactive capabilities are changing the power relationship between journalists and what he calls the "people formerly known as the audience," and journalists are being forced to share control over news making with these "non-professionals." This power sharing with the audience has created uncertainty about journalists' professional roles and has diminished the occupation's collective ability to shape the terms of its work. In a sense, it is deprofessionalizing news gathering.

At the organizational level, the economic challenges facing the news media are perhaps the biggest threat to professional autonomy. Increasingly, newsrooms are losing the power to protect their terrain and resources. One of the most visible examples is the sacrifice of space on the front and section pages of newspapers to advertising (Pilkington, 2009). At most daily newspapers, the content of these pages previously had been under sole control of the news staff. On television, sponsorships have become more tightly integrated with news programming. In some cases, on-air journalists are now being asked to tout the products of sponsors, which suggests that the separation of news and advertising is no longer all that separate (Clifford, 2008).

Evidence also suggests that the individual-level autonomy of journalists is eroding, though not uniformly. Results from the American Journalist studies have documented a steady 35-year decline in the autonomy that reporters perceive that they have at work (Weaver et al., 2007). In 2007, perceived autonomy was examined for the 315 reporters in the panel using the same three questions that have been asked in these studies since 1971 (Beam, Brownlee, et al., 2009):

- If you have a good idea for a subject which you think is important and should be followed up, how often are you able to get the subject covered?
- How much freedom do you usually have in selecting the stories you work on?
- How much freedom do you usually have in deciding which aspects of a story should be emphasized?

The findings underscore the constraints under which most reporters work. Only about four in ten reporters said they had "almost complete freedom" to select the stories that they worked on and to decide what to emphasize in those stories. Still, over the five years of the panel study, their prerogative to execute these tasks had edged up slightly. However, journalists' perceived ability to get important stories covered—another dimension of autonomy—declined. In 2002, about 55 percent of the reporters in the panel said they could "almost always" get important stories covered. That figure had dropped 5 points by 2007. Changes in working conditions appear to be a factor in understanding the reporters' views about their autonomy (Beam, Brownlee, et al.., 2009). The survey found that when workloads grew—and that was the case for about two-thirds of the reporters in the panel—their perceived ability to get important stories covered suffered. As staff size declined, reporters believed that their freedom to select the stories to work on or to choose what to emphasize in those stories slipped (Table 13.3).

TABLE 13.3 Autonomy Indicators for 2007 by Workload and Staff Size Change[a]

	Workload Change[b]		Staff Size Change[c]	
	Workload Same, Less	Workload Increased	Staff Size Same, Larger	Staff Size Declined
Ability to get subject covered[d]				
Occasionally or more often than not	41.8%	53.4%	45.6%	54.3%
Almost always	58.2%	46.6%	54.4%	45.7%
	χ^2 = 3.856 (1 df)★		χ^2 = not significant	
Freedom to select stories to work on[e]				
No or some freedom	6.4%	18.6%	9.4%	20.0%
A great deal of freedom	51.4%	39.7%	40.0%	46.7%
Almost complete freedom	42.2%	41.7%	50.6%	33.3%
	χ^2 = 9.577 (2 df)★		χ^2 = 12.295 (2 df)★	
Freedom to decide aspects to emphasize[f]				
No or some freedom	7.3%	12.8%	9.4%	12.8%
A great deal of freedom	41.3%	44.8%	38.1%	48.3%
Almost complete freedom	51.4%	42.4%	52.5%	38.9%
	χ^2 = not significant		χ^2 = 5.757 (2 df)★★	

Notes. ★$p \leq 0.05$ for chi-square; ★★$p \leq 0.10$ for chi-square.

a   2007 respondents who say they report regularly or occasionally ($n = 315$).
b   Respondent's workload decreased or stayed the same during previous 12 months ($n = 109$) vs. increased ($n = 203$). n varies slightly by item; lowest n reported.
c   Size of staff at respondent's news organization grew or stayed the same in previous 12 months ($n = 160$) vs. shrunk ($n = 149$). n varies slightly by item; lowest n reported.
d   "If you have a good idea for a subject which you think is important and should be followed up, how often are you able to get the subject covered?"
e   "How much freedom do you usually have in selecting the stories you work on?"
f   "How much freedom do you usually have in deciding which aspects of a story should be emphasized?"

The impact of the difficult economic circumstances under which journalists are working is also evident in other findings from the panel study. In both years—2002 and 2007—journalists were asked to talk briefly about the most significant limits on their freedom as a journalist. Most of the 328 journalists who answered this question in both years cited one or more of these four broad categories of constraints:

- *Commercial imperatives*, which related to the financial health of their news organization or to its economic or commercial goals, such as increasing profits or revenues.
- *Constraints of the profession*, which related to limitations inherent in the norms or conventions of the profession, such as objectivity or conventional writing styles.
- *Organizational policies, procedures, and customs*, which related to non-economic constraints imposed by the news organization, such as its policies for handling sensitive stories or the journalistic decision-making of newsroom managers.
- *Outside influences*, which related to efforts by social actors outside the newsroom, such as advertisers, sources, or government agencies, to shape news gathering.

The most notable change across the five years was the growth in the percentage of journalists citing commercial limitations on their freedom (Table 13.4). The increase was about 14 points overall and about 21 points for the roughly 175 daily newspaper journalists who answered the question—that is, the segment of the news industry that has been under the greatest financial stress. Often, the issue was resources. "The lack of time, money, equipment and human capital makes it difficult to pursue the type of watchdog investigative reporting that readers want and have come to expect from newspapers," one journalist explained. "In addition, the corresponding decline in quality has increased the credibility gap and created more skepticism from the public about whether

TABLE 13.4 Percent of Narratives Mentioning a Limit on "Freedom as a Journalist"

Nature of Limitation	2002	2007
Commercial limitations	24	38
Organizational policies, procedures	36	27
Influence of outside agents	29	25
Professional constraints	10	7

Notes. $n = 328$. Percentages do not total to 100 percent because journalists could mention more than one limitation or provide an uncategorized response.

we are telling the truth." Or, as another succinctly put it: "So many stories, so little time."

By 2007, the panel journalists were less likely to cite organizational practices and the influence of outside social actors, such as advertisers, as important limits on their professional autonomy. The drop was much greater for organizational constraints—about 9 points. It's difficult to pinpoint exactly why organizational constraints declined as much as they did. In part, it's probably because the importance of commercial constraints grew so much, absorbing some of the attention that organizational limitations had received in the past. However, references to editors or managers as a constraint on journalistic freedom—one aspect of organizational constraints—were less common in the journalists' responses. Perhaps as news organizations slimmed down, a smaller number of editors simply had less time to tinker with their reporters' stories. Also, this period coincided with efforts by many types of organizations to flatten their organizational structures, eliminating middle managers and putting more control in the hands of rank-and-file employees (Gade, 2004).

Can Journalism Adapt?

As economics and technology transform the conditions under which news work is done, a critical issue is how—or even whether—journalists and their news organizations can adapt to this changing environment. Redefinition of mission will be essential to the survival of news organizations, and an entrepreneurial spirit will be essential to the survival of journalists as professionals.

To remain viable, most large legacy news organizations will need to develop products that meet the needs of smaller, homogeneous audiences. They must shrink their focus. For many organizations, that will require a fundamental change in their mission, and that will be challenging. The precarious state in which these legacy media organizations find themselves today is often attributed to the impact of the Web. However, a more comprehensive explanation for their predicament would also take into account the gradual segmentation of consumer markets, a process that stretches back 50 years or more. That segmentation is largely responsible for the drift of news organizations away from their traditional financial moorings.

These days, most products and services are designed to meet the needs of comparatively small segments of a market. Even products that everyone uses, such as laundry soap, come in formulations or packaging intended for discrete market segments—liquid or powder, with or without fabric softener, instructions in English or Spanish. The biggest legacy players in the U.S. news industry—newspapers and broadcast television—have traditionally made products targeted at large, heterogeneous audiences. Today, those products simply aren't efficient ways for advertisers to reach segmented markets. The

Web and other digital communication tools are more efficient. One proven strategy for serving segmented markets—a strategy that magazines and cable TV have adopted—is to offer focused content to narrow slivers of the audience. To survive, mass audience news organizations like daily papers will need to redefine their mission to become producers of niche market products, not mass market products. In that process, they will once again be forced to redefine the nature of their news work.

To survive in the long run, news organizations also will need to learn what gives content real economic value (Picard, 2009). End consumers—readers, viewers, listeners—will be expected to pay a larger share of the cost of making news. Figuring out what they'll pay for will be essential. That's not to imply that news organizations must abandon public service journalism to survive. To the contrary, they may improve their odds of surviving by embracing it. Consider the TV show *60 Minutes*. After 40 years, it remains one of the most successful programs on television *because* it vigorously embraces public service journalism and invests in compelling journalistic storytelling. Today, too many news organizations squander their scarce resources on content that has only commodity value. If these news organizations are to survive, they must focus on providing their audiences with packages of content that are narrower in scope but higher in quality.

Journalists will need to redefine their own professional missions too. If news work becomes more temporary and more contingent, as Mark Deuze (2007) predicts, journalists' career paths will be less likely to lead to the newsrooms of large, stable media companies. Jeff Jarvis (2009), author of the media blog Buzz Machine, predicts that the future of news will be entrepreneurial. He says this means, among other things, that the production of news will no longer be dominated by a few corporations; that news will look messy and disordered; that journalists will need to understand business; and that it won't be clear what kind of journalism the market will support.

The journalists who will have the greatest control over the terms of their work—the greatest autonomy—may be those who learn to thrive in this entrepreneurial environment. They will be the journalists who want to find new ways to produce meaningful content for niche audiences. They will be the journalists who like to experiment and who are not paralyzed by stale professional practices that don't work in a networked society. And they will be journalists who know how to create content with real economic value for audiences. "Content with real economic value" doesn't mean trivial content. At its best, public service journalism has real economic value. Successful entrepreneurial journalists, operating outside the constraints of big media organizations, ultimately may be among those best positioned to pursue true public interest journalism. Their challenge, of course, will be raising money to support their work. But if they are able to do so, they can capitalize on their autonomy to do journalism that nurtures democracy. They will be the journalists who best understand how to adapt successfully to the uncertain environment in which news will be made in the future.

Thought Questions: Contemplating Change

Economics and technology are conspiring to reshape journalism in the United States. You've read about how this has brought about a redefinition of news work; about the challenges to journalism's public service mission; and about implications for journalists' professional autonomy. The chapter also briefly discussed some implications of these changes for journalism's normative role in a democracy. Here are two issues to consider:

1. How might economic and technological changes affect other aspects of journalists' professional culture? How might they affect journalists' ethics? Their social roles? Their news values? What are three or four ways that you might study such changes?
2. The chapter suggests that too much news today has only commodity value. In effect, nothing makes it special—at least special enough that people will pay to get it on the Web. What characteristics would news need to have to make it special? In its value to readers, viewers, or listeners, what would distinguish news from other information that's available on the Web? And what changes in professional practices would journalists need to make to create this content with real economic value?

Acknowledgements

The authors acknowledge the contributions of David H. Weaver and Bonnie J. Brownlee of the Indiana University School of Journalism, who helped design the American Journalist panel survey on which some of this chapter is based. Funding for that survey was provided by the Sigma Delta Chi Foundation; the Carnegie-Knight Task Force on Journalism and the John S. and James L. Knight Foundation; the Dart Center for Journalism and Trauma; the Indiana University School of Journalism (Bloomington, IN); and the Department of Communication at the University of Washington (Seattle, WA).

Notes

1 The news workers were interviewed first as part of the 2002 American Journalist survey. The American Journalist surveys began in 1971 and have been conducted about every 10 years since. These large national telephone surveys track changes in the social characteristics, working conditions, attitudes, and values of journalists who work full time for daily or weekly newspapers, for television and radio news organizations, for news magazines that publish more than once a month, and for news services such as the Associated Press and Reuters. In 2007, a subset

of 400 respondents from the 2002 survey was contacted and interviewed again by telephone, forming the second wave of a panel study.

2   Reporters were respondents who said that they reported "regularly" or "occasionally."

References

Abbott, A. (1988). *The system of professions: An essay on the division of expert labor*. Chicago: University of Chicago Press.

Accountability journalism is at risk, says Clay Shirky (2009, September 22). Joan Shorenstein Center on the Press, Politics and Public Policy. Retrieved November 25, 2010, from http://www.hks.harvard.edu/presspol/news_events/archive/2009/shirky_09–22–09. html

Baker, C. E. (2007). *Media concentration and democracy: Why ownership matters*. New York: Cambridge University Press.

Beam, R. A. (1990). *Journalism professionalism as an organizational-level concept*. Journalism Monographs, 121. Columbia, SC: Association for Education in Journalism and Mass Communication.

Beam, R. A. (2003). Content differences between daily newspapers with strong and weak market orientations. *Journalism & Mass Communication Quarterly, 80*, 368–390.

Beam, R. A., Brownlee, B. J., Weaver, D. H., & DiCicco, D. T. (2009). Journalism and public service in troubled times. *Journalism Studies, 10*, 734–753.

Beam, R. A., Weaver, D. H., & Brownlee, B. J. (2009). Changes in professionalism of U.S. journalists in the turbulent twenty-first century. *Journalism & Mass Communication Quarterly, 86*, 277–298.

Becker, L. B., Vlad, T., Gans, E. M., Edwards, H. H., Daniels, G. L., & Park, N. (2005). Professionalism of news workers: The creation and evolution of the concept. In S. Dunwoody, L. B. Becker, D. M. McLeod, & G. M. Kosicki (Eds.), *The evolution of key mass communication concepts: Honoring Jack M. McLeod* (pp. 79–112). Cresskill, NJ: Hampton Press.

Boczkowski, P. J. (2004). *Digitizing the news: Innovation in online newspapers*. Cambridge, MA: MIT Press.

Christians, C. G., Glasser, T. L., McQuail, D., Nordenstreng, K., & White, R. A. (2009). *Normative theories of the media: Journalism in democratic societies*. Urbana: University of Illinois Press.

Clifford, S. (2008, July 22). A product's place is on the set. *The New York Times*, p. C1.

Cook, T. E. (1998). *Governing with the news: The news media as a political institution*. Chicago: University of Chicago Press.

Cottle, S. (2003). Media organization and production: Mapping the field. In S. Cottle (Ed.), *Media organization and production* (pp. 3–24). London: Sage.

Cranberg, G., Bezanson, R. P., & Soloski, J. (2001). *Taking stock: Journalism and the publicly traded newspaper company*. Ames: Iowa State University Press.

Dennis, E. E., & DeFleur, M. L. (2010). *Understanding media in the digital age: Connections for communication, society, and culture*. New York: Allyn & Bacon.

Deuze, M. (2007). *Mediawork*. Cambridge: Polity.

Freidson, E. (1994). *Professionalism reborn: Theory, prophecy, and policy*. Chicago: University of Chicago Press.

Gade, P. (2004). Newspapers and organizational development: Management and journalist perceptions of newsroom cultural change. *Journalism & Communication Monographs, 6.*

Gade, P., & Raviola, E. (2009). Integration of news and news of integration: A structural perspective on news media changes. *Journal of Media Business Studies, 6,* 87–111.

Hallin, D. C. (2000). Commercialism and professionalism in the American news media. In J. Curran & M. Gurevitch (Eds.), *Mass media and society* (3rd ed.) (pp. 218–237). London: Arnold.

Hardt, H. (2000). Conflicts of interest: Newsworkers, media and patronage journalism. In H. Tumber (Ed.), *Media power, professionals and policies* (pp. 209–224). London: Routledge.

Hermans, L., Vergeer, M., & Pleijter, A. (2009). Internet adoption in the newsroom: Journalists' use of the Internet explained by attitudes and perceived functions. *Communications: The European Journal of Communication Research, 34,* 55–71.

Jarvis, J. (2009). *The future of news is entrepreneurial.* Buzzmachine.com. Retrieved December 1, 2009, from http://www.buzzmachine.com/2009/11/01/the-future-of-journalism-is-entrepreneurial/

Johnson, T. J. (1972). *Professions and power.* London: Macmillan Press.

Jones, A. S. (2009). *Losing the news: The future of the news that feeds democracy.* New York: Oxford University Press.

Kaufman, R. (2009, July 15). *TV job losses could be slowing.* Mediabistro.com. Retrieved June 21, 2010, from http://www.mediabistro.com/mediajobsdaily/television/tv_job_losses_could_be_slowing_121718.asp

Kennedy, D. (2008). *Can GateHouse media stop the shrinkage of community newspapers in the Bay State?* Retrieved June 21, 2010, from http://www.capecodtoday.com/blogs/index.php/2008/10/22/can-gatehouse-media-stop-the-our-newspap?blog=14

Kimbrough-Robinson, C. (2008). Change happens: Deal with it. *Quill, 96*(2), 35.

Lacy, S., & Blanchard, A. (2003). The impact of public ownership, profits, and competition on number of newsroom employees and starting salaries in mid-sized daily newspapers. *Journalism & Mass Communication Quarterly, 80,* 949–968.

Machill, M., & Beiler, M. (2009). The importance of the Internet for journalistic research. *Journalism Studies, 10,* 178–203.

Mauro, R., & Dindino, C. (October 26, 2007). *Tools, anxieties increasing in nation's newsrooms, survey shows.* Retrieved November 30, 2009, from http://www.newsline.umd.edu/business/newsroomsurvey102607.htm

McChesney, R. W. (1999). *Rich media, poor democracy: Communication politics in dubious times.* Urbana: University of Illinois Press.

McManus, J. H. (1994). *Market-driven journalism: Let the citizen beware?* Thousand Oaks, CA: Sage.

McNair, B. (2005). What is journalism? In H. de Burgh (Ed.), *Making journalists: Diverse models, global issues* (pp. 25–43). London: Routledge.

Meyer, P. (2004). *The vanishing newspaper: Saving journalism in the information age.* Columbia: University of Missouri Press.

Mutter, A. D. (2009, March 16). *The best and worst time for journalism.* Reflections of a Newsosaur. Retrieved March 26, 2009, from http://newsosaur.blogspot.com/2009/03/best-and-worst-time-for-journalism.html

Papacharissi, Z. (2009). Preface. In Z. Papacharissi (Ed.), *Journalism and citizenship: New agendas in communication* (pp. vii–xiii). New York: Routledge.

Phillips, A., Singer J. B., Vlad, T., & Becker, L. B. (2009). Implications of technological change for journalists' tasks and skills. *Journal of Media Business Studies, 6*, 61–86.

Picard, R. G. (2005). Money, media and the public interest. In G. Overholser & K. Hall Jamieson (Eds.), *The press* (pp. 337–350). New York: Oxford University Press.

Picard, R. G. (2009, May 19). *Why journalists deserve low pay*. Retrieved May 5, 2010, from http://www.csmonitor.com/Commentary/Opinion/2009/0519/p09s02-coop.html

Pilkington, E. (2009, January 6). All the news fit to print. (And a page 1 advert). *The Guardian.* Retrieved November 30, 2009, from http://www.guardian.co.uk/media/2009/jan/06/new-york-times-advertisement

Project for Excellence in Journalism. (2010). News leaders and the future. *The state of the news media 2010.* Retrieved June 9, 2010, from http://www.stateofthemedia.org/2010/specialreports_survey_executives.php

Riggio, L. (n.d.). *Blogs and citizen journalism: The effect on our culture.* Retrieved June 9, 2010, from http://mediacrit.wetpaint.com/page/Blogs+and+Citizen+Journalism:+The+Effect+on+Our+Culture

Rosen, J. (2005, March 17). Blogging, journalism and credibility. *The Nation.* Retrieved November 30, 2009, from http://www.thenation.com/article/blogging-journalism-and-credibility

Schudson, M., & Anderson, C. (2009). Objectivity, professionalism, and truth seeking in journalism. In K. Wahl-Jorgensen & T. Hanitzsch (Eds.), *Handbook of journalism studies* (pp. 88–101). New York: Routledge.

Straubhaar, J., LaRose, R., & Davenport, L. (2010). *Media now: Understanding media, culture and technology* (6th ed.). Belmont, CA: Wadsworth.

Tumber, H., & Prentoulis, M. (2005). Journalism and the making of a profession. In H. de Burgh (Ed.), *Making journalists: Diverse models, global issues* (pp. 58–74). London: Routledge.

Wallace, S. (2009). Watchdog or witness? The emerging forms and practices of video-journalism. *Journalism, 10*, 684–701.

Walsh, J. (n.d.). *Who killed Dan Rather?* Retrieved November 30, 2009, from http://dir.salon.com/story/opinion/feature/2005/03/09/rather/index.html

Weaver, D. H., Beam, R. A., Brownlee, B. J., Voakes, P. S., & Wilhoit, G. C. (2007). *The American journalist in the 21st century: U.S. news people at the dawn of a new millennium.* Mahwah, NJ: Lawrence Erlbaum.

Wilson, K. (2008, February/March). High anxiety. *American Journalism Review, 30*(1), 46–47.

14

WHERE PROFESSIONALISM BEGINS

Lee B. Becker and Tudor Vlad, University of Georgia

In the United States, entry to journalism, public relations, advertising, and many of the other communication occupations comes almost always after completion of a university degree. For journalism, at least, the degree most often is from a specialized university program in the field of study called journalism and mass communication.

The linkage between the demands of the labor market and the supply of the educational institutions, however, is not a simple one. The job market for those leaving university journalism and mass communication programs in the United States has varied considerably across time, reflecting changes in the national economy (Becker, Vlad, Olin, Hanisak, & Wilcox, 2009). Enrollments in journalism and mass communication programs have varied less, and for most of the last two decades they have increased on a year-to-year basis despite fluctuations in the labor market (Becker, Vlad, & Olin, 2009).

The sharp downturn in the U.S. economy and the collapse of the economic model for media industries in the country at the end of the first decade of the new century had a dramatic impact on the job market for graduates of the nation's university-level professional journalism and mass communication education programs. The drop in the level of full-time employment six to eight months after graduation—from 70.2 percent of graduates in 2007 to 60.4 percent in 2008—was the largest change recorded in the 23 years that the same methodology had been used to track these statistics (Becker, Vlad, et al., 2009).

The turmoil was not limited to the entry-level segment of the job market. An estimated 5,900 full-time jobs were cut in U.S. newspaper newsrooms in both 2008 and 2009 (Project for Excellence in Journalism, 2009, 2010). Television, radio, and news magazines also trimmed their staffs, often by eliminating positions at the top. Many of those journalists continued to practice their occupation by setting up their own Web operations or joining others in doing the same. If successful, these activities mean that journalism no longer will be the province only of those working at or for established media companies.

Perhaps what is more important, the journalists continuing to work at the established media and those who have gone out on their own have found themselves in competition with another group of individuals, often labeled "citizen" journalists (Keen, 2008; Project for Excellence in Journalism, 2009, 2010). The terminology is important, for it suggests a transformation and deprofessionalization of the journalistic occupation itself (Nossek, 2009). Given the uncertainty of the financial models for the old journalistic organizations and for the start-up companies being formed by former journalists, it is even possible to question whether journalism will remain an occupation. Chris Anderson, editor in chief of *Wired* magazine, speculated that journalism may simply become a hobby (Hornig, 2009).

The competition of the "professional" journalist with the "citizen" journalist raises questions anew about the relationship between journalism and citizens. This is a relationship that Carey (1969), among others, has questioned and challenged in the past.

The turmoil has affected other communication occupations as well. The easy access of amateurs to the tools of graphic design, databases needed for sales, and the distribution capabilities of the Web also mean that everyone can become an advertising or public relations professional.

Any deprofessionalization of an occupation raises questions about the necessity for and components of the educational paths that lead to it. Those questions are the central topic of this chapter. In the same way that changes in the media landscape have created uncertainty for those who work in various communication occupations, those changes and their effects on the labor market have created uncertainties for journalism and mass communication education. How the educational institutions will respond is unknown. It is possible to speculate, however, based on some basic assumptions about the relationship between the market and its supplier, and it is possible to offer some suggestions growing out of that speculation.

Although most of the discussion here is about communication occupations and educational institutions in one country, namely the United States, the questions are likely to generalize to other settings. Although all media systems have their unique characteristics, as the work of Hallin and Mancini (2004) shows, media systems also have characteristics in common. The same can be said about educational institutions (Froehlich & Holtz-Bacha, 2003). For example, the educational institutions all are tied to the labor market in some fashion, though that tie can be rather strong, as in the United States, or more tenuous, as in most European countries.

Professionalization

In the sociology of work literature, an occupation is defined as a social role played by adult members of society that directly and indirectly yields social and financial consequences (Hall, 1994). Occupations can be and frequently are compared with an ideal type, a profession. In Wilensky's (1964) classic characterization, occupations go through four key, defining steps in the process of becoming a profession. First, the occupation establishes training schools for admission. Second, the occupation forms professional associations. Next, it attempts to regulate the practice of the profession through legal protection. Finally, it adopts a formal code of ethics. In addition, professions have been viewed as occupations with a special service orientation toward society.

Across time, however, this positive view of professions and their service orientation has come under challenge. As summarized by Freidson (1994), a more critical view has focused on the political influence of professions, on the relation of professions to political and economic elites and the state, and on the relation of professions to the market and the class system. Freidson's own work (Freidson, 1970, 1986, 1994), as well as that of Larson (1977), has been particularly important in examining the issues of market and class as they relate to the professional classification of occupations. Freidson (1994) also has argued that the professional model is a product of the Anglo-American work culture and may be limited to it. A similar argument had been made by Haug (1977), who found large differences in how professionals were defined even within Western societies.

Particularly influential in the critical discussions of professions has been Freidson's concept of a market shelter. In this view, professions gain control in the economic marketplace by building such a shelter, which keeps out competitors and controls who qualifies for the profession. Once a market shelter is in place, professionals control both the supply and demand of workers and the work they do. The control over qualification is based on presumed skills needed for practice in the profession. The members of the profession claim that they possess a set of skills that requires protection through licensing, credentialing, and restricted training (Timmermans, 2008).

Despite the differences in approaches to professionalization, one common concern has been education. Haug (1977) finds that, even with the varied conceptualizations of what it means for an occupation to be a profession in Eastern and Western Europe, all agree that professions require training in, and command of, a specific body of knowledge. For Larson (1977), the existence of a body of abstract knowledge is essential for the success of an occupation in making the case for market control. The codification of this knowledge, in turn, leads to increased emphasis on formal training in which transmission of that knowledge to the future professional is crucial. Abbott (1988) says that the ability of a profession to sustain its jurisdiction results partly from the power, prestige, and abstract nature of its academic knowledge. Education thus becomes an essential prerequisite for entry into occupations that are labeled as professions, and occupations that are seeking to become professions give prominence to educational training.

A concern with the professional status of journalism has been long-standing in the academic literature, as a review by Becker et al. (2005) has made clear. Particularly influential was the work of Jack McLeod and his students, who drew on the sociological literature on professionals to develop a measure of the degree of professional orientation of journalists (McLeod & Hawley, 1964; McLeod & Rush, 1969a, 1969b). Related research has looked at the professional orientations of public relations and advertising workers, and at efforts by both occupations to establish professional credentials (Johansen, 2001; Kreshel, 1990; Sallot, Cameron, & Weaver-Lariscy, 1997, 1998).

University programs in journalism and mass communication play an important role in discussions about the communications occupations and their efforts at professionalization (Becker, Fruit, & Caudill, 1987; Froehlich & Holtz-Bacha, 2003). By the most recent estimate, 85 percent of those entering daily newspaper newsrooms in the United States come from a university journalism and mass communication program (Becker, Vlad, Pelton, & Papper, 2006). For television newsrooms, the figure is 92 percent.

Deprofessionalization

Consistent with Freidson (1994), the process of professionalization can be seen as an effort at claiming the right to erect market shelters. Timmermans (2008) argues that a key claim in this process is that the profession possesses a highly desirable skills set that requires protection through licensing, credentialing, and restricted training. What is unclear, in Timmermans' view, is how the professions adapt to changes in the social and economic environment within which they operate. What is required, he says, is continuous legitimization of the profession so as to justify the market shelter. The difficulty, according to Timmermans, is that the market shelter, which shields the professionals from competitors and criticism, also can stifle innovation. The professionals thus find it difficult to adapt to a changing scientific and economic landscape. Abbott (1988) argued that, if the academic knowledge base does not adapt and provide solutions to emerging problems, the claim of professional jurisdiction becomes weak. Implicit in this notion is the recognition that occupations can deprofessionalize over time as well as professionalize.

Haug (1975, 1977, 1988) is most closely linked to the deprofessionalization argument about occupations. She holds that professions are successful in their efforts at control when they have a monopoly on esoteric knowledge, maintain authority over clients, and have autonomy in work performance. Haug (1988) uses medicine as an example to illustrate how threats to monopoly, authority,

Westview Press

5500 Central Avenue • Boulder, Colorado 80301
Frederick A. Praeger, President and Publisher

Here is your review copy ___x___ advance copy _____
Title:

THE UNITED STATES AND THE WORLD ECONOMY:
POLICY ALTERNATIVES FOR NEW REALITIES

Author:

edited by John N. Yochelson

Publication Date: Price:
July 2, 1985 $15.00

Comments:

CSIS Significant Issues Series

PLEASE SEND US COPIES OF ANY REVIEWS.

and autonomy have weakened the profession. Though the medical profession has restricted access to training, the media have popularized much of the medical knowledge and made it accessible to an increasingly well-educated public. The public demands participation in medical decision-making, undercutting the authority of the physician. The autonomy of the doctor is undercut by group practice and health maintenance organizations, by medical review boards that involve lawyers as well as doctors, and by legally mandated peer-review systems. Ritzer and Walczak (1988) came to a similar conclusion based on a different argument. Their view is that medicine increasingly relies on rules, regulations, laws, bureaucracies, and economies as a result of greater external control. Autonomy is lost in the process.

Critics of Haug's position, particularly as it relates to medicine, exist. Freidson (1994), prominent among them, says the case for demonopolization of knowledge is particularly weak, as in the case of medicine. Muzio and Ackroyd (2005) argue that changes in the legal profession support Freidson's argument that professions find a way to adapt in order to maintain their special market shelters. Randall and Kindiak (2008) say that parts of social work have actually competed successfully with other professions by broadening the educational programs leading to admission. Hardley (1999), however, argues that the Internet in particular is the locus of renewed struggles over expertise in the medical professions.

Another argument about change in the professions is labeled by Freidson (1994) as proletarianization. Those advancing this argument hold that the location of the work of the professional has changed over time. Professionals are less likely to be working for themselves than in the past and more likely to be working in bureaucratic settings. Freidson says that the evidence that workers in the United States are less likely to be self-employed than in the past is contaminated by large changes in the number of people working in farming. With that group eliminated, there is stability in terms of level of self-employment. Also, those organizations for which professionals work are rarely highly bureaucratized, he contends. The organizations have adapted to reflect the fact that they hire professionals.

Deuze (2007), in his study of media work in the era of the Internet, argues that responsibility has increasingly shifted from the organization to the individual. Cultural production employers and managers stress the importance of enterprise as an individual outcome, rather than as an organizational one. Work is much more flexible than in the past, he argues.

What seems clear from Deuze's example is that occupations have confronted the current technological changes in work at different stages of professional development—whatever that term means—and are likely to respond to those changes in different ways. Journalism in particular and the communication occupations in general have struggled to make the case that their practices were based on unique skills sets acquired through education and training. To be sure, those preparing for the occupations did acquire specific technical skills as part of their training. They learned how to record and edit video and audio. They learned how to write headlines, shoot and crop pictures, and create graphics. They learned how to create stories using the inverted pyramid style of writing.

The argument that the communication occupations relied on a knowledge base for their work has been more difficult to articulate. Journalists have argued that they know news when they see it because of their skills. Advertising and other promotional practitioners have argued that they could create messages based on artistic skills they possessed and honed. The creative producer could say she or he knew good art.

Often these statements of expertise were made in comparison with the audience; that is, the communication worker claimed expertise not shared by the general audience. Carey (1969) said this put the worker at odds with the audience. The journalist, Carey argued, mediates between the audience and the source and is pulled in both directions. The result often is contempt on the part of the journalist for both the audience and the source. Contempt derives from a perception that the audience is apathetic and uninterested, and that the source is often dishonest. Ettema and Whitney's (1994) review of research of media–audience relationships shows that journalists actually know little about their audiences. McQuail (1997) contends that the professional journalist often holds the audience in low regard and resents the influence of the audience on journalistic decisions. Many journalists, McQuail argues, think that audience members lack the skills and qualifications needed to judge their work. The market shelter, with its emphasis on esoteric knowledge—in this case, a knowledge of the characteristics and consequences of news—has protected the professional from the sources and the audience.

Routines of News Construction

In fact, quite a lot is known by inference about the relationship between the journalist and the audience from the literature on news construction and news-making routines (Becker & Vlad, 2009). The literature on routines shows that journalists rely on official sources for their news and give little attention to the articulated concerns of the general public.

Integrated into the discussion of news routines is the concept of news beats. News organizations generally organize themselves so as to be able to observe events and gather the raw materials that are used to produce news. Tuchman (1978) said that news organizations use a "news net" as a means of acquiring the raw materials that become news. Fishman (1980) noted that, although there are multiple ways in which news organizations could organize themselves so as to gather materials for news, "for at least the past one hundred years American newspapers have settled on one predominant mode of coverage known as the beat" (p. 27). For Gans (1979), the key process in news creation is story suggestion. Reporters have the responsibility for thinking up story ideas. To this end, they are required to "keep up with what is going on in the beats they patrol or in the areas of the country assigned to their bureaus, and they are evaluated in part by their ability to suggest suitable stories" (p. 87). Beats are either geographic, such as a beat focused on the offices of government, or topical, such as a beat focused on health. For the most part, the beat reinforces the idea that news is generated by official sources and reflects societal structure. At present, there is no evidence that the creation of work teams in newsrooms as more flexible alternatives to the historic beat structure has substantively changed how news is defined (Gade, 2004).

Gans' conceptualization is particularly informative, for it focuses on the generation of the idea that lies behind the story and links this generation of ideas to beats. In this view, raw material has the potential to become news only if it is recognized as having that potential by someone in the news construction business. Bantz, McCorkle, and Baade (1981) called this process of story idea generation "story ideation." Because newsrooms use beat systems, or other techniques such as work teams that reflect societal structure, research has shown that story ideation is conservative as well (Phillips, Singer, Vlad, & Becker, 2009). Journalists depend on people like themselves and on those they encounter as they cover specific areas to help them generate ideas they turn into stories. This very conservative nature of reporting has been confirmed in a study of sources of news in the Israeli press (Reich, 2009).

Citizens are not often treated as news sources except when they encounter the official structural outcroppings of society, for example when they meet up with authority figures such as the police or when they are assigned some official duty, such as to chair a citizen advisory committee. A citizen with a complaint is not likely to be taken seriously by journalists until governmental officials respond. Citizens on their own lack authority, so they are not considered authoritative sources.

Citizen activists who thrust themselves forward are suspect to journalists for another reason: they are engaged, they have a point of view. Because journalists embrace the ideas of detachment that are central to the notion of a profession, they are at odds with activists who are not detached.

Citizen journalists are often drawn from the ranks of citizen activists, and it is these more activist journalists that the journalists being tossed out of traditional media organizations confront. It should not be so surprising that the traditional journalist, clinging to traditional notions of professionalism, is not enamored with the competition.

The routines that produce news are what journalists learn in their university studies, where classrooms are often designed to mimic the real-world environment of broadcast and print organizations. The students are taught how to work a particular coverage area, how to identify sources, and how to define what is news. This last point is what comes closest to the "esoteric" knowledge required of a profession, and it helps explain why journalists treat citizens with less respect than official sources, who are expected to have a better sense of what news is. What is questionable is the extent to which that knowledge has a scientific footing. Scientific literature on the effects of media messages or on audiences' uses of media messages is available for journalists to reference, and is often part of curricular instruction. However, that literature is disjointed, reflecting the very nature of the field of communication itself (Donsbach, 2006).

Although less is known about the work habits of other communication workers, the existent research suggests that routines exist. Beurer-Zuellig, Fieseler, and Meckel (2009) have found, for example, that the activities of public relations workers in Europe cluster into five broad categories: lobbying external constituencies, advising and consulting to management, advertising and marketing, aiding internal communication, and carrying out technical tasks such as writing press releases and speeches. Such routines would be justified through a link to the same communication science knowledge base.

Empirical Evidence about the Job Market

The changing nature of journalism and other communication work has implications for those entering the labor force for the first time. The disruption of the work brought about by technological change is now exacerbated by the disruption of work brought about by the severe international economic crisis.

In the United States, these changes are reflected in data gathered as part of the *Annual Survey of Journalism & Mass Communication Graduates*, which is designed to monitor the employment rates and salaries of graduates of journalism and mass communication programs in the United States, including Puerto Rico, in the year after graduation (Becker, Vlad, et al., 2009). In addition, the survey tracks the curricular activities of those graduates while in college, examines their job-seeking strategies, and provides measures of the professional attitudes and behaviors of the graduates upon completion of their college studies.

For several years, as negative news swirled around about the changes in media industries, and particularly in the daily newspaper industry, graduates of journalism and mass communication programs around the country seemed protected. The dramatic weakening of the job market after 2000 seemed to have halted in 2003, and recovery appeared to be on the way. There was evidence of a slowing of that recovery in 2007, but little evidence yet that the entry-level part of the job market for journalism and mass communication graduates was in decline. In the second half of 2008 and the first half of 2009 all that changed.

By almost all indications, the 2008 graduates of the nation's journalism and mass communications programs found themselves in a disastrous job market.

Job offers on graduation were down. Opportunities for job interviews had declined. The level of full-time employment at the benchmark October 31 reference point was 8 percentage points lower than a year earlier. Full-time employment based on a second measure—respondents returning the survey instrument—was at its lowest point going back at least to 1986, and the drop from a year earlier was unprecedented. The data for bachelor's degree recipients, who make up more than 90 percent of those earning degrees in journalism and mass communication, are shown in Figure 14.1.

Salaries were stagnant at best. Those graduates who found full-time employment outside the field had a higher median annual salary than those who had work in the field. Even graduates lucky enough to find a job working for a Web publishing company had an annual salary significantly below the annual salary of those who found similar jobs a year earlier. The news in terms of benefits was even more discouraging. Across nine different comparisons, graduates in 2008 reported fewer benefits, and fewer of those were fully employer paid.

Although this is a dreary picture for journalism and mass communication graduates, with an unemployment rate for graduates of journalism and mass communication programs that is higher than for the broader 20- to 24-year-old cohort of which they are a part, there is evidence that some felt the pain more than others. This difference may say much about the future of the journalism and mass communication occupations.

Those students who studied public relations at the university found the job market in 2008 to be considerably less hostile than did those who studied for print media jobs, for telecommunications jobs, or even for advertising jobs. Of the public relations graduates, nearly 71 percent had a full-time job when they returned the survey instrument, compared with 65 percent of the advertising graduates, 59 percent of the print journalism graduates, and 57 percent of the telecommunications graduates. The public relations students also earned above-average salaries—something that the graduates who took jobs in advertising, at dailies and weeklies, and with television (except for cable) could not say.

Public relations graduates are different from others in a key way: They are less likely to seek and find jobs in their own field. In 2008, only 17 percent took a job in traditional public relations, compared with 24 percent of advertising students who went into advertising agencies and departments, 30 percent of the telecommunications students who went into that field, and 23 percent of the print journalism students who went into newspapers or wire services. Public relations students are more likely to say that they are doing communications of some sort in jobs outside traditional employment circles than are any of the other students. In 2008, 38 percent of the public relations students said they found "communications" work that was not with a public relations department or agency, not with an advertising department or agency, not with a newspaper or wire service, and not with a telecommunications company.

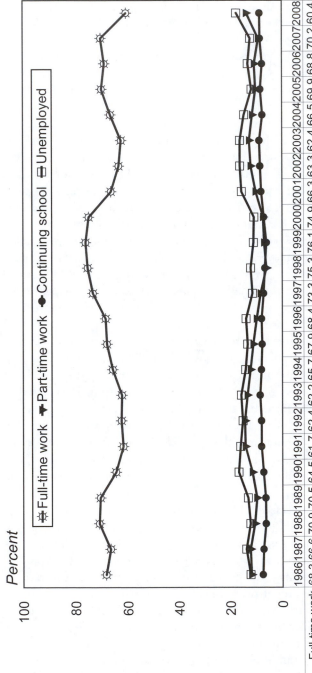

FIGURE 14.1 Employment Status of Bachelor's Degree Recipients When They Returned Questionnaires. Source: *Annual Survey of Journalism & Mass Communication Graduates* (Becker, Vlad, et al., 2009).

Overall, public relations graduates had salaries that were $1,000 above the median for all graduates.

The evidence suggests that public relations students may be less tied to traditional definitions of what is communication work. They may be more entrepreneurial, more flexible about what kinds of work they actually do. They did better in the job market in 2008, in terms of both finding jobs and level of compensation, and that may say a lot about the future of employment for graduates of the nation's journalism and mass communications programs.

Implications for Research

As Deuze (2007) has observed, the literature on news construction, with its heavy emphasis on organizational constraints, is likely to have limited relevance to a future in which journalistic work is less likely to be carried out in organizational settings. Recent empirical studies of news work have remained focused largely on established media settings (Phillips et al., 2009; Reich, 2009). Future research will need to shift to the more entrepreneurial environment of the individual and citizen journalist. The interaction between these two types of news workers will become particularly important. Work in this area is only in its infancy (e.g., Lowrey, 2006; Singer, 2006; Wall, 2005).

Because of the weakened institutional setting, the characteristics of the journalists themselves will become more important. In an organizational setting, the individual characteristics of the journalists can be muted. Journalists are assigned stories by more established managers. Editors handle and modify copy the journalists produce before it appears in print or online.

Among the characteristics of the journalists that are likely to be particularly important in this new setting is the knowledge base upon which the journalist draws. A journalist with expertise in the medical sciences is more likely to be able to cover developments in health care than is a journalist without this expertise. A journalist with an understanding of economics is more likely to be able to write about that topic. A journalist with a background in the performing arts is going to be more able to write meaningfully about theater.

It also should be the case that a journalist with a background in the law and history of the occupation will address legal and ethical issues differently from a journalist without this training. And a journalist with knowledge about the consequences of media messages and of the limitations of news-gathering techniques will produce different kinds of stories from a journalist without this expertise.

The journalists with these specializations, founded on a base of knowledge not readily available to the general public, should be better able to maintain the market shelter crucial to the profession. These references to knowledge should allow the journalist to differentiate herself or himself from citizens who might more readily posses the routine skills of note taking, writing in an inverted pyramid format, taking still pictures, or using a video camera. At the same time, because of new communication technologies, people with expertise in areas such as economics, the law, and medicine can compete with journalists in attracting audiences. For that reason, the professional journalist will need to draw on a knowledge base that combines communication with the specialty areas to make the case for market protection.

These same arguments can be made about public relations or advertising practitioners. Their work has come under less scrutiny in research than is the case for journalists. The exception is where public relations work has had an impact on news production (Cameron, Sallot, & Curtin, 1996). Clearly more needs to be known about the work of public relations and advertising practitioners. However, the expectation is that the public relations practitioner who can draw on esoteric knowledge of audience effects, or the advertising copywriter who knows the literature on the appeal of visual images, will be better protected by the market shelter than those who cannot do this.

Empirical Evidence about Journalism Education

The need for a knowledge base to justify a professional market shelter has significant implications for journalism and mass communication education, which historically has relied on its link to the labor market to justify its existence.

Most likely because of the link to the labor market rather than to the fundamental curricular goals of higher education, journalism and mass communication educators began tracking enrollments as early as 1934 (Banner, 1934). Different methodologies were used until 1988, when the current method for what is now known as the *Annual Survey of Journalism & Mass Communication Enrollments* was put into place. Schools included in the survey since that time are those listed in either the *Journalism & Mass Communication Directory* (2009), published by the Association for Education in Journalism and Mass Communication (AEJMC), or *The Journalist's Road to Success: A Career Guide* (n.d.), formerly published and printed by the Dow Jones Newspaper Fund, Inc., and now available on the Web. All degree-granting senior colleges and universities with courses organized under the labels of journalism and mass communication are invited to be listed in the AEJMC directory. To be included in the career guide, the college or university must offer at least 10 courses in news-editorial journalism, and those courses must include core courses such as an introduction to the mass media and press law and ethics as well as basic skills courses such as reporting and editing. Since 1992, the two journalism programs listed in the AEJMC directory in Puerto Rico have been included in the population. In 2008, data were obtained for all of the 480 active programs in the population (Becker, Vlad, & Olin, 2009). This is the largest number of journalism and mass communication programs since 1988.

In the autumn of 2008, journalism and mass communication programs in the United States enrolled 216,369 students, 201,477 of them seeking undergraduate degrees and 14,892 of them seeking graduate degrees. The total enrollment figure was up 0.8 percent from the year earlier, and the undergraduate figure represented an increase of 0.9 percent. Graduate enrollments declined 0.3 percent overall, with 0.1 percent at the master's level and 1.7 percent at the doctoral level.

Undergraduate students made up 93.1 percent of the students enrolled in the nation's journalism and mass communication programs, and that percentage has been stable across time. In 1988, 93.8 percent of the enrolled students were seeking an undergraduate degree. So the pattern in undergraduate enrollments across time is most informative.

The 0.9 percent growth rate from 2007 to 2008 compares with a growth rate of 1.9 percent a year earlier and 0.3 percent the year before that. The last period of substantial growth was from 1999 to 2003, after which enrollments have grown only slightly year to year (Figure 14.2). Undergraduate enrollments have grown from 1995 to 1999 at a more moderate rate. The number of students enrolled in journalism and mass communication undergraduate programs in the country actually declined from 1989 to 1995. Every year since 1995, undergraduate enrollments have grown, and the number enrolled in those programs in the autumn of 2008 was the largest it has ever been.

Those patterns of growth and decline shown in Figure 14.2 can best be understood in the context of national trends in enrollments across all majors. From 1992 to 1996, the total number of students enrolled in undergraduate programs at all degree-granting post-secondary institutions actually declined before growth returned in 1997 (National Center for Education Statistics, 2009). Rapid growth took place from 1999 to 2003, followed by more moderate growth. Clearly the pattern of enrollments in undergraduate journalism and mass communication largely reflects enrollment patterns across all fields.

At the graduate level in the field of journalism and mass communication, enrollments moved in the opposite direction from undergraduate enrollments until 2001, when enrollment increased at both the undergraduate and graduate levels (Figure 14.2). Across all fields, enrollments flattened when they were declining in journalism and mass communication, and then they grew since 2001, consistent with the data for journalism and mass communication.

The key predictor of these enrollment trends is the economy. The weak economy of the early 1990s kept students out of undergraduate programs. In such an economy, it is better to enter the labor market rather than defer entry for further study. However, if one loses a job, it is a good time to go back to school to improve the chances of getting back into the market through increased training and certification. This would suggest that undergraduate enrollments will weaken in the current fiscal crisis, as students and parents question the value

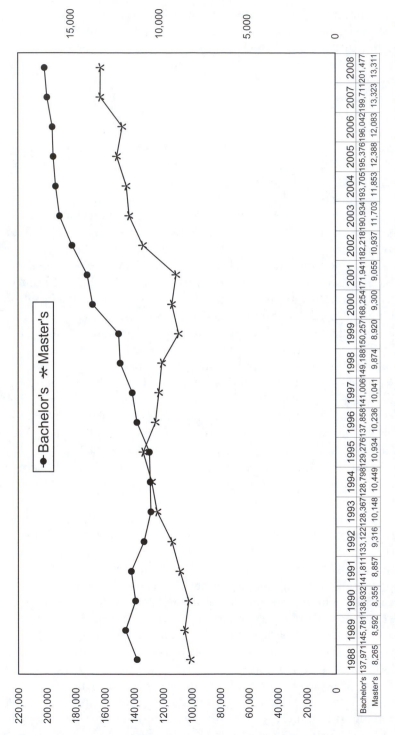

	1988	1989	1990	1991	1992	1993	1994	1995	1996	1997	1998	1999	2000	2001	2002	2003	2004	2005	2006	2007	2008
Bachelor's	137,971	145,781	138,932	141,811	133,122	128,367	128,798	129,276	137,858	141,006	149,188	150,257	168,254	171,941	182,218	190,934	193,705	195,376	196,042	199,711	201,477
Master's	8,265	8,592	8,355	8,857	9,316	10,148	10,449	10,934	10,236	10,041	9,874	8,920	9,300	9,055	10,937	11,703	11,853	12,388	12,083	13,323	13,311

FIGURE 14.2 Journalism and Mass Communication Enrollments: Bachelor's and Master's (dual Y axes). Source: *Annual Survey of Journalism & Mass Communication Enrollments.*

of investing in college, but at the graduate level, the stable enrollments of 2008 compared with a year earlier should be followed by growth.

In 2008, only 6.7 percent of the students enrolled in journalism and mass communication undergraduate programs were in news editorial, or print, journalism. That was a drop from 8.9 percent a year earlier and represented the lowest level of enrollment in news editorial journalism back to 1989. The percentage of students enrolled in broadcast journalism was 8.3 percent, up from 7.8 percent a year earlier. The percentage of students enrolled in journalism programs that did not differentiate by industry was 14.2, compared with 15.2 percent a year earlier. The percentage of students enrolled in one of these three journalism programs in 2008, thus, stood at 29.2, down from 31.9 percent a year earlier. The 2008 percentage, however, was up from 27.5 percent in 2006 and higher than the 26.8 percent figure back in 1989. Journalism, in other words, has held its own across the last 20 years.

In comparison, telecommunications (minus broadcast journalism) has dropped from 10.1 percent in 1989 to 7.4 percent in 2008, and advertising has dropped from 15.3 percent in 1989 to 9.1 percent in 2008. Public relations was the specialty of 13.2 percent of the majors in 1989, and it was the specialty of 14.7 percent in 2008. The percentage of students in majors other than journalism, telecommunications, advertising, and public relations has gone up from 34.6 percent in 1989 to 39.6 percent in 2008, as the number and types of majors has increased, including such specialties as strategic communication, media and communication management and speech. None of those other specialties attracted large numbers of students in 2008. The 39.6 percent figure in 2008 for undergraduate enrollments in communication specialties other than journalism, telecommunications, advertising, and public relations even is a bit misleading, as 9.3 percent of the enrolled students in 2008 were still undecided.

Implications for Communication Education

Cooper (2001) lists three criteria for the development of a field of study. The first is the existence of a group of scholars with a sustained interest in the subject, at least some of whom identify themselves as specialists. The second criterion is a consistent flow of materials in published books, leading journals, and conference sessions devoted to the advancement of theory. The third criterion is the establishment of academic courses in university professional education programs.

Journalism as a field of study began in U.S. universities at the end of the nineteenth century and developed fully in the early years of the twentieth century (Becker et al., 1987). Across time, the field has expanded to include instruction leading to entry to a variety of communication occupations, including journalism, public relations, and advertising. Journalism and mass communication education generally is seen as part of a broader field of communication education, and a part closely tied to the communication occupational labor markets.

As Ma (2009) has argued, knowledge about the sociological determinations of student choice of college major, or field of study, is quite limited. It is reasonable to expect, however, that uncertainty in the job markets associated with a field would create uncertainty in journalism education. The data at hand do not make any strong case for a shift within journalism and mass communication from one specialty to another. The loss of jobs in the core fields of journalism has been quite prominent in the news, yet, as noted, the percentage of students picking that specialty has not changed dramatically in recent years. It is possible that reports of job losses at traditional media are offset by reports of hiring at new players, such as Yahoo and AOL, which are working hard to create content networks on the Internet. It also is reasonable to expect, of course, a lag between market forces and student choices.

Becker (2008) has suggested a number of possible activities that journalism and mass communication programs should consider undertaking in this new occupational environment. Chief among these is credentialing. Universities might want to put more emphasis on degrees and titles, and perhaps create easy verification of these degrees via Internet links. Universities might even list people who have degrees from their programs in easily accessible databases.

Stronger distinctions might be made between the American first degree, the bachelor's degree, and the second degree, the master's degree. Donsbach and Fiedler (2008) made a similar suggestion in their report of the Carnegie-Knight Initiative of the future of journalism education. Also, there might be some consideration of what a doctorate degree could contribute to the non-academic occupational world.

Rather than a single certification, universities might develop a series of certifications, such as in open records searches or in database analysis. Students might be certified as trained in editing procedures or with graphic design software. Journalism students might be certified as having special training in health issues, and public relations students might be certified as expert in conducting and evaluating health campaigns.

The communication curricula will almost certainly need to focus more on skills of entrepreneurial operation. All communicators will need to know how to survive as small businesses. They are going to need the skills to maneuver in very competitive environments in which their own skill sets will be challenged and mimicked by others. Here the public relations and advertising market experience is likely to be particularly informative.

In the past, journalists have not worried much about the audience for their products. They have relied on their news organizations to assemble audiences. Without an organization, journalists will need to understand how to create and manage an audience. Here, too, public relations and advertising have an advantage. They have not had ready access to an audience for their messages in the past, and they have a heightened sensitivity to audiences and the techniques for gaining access to them.

Journalism and mass communication programs in the United States have considered journalism to be their core, because it is from that journalism heart that the curricula in public relations and, to a lesser extent, advertising have grown. It might well be the case that the academic enterprise needs to examine more fully the experiences of those who have been working in public relations and advertising, and make some of those experiences the centerpiece of curricular reform and certification.

If all communication occupations are becoming more individualized, in at least some sense more deprofessionalized and open to amateurs, then parts of the field such as public relations that have experience in such an environment could provide guidance for the future.

Communication education, at a minimum, needs to be aware of the open-source world in which future graduates will work. Everyone can create and edit code. Everyone can make entries into what many would consider to be an encyclopedia. Everyone can issue at least primitive public relations releases and develop some type of advertising. And everyone can produce what would be considered by many to be news. These all require technical skills, and on at least some level they do not draw on the esoteric knowledge allowing an occupation to create a market shelter.

In an environment in which everyone can easily acquire and use technical skills, communication education will either help provide knowledge skills for differentiation of the professional from the amateur, or contribute to the demise of the communication occupations as they exist today. Such inaction could result in the creation of the communication hobby—an activity for which there is no longer any real financial compensation.

Thought Questions: Contemplating Change

1. The nature of communication work is changing dramatically, raising serious questions about the nature of the communication occupations themselves. The work in the future will more likely be carried out in competition with amateurs, that is, individuals without specialized training in the occupations. Also, it will more likely be carried out in a context in which claims about expert knowledge and service to the community are challenged. Are these changes necessarily bad for the communication occupations? Are there advantages to moving away from the professional model of detachment, separation from the client, and claims of specialized expertise? Might journalists and other communicators serve themselves and society better if they abandon the professional model?

2. Journalism and mass communication education historically has been tightly linked to the labor markets of the communication occupations. The assumption is that if those markets falter, journalism and mass communication must adapt or suffer consequences. Are these assumptions correct? Can you imagine reasons why students might select journalism and mass communication as a field of study even if there is no promise of employment at the end of the studies?

3. So the occupations of communications and the educational institutions built up over time to help young people enter those occupations both are facing uncertain futures. That makes it very difficult for educational institutions to know how to prepare students. Offer suggestions to the educational institutions under these uncertain circumstances. What can they do to help students? How can and how should they adapt to the market so as to help people enter it and even shape it in the future?

References

Abbott, A. (1988). *The system of professions*. Chicago: University of Chicago Press.

Banner, F. (1934). News notes. *Journalism Quarterly, 11*, 426–431.

Bantz, C. R., McCorkle, S., & Baade, R. C. (1981). The news factory. In G. C. Wilhoit & H. deBock (Eds.), *Mass communication review yearbook* (Vol. 2, pp. 366–389). Beverly Hills, CA: Sage.

Becker, L. B. (2008). The most pressing challenge for journalism and mass communication education. In A. C. Osborne (Ed.), *The future of journalism and mass communication education* (pp. 78–79). Baton Rouge, LA: LSU Manship School of Journalism.

Becker, L. B., Fruit, J. W., & Caudill, S. L. (1987). *The training and hiring of journalists*. Norwood, NJ: ABLEX.

Becker, L. B., & Vlad, T. (2009). News organizations and routines. In K. Wahl-Jorgensen & T. Hanitzsch (Eds.), *The handbook of journalism studies* (pp. 59–72). New York: Routledge.

Becker, L. B., Vlad, T., Gans, E. M., Edwards, H., Daniels, G., & Park, N. (2005). Professionalism of news workers. In S. Dunwoody, L. B. Becker, D. M. McLeod, & G. M. Kosicki (Eds.), *The evolution of key mass communication concepts: Honoring Jack M. McLeod* (pp. 79–111). Creskill, NJ: Hampton Press.

Becker, L. B., Vlad, T., & Olin, D. (2009). 2008 Enrollment report: Slow rate of growth may signal weakening of demand. *Journalism & Mass Communication Educator, 64*, 232–257.

Becker, L. B., Vlad, T., Olin, D., Hanisak, S., & Wilcox, D. (2009). *2008 Annual survey of journalism & mass communication graduates*. Retrieved July 12, 2009, from http://www.grady.uga.edu/annualsurveys/Graduate_Survey/Graduate_2008/Grad2008Fullcolor.pdf

Becker, L. B., Vlad, T., Pelton, R., & Papper, R. A. (2006, August). *2005 Survey of editors and news directors*. Paper presented at the conference of the Association for Education in Journalism and Mass Communication in San Antonio, TX. Retrieved August

16, 2009, from http://www.grady.uga.edu/annualsurveys/Editors_News_Directors_Survey/Editors_News_Dir_2005.php

Beurer-Zuellig, B., Fieseler, C., & Meckel, M. (2009). A descriptive inquiry into the corporate communication profession in Europe. *Public Relations Review, 35*, 270–279.

Cameron, G. T., Sallot, L. M., & Curtin, P. A. (1996). Public relations and the production of news: A critical review and theoretical framework. In B. R. Burleson (Ed.), *Communication yearbook, 20* (pp. 111–155). Thousand Oaks, CA: Sage.

Carey, J. (1969). The communications revolution and the professional communicator. In P. Halmos (Ed.), *The Sociological Review Monograph, 13*, 23–28.

Cooper, T. L. (2001). The emergence of administrative ethics as a field of study in the United States. In T. L. Cooper (Ed.), *Handbook of administrative ethics* (2nd ed.) (pp. 1–36). New York: Marcel Dekker.

Deuze, M. (2007). *Mediawork.* Cambridge, UK: Polity Press.

Donsbach, W. (2006). The identity of communication research. *Journal of Communication, 56*, 437–448.

Donsbach, W., & Fiedler, T. (2008). *Journalism school curriculum enrichment.* Boston: Harvard University Press.

Ettema, J. S., & Whitney, D. C. (1994). The money arrow: An introduction to audiencemaking. In J. S. Ettema & D. C. Whitney (Eds.), *Audiencemaking: How the media create the audience* (pp. 1–18). Thousand Oaks, CA: Sage.

Fishman, M. (1980). *Manufacturing the news.* Austin: University of Texas Press.

Freidson, E. (1970). *Profession of medicine: A study of the sociology of applied knowledge.* Chicago: University of Chicago Press.

Freidson, E. (1986). *Professional powers: A study of the institutionalization of formal knowledge.* Chicago: University of Chicago Press.

Freidson, E. (1994). *Professionalism reborn: Theory, prophecy and policy.* Chicago: University of Chicago Press.

Froehlich, R., & Holtz-Bacha, C. (Eds.). (2003). *Journalism education in Europe and North America.* Cresskill, NJ: Hampton Press.

Gade, P. J. (2004). Newspapers and organizational development: Management and journalist perceptions of newsroom cultural change. *Journalism & Communication Monographs, 6*, 4–55.

Gans, H. (1979). *Deciding what's news.* New York: Random House.

Hall, R. H. (1994). *Sociology of work.* Thousand Oaks, CA: Pine Forge Press.

Hallin, D. C., & Mancini, P. (2004). *Comparing media systems.* Cambridge, UK: Cambridge University Press.

Hardley, M. (1999). Doctor in the house: The Internet as a source of lay health knowledge and the challenge to expertise. *Sociology of Health and Illness, 21*, 820–835.

Haug, M. R. (1975). The deprofessionalization of everyone? *Sociological Focus, 8*, 197–213.

Haug, M. R. (1977). Computer technology and the obsolescence of the concept of profession. In M. R. Haug & J. Dofney (Eds.), *Work and technology* (pp. 215–228). London: Sage.

Haug, M. R. (1988). A re-examination of the hypothesis of physician deprofessionalization. *The Milbank Quarterly, 66*(Supplement 2), 48–56.

Hornig, F. (2009, July 28). *Who needs newspapers when you have Twitter?* Retrieved November 25, 2010, from http://www.salon.com/news/feature/2009/07/28/wired

Johansen, P. (2001). Professionalisation, building respectability and the birth of the Canadian Public Relations Society. *Journalism Studies, 2*, 55–71.

Journalism & mass communication directory 2009–2010. (2009). Columbia, SC: Association for Education in Journalism and Mass Communication.

The journalist's road to success. (n.d.). Dow Jones News Fund Inc. Retrieved December 22, 2010, from https://www.newsfund.org/PageText/JournRoad.aspx?Page_ID=JrRdInt

Keen, A. (2008). *The cult of the amateur.* New York: Doubleday.

Kreshel, P. J. (1990). The "culture" of J. Walter Thompson, 1915–1925. *Public Relations Review, 16*, 80–93.

Larson, M. S. (1977). *The rise of professionalism.* Berkeley: University of California Press.

Lowrey, W. (2006). Mapping the journalism–blogging relationship. *Journalism, 7*, 477–500.

Ma, Y. (2009). Family socioeconomic status, parental involvement, and college major choices—gender, race/ethnic, and nativity patterns. *Sociological Perspectives, 52*, 211–234.

McLeod, J. M., & Hawley, S. E., Jr. (1964). Professionalization among newsmen. *Journalism Quarterly, 41*, 529–539.

McLeod, J. M., & Rush, R. R. (1969a). Professionalization of Latin American and U.S. journalists. *Journalism Quarterly, 46*, 583–590.

McLeod, J. M., & Rush, R. R. (1969b). Professionalization of Latin American and U.S. journalists: Part II. *Journalism Quarterly, 46*, 784–789.

McQuail, D. (1997). *Audience analysis.* Thousand Oaks, CA: Sage.

Muzio, D., & Ackroyd, S. (2005). On the consequence of defensive professionalism: Recent changes in the legal labour process. *Journal of Law and Society, 32*, 615–642.

National Center for Education Statistics. (2009). *Projections of education statistics to 2018.* Retrieved September 18, 2009, from www.nces.ed.gov/edstats

Nossek, H. (2009). On the future of journalism as a professional practice and the case of journalism in Israel. *Journalism, 10*, 358–361.

Phillips, A., Singer, J. B., Vlad, T., & Becker, L. B. (2009). Implications of technological change for journalists' tasks and skills. *Journal of Media Business Studies, 6*, 61–85.

Project for Excellence in Journalism. (2009). *The state of the news media 2009.* Pew Project for Excellence in Journalism. Retrieved August 12, 2009, from http://www.stateofthemedia.org/2009/index.htm

Project for Excellence in Journalism. (2010). *The state of the news media 2010.* Retrieved June 15, 2010, from http://www.stateofthemedia.org/2010/

Randall, G. E., & Kindiak, D. H., (2008). Deprofessionalization or postprofessionalization? Reflections on the state of social work as a profession. *Social Work in Health Care, 47*, 341–354.

Reich, Z. (2009). *Sourcing the news.* Cresskill, NJ: Hampton Press.

Ritzer, G., & Walczak, D. (1988). Rationalization and the deprofessionalization of physicians. *Social Forces, 67*, 1–22.

Sallot, L. M., Cameron, G. T., & Weaver-Lariscy, R. A. (1997). Professional standards in public relations: A survey of educators. *Public Relations Review, 23*, 197–216.

Sallot, L. M., Cameron, G. T., & Weaver-Lariscy, R. A. (1998). Pluralistic ignorance and professional standards: Underestimating professionalism of our peers in public relations. *Public Relations Review, 24*, 1–19.

Singer, J. B. (2006). The political j-blogger. *Journalism, 6*, 173–198.

Timmermans, S. (2008). Professions and their work: Do market shelters protect professional interests? *Work and Occupations, 35*, 164–188.

Tuchman, G. (1978). *Making news*. New York: Free Press.

Wall, M. (2005). Blogs of war. *Journalism, 6*, 153–172.

Wilensky, H. (1964). The professionalization of everyone? *American Journal of Sociology, 70*, 137–158.

15

CONNECTIVE JOURNALISM

Wilson Lowrey, University of Alabama, and Peter J. Gade, University of Oklahoma

The 2009–2010 recession hit towns and cities across the United States hard, including the city in this vignette—hit especially hard because of its dependence on a single strug-gling industry.[1] Thousands lost jobs in the wake of plummeting ad revenue, among them employees of the city's legacy print and broadcast media. The city's major daily shrunk its newsroom staff by half from 10 years earlier. In the shadows of hard times, small online media efforts sprouted in abandoned coverage areas, including community news sites, partisan bloggers, and specialized non-profit media. Some start-ups included journalists laid off by legacy media. During the depths of the crisis, unemployed and underemployed journalists, bloggers, community news site publishers, and some innovating members of the legacy media began meeting at an all-night midtown restaurant, swapping ideas and brainstorming about possibilities for collaboration and new media efforts. Organizers Skyped in nationally known online innovators to aid the brainstorming, and these meet-ups fueled a citywide community news site that hosted specialty writers and neighborhood journalists. A number of blogs devoted to covering neighborhood crime appeared around the same time, as legacy media resources for covering crime diminished. The city's daily paper ratcheted up its own innovation efforts, reaching out to hyperlocal journalists. Facebook and Twitter activity blossomed, with media outlets of all types and sizes corresponding about the city.

Over time, the local economy gained a pulse, supporting some legacy media hiring, but providing too little to maintain all start-ups. The citywide community site struggled to attract revenue, some online ventures folded, and entrepreneurial enthusiasm waned. Legacy media continued to seek hybrid partnerships, though newsrooms showed a reluc-tance to publish citizen content. Social media interaction across most local media became increasingly fervent. And even as media around the city expressed excitement over emerg-ing opportunities, they continued to look to the city's paper for leadership, voicing concern over its weakened state . . .

As this vignette shows, challenges in the environment lead to uncertainty, and uncertainty can spark fear and creativity, experimentation and collaboration—and often more uncertainty. However, the vignette also shows that responses to uncertainty can be uneven, quickly gaining and losing momentum. Efforts to adapt are hard to sustain, and old ways of thinking and doing die hard. Challenges to change lie in wait at professional, organizational, and community levels.

This book is about journalistic change. As is clear from the preceding chapters, journalism in the United States as elsewhere is facing profound disruption, leaving managers and staff journalists unsure about next steps. Uncertainty has a number of vantage points, as we discussed in Chapter 1. It may be seen as opaque, a product of contexts so complex that the sense can't be perceived. Alternatively, uncertainty may merely obscure—although our limited cognitive abilities keep us from taking in all of our environment's complexities, we can still see well enough to make decisions and move forward. A premise of this book is that journalists have agency and can reduce uncertainty. They can gain knowledge of their complex environment and its interconnections, though it is not a foregone conclusion that they will do so—witness the waning enthusiasm for innovations mentioned in the opening vignette.

The unique position with the commanding view that journalism has occupied for so long is starting to feel merely isolated and remote. Therefore journalists are finally trying new things, looking to integrate with different norms, values, and knowledge areas across their network—found beyond journalism's traditional jurisdiction, or encroaching into it, or even found within journalists' own newsrooms. More thorough integration with their new, complex environments should aid journalists' understanding about these environments, reshaping journalism's culture, even as journalists seek to hold on to core norms, values, and knowledge areas.

Our contributors cover a great deal of conceptual ground as they address these issues: from Enlightenment Era rationality to postmodernism; from the shifting imperatives of economic resources to the less calculable benefits of professional legitimacy and autonomy; from financial markets to labor markets; and from the constraints of organizational structures to networked human agency. Chapters explore uncertainty, complexity, and change from varied theoretical perspectives and levels of analysis, from expansively philosophical frameworks to frameworks grounded in the world journalists work in every day.

This is not primarily a prescriptive book. In this final chapter we do point to a possible way forward for journalism, but we acknowledge that there are no simple solutions. We endorse the logic of our approach—that the first step toward addressing uncertainty is to map the varied and complex contexts within which it originates and grows, so we may better understand the ways journalists perceive it, and the impact it has.

Our initial challenge in this chapter is to connect the dots, identifying patterns that emerge across the book. The chapter begins by discussing patterns in the ways the book's contributors have examined journalism's complex environments. The discussion moves to the uncertainty that complexity spurs, efforts to reduce uncertainty, and factors shaping these efforts. The chapter then takes a twist, proposing uncertainty as a benefit, as a catalyst for change. We end by proposing a *connective journalism*: a journalism that embraces uncertainty, active engagement with diverse social networks, and a commitment to crafting logical but negotiable narratives across emerging specializations. We also embrace the notion that journalism has a democratic mission—and so connective journalism must maintain a connection with the enduring norms and values grounded in this mission. The chapter takes a particularly close look at social networks, as chapters throughout the book touch on their increasing importance for journalism. We discuss the necessity of developing a new knowledge base for this type of journalism, as well as economic implications.

Journalism's Complex Environments

Complexity in this book refers to the multiplicity of components and contexts in an environment. It also refers to the intricacy and dynamism of their interconnections (Tolbert & Hall, 2009). As mentioned, complexity coupled with cognitive limitations leads people to uncertainty in their perceptions. This loose definition of complexity also fits well with the phenomenon of social networks, those negotiated arrangements of diverse and decentralized participants (Stalder, 2006). More and more, the structure of journalism's environment looks like a complex network—egalitarian, interactive, and temporary.

The book's contributors discuss the daunting nature of complexity from social and economic perspectives, at different levels of analysis. Depictions differ, but a common theme is the loosening of hierarchical control and traditional routines and conventions. This is found within news organizations and across news organizations' social environment. As typically seen in network structures, this new news environment may no longer have "a legitimate organizational authority to arbitrate and resolve disputes that may arise during [an] exchange" (Polodny & Page, 1998, p. 59), or at least this authority is weak. As will be discussed, the "freedom" that results from this loosened control can both enliven and confound.

Early chapters in the book map out ideological and philosophical complexities that challenge change efforts. Merrill poses the quandary that concepts of freedom and responsibility in journalism are not compatible. Although interactive digital media would seem to foster freedom through a "people's journalism," it is not clear that "the people" are able or motivated enough to take on the responsibility that is the other side of freedom. Meanwhile, the push for social responsibility by outside agents—by the government particularly—may weaken journalists' autonomy, and therefore their ability to bring about socially responsible change. Gade points to postmodern culture as a source of complexity, fragmentation, and incoherency for journalism. He hopes increased connectedness with the public in the construction of news, and more open, democratic ways to judge veracity and quality, signal a richer type of "freedom and responsibility." However, this new freedom seems a threat as well. For example, opening the gates to news aggregation sites may undermine the role of original reporting.

In different ways, Sylvie, Rivas-Rodriguez, and Hindman all point to a complex society that keeps shifting identity, and to journalists' troublesome task in representing it with fairness, inclusiveness, and accuracy. These changes reflect more open, egalitarian constructions of the national identity, which challenge traditional journalistic norms and traditional interpretive frames. Sylvie notes the difficulty journalists face in trying to get their heads around our increasing social diversity, which by its complex nature defies a singular, dominant definition. Rivas-Rodriguez sees great demographic shifts at the national level as evidence that journalists must be willing to look past their own conventional frames—for example, the traditional "melting pot" frame—to really see the uniqueness and validity of varied new communities. Hindman looks at the confusion local journalists run into when their representations of their communities become entangled in a national polarizing political discourse—a discourse far removed from the diverse particularities of community members' daily lives.

Several authors explore complexities in the relationship between the daily work of journalism and journalists' immediate environments. Singer, and Beam and Meeks point to changing technologies and the leveling of a field that is allowing more give and take between journalists and non-journalists. These complexities challenge journalists' traditional practices and norms. They make journalists uncertain about their stance toward their public. Lowrey shows how managers and staff journalists striving for change are constrained by a social need for a widely understood logic—a common grammar—for the content, practices, and forms of news. Becker and Vlad discuss the uncertainty that shifting tasks, technologies, and knowledge areas present to administrators and faculty of communication schools, as they try to grasp journalism's increasingly slippery knowledge domains, and plan curricula.

The economic environment, like the social environment, is increasingly complex. Just yesterday, legacy news media competed in stable, geographically defined markets, with their limited competition in plain view. Entry barriers to media industries were high, and news media controlled the production and dissemination of news, their main product. No more. Our interactive, networked world lends itself to individual-level control more than institutional control, and news media are looking for ways to adapt. Dimmick, Powers, and co-authors outline individualizing patterns of media consumption, saying that media firms need to evolve in ways that connect with more personalized and niche expectations. However, the legacy product's core audience has been hesitant to embrace the online product. More uncertainty results. Managers are unsure whether to limit change, or to "burn the boats and commit" to a future that apparently will be populated by digital natives.

Lacy and Sohn discuss the inherent conflict between journalism's dual markets as an ongoing cause of uncertainty for managers, and Hollifield says public ownership introduces the further complexity of a third market, the capitals market, which demands news managers' attention. Each market's activity—the selling of content to audiences, audiences to advertisers, and ownership in the corporation to investors—implies different assumptions and organizational goals. Further, Hollifield discusses the complexity introduced by our increasingly small world, as media companies diversity their products into international non-media markets. This has led to some loss of control in the face of unfamiliar product demands and unfamiliar cultures. All of this adds up to a difficult decision-making environment for news managers, who increasingly must think as much about changing markets for the "news product" as they do about editorial decisions that affect their public or community.

Changing ownership structures also confuse and constrain. Lacy and Sohn note that the growth of large publicly traded media firms in the late twentieth century shackled news media to high profit expectations in order to satisfy and attract investors, inducing initiatives to control costs. News staffs are smaller and overworked, causing news outlets to steer away from resource-intensive public interest journalism, as Hollifield notes as well. Though large corporate, publicly owned firms have greater resources to confront uncertainty, they are entangled in complex markets, leaving them with conflicting missions. This is particularly challenging given their bureaucratic structures, unfriendly to change.

Uncertainty and Its Responses

Increasing complexity and interconnectedness in social and economic environments lead to uncertainty in the mind. Where should journalists step first in this murky, tangled environment? Uncertainty is inherently uncomfortable, and it prompts agency; the natural tendency is to take steps to reduce it. As Sylvie says, uncertainty grows out of a lack of knowledge in the midst of complexity. It makes planning and controlling outcomes difficult or even impossible. Throughout this book, uncertainty is generally viewed as a condition that cannot be eliminated entirely, but it is not seen as incalculable. Authors suggest a variety of paths journalism might take toward greater certainty, knowledge, and control. Some paths lead toward loosening current methods, practices, and norms both internally and externally. Others lead toward tightening connections with multiplying voices in the network, and learning from them.

Some paths stay closer to home, leading toward efforts to maintain institutional and professional authority. In fact, many journalists and managers have not embraced change. Singer notes that in the 1990s, news managers tended to dismiss the significance of technological change, and some continue to close their ears and eyes. Also, as Lowrey says, news managers may pay lip service to fundamental change, altering the "window dressing." Skin-deep change may be an easier path for institutions, which are bound by their own bureaucratic structure and by traditional co-dependencies with other institutions. A conservative approach can have its advantages, given the considerable risk in an uncertain environment, and the continuing (if diminishing) value of long-earned institutional connections.

Some journalists and managers are open to change but protective of journalistic values, norms, and practices associated with a democratic mission. A number of contributors echo these sentiments. Merrill sees allegiance to libertarian, democratic principles as a guiding light through change and uncertainty. Singer says traditional journalistic norms are a last line of defense for journalism as journalists seek "occupational turf markers" that are "more durable than the ones the Internet is obliterating." Beam and Meeks say journalists have a better chance of surviving the current upheaval if they keep public service journalism at the heart of their mission, and don't squander resources on content with only "commodity value."

However, the line between agelessness and stagnancy is a fine one. Do norms and values also need to evolve or else risk irrelevance? Gade sees values such as freedom and responsibility and accuracy as enduring, but as necessarily evolving, as journalists find themselves in increasingly postmodern, networked, and transparent contexts. Society's spreading network structures, a social model that makes traditional hierarchical structures seem strangely unworkable, are a significant source of uncertainty. Several authors say journalists should respond by reaching out and embracing the networks' multiplying perspectives. Journalists can learn from them rather than avoid them. Gade says journalists should become more "responsive and responsible" to the network by seeking other voices and using the "crowd" to help verify content. Similarly, both Lowrey and Singer envision journalists continuing to verify and analyze, but also see them revealing socially meaningful connections across disparate nodes in the network, and helping to make sense of them—a "seminar leader" role, Lowrey suggests. Both Rivas-Rodriguez and Hindman say journalists should pursue a path to stronger connection with their communities. This path lies through thorough reporting, fine-grained local detail, and a willingness to look beyond vague, traditional frames.

Maintaining core values, norms, and practices in some form makes economic sense as well. Long-held connections, competencies, and expert knowledge in such areas as establishing veracity and investigating the powerful are well-guarded jurisdictional areas for journalism. These core areas are "high-hanging fruit" for those hungry to encroach on journalism's turf. Accordingly they provide value for journalism, as Robert Picard (2009) has noted, and presumably for society, if they are pursued with purpose. Organizations take on big risk by overthrowing these kinds of core areas. It makes sense to maintain much of the core and innovate on the periphery.

Finally, there is a pushmi-pullyu quality to newsrooms' strategies for reducing uncertainty: a push toward convergence, coupled with a pull toward specialization. On the one hand, converging organizational roles, tasks, and technologies seems to make sense, as this encourages free and open internal communication needed to learn from a changing environment. Convergence also makes it easier to disseminate content across multiple platforms, an argument made by Dimmick, Powers, and co-authors. On the other hand, because of market fragmentation, it would seem wise to increase specialization and entrepreneurialism.

Hollifield says that converged newsroom tasks do allow for greater creativity and open news decision-making to new voices and ideas; however, convergence may also lead to a wider range of tasks and increased workload for journalists, giving them "little time to develop new ideas or do in-depth reporting." Singer, and Beam and Meeks make similar arguments. Beam and Meeks note that two-thirds of respondents to the American Journalists survey reported an increased workload from 2006 to 2007, a figure unlikely to have decreased since then.

Several authors call for journalists to specialize content. Beam and Meeks argue that mass distribution of content will no longer effectively lure advertisers because of increasing segmentation in the market. Similarly, Lacy and Sohn say that journalists should strategically diversify and specialize, guided by audience research. Specialization for Becker and Vlad has educational implications: the media labor market has been kinder to individuals in occupations such as public relations that flexibly adjust to the economic market, that are less organizationally bound, and that can easily specialize. Perhaps, they suggest, schools should certify mastery of specialized knowledge areas, and encourage entrepreneurialism.

Factors Shaping Responses to Uncertainty

A number of factors complicate efforts to reduce uncertainty, among them assumptions and oversimplifications. Rivas-Rodriguez points to the narrow frames that blind journalists to alternate visions of American identity, suggesting that diminished staffs and time constraints encourage pursuit of familiar routines and frameworks. Similarly, Hindman says depleted newsrooms are more susceptible to political polarization at the national level, a force that obscures complex meanings and ultimately confuses both journalists and audiences.

The response to uncertainty itself can become an obstacle, as there is no guarantee that change leads to benefits. Both Hollifield, and Lacy and Sohn point out news industry blunders in seeking to reduce uncertainty, such as cutting circulation in peripheral areas. These expensive mistakes continue to siphon off resources needed for change. Lowrey points out that ceremonial change, avoidance of change, and mimicry by news outlets can hold meaningful change at bay. Gade says the emergence of collaborative structures in news organizations can get in the way of adapting to networked, individualized environments. For example, integrated work teams within news organizations may decouple work from reporters' expertise, leading to news that is more a product of newsroom planning than a discovery of things happening out in the world.

A significant problem is the dearth of guiding conventions and routines for dealing with social, economic, and technological changes. This situation does offer freedom, but can journalists (or anyone) really deal with such limitlessness? Singer says confusion results from "rules for engagement . . . being written on the fly, if they are written at all." Sylvie says unplanned diversity leads to ambiguity and hesitation because of a lack of knowledge and control, and Lowrey points to the paralysis that results from a lack of routines and conventional boundaries. Paradoxically, although conventions constrain, they also encourage agency by maintaining paths, as Giddens (1976) points out.

Learning to Live with Uncertainty

We said in Chapter 1 that uncertainty is generally not seen as a friend. The common response to reduce uncertainty, detailed in the previous section, gives evidence to this: Uncertainty is uncomfortable for managers, staff, and even for audiences. However, would journalism and society be well served if journalists were to rid themselves of uncertainty, as unlikely as that is? Would benefits be lost?

Uncertainty may be viewed as, if not a friend, then a spur to end complacency, a productive irritant, a grain of sand in the oyster. The vignette at the top of this chapter speaks to this, as do contributors' chapters. Lacy and Sohn call for journalists to respond to uncertainty by reacquainting themselves with communities, audiences, and advertisers. Likewise, Dimmick, Powers, and co-authors say that uncertainty from shifting resource niches requires managers to be open-minded. Rivas-Rodriguez sees increasing uncertainty over national identity as an opportunity for journalists to rethink this identity, embrace new ideas, and challenge assumptions, and Merrill sees the disruption of digital technology and the new *vox populi* as an opportunity for journalists to exercise moral responsibility.

Uncertainty is double-edged. It can paralyze, overwhelm us cognitively, as we need some agreed-upon paths in order to move forward. We have referred to this as fundamental uncertainty. However, uncertainty may also be viewed as part of a process, as a loosening of the institutional grip. It may allow an environment with many paths for creative agency, and so prompt needed changes. A number of authors suggest that these changes strengthen journalists as individual practitioners. Journalists stand less protected in the midst of diminishing resources and weakening organizations, but also less constrained. Beam and Meeks think it likely that individual journalists will continue their commitment to public service journalism, even with dwindling support from their news organizations, and they also forecast increasing entrepreneurialism and specialization, as do Becker and Vlad. Singer also thinks individual journalists will continue their commitment to journalistic principles and ethics; this important jurisdictional area remains open to journalists, even as they try to adapt to new surroundings.

It's not clear whether journalism loses too much by striving for certainty, which tends to close off avenues for thought and exploration, or if there is simply too much complexity and too many options for audiences and over-taxed journalists to handle. Greater uncertainty generally dovetails with less control, as uncertainty hinders planning and prediction. Should journalism pursue less uncertainty and greater control? This question leads to different answers depending on the frame of reference.

From a management/economics standpoint, the answer is a qualified "yes." Although managers have tried to decentralize authority in many newsrooms, decentralization is really a strategy to regain the firm's strategic control. Learning about a complex, fluid environment requires flexibility in the assignment of the boundary spanners who monitor the environment. Learning helps prediction, which aids control. Both Lacy and Sohn, and Dimmick, Powers, and co-authors speak to this strategy, calling for more careful monitoring of shifting audiences and emerging niches.

From a more philosophical viewpoint, it is less clear that journalists should pursue certainty and control. Certainty and control in the form of routines, tight coordination, and organizational buffers may dampen individual journalists' initiative, encouraging their "escape" from freedom's responsibilities, as Merrill suggests. Sylvie suggests that to increase certainty about newsroom diversity would shut off needed discussion about the role of diversity, potentially choking off some freedom for journalists and shutting out alternative voices.

In fact, Sylvie says, diversity and uncertainty go hand in hand, as diversity casts doubt on dominant thoughts and accepted practices. We are more likely to change in substantive ways during times of upheaval, when the institutions of control have let down their guard and voices from the margins can be heard, as Rivas-Rodriguez says. According to Gade, postmodern impulses—society's embrace of subjectivity, relativity, and ambiguity—suggest that our society has already become more comfortable with uncertainty, or at least more comfortable with multiple perspectives and flexible meanings. An embrace of one set of values, an advocacy of one best method for finding and reporting truth, a claim of authenticity based on institutional knowledge and professionalism—all are now cast in doubt.

Digital interactive technologies give nearly everyone the ability to publish, and so any attempts by journalism to restore complete control over, and certainty about, information flow, news creation, and agenda setting are not logical anyway. They are also likely to be fruitless. It is understandable that a threatened journalism would try to adapt in ways that hold on to authority, and in fact journalism may regain some authority. However, thanks largely to the Internet, the public now views publication as a right. There's no going back.

So it seems journalists are stuck with significant uncertainty and diminished control. Actually, this may be to the benefit of both journalism and society, though it may not feel like it from within the journalism field. Some curb on certainty of processes and practices may provide the flexibility needed to integrate traditional journalistic practices, norms, and values with the many minds and voices beyond newsrooms. And then integrating with the network can bring more knowledge, alleviating uncertainty to a degree.

New Directions: Connective Journalism

Uncertainty is Janus-faced in the classical sense, with one face looking back and the other into the future. Uncertainty may create confusion and disorder of the sort that makes us avoid change, that makes us close our eyes and ears as Singer says, and long for simpler times. However, uncertainty also leaves doors and possibilities open. The cognitive discomfort it causes can spark efforts toward change, maybe even productive change, though that's not guaranteed (an important point to keep in mind—change can lead to disaster as well, a fact that change advocates don't dwell on).

We will be living with uncertainty for the foreseeable future, and so journalists may as well look bravely into uncertainty's forward-looking face. Calls to wrestle honestly and productively with uncertainty without squelching it are heard throughout this book, and it seems clear that journalists should come to view uncertainty as a dynamic foundation for their work. Such a foundation would spur the profession to engage outwardly and actively, would curb automatic tendencies to build barriers and buffers, and would encourage journalists to be responsive and responsible to society.

However, uncertainty tends to foster confusion as well as diversity and freedom. This creates an opportunity for journalists to exercise social responsibility in a fractured postmodern culture. Journalism can be an indispensable and intelligent vehicle for coherence, for identifying broader interests and varied frames of reference, and for drawing connections across these. This goes hand in hand with a core aspect of journalism's democratic mission: the creation of a marketplace of ideas and the rigorous representation of varied constituent groups in society, norms rooted in both the libertarian and social responsibility theories of the press.

Toward this end, journalists may reposition journalism as a profession with a knowledge base that moves connectivity, as a value and as a competency, to its core. *Connective journalism* (1) unearths disparate points of view, juxtaposing and linking them in meaningful ways; (2) helps resolve confusion for people by coaxing forth logical, coherent, and valid narratives with meaningful contexts; and (3) embraces uncertainty, experimentation, and a willingness to negotiate meaning. This is not a move away from core values and competencies related to a democratic mission—establishing veracity, critically analyzing claims, monitoring the powerful. Rather, these remain the bedrock upon which journalism shifts—journalism can keep the faith while changing the church, as Clay Shirky (2008) has said. The remainder of this section explores the nature of networks, so central to a connective journalism, and looks at the benefits and complications of adopting connective journalism.

Repositioning the Profession within Networked Environments

Connective journalism is networked journalism, but with an eye on meaningful coherency. We find that the concept of networks as a useful organizing logic has emerged gradually throughout the book, moving from the background to the foreground. So we take a moment here to explore the concept more fully.

Participants within network structures seek to reposition themselves and secure their footing through ongoing negotiation, in response to internal and external factors. We also see this idea of negotiation for jurisdictional control in approaches such as Abbott's system of professions and Bourdieu's field theory (perspectives touched on throughout the book), and both approaches have network qualities. Stalder's (2006) definition of the network, based on the scholarship of Manuel Castells, describes the news media's emerging new environment: "an enduring pattern of large-scale interaction among heterogeneous social actors that define one another . . . [and] coordinate themselves on the basis of common protocols, values and goals" (p. 180). Rather than having predetermined roles and hierarchical structures, networked participants mutually adjust and readjust in response to changing internal interaction patterns, and in response to outside factors (Castells, 2000). In so doing, participants continuously define one another and one another's goals, norms, and practices.

Yet networks have structure—a structure looser than the hierarchy, but more enduring than the market, with its fleeting transactions (Stalder, 2006).

Network participants are diverse in their norms and processes, but they share common purpose, which serves as a weakly cohering glue (Stalder, 2006). Such a purpose enables agency, similar to Giddens' (1976) notion of a common language structure enabling the agency of speech. We see this weak cohesion in journalism's traditional network, with journalists and corporate and government sources sharing a common purpose in getting information to publics—but conflicting in their professional norms and values. In a new, increasingly expansive and complex network, it gets harder to see shared purposes clearly, but they need to be there.

Although theoretically networks are non-hierarchical, having no set legitimate authority to resolve conflict during exchanges (Polodny & Page, 1998), networks do have a dynamic pecking order, based largely on the network's history. The more a "node" (connecting point) has contributed to a network, the more importance it assumes (Castells, 2000). Also, networks exhibit some measure of social control, negotiating common purposes and protocols and shared sets of goals, without which networks would disintegrate (Stalder, 2006). These ideas are important in considering journalism's responses to volatile, fluid, networked environments. Although uncertainty and heterogeneity are likely to persist, journalism's most fundamental, long-held jurisdictional area is grounded in its democratic mission, as many of the chapter authors note. What seem to be weakened in current hybrid journalism–citizen efforts, as well as popular personality-driven news sources, are the core norms and practices related to serving a democratic public. To date, where such efforts are sustainable, they tend to emphasize entertainment, personal stories, and commentary. There's nothing wrong with these forms, of course, in and of themselves. But a dearth of thoroughly reported, verified, and analyzed information serving democratic publics—that is a problem.

It seems that a network with a whiff of hierarchy is called for. In fact, this may be inevitable, given the tendency of flat structures to move toward hierarchy (Michels 1962 [1911]; Tolbert & Hiatt, 2009). That's an important factor to keep in mind, given the various powerful institutions that could assume control of such a hierarchy.

Continuing uncertainty and diversity demand a journalism that is more flexible and fluid than hierarchical bureaucracy allows. But the normative need for a sense of coherency and a common grammar for talking about public issues in context—these suggest we need a journalism that exerts influence over the network's common purposes. Connective journalism should possess the public and institutional legitimacy to arbitrate exchanges and lend some order to information, enabling agency and action on the part of both media and society. The vignette that led this chapter suggested as much, with smaller media in the city continuing to look to the daily paper for leadership.

A New Knowledge Base

The ability to practice connective journalism and to gain some jurisdiction over it requires a body of abstract knowledge—knowledge that allows journalists to see more clearly through the uncertainty. This knowledge would inform journalists' abilities to locate varied and valuable knowledge domains and link them logically, to broaden contexts of specialized knowledge domains, and to perceive and offer multiple framings.

Journalists must also fully understand the roles that information, knowledge, and public discussion play in the democratic process. They must hold on to core competencies such as finding likely stakeholders and special interests, and ferreting out questionable, unverified information. And they must be able to articulate the value of freedom, the basis for an independent voice.

As long as journalists work within organizations, they must have the organizational flexibility to exercise such knowledge. As Hollifield points out, journalists have traditionally been able to exercise some professional autonomy within newsroom hierarchies, though this autonomy is increasingly constrained, as Beam and Meeks note. Both Hollifield and Gade note the importance of loose collaborative structures in encouraging creative, innovative thought and practice, which would certainly be required in a connective journalism—although not so loose as to cause confusion.

Journalists must gain specialized knowledge as well, as Becker and Vlad say. This is partly because knowledge areas and audiences are fragmenting, and partly because networks reward the engaging expert. But it is also because journalists must have some understanding of specialized knowledge areas—for example, business, urban planning, environmental science, the historical context of a community—if they are to connect them in logical ways. Like a seminar leader, the connective journalist must listen carefully, draw thoughtful, clarifying connections, and be ready for ongoing discussion. In a community's discussion of development along a local river, for example, viewpoints and information may be provided by city officials, everyday citizens, neighborhood activists, chambers of commerce and local businesses, and environmental and economic experts. Constraints may be imposed at state and federal levels. Traditional journalists too will provide information and commentary, but would also help find and juxtapose these diverse voices, provide meaningful connective links across them, expose inaccuracies and spin, and suggest meaningful syntheses and areas of agreement.

In striving for sense-making, journalists should not be too eager to reach concrete consensus about "acceptable discussion." Conceptual boundaries must be drawn in pencil, as socially shared understandings have a way of slipping into certainty, getting "into their uniforms" as taken-for-granted, conventional wisdom (Cohen & Gooch, 1991, p. 44), as mentioned in Chapter 1. In the river development case, for example, the outcome could become framed as a choice between two different plans for commercial development, with citizens being blinded to third ways, such as expanding green space.

Economic and Organizational Implications

To tolerate uncertainty is to undercut predictability, a key factor for planning business success. That's a problem for the type of journalism proposed here, which tolerates uncertainty. Still, conventions and routines that enable prediction, planning, and assessment are likely to emerge over time for this type of work—all professions have routines. True, routinization can take on a life of its own, but active connections with diverse networks work against tendencies to over-routinize and calcify.

A journalism that seeks connections does have its economic advantages. It has the capacity to attract specialized niche audiences, and to add value through intelligent aggregation—aggregation that brings in disparate viewpoints, links to enlightening information, and organizes prominent ways of thinking on these topics. In contrast, the back-and-forth polemic screaming matches in many news-story forums are of little value. Lacy and Sohn note the economic wisdom of cross-promoting specialist websites, given consumers' variety of interests. They say this economic strategy should benefit the public as well, as "cross-promotion would allow a community to share a larger amount of knowledge about itself."

It is not at all clear what funding models would be best sustaining financially. Journalists must continue to explore different sources of funding, from foundations, to think-tanks, to models based on some mix of sponsorships, donations, and advertising; and to explore different forms of journalism–citizen hybrids. Continued experimentation and relaxing of control—consistent with the ethic of connective journalism—should eventually aid the emergence of new models, even "populations" of media that demonstrate relatively greater advantages and accumulate the social and economic capital needed to achieve the legitimacy and shared understanding that ongoing success requires.

Connective journalism may be a risky proposition economically: Many may crave only media that reinforce specialized, existing interests and values—media that look like them. However, doubtless others will desire information that expands horizons, offers diverse views, and employs social scientific methods to seek truth. This audience would not be a twentieth-century-style "mass" audience. Still, we argue that there will be a strong perceived need for a journalism that unearths and connects disparate views, sorts through the polemic shouting and confusion, and aids sense-making—and ultimately legitimizes or contextualizes the messages examined. Such a journalism would have value at multiple levels, for publics, and for political and economic institutions. That would seem a niche deserving of resources.

The Journey toward Connective Journalism

A dual legitimacy is at work in connective journalism, anchored in both a dynamic, networked approach and traditional commitments to truth seeking. There is a tension here, between listening and engaging widely on the one hand, and leading through sense-making and truth-seeking on the other. This reflects the ongoing tension between the views of news as a "communal force" and as a resource for rational public discourse (Schudson, 2003, p. 212). It is not unlike the tension Sylvie ascribes to the concept of diversity in Chapter 5. Connective journalism is fluid and egalitarian, but only to a degree. Networks have some cohesiveness and structure, and we have cautiously called for some measure of hierarchy—likely anyway, as we have noted. This is demonstrated in the opening vignette, in the deference many small media showed the city's daily paper even as media networks developed.

A note of caution: The diminished control of connective journalism may open the doors to unintended consequences—to agendas of the powerful and well-heeled outside of news organizations, and to internal agendas by those on the inside. As mentioned in Chapter 1, organizations are tools, and, as such, their resources and goals "are up for grabs, and people grab for them continually" (Perrow, 1986, pp. 12–13). Someone will take the reins, and, as Merrill notes, better that the driver be professionally (if imperfectly) committed to a broad democratic mission than to the narrow interests of powerful institutions. According to both Merrill and Gade, a people-focused journalism may leave the powerful unchecked and more able to frame and control discussion; Hindman's call to challenge simplistic frames that serve narrow, powerful interests is dead on. We need a journalism that can stand toe-to-toe with other powerful institutions in society, for as long as these institutions hold forth. A long tail of hyperlocal and highly specialized outlets won't cut it.

The goals for a connective journalism as discussed in this chapter are ambitious and demanding, a fact that should not be glossed over. Several contributors to this book note the increasing burdens under which journalists labor. Doing more with less is the norm, and the squeeze continues to tighten. Connective journalism asks a lot in calling for journalists to embrace uncertainty and continue experimentation. And the abstract knowledge of a connective journalism demands a lot of the schools that support journalism. So while we lay out an ideal-type direction here, it is important to keep in mind the daily lived realities that limit journalists' abilities to move beyond routines, and to exercise abstract professional knowledge.

We should also keep in mind that the journey from these ideal-type discussions of connective journalism to its daily practice is an arduous one. Professional and organizational cultures are change resistant, both in news organizations and in the schools, and, for connective journalism to take root, shared meanings about the nature of professional journalism must shift and coalesce again, both within the professional culture and throughout the relevant wider culture.

Management has a limited ability to spur cultural change—rearranged organizational structures and processes can accomplish only so much. As discussed, uncertainty can be a catalyst for this change, though the forces constraining responses to uncertainty should be recognized, including the narrow, rigid frames that constrain journalists' thinking and the dearth of guiding principles for new kinds of journalism. But change has a way of emerging. We should keep in mind Singer's point about changing labor markets: "As more 'digital natives' enter the newsroom, uniting their knowledge of the medium with older colleagues' knowledge of the craft, answers to the 'how' questions that seem so challenging will have more opportunities to emerge."

Of course the goals of connective journalism would be accomplished imperfectly. Most goals are. However, these goals aren't exclusive of, or in conflict with, one another. Rather, this is a journalism that can do many things well. It is a journalism that can position and reposition its abstract knowledge within dynamic social structures and in line with a networked, postmodern world. It is a journalism that does not forget where it has been, and so holds on to core values related to truth-seeking. And it is a journalism that lights the path on the journey toward widely shared understanding, but can also find value in the murkiness of uncertainty.

Thought Questions: Contemplating Change

1. The vignette that opens this chapter describes a city with an increasingly fragmented media environment, with a diminished legacy media and a multiplying but unstable and impermanent group of small media. Do you think a connective journalism as described in this chapter can work in such a community? Why or why not? What are the significant obstacles?
2. What are your opinions about connective journalism, as laid out in this chapter? Is it possible for journalism to be a leader in a community or society while also embracing uncertainty? Can a journalism that is open to many different viewpoints provide democratic society with direction?
3. Do you think a connective journalism can be sustained financially? Why or why not?

Note

1 The information in this vignette derives from interviews conducted in 2010 by one of the chapter's authors for a separate research project. Anonymity was promised to interviewees.

References

Castells, M. (2000). *The rise of the network society* (2nd ed.). Oxford, UK: Blackwell.

Cohen, E. A., & Gooch, J. (1991). *Military misfortunes: The anatomy of failure in war*. New York: Anchor Books.

Giddens, A. (1976). *New rules of sociological method*. London: Hutchinson.

Michels, R. (1962 [1911]). *Political parties: A sociological study of the oligarchical tendencies of modern democracy*. New York: Collier Books.

Perrow, C. (1986). *Complex organizations: A critical essay*. New York: McGraw-Hill.

Picard, R. (2009, May 21). Why journalists deserve low pay. *Christian Science Monitor*. Retrieved November, 23, 2010, from http://www.csmonitor.com/2009/0519/p09s02-coop.html

Polodny, J. M., & Page, K. L. (1998). Network forms of organization. *Annual Review of Sociology, 24*, 57–76.

Schudson, M. (2003). *The sociology of the news*. New York: W. W. Norton.

Shirky, C. (2008). *Here comes everybody: The power of organizing without organizations*. New York: Penguin Press.

Stalder, F. (2006). *Manuel Castells: The theory of the network society*. Cambridge, UK: Polity Press.

Tolbert, P. S., & Hall, R. H. (2009). *Organizations: Structures, processes and outcomes* (10th ed.). Upper Saddle River, NJ: Pearson.

Tolbert, P. S., & Hiatt, S. R. (2009). On organizations and oligarchies: Michels in the twenty-first century. In P. S. Adler (Ed.), *The Oxford handbook of sociology and organization studies* (pp. 174–199). Oxford, UK: Oxford University Press.

AUTHOR INDEX

SUBJECT INDEX

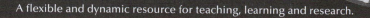